EDUCATIONAL AND PSYCHOLOGICAL MEASUREMENT

contributions to theory and practice

second edition

EDUCATIONAL
PSYCHOLOGICAL

second edition

AND
MEASUREMENT

contributions to
theory and practice

David A. Payne
University of Georgia at Athens

Robert F. McMorris
State University of New York at Albany

GENERAL LEARNING PRESS
GENERAL LEARNING CORPORATION
250 James Street, Morristown, N.J. 07960

0184922

David A. Payne is Professor of Education specializing in educational and psychological measurement at the University of Georgia. He has taught at Michigan State University (where he received his M.A. and Ph.D. degrees) and at Syracuse University. Professor Payne has contributed to many journals, among them the *Journal of Educational Psychology, Educational and Psychological Measurement,* and the *Personnel and Guidance Journal.* He is the author of *The Assessment of Learning* and *Specification in Measurement of Learning Outcome* and is the editor of *Curriculum Evaluation.*

Robert F. McMorris is Professor of Educational Psychology and Statistics at the State University of New York at Albany. He has taught at Syracuse University (where he received his M.S. and Ph.D. degrees). Professor McMorris has done consulting work with the Exploratory Committee on Assessing the Progress of Education and with Southwest Regional Laboratory for Educational Research and Development, and has been program chairman for National Council on Measurement in Education.

Manufactured in the United States of America.

Published simultaneously in Canada.

Library of Congress Catalog Card Number 74-79602

To our parents
Polly and Allen
Ethel and Robert

PREFACE TO THE
SECOND EDITION

The behavioral sciences are receiving important notice from both public and private quarters. Increasing amounts of money are being funneled into research and research training programs. The resulting "knowledge explosion" is one that has led to a tremendous increase in research reports, theoretical papers, and numerous other types of publications. Consequently, there is an obvious problem —how to communicate and digest the increasing amount of data that is being made available to the academic community.

Instructors of graduate and undergraduate courses are being required to increase the amount and speed with which updated information is introduced to students. The instructors of educational and psychological testing courses are particularly aware of this dissemination problem. The primary purpose of the set of readings in this book is, therefore, to assist in the communication of knowledge by providing convenient and readily accessible discussions and research summaries of concern to the student of measurement.

This collection of papers covers a variety of topics and reflects several degrees of sophistication on both theoretical and applied subjects. The primary audience for this volume are students in introductory tests and measurement courses at the college senior and first-year graduate level in departments of psychology, or in schools of education. Advanced graduate students and instructors should also find valuable material for review or reference in this volume.

This book may be used as an adjunct to a general text, or as the basic text, especially if it is supplemented by appropriate experiences such as test development (e.g., item writing and analysis), administration, and interpretation.

The basic intents in preparing this second edition have been to up-date the coverage of topics, to reflect changes in the field, and to respond to the suggestions of instructors who used the previous edition. The result has been to put more "education" into "educational psychological measurement." With increasing specialization in both applied measurement areas it seemed reasonable to present a more comprehensive picture of one area rather than run the risk of diluting the product by trying to do too much and please too many people.

Many changes have been made. The number of chapters has been reduced from twelve to nine, and the number of papers decreased from fifty-four to forty-six (twenty-five of which are new). The chapters on both testing programs and prediction and decision making have been eliminated. A chapter dealing with the important and revitalized area of curriculum evaluation has been added. Some topics are receiving emphasis for the first time (e.g., attitude measurement, creativity, performance contracting and accountability, and unobtrusive measures) and others are being reemphasized (e.g., testing the disadvantaged, instructional objectives, and criterion-referenced measurement). In addition, the research that forms the basis for the two McMorris articles (on statistical estimates and item construction principles) in the present volume resulted from ideas suggested by papers in the first edition.

With some exceptions, the papers have been edited and abridged. Extensive reviews of the literature have been condensed, statistical data summarized, and all but the major references deleted. The remaining references are listed alphabetically at the back of the volume.

The organization of this second edition generally corresponds to the original. The first six chapters parallel the development of a test from theory, to design and construction, on through analysis, refinement, and interpretation. The next two chapters deal with applications of measurement data in curriculum evaluation, and special problem areas. The final chapter focuses on the state of the art and science of educational and psychological measurement.

A foreword that highlights the general significance and the contribution of the individual papers precedes each chapter. In addition a brief introduction prefaces each paper to orient the reader, point up parallel and interrelated themes that recur in the various readings, and to provide leads to relevant literature. Most introductions to individual papers contain several "stimulus questions" to alert the reader to imporant points in the paper or to prod his thinking about possible issues and applications. A reference chart, which relates the various chapters of this book of readings to chapters in current textbooks in tests, measurement, and·evaluation, is also included.

Our major acknowledgement goes to the publishers and authors of each paper. They were more than generous in permitting us to reproduce their publications. To the many colleagues and students who assisted in the identification and selection of the articles, but who are too numerous to mention by name, a sincere general acknowledgement is made. In particular the editors would like to thank Dr. J. Stanley Ahmann and Dr. Max D. Engelhart for their constructive suggestions.

To Miss June McClain fell the major typing task of bringing order out of chaos. To these and many others, especially the always supportive, warm, tolerant, and understanding Mary Ann and Bobbie, we are indebted.

A special remembrance for the late Dr. Raymond G. Kuhlen, Professor of Psychology at Syracuse University, who guided the first volume to publication, is hereby expressed.

D.A.P.
R.F.M.

CONTENTS

CURRENT TEXTBOOKS IN TESTS, MEASUREMENT, AND EVALUATION

ADAMS, GEORGIA S. *Measurement and Evaluation in Education, Psychology, and Guidance.* New York: Holt, Rinehart & Winston, 1964.

AHMANN, J. S. and GLOCK, M. D. *Evaluating Pupil Growth.* Boston: Allyn & Bacon (Fourth Edition), 1971. (*See also* AHMANN, J. S. and GLOCK, M. D. *Measuring and Evaluating Educational Achievement.* Boston: Allyn & Bacon, Inc., 1971.)

AIKEN, JR., L. R. *Psychological and Educational Testing.* Boston: Allyn & Bacon, 1971.

ANASTASI, ANNE. *Psychological Testing.* New York: Macmillan (Third Edition), 1968.

BLOOM, B. S. *et al. Handbook on Formative and Summative Evaluation of Student Learning.* New York: McGraw-Hill Book Co., 1971.

BROWN, F. S. *Principles of Educational and Psychological Testing.* Hinsdale, Ill.: Dryden Press, 1970.

CRONBACH, L. J. *Essentials of Psychological Testing.* New York: Harper and Row (Third Edition), 1970.

DAVIS, F. B. *Educational Measurements and their Interpretation.* Belmont, Calif.: Wadsworth Pub. Co., Inc., 1964.

DOWNIE, N. M. *Fundamentals of Measurement: Techniques and Practices.* New York: Oxford University Press (Second Edition), 1967.

EBEL, R. L. *Essentials of Educational Measurement.* Englewood Cliffs, N.J.: Prentice-Hall, Inc. (Second Edition), 1972.

GREEN, J. A. *Introduction to Measurement and Evaluation.* New York: Dodd, Mead & Company, 1970.

GRONLUND, N. E. *Measurement and Evaluation in Teaching.* New York: Macmillan (Second Edition), 1971.

HORROCKS, J. E., and SCHOONOVER, THELMA S. *Measurement for Teachers.* Columbus, Ohio: Charles Merrill Publishing Company, 1968.

KARMEL, L. J. *Measurement and Evaluation in the Schools.* New York: Macmillan; 1970.

MARSHALL, J. C., and HALES, L. W. *Classroom Test Construction.* Reading, Mass.: Addison-Wesley, 1971.

MEHRENS, W. A., and LEHMANN, I. J. *Measurement and Evaluation in Education and Psychology.* New York: Holt, Rinehart and Winston, 1973.

NOLL, V. H., and SCANNELL, D. P. *Introduction to Educational Measurement.* Boston: Houghton Mifflin Company (Third Edition), 1972.

NUNNALLY, J. C. *Educational Measurement and Evaluation.* New York: Mc-Graw-Hill, 1964.

PAYNE, D. A. *Assessment of Learning: Cognitive and Affective.* Lexington, Mass.: D. C. Heath, 1974.

REMMERS, H. H., GAGE, N. L., and RUMMEL, J. F. *A Practical Introduction to Measurement and Evaluation.* New York: Harper and Row (Second Edition), 1965.

SAWIN, E. I. *Evaluation and the Work of the Teacher.* Belmont, California: Wadsworth Publishing, Inc., 1969.

SMITH, F. M., and ADAMS, S. *Educational Measurement for the Classroom Teacher.* New York: Harper and Row (Second Edition), 1972.

STANLEY, J. C., and HOPKINS, K. D. *Educational and Psychological Measurement and Evaluation.* Englewood Cliffs, New Jersey: Prentice-Hall, Inc. (Fifth Edition), 1964.

THORNDIKE, R. L., and HAGEN, ELIZABETH. *Measurement and Evaluation in Psychology and Education.* New York: John Wiley (Third Edition), 1969.

TEXTBOOK REFERENCE CHART

Cell Entries Relate Chapters (Roman Numerals) or Selected Articles (Arabic Numerals) of This Book to Chapters in Current Textbooks Listed on Two Preceding Pages.

Text Author / Text Chapter	Adams	Ahmann and Glock (Fourth Edition)	Aiken	Anastasi (Third Edition)	Bloom and Others
1	I, IX	I, IX	I, 9		I
2	VI, 9	14, 17	IV, V	I	14
3	II	V	II, III, 29	VI, 9	5, 16 ,17
4	III	V	4, 36	II	II, III, IV, V
5	32	23	25, 30, 40	III	16
6		26, 27		VI, 29	IV, V
7			42	26, 27	IV, V
8		VI, 9	24		IV, V
9		III			
10	IV, V	II	IX		15, 24
11	14				
12					VII, IX
13	VII				
14		VII, 37		42	
15	4	39		IV, V, VII, 37	
16	39	4			
17					42
18					
19					
20				24, 18	
21				IX, 30, 39	
22				41	
23					
24					

Brown	Cronbach (Third Edition)	Davis	Downie (Second Edition)	Ebel (Second Edition)	Green
I, 9	I, IX	I, IX	I, IX		I, IX
IV, V	I	II, III	9	I, II, VII, 32	
II	22, 30, 40	22	VI	14, 15, 16	VI, 9
II, 8, 9	VI, 9, 16, 17	23	II, III	IV, 17, 32	II, III
III, 29	III			IV, 22	25, 30, 40
III, 17	II		IV	23	
VI			20, 21		
		VI		20, 21	
			23		IV, V
		37	26, 27		
			VII		
	42	IV, V		39	
IX, 40		39			24
				26, 27	28, 39
				II	4
				III	VII
				1	
			VII	4	
				VI	
				4	

TEXTBOOK REFERENCE CHART *Continued*

Text Chapter / Text Author	Gronlund (Second Edition)	Horrocks and Schoonover	Karmel	Marshall and Hales	Mehrens and Lehmann
1	I, IX	I	I	I	I
2	IV		IX	IV	IV
3	IV			IV	VII, 14-15, 17
4	III, 18, 19, 29	II, III	II, III	23	
5	II		VI, 9		II, III, 29, 37
6	IV, V				VI
7	20		25, 30, 40	20	3, 20
8	20, 21, 22			20, 21	23
9	14			20	20
10	23				20, 21, 22
11	26, 27		31	VI, 9, 39	19, 26-27
12	1		24	II, III	18, 24
13	25, 40, 42	40	IV, V	26, 27	1, 32
14	VII, 4, 5		23		25, 29-31, 40
15	VI		IV, V		2
16	18		39		18, 19, 24, 41-42
17	15, 24, 41		VII, 4		16, 28, 39
18	2, 28, 37, 39				4, 5, 18, 36
19		24			9, 25, 30, 32, 40
20					
21		IV, V			
22		23, 39			
23		VI, 4			
24		IX			

Noll and Scannell (Third Edition)	Nunnally	Payne	Remmers, Gage, & Rummel (Second Edition)	Sawin
I, IX	I, VII	VII, 5, 35, 37, 38	I, IX	IX, 2, 14, 15, 16, 17
	I, IX		I	
9	VI	15	VI, 9	I, II, III
VI	II	18, 19, 22, 25	VII, 4	IV
II, III	IV	20, 21	II, III	
14, 16, 17	V	23	22	
IV, V	39		IV	24
26, 27			V	V
		9	39	
		28, 29, 30, 31, 40	24	18, 41
		II, III		
42	40	26, 27		VII
24		17		28, 39
	42	1, 4		
4, VIII	24			
VI, VII, VIII	18, 41			
	4, IX	16, 39		
		IX, 32, 36, 41, 42		

TEXTBOOK REFERENCE CHART *Continued*

Text Chapter / Text Author	Smith and Adams (Second Edition)	Stanley (Fifth Edition)	Thorndike and Hagen (Third Edition)
1	I, IX	I, IX	I, IX
2	I, VII	9	
3	VI, 9	VI	IV
4	II, III	III	V
5	IV	II	9
6	IV	19, 25, 30, 40	II, III
7	V		VI
8		IV, 22	
9	23	23	
10		20, 21	
11	15, 24	26, 27	
12	II, III, 27	24	
13	39	39	
14	4		
15	31, 32, 37	37, 38	
16			VII, 4
17	15, 24	VII, 4	39
18	VI, 40		
19			
20			
21			
22			
23			
24			

"Examinations are formidable, even to the best pre-pared, for the greatest fool may ask more than the wisest man can answer."

C. C. Colton

LACON (REVISED EDITION), 1836

INTRODUCTION
FOR STUDENTS
AND INSTRUCTORS

This collection of readings is intended for use by students of educational and psychological measurement. It is concerned with many technical and philosophical problems which are encountered in any attempt to assess human behavior. The study of educational and psychological measurement might be undertaken on the basis of its academic merits alone. As a subject for study, measurement offers much to the individual interested in relating and integrating theoretical, research, and applied developments within the behavioral sciences. For without the availability of measurement devices, most of the significant behavioral research completed in the last 100 years could not have been accomplished. In addition the practicing educator and psychologist will derive much information from an extensive and intensive study of measurement which should prove helpful in meeting day-to-day problems.

This introductory section has several purposes: first to point up the significance of measurement; second to discuss some possible uses of the book and guidelines involved in selecting and editing the papers; and third, to set forth the major framework of the volume.

Our ability to quantify human behavior has many practical implications. But sound measurement practice must rest on a solid theoretical base. The use of theory allows us to integrate research findings as well as to derive hypotheses which, after testing, should stimulate further applications. A practitioner must be aware of both research results and theory.

THE SIGNIFICANCE OF EDUCATIONAL AND PSYCHOLOGICAL MEASUREMENT

The intelligent application of tests and measurements constitutes a powerful force which can be used to improve the human condition, particularly in the realm of education. The use of poor instruments, on the other hand, or the improper use of good ones can adversely affect individuals and society. Even though misuse sometimes occurs, the demonstrated and potential benefits that can be derived from scientific and valid assessment cannot be denied.

It is almost a truism that the results of measurement permeate the lives of all people. It would indeed be an unusual individual who has not taken a test and whose life has not in some way been directly influenced by a test. Tests have been devised to assist in the determination and analysis of individual differences primarily in the areas of general intelligence, specific aptitudes, educational achievement, occupational competency, and personality development. Tests are not limited to use only with individuals, but have also frequently been applied to groups and institutions in a variety of employment, educational, psychological, military, and sociological settings, often for the purpose of arriving at major policy decisions.

It is axiomatic in science that unless something can be measured it cannot be studied. Thus measuring procedures are an important base of science and provide means of testing scientific hypotheses. Consequently the research applications of measurement methods are receiving increased attention, especially in the behavioral sciences with which this book is primarily concerned. Some idea of the scope of the research applications can be seen in Freeman's (1962) enumeration of test uses in psychology. He notes that:

> Among . . . studies, the following have been most common and include the most important fields of investigation: the nature and course of mental development, intellectual and non-intellectual personality differences associated with age, sex, and racial membership; differences that might be attributed to hereditary or environmental factors; differences among persons at different occupational levels; intellectual and other personality traits of atypical groups such as the mentally retarded, the mentally gifted, the neurotic, and the psychotic (p. 1).

The foregoing partial list, if extended and expanded to include other current and future applications, would become encyclopedic. Tests are probably used more extensively for educational classification, selection, and planning than for any other purpose. Furst (1958), for example, notes ten major purposes served by educational measurement and evaluation. These are (1) determining the effectiveness of courses and programs, (2) testing assumptions about instructional practices, (3) selecting, clarifying, and appraising objectives, (4) discovering and understanding learning difficulties, (5) planning instruction, (6) motivating learning, (7) guidance, (8) selection, (9) placement, and (10) certification. Obviously then tests influence the entire educational career of an individual.

Not to be overlooked are business, industry, and the military, where tests are helpful in selecting and classifying personnel for placement in positions ranging from semi-skilled to top-level management. In any decision making or evaluation situation, however, test data constitute only one source of valuable information.

It is clear that measurement methods have great utility. Many different procedures are available for use. The papers in this book deal almost exclusively with the so-called paper and pencil variety. Rating scales, checklists, sociometric and observational methods, and projective devices are, in addition, valuable components of the psychometrists' arsenal. All of these techniques have one thing in common; they are methods that can be used to quantify behavior. Stated in another way, they constitute procedures for assigning numerals to represent objects or events according to rules. The problem is that they are fallible and subject to error. Some of the methods used to reduce, control, or eliminate these errors of measurement, as well as related topics, are covered in this book of readings.

WHY A BOOK OF READINGS?

Textbooks are dull! How often have college and university professors heard this or similar comments from their students. Why is this the case? It is in part probably because of the author's style, perhaps to the selection of subject matter, or perhaps to level of instruction. Very frequently it is not just *what* one says but *how* one says it that influences communication. But communication is also how the basic concepts, principles, and pertinent research are integrated into the body of the text. Generally these are briefly summarized with scholarly footnotes attached. Frequently something is lost in the translation and interpretations. What is this "something"? Perhaps it is the transmitted enthusiasm of a researcher discussing his original investigation or experiment. Or the clarity with which a creative scholar presents his logical and well thought out contribution. It is indeed an unusual textbook author who can draw upon the thoughts and data from a variety of original sources and authors and mold them into a readable and concise communication. It would perhaps even be unreasonable to expect an author to be able to address himself with equal clarity to a large number of topics. Some writers, by virtue of their command of the language, and mechanics and style of expression can frequently "instruct" more effectively than others. And they may also be more knowledgeable about the subject matter. A book of readings which contains original presentations should then facilitate communication and learning.

The problem of motivating the student to seek and digest the original source is ever present. An instructor may assign readings in selected journals or go so far as to require an "integrative" term paper which will, hopefully, result in a meaningful learning experience. Such efforts most would probably agree fall short of intentions. This is due in part to the fact that many of the original sources may be difficult either to obtain or comprehend. It was a primary intention of the editors of this volume to collect some of the significant original research and theoretical discussions in the area of educational and psychological measurement and make these available for possible use as text materials.

SELECTION AND EDITING OF PAPERS

Several criteria guided the selection of papers. It was hoped that within the general sections papers of variable difficulty level could be placed and sequenced in such a way as to allow an instructor to select appropriate readings for his students.

The editors have included some papers presenting theory or research which represent the frontiers of knowledge; also some of the "classic" discussions in the area of psychometrics have been included. The research studies reported deal with both application and theory-testing. The student's exposure to original research should provide him with both perspective on current practices in measurement as well as justification for the various theoretical positions assumed. The approach taken in general was toward providing a broad perspective on measurement. If a bias exists, it is in the direction of placing greater weight on the assessment of learning outcomes, i.e., on educational measurement. Some attempt has been made to select articles which will generate discussion. This was done by including somewhat controversial material or unusual conceptualizations of certain topics.

To help insure appropriate selection many of the articles were "tried out" either in edited or original form with students in courses in tests and measurements. A large number of these articles have been rated by students on such factors as readability, aid in understanding course material, clarity of author's presentation of main points, number of readings necessary for comprehension, and relevance to professional needs. These data influenced the selection of the majority of the papers included in this book.

With only minor exceptions, articles in the present book have been edited in an effort to emphasize the most salient points in each of the authors' original presentations. It will be noted that the editing has often been quite extensive: by saving space it was possible to include a wide sampling of significant studies and discussions. The elaborate reviews and references to the literature that frequently accompany research articles have been abridged or eliminated. An attempt has been made to simplify the statistical presentation so as to minimize the knowledge of statistics required for comprehension of the material. One technique employed was the simplification of selected tables through elimination of all but descriptive data. Reference to various introductory statistics texts should provide the reader with sufficient background for comprehension of the research articles.[1]

Each group of papers (chapter) is introduced by a brief discussion of the general topic with which the papers are concerned for the purpose of providing a perspective in which the individual papers may be viewed. In addition each paper is introduced by a brief paragraph that includes several "focusing questions." It is hoped that these introductions and questions will serve to guide the reader through the papers and alert him to important ideas in each article.

ORGANIZATION OF THE VOLUME

The organization of the papers is somewhat unlike most of the topical outlines that might be found in traditional textbooks in the area of testing, measurement, or evaluation. The forty-six articles included in this volume are *not* intended to serve as a systematic integration of either the theoretical or empirical literature of measurement. The book is intended to provide for student use a collection of research reports and discussions that have historical significance, represent contemporary thought, or will assist him in dealing with measurement concepts and devices.

What is measurement all about? The five articles of Chapter I present summaries of the thinking of a number of authorities about the purposes and processes of measurement. These papers also contain a synopsis of the characteristics of a "good" measuring instrument. The central measurement concepts of reliability and validity are treated in the next two chapters. Aspects of both the technology and theory associated with these topics are treated in detail. Chapters IV and V deal with test construction techniques. Subtopics such as planning the test, item writing, and test analysis are approached from both discursive and empirical angles. The reader is next introduced to a systematic consideration of some of the many factors involved in test interpretation. Curriculum evaluation is given attention in Chapter VII. The uses and design of curriculum evaluation studies are discussed, and a cross-national example described. Some special problem areas that measurement techniques directly influence or only touch are next considered. Such areas as grading and marking, testing the disadvantaged, measuring environments, and creativity are explored. And finally in Chapter IX an effort is made to present a balanced philosophical view of testing. Both positive and negative comments are made. In total this collection of papers represents a crossection of measurement theory and practice. Close examination of them will bring about changes in cognitive behavior, and in addition will assist in developing critical attitudes toward testing. Bon Voyage!

[1] See for example Adkins, 1964; Blommers and Lindquist, 1960; Bradley and McClelland, 1963; Edwards, 1969; Glass and Stanley, 1970; Gotkin and Goldstein, 1964; Guilford, 1965; McCullough and Van Atta, 1965, 1963; Minium, 1970. *Note:* All bibliographic references have been drawn together at the end of the book.

I

OVERVIEW OF THE
PURPOSES AND PROCESSES
OF MEASUREMENT

The study of individual differences is a fascinating and worthwhile endeavor. It is one field within the behavioral sciences which holds interest for both casual observer and scholar. Part of the fascination and value of such studies derives from the fact that information concerning individual differences touches on vital questions in all aspects of our lives. Educators and psychologists are particularly sensitive to the importance of individual differences as they are continually being called upon to make decisions and evaluations about people.

Many dimensions of human behavior are in need of assessment. The techniques that may be employed are many, and the task itself is complex and arduous. What is assessed will, of course, depend upon the requirements of the particular situation. It may be an on-the-job training program, ability to take shorthand at a specified rate, or effective teaching.

The standardized test is a frequently used technique to gather data reflecting individual differences. Cronbach (1970) notes that tests are used to make decisions with respect to the selection and classification of individuals, evaluation of educational or treatment procedures, and acceptance or rejection of scientific hypotheses. But what is standardized about a standardized test? Obviously the content is fixed; i.e., all examinees will be required to respond to the same stimuli. The administration and scoring procedures are also controlled. In addition virtually all manuals accompanying standardized

7

tests provide tables of norms which summarize the test performances earned by specified and representative subjects. The procedures involved in the process of standardizing a test are outlined by Angoff and Anderson in the first article in this chapter. Their presentation provides a good summary of the processes involved in the construction and refinement of a standardized test. When we hear the term "standardized" used in conjunction with a test, we generally think of an instrument published by a commercial organization. But there is no reason why a classroom test could not be considered as a standardized test. The only element lacking perhaps is the availability of normative data. Of course, this kind of information could be accumulated over time, if desired. Norms may be thought of as providing frames of reference for interpreting test scores. But the type of norm developed will obviously depend on the "purpose of testing."

Just as the "purpose of testing" may dictate the type of normative data gathered, it will also determine the general approach taken to test development and interpretation. But test development assumes an educationally sound, viable, and rational philosophy and curriculum. The schools are changing. In our second article Coffman suggests some ways in which these changes are modifying how we look at and measure achievement. He poses some important questions.

One of the major purposes of testing is to assess educational achievement. In the third article in this chapter Robert Ebel has specified some of the knowledge and skills that a classroom teacher must possess if he is to evaluate adequately student learning. It is interesting to note that Ebel considers principles that range from the philosophical to the technical, thereby underscoring the complexity of the measurement task.

Most of the tests in use today by educational, industrial, and governmental agencies are objective paper and pencil instruments. Historically the term "objective," when used in conjunction with measurement, has meant consistency of scoring. It has required that a standard key be applied in the same way to all examinees. Ebel (1965, p. 296) takes this definition a little further by including the notion that not only must the scoring key be applied fairly, but also that the responses keyed as correct must in fact be correct. The keyed answers must therefore be evaluated by a number of experts in addition to the test constructor.

Our attention is next turned to the school testing program. Almost everyone is aware of the increasing number of blocks of time that are being given over to formal and informal testing in our schools and colleges. In addition, external testing programs (e.g., scholarship and admissions testing) appear to be taking on increased importance. One wonders whether the public, or a great proportion of school personnel for that matter, are really aware of the economic, social, and psychological implications of increased test "use." The word "use" is purposefully enclosed in quotation marks as it may take on many definitions in a testing context. All too often tests are administered, scored, and then filed away, never to be seen by teacher, counselor, or student. Unfortunately, many individuals involved in establishing and administering the testing programs, be it for the purpose of curriculum evaluation or counseling, are not trained in measurement. Many of the problems in test "use" can, therefore, be traced to ill-conceived, poorly administered, and inefficient testing programs.

Whether the testing program is administered to (1) secure information useful in improving instruction, (2) facilitate curriculum revision, (3) provide information for educational and vocational counseling, or (4) assist the administrative staff in appraising the total educational program, the testing program itself needs to be continually monitored. As the program undergoes periodic reappraisal, the criteria supplied by Arthur Traxler in the fourth article in this chapter might be applied. The criterion questions raised by Traxler are for the most part of a common-sense variety. But often because questions are viewed as common sense, their importance is overlooked. The author does a commendable job in emphasizing their importance. The necessity of involving the total faculty in conducting the testing program is a particular point worth underscoring. Those interested in further reading about testing programs are referred to a book by Bauernfeind (1963), one edited by Findley (1963), and an article by Womer (1961).

The final article of the chapter considers some of the measurement problems generated by the so called "accountability" movement. In it Ralph Tyler discusses applications of norm-referenced and criterion-referenced measures.

As noted at the outset of this introduction, educational and psychological tests and measures touch all our lives, particularly during the periods of educational and occupational development. The editors have attempted to show with appropriate articles and commentaries how society provides the impetus for developing various types of tests, measures, and evaluation systems. The changes in our schools, with significant innovations being made seemingly yearly, require the establishment of new and different methods and the up-dating of teacher skills in all areas including measurement. The public also is involved as it demands dollar value received for dollar spent. School testing programs can provide the data necessary to evaluate progress toward educational accountability.

1   The Standardization of Educational and Psychological Tests

WILLIAM H. ANGOFF AND SCARVIA B. ANDERSON

The development and standardization of a mental test is a very complex, expen-

sive, and time-consuming project. In this article Doctors Angoff and Anderson present a lucid overview of the test development process. Although they are primarily concerned with tests which become commercially available, their comments apply equally well to any "homemade" instrument, be it for classroom or research use. The following questions should guide the reader through this article. What does the term "standardization" mean? What are the primary purposes of "scaling" a test? What might be some applications of scaling procedures for a classroom test or for a college qualification admissions test? What purposes might a teacher have in mind in developing norms for his classroom tests? Some of the positive and negative consequences of the use of standardized tests are considered in later articles by Womer (#32), Goslin (#44), and Ebel (#46).

The development and application of standardized tests probably represent one of the major contributions to educational progress of the last fifty years. But its success has not come without criticism; indeed, some of the success would not have been possible without the constructive criticism which has spurred test makers into improving their procedures and seeking new methods of assessing human mental processes. Some of the least constructive of the criticisms have stemmed from a fundamental view that testing is motivated by a mechanistic philosophy by which all men are cast into one mold, without regard for their essential individuality. The test makers, on the other hand, take the view that not only do they *not* disregard the essential differences among individuals, but also that these differences are precisely what they seek to understand. They also maintain that the pursuit of this understanding is best accomplished by adopting the methods of scientific inquiry by which they imply that all aspects of measurement be held constant and uniform, except for the individual's own performance. Only then can the variability in performance from one person to another be taken as evidence of the *abilities* of the individuals and of nothing else.

The test makers will also take the position that because it provides *uniform methods* and *uniform standards* for everyone standardized testing necessarily yields fair and equitable assessments of performance for everyone. Thus the process of standardization permeates all aspects of a test; the construction, administration, scoring, reporting, and evaluation of test results.

TEST CONSTRUCTION

Ordinarily a standardized test poses the same questions for all students. The test maker attempts to write questions that will be regarded in the same way by all students who take the test. He pretests his questions in an effort to weed out

Reprinted with permission of the first named author, and publisher (Ray Page, State Superintendent of Public Instruction) from the *Illinois Journal of Education*, (February) 1963, pp. 19–23.

ambiguities that result in different meanings to different people. (Pretests are conducted for other reasons as well: to insure the proper degree of difficulty for the test and the highest degree of reliability.) In most cases he writes a variety of test questions in order to sample as widely as possible the distribution of knowledge covered in a particular test. In this way he avoids giving special advantage to a student for whom the test is heavily weighted with questions in which he happens to have special competence or for which he did special intensive preparation in an attempt to "beat the test." In order to achieve a test which gives uniform opportunity to all students, a test maker asks not one or three or five questions but fifty or a hundred, because only with large numbers of questions can he be confident of achieving an adequate sampling of knowledge. He also writes questions which will test specifically what he intends to test, say knowledge and understanding of the events leading up to World War II—not "test wiseness," not general intelligence, not handwriting ability, nor neatness, nor English composition. This is not to say, of course, that some of these other characteristics are unimportant; but fair assessment demands that they must be measured separately.

ADMINISTRATION AND SCORING

The test maker also prescribes that the test be administered under uniform conditions—the same directions for all, the same presentation of questions, the same time limits, and insofar as possible the same favorable environmental conditions: proper light, ventilation, and temperature; convenient working space; general quiet, with freedom from extraneous disturbances.

Uniformity is also achieved in the scoring process. By restricting the nature of the student's responses and by removing from the task any opportunity the student may seize upon to bias the grading of his paper, the test maker insures virtually perfect scoring reliability. On a subjectively scored test the teacher's ratings can be influenced by such diverse factors as neatness and legibility, good or poor prose, his own fatigue or boredom with the scoring task, his general feeling of well-being, and, not of least importance, *his prior biases toward the student.* The standardized test, on the other hand, is scored only for the student's performance on the questions that are asked him. Again this is not to say that such factors as prose style or legibility of handwriting should not be tested. But if they are considered important enough to be tested, they should be tested independently. They should not appear as unreliable riders to another purpose to be considered as part of the score or not, depending on the particular mood and predilections of the person who happens to be scoring the paper at the time. As in the administration of the tests, what is sought here is a fair and equitable score, uncontaminated by factors that can only be considered as irrelevant or biasing in terms of the stated purpose of the test.

Of course all standardized tests are not "multiple-choice" tests. There are numerous instances in which a student is asked an "open-ended" question, as in the Stanford-Binet, the Wechsler-Bellevue, and the Interlinear Section of the College Board English Composition Test. In such cases the rules for scoring are agreed upon in advance by a group of experts and set down to be followed rigidly in the scoring process. Thus, even with tests that call for some subjectivity in scoring, attempts are made in the standardized test to reduce to a minimum the influence of extraneous factors and to set uniform standards to be applied to all examinees without bias.

SCALING

Standardization is also achieved in the development of an appropriate score scale system. Very frequently tests are constructed in more than one form—to discourage students from memorizing the questions either for their own benefit on retest or to help other students achieve higher scores, to avoid the effects of practice in studies of educational change, and to allow a second measurement when the validity of the first is open to question. Even when the various forms are constructed according to common specifications and precautions are taken to adopt an item-sampling scheme that will yield a similar "mix" of items in all forms, there are almost certain to be small differences between forms. Occasionally the differences are large, not only with respect to the general level of talent for which the forms are appropriate, but also with respect to the range of talent for which they are appropriate. In such cases it would be grossly unfair to compare the raw score earned by one student who is given an easier form with the raw score earned by another student who is given a more difficult form. Therefore, in order to correct the differences between forms and to provide scores that are independent of the particular form that happened to be administered in any instance, scores on the various forms of a test are equated—or "calibrated"—and converted to a common reporting scale. (In order to avoid confusion this scale is made independent and different from the raw-score system for any single form.) Then, within the limitations imposed by the reliability of the equating method one can be confident that a student's score was unaffected by the difficulty of the particular form he took. Teachers, admissions officers, and counselors are relieved of the obligation of taking into consideration the difficulty characteristic of each test form.

There are other advantages to equating. If the reporting scale is maintained intact and without change over a period of time during which new forms are introduced, it is possible to trace the quality of successive groups of examinees, to make studies of trends, and to compare individuals and groups tested at different times, in different places, and for different purposes.

The methods by which a scale is established and the methods by which it is maintained in the face of multiple forms constitute a sizable field of study by themselves. Frequently a representative group of individuals ("representative" in terms of the population for which the test is designed) is tested to become the "standard group" on whom the scale is based. In later uses of the test the "standard group," whose average performance provides the focal point of the scale, is used as the basic reference or normative group for the purposes of evaluating individual scores. This procedure expresses the view that the "standard group" gives normative meaning to the scale. Multiple forms of the test that are introduced at later times are equated, by procedures to be described below, to the scale defined by the original group, a process which allows scores on all of the forms to be reported in terms of this single standard scale.

There are other approaches to the problem of scale definition. One of these is based on the philosophy that because of changes in the population it is not always possible to give the scale lasting normative meaning. Moreover, even in those instances when the characteristics of the group may be expected to remain fairly constant, there is some question whether the scale should have any normative meaning or whether it should be a purely arbitrary scale of measurement, like the commonly used scales of inches, pounds, and Fahrenheit. The proponents of this view maintain that a measurement should be just a measurement and no more; that the evaluation of that measurement, as of the measurement of physical objects, should come from other sources: from continued experiences and increased familiarity with the scale and from comparison with the performance of groups of individuals who are either known to the test user or easily characterized for him.

The methods of equating two forms of a test all pre-suppose that the conversion of scores from one form to another involves simply an adjustment of units to account for differences in difficulty of the forms. Ideally this adjustment would be determined by administering both forms to all members of a group and observing the differences in performance on the forms—after first removing the effect of practice or fatigue on the form administered second. Variations on the approach, necessitated by practical considerations, include (a) dividing a large group of individuals into two random halves, administering one form to each half and observing the differences in the statistics on the test form that each group took; and (b) administering the same "equating" test to two groups, each of which has been tested with one of the major test forms. Here, too, the differences in performance on the two test forms are observed, but with adjustments made for any differences in the two groups by use of the equating test.

NORMING

An essential characteristic of the test standardization process is the presentation of reference data for appropriate norms groups. In some cases, as was just noted, the characteristics of the norms sample are built directly into the test scale itself. Tests which yield I.Q. scores fall into this category. In other cases an arbitrary scale is maintained, and the test is accompanied by norms appropriate for the principal uses for which the test is intended.

Tests designed for general surveys of ability, aptitude, and achievement are frequently related meaningfully to "national" norms collected by grade or age. But for these tests and for other tests in specific areas other types of norms may be desirable—norms differentiated by sex, geography, type of curriculum, rural-urban-suburban, public-private-parochial, etc. It is then the task of the test user to choose the appropriate norms from those that are available and to apply them in evaluating the performance of the individuals he has tested.

The norms that are developed for a test may be as elaborate as the test demands or the test maker can afford. The process of norms development, however, is fundamentally the same, regardless of the number and type of norms that are constructed. The test maker defines the characteristics of the population from which he decides to sample, and proceeds to select a sample from this population which will be as nearly representative of the population as possible. Ideally this would mean selecting all individuals at random from the population; however, for practical reasons other procedures are ordinarily employed. Typically the schools in the nation are grouped into categories or strata, homogeneous by type, size, socio-economic level, or location, or by combinations of these characteristics; and entire schools are chosen at random from these strata. Sometimes multistage cluster sampling techniques are employed, involving several steps: random sampling of communities, random sampling of schools within those communities, random sampling of classes within those schools, and occasionally random sampling of students from those classes. When possible, the methods of stratified sampling and cluster sampling are combined to yield norms samples that are not only economical as to size, but also possess the desired levels of reliability and representativeness.

When any particular student is to be evaluated, the best comparison group is a group of students with whom he is in competition or with whom he aspires to compete (or a group as similar to one of these as possible). Thus, if a test is to be used for educational guidance, an appropriate norms group consists of those students with whom the student will be in competition if he undertakes a particular course of study. If the test is to be used for selection at a given college, the appropriate norms group is the group of candidates with whom the student is competing for a place. If a test is to be used for evaluation of achievement in a specific school course, then the ideal group is the rest of the class.

Increasingly the major test publishers are coming around to the point of view that the most valuable norms group may be one that is locally assembled by the test user himself. This does not relieve the publisher of the responsibility of providing more general norms; however, his norms may be considered only supplementary to the data collected on the local group.

OTHER TEST CHARACTERISTICS

Finally, the producer of a standardized test will make available to the test user for his information in selecting and using the instrument a set of data describing the various characteristics of the test: the use to which it is intended or for which it is recommended; an outline of the test content; the item difficulties and discrimination indices; data on the speededness of the test; its reliability and standard error of measurement; its predictive validity for various pertinent criteria; the pattern of growth if the test is designed for use at more than one level; relationships with other tests or forms; and, finally, an evaluation of the strengths and weaknesses of the test for various purposes to which it might be put. The makers of standardized tests are committed to the methods of scientific inquiry; they must also assume the obligations of science—making the results of their inquiry available to the public.

The procedures involved in the process of standardizing tests as they are discussed here are not by any means intended to constitute a set of minimum criteria for a test to be considered "standardized." Some highly useful tests follow the procedures of standardization in somewhat different ways from those that are outlined here. However, aside from the details of procedure, it is certainly reasonable to say that taken together the characteristic features of a standardized test are what make it a scientific measuring instrument, capable of precision and predictive of future achievement. For both human and practical reasons the standardized test is a necessary outcome of the philosophy of a modern democratic society in which large masses of individuals competing for educational awards, or simply seeking better self-understanding, assemble for an objective, unbiased evaluation of their abilities. No other method that we know of today can provide measurement for the tremendous number of individuals who demand objective consideration of their talents. Certainly no other method that we know of today can accomplish this measurement as equitably as can the standardized test.

2   *Concepts of Achievement and Proficiency*

WILLIAM E. COFFMAN

The author of this article considers several philosophical dilemmas concerning the concept of achievement in our schools. What should be the goals of education in our schools—acquisition of subject matter or development of command of this substantive knowledge? The author feels that moving to a relative standard for specifying expected student performances would be reasonable. The idea of absolute standards, given the validity of individual differences, perhaps places too great demands on students. There is also the attendant problem of grading and reporting. But the schools must change. The question is in what direction. Some possible alternatives are discussed. There are many challenges to those who teach and test.

What are the relative advantages and disadvantages of using absolute or relative standards in judging the accomplishments of our students? What are some measurement problems likely to be encountered if we move toward a system of education in which each student pursues his own interests, satisfies his own curiosity, and develops his abilities and skills? Is the concept of mastery learning à la Bloom and Carroll reasonable for all levels of education and subject matter? Why?

One of the episodes in the motion picture *Isadora* depicts the birth of Isadora's first child. There are two scenes. In the first, Isadora, obviously in pain and taking her usual positive approach to events, is demanding that the attending physician *do something.* The doctor, wearing the frock coat of the turn-of-the century practitioner of the healing art, just stands there waiting for nature to take its course. The second scene opens as the newborn baby is placed into the arms of a tired but obviously triumphant mother who shouts, "I did it all myself! I did it all myself!"

The viewer of the film does not doubt that he has witnessed an achievement in the sense of definition 2a in *Webster's Seventh New Collegiate Dictionary:* "a result brought about by resolve, persistence, or endeavor." If he is a medical educator, or if, like me, he has agreed to speak at an Invitational Conference on Testing Problems, he might wonder whether the achievement represented the ultimate in proficiency. What, for example, would have been the effect if Isadora had been able to consult, prior to the labor, one of today's specialists in natural childbirth? Or if the attending physician had been more inclined toward intervention? I doubt, however, that Isadora at the moment of achievement was concerned with such questions. The labor was accomplished, the product was good, and the satisfaction was complete.

Now, one might draw a more or less extended analogy between the achievement of Isadora and the achievement in today's schools depending on his educational philosophy and his conception of the nature of human learning. At this point, let us simply note that the achievement was a tangible product, that the achiever had had some choice in the matter of whether or not to risk pregnancy, that the achiever had immediate knowledge of results, that the evaluation was made by the achiever herself, and that the judgment was absolute, not relative. The same cannot often be said in the case of achievement in school.

Those who undertake to propose goals of instruction in school are usually careful to be comprehensive; after all, the school is concerned with the well-being of developing human beings, and developing human beings have many legitimate needs. On the other hand, time is limited and so choices have to be made. Implicit in the choices of things to emphasize are the differing viewpoints about what achievements and proficiencies should be the outcomes of schooling.

One well-established viewpoint is that the schools exist primarily for the purpose of transmitting accumulated knowledge. Through successive generations, mankind has accumulated a vast store of knowledge about himself and his environment and has organized this accumulation of systematic ways that facilitate its transmission and use. It is the responsibility of the educator to abstract from this accumulation those elements that are of greatest significance and organize them into teachable units. The viewpoint is well expressed by Ausubel (1963, p. 13) :

> Actually . . . the transmission of subject matter can be considered the primary function of the school. Most of the thinking that goes on in school is and should be supplementary to the process of reception learning, that is, concerned with having students assimilate subject-matter content in a more active, integrative, and critical fashion. Development of thinking or problem-solving ability can also be considered an objective of schooling in its own right, although it is a lesser objective than the learning of subject matter and is only partly teachable; but under no circumstances is it a proper substitute for reception learning or a feasible primary means of imparting subject-matter knowledge.

Ebel (1965, pp. 38–39), after recognizing the complexity of the problem of deciding what pupils should achieve in school, comes to much the same conclusion as Ausubel:

> If we look at what actually goes on in our school and college classrooms and laboratories, libraries and lecture halls, it seems reasonable to conclude that the major goal of education is to develop in the scholars a *command of substantive knowledge*. Achievement of this kind of cognitive mastery is clearly not the only concern of teachers and scholars engaged in the process of education. But the command of substantive knowledge is, and ought to be, the central concern of education.

For Ausubel, school achievement is marked by progress in the construction in the minds of students of an ever increasingly complex set of cognitive structures that will enable the student to interpret experience. By capitalizing on the work of generations of scholars, the school can short-cut the agonizingly slow process of building cognitive structures through direct experience. To a considerable extent, the abstractions that constitute the structure of the networks can be taught directly so that the bits of information can be incorporated without the necessity of wasting time trying to "discover" how things go together in meaningful ways. For Ebel, the task of the test maker is to construct questions that differentiate between automatic, rote verbalizations and responses reflecting meaningful relating of the questions to the structure that has been developed in the mind of the student.

This view of the purpose of schooling, often simplified or distorted, is probably held by a majority of teachers today. A systematic survey would probably show that pupils, too, think of school as a place where they are to learn subject matter, organized and communicated through textbooks, lectures, and discussions and examined by questions of one type or another for which there exist right answers that the informed can recall or figure out in one way or another. The frame of reference is generally that of some standard, more or less flexible, set by the teacher—or perhaps by some impersonal "they" representing the authority of the school or the society. To achieve in this setting is to accumulate points—by answering questions in class, handing in homework, supplying answers to periodic quizzes, and writing a final examination. If one accumulates enough points, usually a certain percentage of all the possible points one might accumulate, one has achieved. If one accumulates fewer points, one fails and must have another try at it or withdraw from the competition. My recollection is that I thought of school achievement in this manner when I was passing through the system some 40 odd years ago. And my daughters did not appear to have a very different conception 30 years later in spite of subsequent developments in the field of testing. I recall vividly their discussions of the importance of accumulating 85 percent rather than 84 percent since that seemed to be the difference between a B and a C on the periodic report card. True, the school did administer standardized tests at periodic intervals on which were reported grade-equivalent or percentile scores, but these were strictly peripheral. The thing that counted was doing the "regular" class work.

Anybody who has taken the trouble to look closely at what goes on in schools knows that there is great variability in the extent to which pupils do learn what teachers attempt to teach them. There was a time when the problem could be solved by a process of attrition; those who didn't learn simply dropped out of school. Today, however, individuals stay in school even if they don't learn the subject matter or develop the skills taught at a particular level. So long as they do not become too troublesome, they are simply ignored. In extreme cases, however, such as in certain inner-city schools, teachers have become primarily disciplinarians leading the class through a caricature of meaningful learning. And even in more affluent settings, all is not well. A teacher like John Holt, who takes seriously his commitment to guiding meaningful learning, becomes an angry man as he struggles to reconcile the objectives of instruction with the facts of individual differences.

One solution to the problem is to throw out the concept of absolute standards and replace it with one of relative standards: individual differences are inevitable. And even the good student soon forgets much of the detailed content of instruction. Identify the broad skills and understandings that remain after the specifics are forgotten and measure them with general examinations appropriate for a wide range of ability. Report scores in units that are related to the actual performance of reference groups of school children. Over time, it will then be possible to chart the progress of individuals in this frame of reference. This is the system characterized by ability grouping, some choice of courses at the secondary school level, and the school testing program as the monitor.

Some years ago I made a study of the achievement of two classroom groups in a small city school system. The groups were measured annually beginning in Grade 4 and continuing through Grade 8 with tests in the Stanford Achievement Battery. There were a few striking individual growth patterns, but in general, when fluctuations attributable to errors of measurement were discounted, the picture that emerged was one of constantly increasing scores on a gradient the slope of which was determined by the initial status. In other words, in this particular system, children seemed to be increasing in their ability to answer the kinds of questions in the test at a rate proportional to their initial level of ability. At the time I noted that even those in the lower third of the distribution seemed to be improving over time and commented: "It is also interesting to speculate on the attitudes which have been built up in this group of pupils, who, over a four-year period, have increased their scores as much as an average group would be expected to increase in about three and one-half years. They have been in the bottom third of their class. They have received the D's and F's. To my knowledge they have not had an opportunity to see plots of their growth lines. I suspect that periodic reports of scores on standardized tests might be more rewarding to them than periodic grades reflecting their position in the group" (Coffman, 1960).

There's some question, however, whether it would be possible to substitute a record of systematic improvement in broad areas of cognitive skills for relative position in the group as a measure of success in school. I recall with deep concern the remark of one mother on hearing that I was the Director of the Iowa Testing Programs. "Oh yes," she commented, "some of my friends report proudly each year how their children have scored at the 99th percentile. I keep quiet, because mine never seems to be able to get above the 75th percentile." For her, and possibly for her children, success in school consisted of scoring at or near the top of the examinations, whether they were teacher-made tests graded on some absolute scale or standardized tests reflecting relative position in the group on broad intellectual skills. In his book *Schools Without Failure*, William Glasser (1969, p. 63) reports his findings with respect to this matter:

> From talking with many children over the past several years about grades, I find that they believe that the line between passing and failing in our grading system lies just below B; that is, a child who gets mostly C's is essentially a failure in school because the only real passing grades are B and A.

For Glasser and for Holt, the solution to the problem lies in fomenting a revolution that would transform the schools into markedly different institutions. Stop trying to plan in detail the content of the curriculum and pass it out in little doses to children. Stop grading, and stop the testing that is the basis of grading. Get rid of this whole rigid system. Toward the end of his book *How Children Fail*, Holt (1968, p. 180) writes:

> The alternative—I can see no other—is to have schools and classrooms in which each child in his own way can satisfy his curiosity, develop his abilities and talents, pursue his interests, and from the adults and older children around him get a glimpse of the great variety and richness of life. In short, the school should be a great smorgasbord of intellectual, artistic, creative, and athletic activities from which each child could take whatever he wanted, and as much as he wanted, or as little.

Presumably, in such a system each child, like Isadora, would make his own evaluation after examining the product. Teachers, like those described by Phil Jackson in his book *Life in Classrooms* (1968), would make their evaluations by examining the process rather than the product. If children were engaged in meaningful activities that experience had indicated might lead to useful learning, then the educational program in that classroom would be judged effective. Presumably, the administrators would obtain evidence for their evaluation by looking at the process of interaction of teachers and pupils. And given the drive of the human organism to make sense out of his world, it just might be that such a system could provide the society with enough scientists to keep the machinery going and expanding, enough artists to interpret and beautify the culture, enough politicians to manage the human interactions, and a host of happy people able to do their thing. There may be a place for freedom of choice in the market place of education as well as in the market place of the economic system.

It is likely, however, that the cost in a free market of educational activities would be as high as that in a completely unregulated free market in goods and services. Not all teachers are likely to have the sensitivity of a Holt or the skill in questioning of a Glasser or the ability to recognize good learning situations of the teachers observed by Jackson. Furthermore, how shall the content of the smorgasbord be developed? And how shall the output of the system be assessed if not in comparison with the performance of reference groups?

Over 10 years ago, Dorothy Adkins (1958), after analyzing and evaluating the implications of Skinner's learning theory, proposed that the solution was in teaching each learner to the mastery level those materials that he is capable of mastering. Such a procedure would require a variety of teaching methods and more or less continuous progress appraisals based on tests of defined educational objectives. The work of Gagné (1965, 1968) offers one possible solution to the problem of developing suitable teaching methods and testing procedures.

Identify, by detailed analysis, the hierarchical structure involved and aim test questions at key points in the structure, insuring that the prerequisites are mastered before proceeding to the next level. Glasser (1963) has pointed up the implications of such an educational program for testing. If all students master a unit, the concept of item difficulty as the percentage of the group marking the correct answer and the concept of test score as relative position in the group becomes meaningless. What are needed are criterion-referenced measures: The pupil demonstrates achievement by answering the questions correctly.

In 1963, Carroll suggested that perhaps the major factor accounting for individual differences in learning was not, as Adkins assumed, difference in the capacity of the pupils to reach higher and higher levels of cognitive organization but rather differences in the time required to incorporate and organize experience. If so, by individualizing instruction and by using carefully prepared unit materials, it should be possible to insure that all students achieve mastery of the units they have the time to complete. There should be no failure, only differences in the number of units completed. Bloom (1968) states the expectations thus:

> Most students (perhaps over 90 percent) can master what we have to teach them, and it is the task of instruction to find the means which will enable our students to master the subject under consideration.

Does this mean the end of educational achievement testing as we have known it for many years? I doubt it. In the first place, it is not yet clear that children will necessarily accept the adult value system implicit in the subject-matter specialists' view of what ought to be taught. What if Snygg (1963) is right in his view that phenomenal field theory is applicable to all school learning? Bloom has demonstrated that the concept of mastery learning is dramatically successful for the highly selected students at the University of Chicago who, like Isadora, have chosen to try for the prize. It will be interesting to see how he fares with a representative sample of elementary or secondary school pupils. Some may point to the reported success of Bereiter and Engelmann with disadvantaged preschool children (1966). It's my impression, however, that they are simply providing the children with the minimum tools required to play the educational game so painfully described by Holt and Glasser.

Secondly, there's some doubt in my mind just how long the demonstrated mastery can be guaranteed to persist unless there are solid anchors in the world of ongoing experience. Once we have learned to drive a car, we don't forget, but then, every time we take hold of the wheel and press the accelerator, we receive immediate feedback. I imagine that the society will want some program of periodic testing to monitor even a system based on the concept of mastery learning.

There is a mountain of unfinished business in this area if we are to provide something more than a distorted view of a small aspect of the output as we do today through tests of cognitive skills and subject-matter knowledge. Lindquist (1951, p. 137) posed the challenge almost 20 years ago, and we have not yet found a way of meeting it. In his chapter in *Educational Measurement* he wrote:

> If the descriptions of educational development of individual students provided by tests are to be truly comprehensive, tests and measuring devices must be developed for many more educational objectives than are now being measured at all. In general, satisfactory tests have thus far been developed only for objectives concerned with the student's *intellectual* development or with his purely *rational* behavior. Objectives concerned with his non-rational behavior, or with his emotional behavior, or objectives concerned with such things as artistic abilities, artistic and aesthetic values and tastes, moral values, attitudes toward social institutions and practices, habits relating to personal hygiene and physical fitness, managerial or executive ability, etc., have been seriously neglected in educational measurement.

I would only add that we need to be concerned not only with what the schools are trying to accomplish—that is, the educational objectives—but also with what the unintentional concomitants are. We do not intend that an educational program produce fearful or deeply anxious children or teachers. We ought to know when it does if we are to reach valid conclusions about its effectiveness.

3   *Measurement and the Teacher*

ROBERT L. EBEL

After reading this article, the reader may say to himself, "That's only common sense," or "Everyone knows that." Unfortunately the ten principles summarized by Dr. Ebel are not always considered in developing tests. He has spelled out tacit assumptions which form the basis for much of what we do in evaluating instructional outcomes. The principles are well worth reviewing. A teacher might ask himself how his tests and evaluation philosophy stack up against Dr. Ebel's requirements. Some of the author's statements might be considered controversial. For example, can every important educational outcome or classroom experience be practically assessed? Is the acquisition of useful knowledge the most important outcome? Are the listed criteria for judging the quality of a test exhaustive? What is the relationship between test reliability, item discrimination, and item difficulty? Many of the points covered in this article will be treated in more detail in presentations later in this volume.

Reprinted and abridged with permission of the Association for Supervision and Curriculum Development and the author. Copyright 1962 by the Association for Supervision and Curriculum Development. From an article which appeared in *Educational Leadership*, 1962, Vol. 20 (October), pp. 20–24 (43).

The principles of measurement of educational achievement presented in this article are based on the experience and research of a great many people who have been working to improve classroom testing. The particular principles discussed here were selected on the basis of their relevance to the questions and problems which arise most often when tests of educational achievement are being considered, prepared and used. While some of the principles may seem open to question, we believe a case can be made in support of each one.

1. *The measurement of educational achievement is essential to effective education.* Learning is a natural, inevitable result of human living. Some learning would occur even if no special provision were made for it in schools, or no special effort were taken to facilitate it. Yet efficient learning of complex achievements, such as reading, understanding of science, or literary appreciation requires special motivation, guidance, and assistance. Efforts must be directed toward the attainment of specific goals. Students, teachers, and others involved in the process of education must know to what degree the goals have been achieved. The measurement of educational achievement can contribute to these activities.

It is occasionally suggested that schools could get along without tests, or indeed that they might even do a better job if testing were prohibited. It is seldom if ever suggested, though, that education can be carried on effectively by teachers and students who have no particular goals in view, or who do not care what or how much is being learned. If tests are outlawed, some other means of assessing educational achievement would have to be used in their place.

2. *An educational test is no more or less than a device for facilitating, extending, and refining a teacher's observations of student achievement.* In spite of the Biblical injunction most of us find ourselves quite often passing judgments on our fellow men. Is candidate A more deserving of our vote than candidate B? Is C a better physician than D? Is employee E entitled to a raise or promotion on his merits? Should student F be given a failing mark? Should student L be selected in preference to student M for the leading role in the class play?

Those charged with making such judgments often feel they must do so on the basis of quite inadequate evidence. The characteristics on which the decision should be based may not have been clearly defined. The performances of the various candidates may not have been observed extensively, or under comparable conditions. Instead of recorded data, the judge may have to trust his fallible memory, supplemented with hearsay evidence.

Somewhat similar problems are faced by teachers as they attempt to assess the achievements of their students. In an effort to solve these problems, tests have been developed. Oral and objective examinations make it easier for the teacher to observe student behavior under controlled conditions.

The price that must be paid for a test's advantages of efficiency and control in the observation of student achievements is some loss in the naturalness of the behavior involved. In tests which attempt to measure the student's typical behavior, especially those aspects of behavior which depend heavily on his interests, attitudes, values, or emotional reactions, the artificiality of the test situation may seriously distort the measurements obtained. But this problem is much less serious in tests intended to measure how much the student knows, and what he can do with his knowledge. What is gained in efficiency and precision of measurement usually far outweighs what may be lost due to artificiality of the situation in which the student's behavior is observed.

3. *Every important outcome of education can be measured.* In order for an outcome of education to be important, it must make a difference. The behavior of a person who has more of a particular outcome must be observably different from that of a person who has less. Perhaps one can imagine some result of education which is so deeply personal that it does *not* ever affect in any way what he says or does, or how he spends his time. But it is difficult to find any grounds for arguing that such a well-concealed achievement is important.

If the achievement does make a difference in what a person can do or does do, then it is measurable. For the most elementary type of measurement requires nothing more than the possibility of making a verifiable observation that person or object X has more of some defined characteristic than person or object Y.

To say that any important educational outcome is measurable is not to say that every important educational outcome can be measured by means of a paper and pencil test. But it is to reject the claim that some important educational outcomes are too complex or too intangible to be measured. Importance and measurability are logically inseparable.

4. *The most important educational achievement is command of useful knowledge.* If the importance of an educational outcome may be judged on the basis of what teachers and students spend most of their time doing, it is obvious that acquisition of a command of useful knowledge is a highly important outcome. Or if one asks how the other objectives are to be attained—objectives of self-realization, of human relationship, of economic efficiency, of civic responsibility —it is obvious again that command of useful knowledge is the principal means.

How effectively a person can think about a problem depends largely on how effectively he can command the knowledge that is relevant to the problem. Command of knowledge does not guarantee success, or happiness, or righteousness, but it is difficult to think of anything else a school can attempt to develop which is half as likely to lead to these objectives.

If we give students command of knowledge, if we develop their ability to think, we make them intellectually free and independent. This does not assure us that they will work hard to maintain the status quo, that they will adopt all of our beliefs and accept all of our values. Yet it can make them free men and women in the area in which freedom is most important. We should be wary of an educational program which seeks to change or control student behavior on any other basis than rational self-determination, the basis that command of knowledge provides.

5. *Written tests are well suited to measure the student's command of useful*

knowledge. All knowledge can be expressed in propositions. Propositions are statements that can be judged to be true or false. Scholars, scientists, research workers—all those concerned with adding to our store of knowledge spend most of their time formulating and verifying propositions.

Implicit in every true-false or multiple-choice test item is a proposition, or several propositions. Essay tests also require a student to demonstrate his command of knowledge.

Some elements of novelty are essential in any question intended to test a student's command of knowledge. He should not be allowed to respond successfully simply on the basis of rote learning or verbal association. He should not be asked a stereotyped question to which a pat answer probably has been committed to memory.

6. *The classroom teacher should prepare most of the tests used to measure educational achievement in the classroom.* Many published tests are available for classroom use in measuring educational aptitude or achievement in broad areas of knowledge. But there are very few which are specifically appropriate for measuring the achievement of the objectives of a particular unit of work or of a particular period of instruction. Publishers of textbooks sometimes supply booklets of test questions to accompany their tests. These can be useful, although all too often the test questions supplied are of inferior quality—hastily written, unreviewed, untested, and subject to correct response on the basis of rote learning as well as on the basis of understanding.

Even if good ready-made tests were generally available, a case could still be made for teacher-prepared tests, the chief reason being that the process of test development can help the teacher define his objectives. This process can result in tests that are more highly relevant than any external tests are likely to be. It can make the process of measuring educational achievement an integral part of the whole process of instruction, as it should be.

7. *To measure achievement effectively the classroom teacher must be* (a) *a master of the knowledge or skill to be tested and* (b) *a master of the practical arts of testing.* No courses in educational measurement, no books or articles on the improvement of classroom tests are likely to enable a poor teacher to make good tests. A teacher's command of the knowledge he is trying to teach, his understanding of common misconceptions regarding this content, his ability to invent novel questions and problems, and his ability to express these clearly and concisely—all these are crucial to his success in test construction. It is unfortunately true that some people who have certificates to teach lack one or more of these prerequisites to good teaching and good testing.

However, there are also some tricks of the trade of test construction. A course in educational measurement, or a book or article on classroom testing can teach these things. Such a course may also serve to shake a teacher's faith—constructively and wholesomely—in some of the popular misconceptions about the processes of testing educational achievement. Among these misconceptions are the belief that only essay tests are useful for measuring the development of a student's higher mental processes; that a test score should indicate what proportion a student does know of what he ought to know; that mistakes in scoring are the main source of error in test scores.

8. *The quality of a classroom test depends on* (a) *the relevance of the tasks included in it,* (b) *the representativeness of its sampling of all aspects of instruction, and* (c) *the reliability of the scores it yields.* If a test question presents a problem like those the student may expect to encounter in his later life outside the classroom, and if the course in which his achievement is being tested did in fact try to teach him how to deal with such problems, then the question is relevant. If the test questions involve in proportion to their importance all aspects of achievement the course undertakes to develop, it samples representatively. If the scores students receive on a test agree closely with those they would receive on an independent, equivalent test, then the test yields reliable scores.

Relevance, representativeness, and reliability are all matters of degree. Procedures and formulas for calculating estimates of test reliability are well developed, and are described in most books on educational measurement. Estimates of representativeness and relevance are more subjective, less quantitative. Yet this does not mean that relevance and representativeness are any less important than reliability. The more a test has of each the better. While it is possible to have an irrelevant and unrepresentative but highly reliable test, it is seldom necessary and never desirable to sacrifice any one of the three for the others.

Either essay or objective test forms can be used to present relevant tasks to the examinees. Ordinarily, the greater the novelty of a test question, that is, the smaller the probability that the student has encountered the same question before or been taught a pat answer to it, the greater its relevance. Because of the greater number of questions involved, it is sometimes easier to include a representative sample of tasks in an objective rather than in an essay test. For the same reason, and also because of greater uniformity in scoring, objective tests are likely to yield somewhat more reliable scores than essay tests.

9. *The more variable the scores from a test designed to have a certain maximum possible score, the higher the expected reliability of those scores.* Reliability is sometimes defined as the proportion of the total variability among the test scores which is not attributable to errors of measurement. The size of the errors of measurement depends on the nature of the test—the kind and the number of items in it. Hence, for a particular test any increase in the total variability of the scores is likely to increase the proportion which is not due to errors of measurement and hence to increase the reliability of the test.

Figure 1 shows some hypothetical score distributions for three tests. The essay test consists of 10 questions worth 10 points each, scored by a teacher who regards 75 as a passing score on such a test. The true-false test consists of 100 items, each of which is worth one point if correctly answered, with no subtraction for wrong answers. The multiple-choice test also includes 100 items, each of

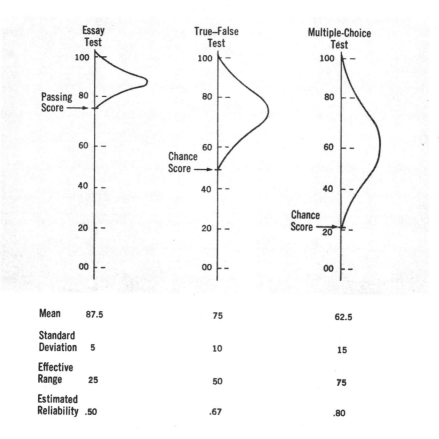

Figure 1. Hypothetical Score Distributions for Three Tests

which offers four alternative answer options. It too is scored only for the number of correct answers given, with no "correction for guessing."

Note in the data at the bottom of Figure 1 the differences among the tests in average score (mean), in variability (standard deviation), in effective range, and in estimated reliability. While these are hypothetical data derived from calculations based on certain assumptions, they are probably reasonably representative of the results most teachers achieve in using tests of these types.

It is possible to obtain scores whose reliability is above .90 using 100 multiple-choice items, but it is not easy to do, and classroom teachers seldom do it in the tests they construct. It is also possible to handle 100-point essay tests and 100-item true-false tests so that their reliability will equal that of a 100-item multiple-choice test. But again, it is not easy to do and classroom teachers seldom succeed in doing it.

10. *The reliability of a test can be increased by increasing the number of*

questions (or independent points to be scored) and by sharpening the power of individual questions to discriminate between students of high and low achievement. Figure 2 illustrates the increases of test reliability which can be expected

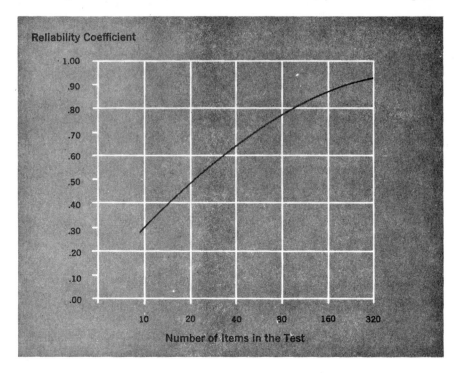

Figure 2. Relation of Test Reliability to Test Length

as a result of increasing the number of items (or independent points to be scored) in a test. Doubling the length of a 10-item test whose reliability coefficient is .33 increases the reliability to .50. Doubling again brings it up to .67 and so on. These estimates are based on the Spearman-Brown formula for predicting the reliability of a lengthened test. While the formula requires assumptions which may not be justified in all cases, its predictions are usually quite accurate.

Figure 3 shows how the maximum discriminating power of an item is related to its level of difficulty. These discrimination indices are simply differences between the proportions of correct response from good and poor students. Good students are those whose total test scores fall among the top 27 percent of the students tested. Poor students are those whose scores make up the bottom 27 percent. An item of 50-percent difficulty does not necessarily have (and usually will not have) an index of discrimination of 1.00. Its discriminating power may be zero, or even negative. But items of middle difficulty have higher ceilings on their discriminating power. What is more important, they not only can have, but

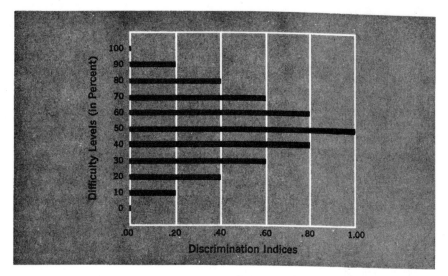

Figure 3. Maximum Discrimination Attainable with Items at Different
Levels of Difficulty

usually do have greater discriminating power than very easy or very difficult items. An item that no one answers correctly or that everyone answers correctly cannot discriminate at all. Such an item adds nothing to the reliability of a test.

4   *Fifteen Criteria of a Testing Program*

ARTHUR E. TRAXLER

The evaluation of the effectiveness of a testing program is an on-going process. It will not only improve periodic subjective appraisals, but will hopefully stimulate frequent empirical investigations into program utility as well. The fifteen significant questions posed by Dr. Traxler in the following article are ones which every school administrator, teacher, and guidance staff member should ask about his own testing program.

Reprinted and abridged with permission of author and publisher from *The Clearing House*, 1950, Vol. 25, pp. 3–7.

The criteria of a testing program are dependent, in part, upon the nature of the school and the grade level of the pupils involved. Certain general criteria, however, are applicable to nearly all kinds of schools and practically all grade levels. These criteria may be phrased in the form of questions.

1. *Is the testing program comprehensive?* Does it include different kinds of tests? It is difficult to interpret a test score in one area, for example, reading comprehension, unless it can be compared with scores in other areas. The level of a pupil's score in a given subject is not as important as the pattern or profile of his scores indicating his strengths and weaknesses.

2. *Does the testing program include all pupils in the school?* If the tests are placed on a voluntary basis, or if they are given only to the pupils who are having difficulty, or if they are administered only to selected groups, or if a large number of pupils are designated as special pupils and are excluded from the class distributions, erroneous conclusions may be drawn concerning the ability and achievement in the school as a whole. What is more important, if some pupils are excluded from the testing, their educational guidance may be impaired by the fact that their records are incomplete. Following each testing program there is a need for a careful check-up and testing of absentees, even though this procedure will inevitably involve a large amount of extra work for the person in charge of the testing program.

3. *Are the tests given at regular intervals?* Are there regular fall and spring testing programs in the school, or are the tests given in a haphazard manner whenever it suits the convenience of the staff member in charge of testing? If the tests are administered at regular intervals, it is possible to study the growth of the pupils from year to year or from the beginning of the school term to the end. But if they are given irregularly, growth studies are likely to be difficult to make and of little value.

4. *Are the tests well timed?* Is the time of administering the different types of tests carefully planned so that the results will be of maximum usefulness? For instance, are tests of reading ability and arithmetic skills given fairly early in the fall so that there will be time to plan and carry out corrective work for pupils found to be retarded in certain skills? Are tests in one-year subjects, such as plane geometry and biology, given toward the end of the year so that the results can readily be reported to the teachers who have the pupils in class, and yet far enough from the end of the term to enable the teachers to make practical use of the results?

5. *Are the tests in the school's testing program comparable?* Are the various tests in a particular fall or spring testing program constructed along similar lines and standardized on similar populations so that it is possible to make comparisons among the results on the different tests? Is an attempt made to keep the tests from year to year comparable through the use of different forms of the same battery?

It has been observed that occasionally a school will deliberately vary its testing program from one year to the next in an effort to get as many different kinds of measures on its pupils as possible. While a certain amount of experimentation, particularly with new and promising tests, is necessary, frequent changes in the tests used are ordinarily undesirable. Such frequent changes are likely to give the test results for the school as a whole a confused picture which even test specialists find difficult to interpret.

6. *Do the tests used agree with the objectives and the curriculum of the school?* In planning a testing program, it is advisable for a school, first of all, to state its objectives, not merely in general terms but specifically and in detail, and then to try to choose tests that are in line with the objectives and the course of study that has been formulated to carry out these objectives. For instance, if a school has an integrated program in the social studies, it will likely find that a general achievement test in social studies is better suited to its program and needs than separate tests in American history, world history, and other specific subjects. No set of standardized tests will fit the objectives and program of an individual school exactly, but there should be a reasonable amount of agreement if the results are to be meaningful.

7. *Are the specific tests carefully chosen?* Does a competent group of persons go over the tests themselves with care and study the available statistical data concerning them? Many different tests are available for various fields, and there is often a great deal of difference in the value of these tests. The work of studying and choosing among specific tests is so time-consuming and has so many technical ramifications that oftentimes it is preferable to have this work done by a committee appointed to represent a group of schools with similar objectives and programs.

8. *Are the tests carefully administered to each group?* No matter how reliable and valid the tests are, the results may be rendered almost worthless by indifferent and careless administration. The question of whether the tests should be administered in large, specially scheduled groups or in the regular classes is one that can be decided only on the basis of local conditions. If the physical equipment of the school is suitable, probably more nearly standard conditions can be achieved through the use of a small number of large groups. But a more natural and less tense atmosphere may attend the administration of the tests in the regular classes.

If the tests are given in the regular classes with all or nearly all the teachers participating, it is important to precede the testing program with a special period of instruction and training of the teachers in test administration. It is highly desirable to make sure that the teachers understand the purpose and value of the tests and that their attitude toward the testing situation is favorable, for an indifferent attitude on the part of a teacher may be reflected in indifference in his pupils. Even with these precautions, it may be necessary to leave some teachers out of the test-giving process, for some excellent teachers seem constitutionally unable to administer tests according to a definite and rigid time schedule.

9. *Are the tests scored accurately?* Test scoring is a difficult and wearisome clerical task. It calls for careful attention to detail, not only in the original scoring but also in the rescoring and checking, and it requires vigilant supervision if large errors in the scores of individual pupils are to be avoided. As a rule, a clerical staff, specially chosen and trained for this task, can score objective tests more rapidly and accurately than the most intelligent group of teachers a school can assemble. It is doubtful whether a school can ever feel confident of the accuracy of the test scores on its records unless it either specially plans and carries through a thoroughly supervised local scoring program or makes use of the services of an outside scoring agency.

10. *Are the test results interpreted in terms of appropriate norms?* National norms based on a meticulous statistical sampling of public schools throughout the country are likely to be very useful for an average public school, but these norms may be almost useless for a public school in a remote rural area of the South or Mid-west, a school in an underprivileged area of a large city, or a college-preparatory group in a suburban public school, or an independent school. The tests scores of an individual pupil or a class group should be compared with norms appropriate to the background, training, and educational and vocational goals of that individual or group.

11. *Are the test results quickly reported to teachers and counselors in understandable terms?* If the test results are to be of maximum value to the school, they must be placed in the hands of the person in a position to use them while the interest in the tests is still strong and while there is still time in the school year to act upon the needs indicated by the results. The scores should reach the teachers and counselors in not more than a few weeks at the most. The test data should be organized in the form of class distributions and alphabetical lists so that the results for both groups and individuals can be quickly and easily apprehended.

The results should be expressed in terms that the individuals who are to use them can understand. For most classroom teachers and many counselors, percentile ranks are the best medium of expression of the results. Where there is a high degree of sophistication concerning tests, the results may be expressed in units whose statistical properties are superior to percentiles, such as standard scores or scaled scores.

12. *Are the test results recorded on individual cumulative record forms?* The results of each testing program have an immediate usefulness, but they also have a long-term value, and this value is enhanced as data are accumulated from year to year. The point cannot be over-emphasized that while it is important to know the level of ability and achievement of a pupil at a given time, it is much more important to know how he is growing in the different areas measured by the tests. Growth can be noted and appraised only when the test results are systematically recorded on individual forms. A school may either prepare its own cumulative record form or use forms generally available through such organizations as the

Educational Records Bureau or the American Council on Education. The cumulative record should include not only test data but also many other kinds of information about the individual.

13. *Is a definite attempt made to relate the test scores to other kinds of information?* Even the most enthusiastic proponent of testing must concede that test results cannot stand alone. They can never give a complete picture of a pupil. There are areas such as effectiveness of oral expression, ability to bring ideas together and synthesize thinking in written expression, various personal factors, and other qualities that are not covered by existing tests. Moreover, even in the skills and understandings that can be measured well by the better objective tests, it is often true that test results can be adequately interpreted only if there is information on some of the less tangible areas which the tests do not cover. For instance, the development of a situation leading to the personal and social maladjustment of an individual may explain what would otherwise be a puzzling and alarming decline in achievement test scores. Up-to-date cumulative records are invaluable in the study of these interrelationships, although even the best cumulative record must oftentimes be supplemented by the collection of current information and case-study procedures for specific individuals.

14. *In addition to the regular testing program, is there provision for special testing as needed?* The all-school testing program should be supplemented by a variety of tests to meet special needs. Several specific needs may be cited by way of illustration. Usually the testing of intelligence or scholastic aptitude in the regular all-school testing program is based on group tests of mental ability, most of which depend rather heavily upon ability to read. Where a reading handicap is suspected, it may be necessary to give a pupil an individual Stanford-Binet Scale to obtain an accurate measure of his intellectual capacity. A pupil who is having difficulty with the usual academic subjects may be given tests of mechanical and clerical aptitude in order to identify aptitudes that have positive significance for educational and vocational guidance.

Guidance of both an educational and a vocational nature may be enhanced by measures of interests, such as the *Kuder Preference Record* or the *Strong Vocational Interest Blank*. In the adjustment counseling of a pupil with whom good rapport has been established, occasional use of inventories of personal qualities, such as the *Bell Adjustment Inventory* or the *California Test of Personality*, may be helpful, provided the counselor has sufficient training and experience to interpret and use the results.

15. *Does the school have an in-service program for educating teachers in the use of test results?* This is without doubt the most important criterion of all. Even a somewhat inadequate testing program from the standpoint of number and kind of tests used may be very helpful to a school if the teachers are prepared to make full use of the test results. But the most thorough and elaborate testing program ever devised will fall flat and be largely a waste of time if the results are placed in the hands of persons untrained in and indifferent to their use. Very few

teachers can ever expect to be experts in testing, but every school should have on its staff one person who makes it his special job to thoroughly understand the testing field, and this person should assume responsibility for training the rest of the faculty. All teachers, even those least mathematically inclined, can learn enough about test scores, class medians, and percentile ranks to interpret and use intelligently the results of the tests in their own subject fields. Understanding of test results can be increased through group discussions, lectures based on lantern slides, non-technical staff clinics, and case studies.

The use of test results is an all-faculty function. When it is accepted as such, pupils and teachers alike can benefit greatly from a comprehensive, regular, systematic testing program.

5   Testing for Accountability

RALPH W. TYLER

The concept of accountability (Lessinger, 1970) is beginning to pervade public education. Based on the notion that those who are given the task of educating our millions of children should be held fiscally and professionally accountable, federal, state, and local governments are requiring periodic audits of both the educational product and process of education. The design of such evaluation programs is complicated and frequently inhibited by difficulties in identifying, selecting or developing appropriate instrumentation. In the following article one of the leading experts in measurement and evaluation discusses in general terms the issues involved in using norm-referenced and criterion-referenced tests. In article 17 of this book Popham and Husek discuss criterion-referenced measurement in detail. See also article 38 in Chapter VIII which deals with a related topic—performance contracting.

Over and above "accountability," what implications does the use of norm-referenced versus criterion-referenced measures have for (1) a classroom teacher, (2) supervisors of instruction, and (3) a school principal or superintendent? If an outside contractor is supplying education, who should evaluate —the contractor, the school, an independent agency, some combination of the three, or no one?

The growing concern about accountability has put new emphasis on measuring what and how much a student has learned in a short period of time. To measure educational outcomes in such a period requires tests designed for this

Reprinted with permission of the author and publisher from *The Nation's Schools*, 1970, Vol. 83, #6 (December), pp. 37–39.

purpose—and the problem for administrators is that most tests currently available are not very suitable.

A good example of the problem is in the area of performance contracting, where schools contract for instruction with private companies on a fee arrangement based on student performance. Since it appears that performance contracts will generally be let to cover students considered to be low achievers from disadvantaged environments, the standard achievement tests in common use do not furnish a dependable measure of how much these children have learned during one school year or less.

They were not constructed to do so.

A typical achievement test is explicitly designed to furnish scores that will arrange the pupils on a line from those most proficient in the subject to those least proficient. The final test questions have been selected from a much larger initial number on the basis of tryouts and are the ones which most sharply distinguished pupils in the tryouts who made high scores on the total test from those who made low scores. Test questions were eliminated if most pupils could answer them or if few pupils could answer them, since these did not give much discrimination.

As a result, a large part of the questions retained for the final form of a standard test are those that 40 to 60 percent of the children were able to answer. There are very few questions that represent the things being learned either by the slower learners or the more advanced ones. If a less advanced student is actually making progress in his learning, the typical standard test furnishes so few questions that represent what he has been learning that it will not afford a dependable measure for him. The same holds true for advanced learners.

This is not a weakness in the test in serving the purpose for which it was designed. The children who made lower scores had generally learned fewer things in this subject than those who made higher scores and could, therefore, be dependably identified as less proficient. Furthermore, a good standard test has been administered to one or more carefully selected samples, usually national, regional or urban samples, of children in the grade for which the test was designed. The scores obtained from these samples provide norms for the test against which a child's score can be related.

These tests—called *norm-referenced tests*—thus provide dependable information about where the child stands in his total test performance in relation to the norm group. But when one seeks to find out whether a student who made a low score has learned certain things during the year, the test does not include enough questions covering the material on which he was working to furnish a dependable answer to that question.

This leads to another problem encountered when one attempts to measure what a child learns in a school year or less. In the primary grades, particularly, each child's learning is dependent on what he had already learned before the year began and what sequence he follows. For example, in reading, some children enter the first grade already able to read simple children's stories and newspaper paragraphs. Measures of what they learn during the first year should be based on samples of reading performance that go beyond this entry level.

On the other extreme, some children enter the first grade with a limited oral vocabulary and without having distinguished the shapes of letters or noted differences in their sounds. Measures of what such a child learns during the first year must take off from his entering performance and be based on the learning sequence used in his school to help him acquire the vocabulary and language skills that are involved in the later stages of reading instruction.

A standardized test, however, is designed to be used in schools throughout the nation, despite the different learning sequences they have and with children coming from a variety of backgrounds and at various stages of learning in the field covered by the test. For this reason, it cannot include enough questions appropriate to each child's stage of development to measure reliably what he has learned during a single school year.

Recognizing that norm-referenced tests can provide dependable information on the relative standing of children, but cannot reliably measure what a child has learned or how much he has learned in a year or less, efforts are now under way to construct and utilize tests that are designed to sample specified knowledge, skills and abilities and to report what the child knows and can do of those matters specified. Since the criterion for a performance contract is that each child will learn specified things, a test that samples them is called a *criterion-referenced* test.

For example, in primary reading, the children who enter without having learned to distinguish letters and sounds might be tested by the end of the year on letter recognition, association of letters with sounds, and word-recognition of 100 most common words. For each of these specified "things to be learned" the child would be presented with a large enough sample of examples to furnish reliable evidence that he could recognize the letters of the alphabet, he could associate the appropriate sounds with each letter, alone and in words, and he could recognize the 100 most common words. A child has demonstrated mastery of specified knowledge, ability, or skill when he performs correctly 85 percent of the time. (Some small allowance, like 15 percent, is needed for lapses common to all people.)

At a higher level of initial performance, a group of children may be expected to read and comprehend typical newspaper paragraphs, simple directions for making or doing something, etc. Similar specifications are made in arithmetic and in writing. Science and the social studies represent greater problems because of the variations in content and the lack of agreement on essential objectives.

The National Assessment of Educational Progress utilizes criterion-referenced tests and reports to the public about the performance of various categories of children and youth rather than individuals. The public is given the percentage of each group—9 year olds, 13 year olds, 17 year olds, and young adults—who know certain facts, can use certain principles in explaining phenomena, are able to do certain things. The reports reveal the exercises that were used and give the percent of each group who answered the question correctly or who demonstrated· the ability or skill involved. The public can get a better grasp of what children and youth are learning by these reports than by trying to interpret abstract scores.

The need for criterion-referenced tests is particularly acute when a contractor undertakes to aid the education of disadvantaged children. Currently used standard tests are not satisfactory tools to appraise the learning of disadvantaged children that can be expected in a single school year. Because most of the disadvantaged begin the year at much earlier stages than a majority of pupils, the standard tests developed for that grade include very few questions that represent what these children are learning.

For this reason, when such a test is given at the beginning of the year and a second test at the end of the year, the changes in score for an individual child may largely be chance variations, since both scores are based on very small samples of knowledge, abilities or skills to which these children could respond. Furthermore, since the number of questions on which the initial score is based is small, coaching for these particular items can give a large relative gain. For example, if a child answered four questions correctly in the initial test, being able to answer four more in the final test will place him very much higher on the relative score of a standard test than would a gain of four points when his initial score was 40.

This fact increases the temptation for coaching in the case of contracts involving disadvantaged children. Criterion-referenced tests constructed for the learning sequences actually being followed will include a much larger sample of appropriate questions.

Although there are few criterion-referenced tests presently available, if performance contracting continues to expand rapidly, both schools and contractors will soon recognize that they do not have the tests they need to furnish dependable measures of performance. Publishers may well respond by a crash program of criterion-referenced test development.

II

DEFINING AND
ESTIMATING RELIABILITY

The term "reliability" as used in everyday language conveys a meaning which is *somewhat parallel* to the meaning ascribed to it by the measurement expert. An example may serve to demonstrate the similarities and differences in meaning. Suppose we said that a worker was reliable. What would this convey? It might be supposed that the worker reports at the same time every day, appears in the same condition, and performs consistently. This similarity of behavior from time to time would be comparable to one of the tester's approaches to reliability. Note, however, that for the tester no judgment of the appropriateness of the behavior is implied. Suppose the worker could be trusted to report to work one hour late, with the same amount of alcohol already consumed, and to fall asleep next to his machine. Following the measurement expert's approach, this man is reliable. His behavior is consistent from time to time, although it probably would not be deemed desirable. Similarly, a test can yield very dependable information but be inappropriate for the particular purpose for which we may be considering it.

For decades the concept of reliability has remained of crucial importance for describing the outcomes of the measuring process. The test manuals containing reliability information as well as the theoretical and research articles devoted to reliability constitute a significant proportion of yearly scholarly production and publication in the field of educational and psychological measurement. The first article in this chapter is a summary of recent authoritative thinking as to the reliability information which should be included in test manuals. It is the product of a joint committee representing the following three associations: American Psychological Association, American Educational Research Association, and National Council on Measurement in Education. The reading of these *Standards* will provide an overview of the chapter, especially with regard to the kinds of variation in test scores that may be considered "error."

The publication date of the next article (1928) should help "validate" the statement made at the beginning of the previous paragraph, i.e., "For decades. . . ." In this paper the late Dr. Percival Symonds presents a diagrammatic assist to the understanding of reliability and validity before discussing what factors affect the various sources of error. Not only should the producer of an instrument consider how to control its reliability, but also the consumer should interpret reliability information in view of the various factors which influence the reliability.

In the above articles the emphasis has been more upon test selection and description than upon the interpretation of scores for an individual. But suppose one finds himself concerned with the accuracy of a score for a particular individual. One knows that the greater the reliability for the group, the smaller the error to expect for the individual. But how small an error would be expected if, for example, the correlation between alternate forms given a week apart were .83? One would want an estimate of the number of points the score is apt to be in error. The problem of estimating the number of points the score is apt to be in error is the problem addressed by Doppelt in the next article of the chapter. Doppelt defines the standard error of measurement and discusses its interpretation. The concept of standard error of measurement is of prime importance when interpreting the results of either informal or standardized instruments, and studying this article should assist the reader in making correct use of this concept.

In the final article of the chapter, McMorris addresses a problem inherent in the use of basic descriptive measures. He presents formulas for approximating the standard deviation, internal consistency reliability, and the standard error of measurement. The reader may judge the accuracy of the approximations from the summary of results given for a sample of classroom tests. He may judge the ease of computing the approximations merely by examining the formulas.

In summary, this chapter has been designed to overview the concept of reliability and various types of errors that affect the accuracy of a test, to consider a variety of influences on reliability, to define and interpret a reliability measure appropriate for use with an individual's score, and to specify and judge approximations for measures used to describe reliability. The chapter contains not only basic conceptualizations but also specific suggestions for classroom applications.

6   *Standards for Reporting and Evaluating Test Reliability*

NATIONAL COMMITTEE ON TEST STANDARDS

In 1954 the American Psychological Association published Technical Recommendations for Psychologieal Tests and Diagnostic Techniques. *The guidelines included in this document were to serve as criteria against which a test publisher would compare his product before it was to be made commercially available. Minimum and more desirable amounts and types of information to be included in the test manual were specified. The focus was on potential users of educational and psychological tests, and was to serve as a kind of "watchdog" for the psychometric fraternity. As with most suggested guidelines, the* Recommendations *have met with varying degrees of acceptance. Their influence can, however, only be evaluated as having been positive.*

The following excerpt from the newly revised Recommendations, *now called* Standards, *describes the essential reliability data required in any test manual for the user to make intelligent evaluations and applications of the instrument. It also represents an integration of the requirements specified by the American Educational Research Association and the National Council on Measurement in Education in their 1955 publication,* Technical Recommendations for Achievement Tests.

The following questions should guide the student's reading. What reliability information should a teacher be most interested in with respect to his classroom examinations? What specific influences would have the greatest impact on the score reliability of an individually administered intelligence test rather than a group administered intelligence test? If you were developing a test to predict success in medical school, what specific recommendations would you need to make about reliability? What are some possible ways by which a tester could control the reliability of the tests he administers? A factory uses a "work-sample" (actual job tryout with a drill press) as a predictor of success on the job. What are some possible sources of measurement error and how could you determine the magnitude of their influence? In a mental health clinic, a psychologist uses a "projective test" (e.g., Thematic Apperception Test) to make a diagnosis of the presence or absence of psychopathology. In what way would reliability be a significant factor in this situation?

Reliability refers to the accuracy (consistency and stability) of measurement by a test. Any direct measurement of such consistency obviously calls for a comparison between at least two measurements. (Whereas "accuracy" is a general expression, the terms "consistency" and "stability" are needed to describe respectively form-associated and time-associated reliability). The two measurements may be obtained by retesting an individual with the identical test. Aside from practical limitations, retesting is not a theoretically desirable method of determining a reliability coefficient if—as usual—the items that constitute the test are only one of many sets (actual or hypothetical) that might equally well have been used to measure the particular ability or trait. Thus there is ordinarily no reason to suppose that one set of 50 vocabulary items, for example, is especially superior (or inferior) to another comparable or equivalent set of 50. In this case it appears desirable to determine not only the degree of response-variation by the subject from one occasion to the next (as is accomplished by the retest method), but also the extent of sampling error involved in selecting a given set of 50 items. These two objectives are accomplished most commonly by one's correlating scores on the original set of 50 items with scores by the same subjects on another set of 50 items—an "alternate form" of the original 50. If the effect of content sampling alone is sought (without the effects of response-variability by the subject), or if it is not practical to undertake testing on two different occasions, a test of 100 items may be administered. Then the test may be divided into two sets of 50 odd-numbered items and 50 even-numbered items; the correlation between scores on the odd and the even sets is a "split-half" or "odd-even" correlation, from which a reliability (consistency) coefficient for the entire test of 100 items may be estimated by the Spearman-Brown formula.[1] Essentially the same type of estimated reliability coefficient may be obtained from item-analysis data through use of the Kuder-Richardson formulas.[2] It should be noted that despite the possible heterogeneity of content, the odd-even correlation between the sets of items may be quite high if the items are easy and if the test is administered with a short time limit.

It is clear that different methods of determining the reliability coefficient take account of different sources of error. Thus, from one testing to the other, the retest method is affected not only by response-variability of the subjects but also by differences in administration (most likely if different persons administer the test on the two occasions). Reliability coefficients based on the single administration of a test ignore response-variability and the particular administrative conditions: their effects on the score simply do not appear as errors of measurement. Hence "reliability coefficient" is a generic term referring to various types of evidence; each type of evidence suggests a different meaning. It is essential that the method used to derive any reliability coefficient should be clearly described.

As a generic term reliability refers to many types of evidence, each of which describes the agreement or consistency to be expected among similar observations. Each type of evidence takes into account certain kinds of errors or inconsistencies and not others. The operation of measurement may be viewed as a sample of behavior; in a typical aptitude or achievement test the person is observed on a particular date as he responds to a particular set of questions or stimuli, and his responses are recorded and scored by a particular tester or system. The occasion is a sample from the period of time within which the same general inquiry would be pertinent; some sampling error is involved in selecting any one date of observation. The items that constitute the test are only one of many sets (actual or hypothetical) that might have been used to measure the same ability or trait. The choices of a particular test apparatus, test administrator, observer, or scorer are also sampling operations. Each such act of sampling has some influence on the test score. It is valuable for the test user to know how much a particular score would be likely to change if any one of these conditions of measurement were altered.

There are various components that may contribute to inconsistency among observations: (a) response-variation by the subject, due to changes in physiological efficiency or in such psychological factors as motivation, effort, or mood— these may be especially important in inventories of personality; (b) variations in test-content or the test-situation; (In "situational tests" which include interacting persons as part of the situation this source of variation can be relatively large.) (c) variations in administration (either through variations in physical factors such as temperature, noise, or apparatus-functioning; or in psychological factors such as variation in the technique or skill of different test-administrators or raters); (d) variations in the process of observation. In addition to these sources of error, scoring error variance in test scores reflects variation in the process of scoring responses as well as mistakes in recording, transferring, or reading of scores.

The estimation of clearly labelled components of error variance is the most informative outcome of a reliability study, both for the test-developer wishing to improve the reliability of his instrument and for the user desiring to interpret test scores with maximum understanding.

Although estimation of clearly labelled components of error variance is the most informative outcome of a reliability study, this approach is not yet prominent in reports on tests. The more familiar reliability study obtains two measures

---

[1] The general form of the Spearman-Brown formula employed to estimate reliability is usually expressed as follows:

$$r_{tt} = \frac{nr}{1 + (n-1)r}$$

where r_{tt} is the reliability of a test lengthened n-times and r represents the original reliability. If the test has been divided into comparable or equivalent halves, r would represent the correlation of these halves, and the formula could be rewritten as follows:

$$r_{tt} = \frac{2r}{1+r}.$$

[2] The most frequently used Kuder-Richardson formula is Number 21, and is usually expressed as follows:

$$KR_{21} = \left(\frac{K}{K-1}\right)\left(1 - \frac{\overline{X}(K-\overline{X})}{KS^2}\right)$$

where $K = \#$ of items in the test, scored as either right (1) or wrong (0), $\overline{X} =$ the mean, and $S^2 =$ the variance of test scores.

and correlates them, or derives a correlation coefficient by applying one of several formulas to part- or item-scores within a test. Such a correlation is often interpreted as a ratio of "true variance" to "true variance plus error variance." Many different coefficients, each involving its own definition of "true" and "error" variance, may be derived from a multivariate reliability experiment with the presence of controls for such factors as those of content, time, and mode of administration. Hence any single correlation is subject to considerable misinterpretation unless the investigator makes clear just what sampling errors are considered to be "error" in the particular coefficient he reports. The correlation between two test forms presented on different days has a different significance from an internal-consistency coefficient, for example, because the latter allocates day-to-day fluctuations in a person's efficiency to the "true" rather than to the "error" portion of the score variance.

In the present set of *Standards* the terminology by which the 1954 *Technical Recommendations* classified coefficients into several types (e.g., coefficient of equivalence) has been discarded. Such a terminological system breaks down as more adequate statistical analyses are applied and methods are more adequately described. Hence it is recommended that test authors work out suitable phrases to convey the meaning of whatever coefficients they report; as an example, the expression "the consistency between measurements by different test-forms as determined by stability over a 7-day interval," although lengthy, will be reasonably free from ambiguity.

GENERAL PRINCIPLES

1. The test manual should report evidence of reliability that permits the reader to judge whether scores are sufficiently dependable for the recommended uses of the test. If any of the necessary evidence has not been collected, the absence of such information should be noted.

The test manual should furnish insofar as feasible a quantitative analysis of the total inconsistency of measurement into its major identifiable components; viz., fluctuations or inconsistency in responses of the subject; inconsistency or heterogeneity within the sample of test content (such as the stimulus items, questions, and situations); inconsistencies in administration of the test; inconsistency among scorers, raters, or units of apparatus; and mechanical errors of scoring.

With group tests of school achievement the principal sources of error to be evaluated usually include (a) inconsistency or heterogeneity within the sample of test content; (Although admittedly in an achievement test the content should be just as heterogeneous as the subject matter or the functions that are involved in successful use of knowledge.) (b) inconsistencies in test administration; and (c) inconsistency in responses of the examinee over time, i.e., instability. The collection of data should be designed to permit evaluation of these three factors. In the case of projective tests fluctuation or inconsistency in the responses of the subject is usually a major source of random error to be evaluated; inconsistency among scorers or raters should also be evaluated.

For instruments that yield a profile having a low reliability of differences between scores, the manual should explicitly caution the user against casual interpretation of differences between scores, except as a source of tentative information requiring external verification.

2. In the test manual reports on reliability or error of measurement, procedures, and samples should be described sufficiently to permit a user to judge to what extent the evidence is applicable to the persons and problems with which he is concerned.

The maturity of the group, the variation in the group, and the attitude of the group toward the test should represent normal conditions of test use. For example, the reliability of a test to be used in selecting employees should be determined by testing applicants for positions rather than by testing college students or workers already employed.

The reliability of a school intelligence or achievement test should generally be estimated separately for each of many classes at each of several grade levels within each of several school systems. The mean and standard deviation for each sample should be reported in the test manual along with its reliability coefficients.

The reliability sample should be described in the test manual in terms of any selective factors related to the variable being measured. Demographic information such as distribution of the subjects with respect to age, sex, socio-economic level, intellectual level, employment status or history, and minority group membership should be given in the test manual.

If reliability coefficients are corrected for range, both the uncorrected and the corrected coefficients should be reported in the test manual, together with the standard deviation of the group actually tested and the standard deviation assumed for the corrected sample.

3. Reports of reliability studies should ordinarily be expressed in the test manual in terms of (a) variances for error components (or their square roots), or (b) standard errors of measurement, or (c) product-moment reliability coefficients.

Reliability is a necessary, but not a sufficient condition of validity. Reliability coefficients are pertinent to validity in the negative sense that unreliable scores cannot be valid. But reliable scores are by no means *ipso facto* valid, since validity depends on what interpretation is proposed. Reliability is of special importance in support of, but not in replacement of, the analysis and estimation of content validity.

COMPARABILITY OF FORMS

4. If two forms of a test are published, both forms being intended for possible use with the same subjects, the means and variances of the two forms should be

reported in the test manual along with the coefficient of correlation between the two sets of scores. If necessary evidence is not provided, the test manual should warn the reader against assuming comparability.

Whenever feasible, the test manual should present a summary of item statistics for each form, such as a frequency distribution of item difficulties and of indices of item discrimination.

Whenever the content of the items can be described meaningfully, it is advisable that a comparative analysis of the forms be presented in the test manual to show how similar they are.

In the instance of two forms of an achievement test, a chart or table should be presented in which not only frequency distributions of item statistics are furnished, but also a tabulation of frequency of items by categories of subject-matter content and of behavioral or instructional objectives. The two forms should represent different samples of items within each category. Artificially close similarity between forms which could be attained by matching item for item from form to form is not desirable because it hides real errors of measurement associated with content sampling, and in this case the inter-item correlation is a spuriously high estimate of the reliability.

Whenever two sets of performances on a test are correlated to determine comparability, the interval of time between the testings should be specified in the test manual.

INTERNAL CONSISTENCY

5. If the test manual suggests that a score is a measure of a generalized, homogeneous trait, evidence of internal consistency should be reported.

Internal consistency is important if items are viewed as a sample from a relatively homogeneous universe, as in a test of addition with integers, a list of general high-school vocabulary, or a test presumed to measure introversion. Nevertheless, measures of internal consistency should not be regarded as a substitute for other measures. When alternate forms are available, alternate-form reliabilities should be reported in preference to coefficients based on internal analysis.

Estimates of internal consistency should be determined by the split-half method or methods of the Kuder-Richardson type, if these can properly be used on the data under examination. Any other measure of internal consistency which the author wishes to report in addition should be carefully explained in the test manual.

Whenever reliability coefficients based upon internal analysis are reported, the test manual should present evidence that speed of work has a negligible influence on scores. If speed is a consequential factor, the internal correlation measures will be too high by an indeterminate amount; in such cases, assuming that alternate forms are not available, the reliability coefficient should be based upon separately timed half tests.

COMPARISONS OVER TIME

6. The test manual should indicate to what extent test scores have stability: that is, how nearly constant the scores are likely to be if a test is repeated after time has lapsed. The manual should also describe the effect of any such variation on the usefulness of the test. The time interval to be considered depends on the nature of the test and on what interpretation of the test scores is recommended.

For most purposes in psychology and education fluctuations of test scores within a few hours, days, or even months will interfere with measurement. The intention in using educational and psychological tests is to draw conclusions about relatively lasting characteristics of the person tested; hence, instability over trails or observations within a short period is regarded as a source of error variance which lowers reliability. For example, a college entrance test which is administered once is intended to measure a characteristic of a person that is related to his accomplishments over the first year of college. To the extent that the test scores fluctuate from day to day about the person's average level, they are in error. In some situations, however, where the test is intended as a measure of a changing characteristic, fluctuation over a period of weeks or months is not to be regarded as a defect in the measurement. A reading readiness test used only once for an initial tentative assignment of first-grade pupils among instructional groups is an example. Even for this test, however, stability over a month perhaps is required if scores are to serve their intended purpose. In experiments on the effects of drugs, on the other hand, it may be desirable to measure meaningful changes in two sets of test scores that represent a time lapse of only a few minutes.

It seems reasonable to require an assessment of stability for projective techniques and other devices for assessing personality dynamics even though it is recognized in some instances that a low retest stability over a substantial period merely reflects true trait fluctuation and hence indicates desired validity. However, clinical practice rarely presumes that the inferences from projective tests are to be applied only on the very day the test is given. Realistically, one must recognize that pragmatic decisions are being made from test data which are meaningful only in terms of at least days, and usually weeks or months of therapy and other procedures following the test administration. If a certain test result is empirically found to be highly unstable from day to day, this evidence casts doubt upon the utility of the test for most purposes even if that fluctuation might be explained by the hypothesis of trait inconstancy.

In any report in the test manual concerning the determination of the stability of scores by repeated testing, alternate forms of the test should have been used to minimize recall of specific answers, especially if the time-interval is not long enough to assure forgetting.

7 *Factors Influencing Test Reliability*

The individuals who construct instruments have to be concerned with how reliably the instruments measure. These individuals, such as teachers, psychologists, and researchers, are concerned not only with how accurately an instrument functions with a specific type of group, but how that accuracy may be improved. For example, should the items be of varying difficulties? Does objectivity of scoring allow for higher reliability? Would making the content more homogeneous be apt to increase the reliability? What influence would each of the following factors have on test reliability: (a) guessing, (b) training, (c) speed, (d) testwiseness, and (e) physical condition?

Many of the comments included in the following article may appear to some readers as naïve and unsophisticated. It must be remembered, however, that when this summary was prepared, little definitive research had been completed. The paper has nonetheless been included in this collection because the generalizations presented are as viable today as they were in 1928. For more recent, comprehensive, or technical considerations of reliability, the reader is referred to any one of the following: Jackson and Ferguson (1941), R. L. Thorndike (1951), Cronbach (1960 & 1970), Cronbach, Rajaratnam, and Gleser (1963), Stanley (1971), and Tryon (1957).

This paper proposes to list and discuss the factors which influence the reliability of tests. Were psychologists more conscious of what it is that makes a test reliable, fewer blunders would be made in devising tests which have low and unsatisfactory reliability. The development of the natural sciences depended on the development of exact measurements, and the development of psychology as a science likewise depends on the perfection of its measuring instruments. Much of the recent work in the development of tests, particularly in the measurement of personality, is practically worthless because the tests do not tell a consistent story.

Reliability in this paper is defined as the correlation between two comparable tests. If a test is split so that one-half contains items 1, 3, 5, 7, etc., and the other half items 2, 4, 6, 8, etc., these two halves constitute in themselves comparable tests. Any two comparable tests may be thought of as being the split halves of a test double the length of either. If the test is an objective test containing homogeneous material, corresponding items of comparable tests may have little resemblance to one another in form, significance, or difficulty.

To use Kelley's (1924) terminology with reference to Figure 4 let the two

Reprinted and abridged from an article by the late Professor Percival M. Symonds entitled "Factors Influencing Test Reliability," which appeared in the *Journal of Educational Psychology*, 1928, Vol. 19, pp. 73–87. Copyright 1928 by the American Psychological Association and reproduced by permission.

48

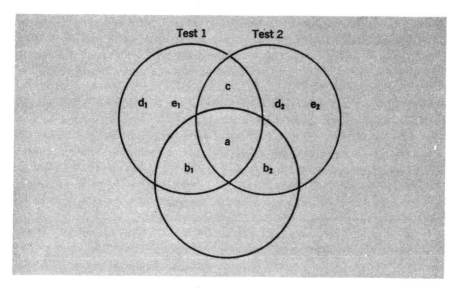

General Field
Figure 4.

upper circles represent the field measured by two comparable tests 1 and 2 and
let the lower circle represent the field that the tests are intended to measure, such
as intelligence, reading, algebra, or French.

> Let a $=$ a factor common to test 1 and test 2 and to
> the field that the test intends to measure
> $b_1 =$ a factor common to test 1 and the general
> field but not to test 2
> $b_2 =$ a factor common to test 2 and the general
> field but not to test 1
> c $=$ a factor common to test 1 and test 2, but not
> to the general field
> $d_1 =$ a factor unique to test 1
> $d_2 =$ a factor unique to test 2
> $e_1 =$ a chance factor found in test 1
> $e_2 =$ a chance factor found in test 2

Kelly defines the reliability of test 1 as

$$\frac{\sigma_a^2 + \sigma_c^2}{\sigma^2}.$$

The validity of test 1 is

$$\frac{\sigma_a^2 + \sigma_{b1}^2}{\sigma^2}.$$

The problem of this paper is to isolate factors a and c and distinguish them from
factors d and e.

It is customary to group the factors influencing test reliability into: (1) factors in the construction of the tests themselves; and (2) factors in the variability of the individuals taking the tests. For certain factors this is a clear cut distinction; for others both irregularity in test and construction and the variability in individuals seem to be operative. Factors concerned with the construction of tests may be divided into: (a) general factors such as the influence of directions, objectivity of scoring, character of printing; and (b) character of specific items such as the affective tinge of items or catch questions. Likewise the variability of individuals may be divided into: (c) the general conditions of the individual such as excitement or nervousness; and (d) specific methods of attack on the test such as speed or accuracy.

1. A very important factor influencing test reliability is the *number of test items*. That is, *the greater the number of the items in a test, the more reliable the test*. The evidence for this is both deductive and experimental. It can be argued that an increase in the number of items in a test (provided the test retains identity in comparability with the original test) increases the reliability. This increase in reliability has a mathematical relationship as given by the Spearman-Brown formula.

The reliability of tests would increase exactly as predicted by the Spearman-Brown formula if the longer tests were exactly comparable to the shorter tests. Since this is never actually true there is deviation from the Spearman-Brown prophecy in actual practice.

Any factor which apparently tends to make a test have a greater or smaller number of items or which is correlated with number of items is a factor in test reliability. Among these factors may be mentioned:

2. Other things being equal, *the narrower the range of difficulty of the items of a test the greater the reliability*. If an item is so hard that no one in the group answers it, that item may be omitted without changing the score of any individual taking the test. Consequently it has no influence upon the reliability of the test and really makes the test equivalent to a test having one item less. Likewise a test including items so easy that everyone in a group answers them correlates perfectly with the same test minus those easy items Hence those items add nothing to the value of the test. That item which has the greatest influence on the reliability of a test is one answered correctly by 50 per cent of the group taking the test.

3. *Evenness in scaling is a factor influencing the reliability of a test*. Other things being equal a test evenly scaled is more reliable than a test that has gaps in the scale of difficulty of its items. Bunching items together in difficulty has the same effect on the reliability of a test as lowering the number of items. For instance, if an extreme case is taken so that items are divided into two groups, the items in one group being passed by the majority of pupils in a class and the items

NOTE: The symbol σ^2 represents a measure of variability referred to as the "variance." When unaccompanied by a subscript it is interpreted as "total variance."

in the other group being failed by the majority of pupils in a class, the test is reduced to little better than a test of two items.

4. Other things being equal, *interdependent items tend to decrease the reliability of a test.* If the answer to one item is suggested in another item, or if the meaning of one item depends upon a previous item, these items act to lower the reliability. For the tendency becomes to answer neither item or both items and thereby produces an effect equivalent to reducing the number of items in a test. Asking several questions on one paragraph in a reading test comes under this head, for if a pupil fails to understand the paragraph he has difficulty with all the items on that paragraph.

5. *The more objective the scoring of a test the more reliable is the test.* One factor which may influence the variability of test scores is the uniqueness of the answers which are given credit. If a test is perfectly objective, i.e., if answers which are given credit are sharply defined in a key and only those answers are given credit, this factor influencing reliability is eliminated. But where judgment of the scorer enters in determining the acceptability or fitness of an answer, as in the verbal completion test, there is a factor causing test unreliability.

6. As a corollary to the last point *scoring inaccuracy is a factor in test reliability.* This factor is eliminated with accurate scoring. But errors in scoring give rise to a variation in scores which lowers the reliability of the test.

7. *Chance in getting the correct answer to an item is a factor in test reliability.* Some of the most objective forms of tests offer the most opportunity for a chance to influence the score. The true-false test is a type in which chance plays a maximum part in determining the score. In the single-answer test and in subjective tests chance plays a negligible part in test reliability because the ratio of the one correct answer to the multitude of possible answers is so small. In the case of multiple-response tests the influence of chance in determining the correctness of any item is $\frac{1}{n-1}$ where n is the number of alternatives provided. A skillful test maker can lower this ratio by including misleading associations among the various alternatives. There has been much speculation as to the influence of chance in lowering test reliability. It is especially important to know the relative influence of chance in lowering reliability as against objectivity in raising it. This has been considered by Ruch, whose results are illustrated in the following reliability data (Form A–Form B) for comparable tests of 100 items.

Type of Test	*Coefficient of Reliability*
Recall	.950
7-response multiple choice	.907
5-response multiple choice	.882
3-response multiple choice	.890
2-response multiple choice	.843
True-false	.837

These data enable one to estimate the loss in reliability which is due to chance. Any factor that causes chance to play a part in determining whether or not an item is to be answered is also a factor that influences test reliability.

8. Other things being equal, *the more homogeneous the material of a test the greater its reliability*. The reason for this may be seen by referring back to Figure 4. If the items of a test are heterogeneous in subject matter or if the factors b, d, and e are more numerous than factors a and c, by definition the reliability becomes less. If a test maker purposely includes items of diverse character in a test in order to sample different phases of the function being measured, he does so at the expense of reliability as the increased heterogeneity of the material only works to lower the reliability.

9. Among chance factors may be mentioned the commonness or uniqueness of the experiences in the test. Other things being equal *the more common the experiences called for in a test are to the members of the group taking the test the more reliable the test*. For this reason tests of things learned in school are more reliable than things learned outside of school. In general, tests of conduct or character will always be less reliable than tests of ability in which there is universal agreement as to rightness or correctness. Tests using material taken from the common environment are the most reliable. A good example of this is found in the Stanford Achievement Test. Even though the test in language usage contains more items than test 1 (reading of paragraphs), test 2 (arithmetic computation), and test 3 (arithmetic reasoning), it has a lower reliability coefficient than these other tests. Part of this may be due to the form, for since each item of the language usage test is a two-alternative item, chance may play a considerable part in the score. But part of the lower reliability may be due to the fact that pupils learn their language habits mainly at home which has its own standard of correctness. On the other hand, tests on subjects learned at school usually have a common standard of correctness.

10. Variations of this factor of commonness or uniqueness of material occur frequently. Other things being equal *the same test given late in the school year is more reliable than when given early in the year.* Given early in the year much of the material of the test will not have been formally covered in class. Whether or not a pupil answers many items in the Powers General Chemistry Test at the opening of the school year will depend on such factors as whether he has read chemistry outside of class, or whether he has had a chemistry experimental set at home, or whether his family discusses matters of intellectual interest at the table.

11. *Another factor similar to the last is the inclusion of extraneous or dead material in a test.* If a test contains material not discussed in class or not given in the textbook, that test is less reliable than a test having the same number of items all of which are relevant. Such a test may be considered as the equivalent of a shorter test with a smaller number of items, with chance determining the answers to the extraneous or dead material. For this reason standardized tests

in a subject are probably less reliable than comparable tests, equivalent in form and length but containing only material relevant to the course as given.

12. Other things being equal, *catch questions in a test lower the reliability of the test.* A test answered by the systematic recall or recognition of orderly facts or experience is more reliable than a test answered by sudden insight because of novelty. Questions which must be answered by sudden insight tend to lower the reliability of the test. Thorndike has noted the incidence of this factor. He says: "The equalization of environmental influence obtained by novelty in and of itself has one notable practical disadvantage. Special coaching for the test is likely to produce many great inequalities in favor of those who receive it." The most reliable tests are those in which special coaching has the least influence.

13. *Subtle factors* in a test item which tend to be misinterpreted or over- or underemphasized help to make the test in which the item is included unreliable. Such factors are:

(a) *The Emotional Tinge of Words in Items.* If words are included in an item which cause the item to be misinterpreted or which lend false clues or associations, that item is a factor of unreliability in the test.

(b) *Length of a Test Item.* The longer a test item the more chance there is that it will be misinterpreted or that certain factors in the item will be over- or underestimated. Items which require extensive reading tend to be less reliable than items which require little reading.

(c) *Choice of Words.* If strange or unusual words are used or if words are used with unusual or technical meanings, they tend to increase the unreliability of an item. Any item which contains trade secrets tends to be less reliable than an item in which all terms are used with their ordinary connotation.

(d) *Poor sentence structure.* Particularly an unusual order of words tends to lead to misinterpretation of an item and is a factor in unreliability.

(e) *Inadequate or faulty directions* in a test or the *failure to provide suitable illustrations* of the task tend to lead to test unreliability.

(f) *Any factor which makes one misinterpret the intention in a test item* tends to make that item and hence the whole test unreliable. Matters of printing, spacing, paragraphing, etc., are all potent in this connection. If a term or phrase is split so that it occupies two lines, or if variations in type are used so that certain parts of the test stand out and others are diminished, the test is liable to be misinterpreted and become unreliable.

The factors to be discussed next are those which have to do with the variability of the individuals being tested.

14. It has been shown that the *speed of taking a test* is a factor in the reliability of the test. Individuals may vary in the speed with which they take a test. At one time they may work more slowly than at another time. Part of this is due to the matter of getting adjusted to the taking of the test. One has to learn how to work the test as well as the requirements of the exercises themselves. Pupils will

differ in the speed with which they adjust themselves to the taking of a test. This is due partly to general mental agility and partly to experiences in taking tests. Practice and experience with tests, particularly with the mechanics of taking the test, helps to diminish the unreliability of tests. A fore-exercise to a test which pupils may experiment with before taking the test itself helps to stabilize this factor of speed. In this connection the *accuracy with which a test is timed* is an important factor in test reliability,

15. *Accuracy in taking a test* is an important factor influencing reliability. A pupil will vary at times in his accuracy on a test. This may be due to the set which he is given by the directions in the test. It is often due to the fact that before a pupil understands what the test requires he will proceed with less accuracy than later when he understands the nature of the test exercises. Part of this factor is due to the way in which we teach pupils to interpret test results. Our insistence on speed and the length of the test leads a pupil to believe that he is expected to cover as much ground as possible, regardless of the accuracy of his work.

16. *Incentive or effort.* Differences in incentive and effort tend to make tests unreliable. The appeal of a test is stronger with some pupils than with others; and is stronger with a pupil at one time than at another. It is commonly assumed that tests have a uniform and a maximum appeal, but this must be far from the case. When one comes to character or personality tests this factor is greatly magnified. Such tests assume that the pupil is being impelled by the same forces of interest and purpose. In the case of achievement tests a strong motive is thrown into the field, like a magnet, and as in magnetization we assume that all of the molecules align themselves in the direction of polarity, so we assume that the motive of the test is equally effective on all pupils taking the test. But in a character or personality test we cannot even assume a uniform motivation. Probably this is as potent as any other factor in causing the unreliability of personality tests.

17. An unknown but probably powerful factor in determining unreliability is the *obtrusion of competing ideas.* This perseveration of previous experience is a factor that must be reckoned with. Children bring to school perseverating experiences from the movies, family life, happenings on the street, playground, and locker room. If a pupil is steeped in the sentimentality of a movie, or worried because of friction at home, or afraid because of a bully who promised to get him after school, his mental mechanism is surely less able to stick to the manipulations required on a test than if his mind is freed from such extraneous factors. Pupils probably differ in their ability to concentrate. Pupils differ also in the number or intensity of outside distracting influences which they encounter. Any one pupil will be more dominated by the compelling idea on some occasions than on others.

18. Following closely on this last point is the matter of *distractions* during the test itself. Any incident that occurs in the schoolroom during the taking of a test influences to some degree the taking of the test. If a test is given while noisy pupils are having recess on the playground under the window or in the school

corridors, or if a test is given at the end of the hour when the pupil is momentarily expecting the bell for dismissal, the conditions are unfavorable for the best results. Distracting incidents in the schoolroom also ought to be avoided. Pupils should not be allowed to leave their seats during a test. No questions from pupils should be permitted after the test is started. Directions should be given concerning what to do if the test is finished ahead of time. Under no conditions should pupils be allowed to leave the examination room early if confusion is to be the result.

19. *Accidents occuring during the examination,* such as breaking a pencil, running out of ink, or defective test booklets influence the reliability of the test. So far as possible accidents should be foreseen, prevented if possible, quickly remedied at any event.

20. *Illness, worry, excitement* probably are minor factors in test reliability. The pupil who has sprained a wrist so that he cannot write with his writing hand is at an obvious disadvantage. Likewise if the pupil is working with a splitting headache or high fever the average results should not be expected. The human machine can submit to marked variations in physical efficiency, however, with no marked change in mental efficiency. In general this factor of general condition of the individual has been much overemphasized in considerations of test reliability. Most persons believe that excitement, worry, and variations in physical efficiency markedly influence test results. Many teachers would entirely discard test results as measures of achievement because they believe that pupils are unable to do themselves justice on an examination. This superstition probably may be traced to one's own experience in taking tests and the rationalization that would excuse a test result on the basis of excitement, worry, or nervousness.

On the other hand experimentation shows that the general condition of an individual is of relative unimportance in influencing the results of a test. A number of experiments have been conducted studying various phases of work and efficiency. The general conclusion is that mental work has a remarkable consistency even during or following a variety of distracting influences. Continuous mental work or fatigue has been found to have little effect on the subsequent efficiency. Loss of sleep, fasting, atmospheric effects all seem to produce no immediate effect on the capacity to do mental work. Concerning this Gates says, "Such facts bear witness to the remarkable stability of the mechanisms involved in well habituated mental activities. It is surprising that those functions, which may be so readily allowed to operate below maximum in the absence of incentives, remain unimpaired in efficiency, during and after such extreme deprivations and exertions. The facts attest, also, to the remarkably effective and facile adaptability of the human organism to unfavorable conditions imposed upon it." In general, therefore, distractions on general conditions of the individual are relatively unimportant as factors in test reliability.

21. Indeed, so little potency have those individual variations in causing unreliability that Woodyard has found that there is little lowering of reliability for

intervals up to a year. In other words, *an interval between repetitions of comparable tests up to a year has little influence on the correlation between comparable tests.*

22. *Cheating* may be a factor in the reliability of a test. Cheating tends to make an individual score higher (or lower) than he otherwise would score and hence tends to lower the correlation between a test and the true score of individuals on that test.

8   *How Accurate Is a Test Score?*

JEROME E. DOPPELT

The degree of relative precision of measurement or accuracy of a set of test scores has been defined as test reliability. This test characteristic may be expressed as a reliability coefficient (e.g., the correlation of scores from two forms of the same test administered a month apart), or in terms of the standard error of measurement as described in the following article. The reliability coefficient is a useful way to describe precision because it is an abstract summary index which is independent of the units of measurement and as such can be applied in making inter-test comparisons even though the score units are not comparable. It has a disadvantage in that it is not independent of the "range of talent" (i.e., the variability of individual differences measured by a particular test). In general the greater the spread of ability the higher the coefficient. On the other hand, the standard error of measurement is relatively independent of the range of talent, and is therefore helpful in making judgments about the relative precision of measurement for intra- or inter-individual comparisons.

What is a "true" score? How does the standard error of measurement relate to an individual's "true" score? How would a teacher or counselor use the standard error of measurement to interpret a test score?

Every user of test scores knows that no test is perfectly accurate. The score on a test is determined principally by the ability or knowledge of the person who takes it, but the score is also affected by the inaccuracy of the test itself.

It would be helpful if we could know each time we see a score whether it is higher or lower than it should be, and by how much. Unfortunately, no one has ever figured out a practical way to determine the precise amount of error in an individual case. Statistics have been developed, however, for *estimating* the margin of error we should allow for in test scores. One of the most useful of these is the *standard error of measurement* (SE_M).

Let us consider a practical situation in which it would be useful to have a

Reprinted and abridged with permission of the publisher from *Test Service Bulletin #50*, New York: The Psychological Corporation, 1956.

measure of the accuracy of a test score. Suppose we have an opening for a junior executive in our company. We have a large number of applicants and among them is Henry Smith. He looks good on most counts, but he has a score of 28 on a test of administrative knowledge. The test norms show that a score of 32 would place an applicant within the upper half of all executive applicants and we desire to make our choice from the upper half. Since Smith looks promising in other ways we begin to wonder about his test placement.

If we could test him again, would he get 28 or some other score? Just what is Smith's *true* score on this test? Before we can make sense in talking about the difference between the *true* score and the *observed* or *obtained* score, we need to specify what we mean by *true* score.

Imagine that we have a very large number of comparable forms of our test. (We need not go into the statistics of comparable forms here; let us simply agree that comparable forms are interchangeable. That is, if we had to choose only one form to measure administrative knowledge, we would be equally happy with any one of the forms.) Now suppose we were able to corner Henry Smith and test him with all our tremendous number of equivalent forms. We would find that our hero does not always get the same score. As the number of forms administered gets larger and larger, we would discover that the distribution of Smith's scores begins to resemble the familiar "normal" curve. In this situation we can reasonably decide that the average of the large number of scores is characteristic of Smith's performance on our test, and we will call this his *true* score.

At the beginning of the article we pointed out that the score on a test reflects primarily what the person tested brings to the task and partly it reflects the error of measurement in the test. The true score measures the performance that is characteristic of the person tested; the variations plus and minus around the true score describe a characteristic of the test.

When we use the standard deviation as a measure of the variation of observed scores around the true score, the result is called the *standard error of measurement*. Since this statistic has direct interpretable meaning in relation to the "normal" curve, we are in a position to make this statement:

> If we could know both an individual's exact true score and the SE_M which is characteristic of the test, we would know that about 68 percent of the scores the individual obtained on the vast number of comparable forms fall within one SE_M of his true score. A band stretching two standard errors above and below his true score would include about 95 percent of his obtained scores, and within three standard errors of the true score would lie over 99 percent of his scores on the many forms of the test.

Obviously it is useful to be able to say, putting it a little differently, that for about two-thirds of all people tested the observed scores lie within one SE_M of the true scores—and that for nineteen out of twenty cases the observed score will not be more than two standard errors away from the true score.

As explained in the Note at the end of this article, we must be quite careful how we make statements like the foregoing. It is not correct to say of an individual with a certain *observed* score that the odds are two out of three that his *true* score is within one SE_M of the score he got. But in the practical instance we can use the SE_M in defining limits around the observed score within which we would be reasonably sure to find the true score. Whether the "reasonable limits" will be one, two, or three times the SE_M will depend on the level of confidence the test user desires. The surer he wants to be of not making a mistake in locating the true score, the broader the margin of error he must allow for and therefore the less definite and precise will be the indication given by the test. The broader the score band we allow for each job applicant, for example, the greater the likelihood that his true score will be within it, but the harder it will be to tell the applicants apart.

Coming back to the case of Henry Smith, let us suppose that the test manual reveals that the SE_M is 3 points. If we establish "reasonable limits" of one SE_M on either side of the observed score, the band for Smith would extend over the score range 25–31. And since a score of 32 is needed before a person may be considered as belonging to the top half of executive trainees, we may decide that Smith does not belong in the top half of the group. We are not willing to act as if his true score is 32.

We could have established wider "reasonable limits," say 2 or 3 SE_M on either side of the observed score. We would then have greater confidence that our location of the true score within the band is correct. This extra confidence costs us something. We pay for it by having more people to be considered as possibilities. When there are many applicants, we usually want to reduce the number of eligible candidates even though we increase the possibility of making a wrong decision about the true score of some of them.

Since in practice we cannot give a large number of equivalent forms of a test in order to find the characteristic standard error of measurement, how do we determine it? The answer to this takes us back to the reliability coefficient.

As measured by the reliability coefficient, reliability means consistency of measurement. If the individuals of a group remain in about the same relative positions or ranks after successive testings, the test is "reliable" for that group. It is unfortunately true that a test will tend to have higher reliability coefficients for groups with a wide spread of scores than for groups with scores bunched more closely together.

The SE_M is less subject to this variation; the formula for computing it takes into account both the reliability coefficient *and* the standard deviation for each group. The formula is simple:

$$SE_M = SD \sqrt{1 - r_{tt}}.$$

Here SD is the standard deviation of the obtained scores of a group and r_{tt} is the reliability coefficient computed for the same group.[1]

Like a true score for an individual, the SE_M for a test should be just one definite number if it is really a characteristic of the test rather than of the people tested. But if we look in a test manual, we may see that there appear to be differences among standard errors of measurement computed for different groups. For example, the SE_M is reported for each of nine groups on the Numerical Test in the *Personnel Tests for Industry* series. The values range from 1.7 to 2.4. The explanation is that we have no way of computing the exact value of the SE_M— the formula merely provides an *estimate* of the SE_M. Estimates of course can be expected to differ. In any situation where we cannot obtain the true value of a statistic it is advisable to have as many estimates of that value as practical. In the case of PTI-Numerical, we can be comfortable with the conclusion that the SE_M is about 2 points.

Many test manuals give both reliability coefficients and standard errors of measurement for the convenience of the user. When the SE_M is not given, it can be estimated readily by use of the reliability coefficient, provided the manual also

TABLE 1. *Standard Errors of Measurement for Given Values of Reliability Coefficient and Standard Deviation*

SD	Reliability Coefficient					
	.95	.90	.85	.80	.75	.70
30	6.7	9.5	11.6	13.4	15.0	16.4
28	6.3	8.9	10.8	12.5	14.0	15.3
26	5.8	8.2	10.1	11.6	13.0	14.2
24	5.4	7.6	9.3	10.7	12.0	13.1
22	4.9	7.0	8.5	9.8	11.0	12.0
20	4.5	6.3	7.7	8.9	10.0	11.0
18	4.0	5.7	7.0	8.0	9.0	9.9
16	3.6	5.1	6.2	7.2	8.0	8.8
14	3.1	4.4	5.4	6.3	7.0	7.7
12	2.7	3.8	4.6	5.4	6.0	6.6
10	2.2	3.2	3.9	4.5	5.0	5.5
8	1.8	2.5	3.1	3.6	4.0	4.4
6	1.3	1.9	2.3	2.7	3.0	3.3
4	.9	1.3	1.5	1.8	2.0	2.2
2	.4	.6	.8	.9	1.0	1.1

This table is based on the formula $SE_M = SD\sqrt{1 - r_{tt}}$. For most purposes the result will be sufficiently accurate if the table is entered with the reliability and standard deviation values nearest those given in the test manual. Be sure the standard deviation and the reliability coefficient are for the same group of people.

---

[1] We cannot automatically say that the more accurate or reliable of two tests is the one which has the lower value for its SE_M. As may be seen from the computing fromula, the SE_M is tied in with the score units in which the standard deviation is expressed. A test with a standard deviation of 16 points may have the same reliability as a test with a standard deviation of 8 points. However, the SE_M of the first test will be numerically twice that of the second.

states the standard deviation of the particular group of people on which the reliability coefficient is based. It is well worth the test user's time to make this computation; Table 1 permits an approximation to be made easily without any figuring.

If, as is too often the case, the manual does not present the standard deviation of the group for which the reliability coefficient is reported, it would be advisable for the user to write a letter to the test author.

NOTE: As textbooks usually point out, it is correct to make a statement of probability (such as "68 per cent of the scores" or "two out of three times") only when the SE_M is applied to the true score. If a test has a standard error of 5.5, it is *not* correct to say of a person who obtains a score of 48 that the chances are two out of three that his true score is between 42.5 and 53.5. This person's true score is a definite number, although we do not know what it is. The statement that his true score lies between 42.5 and 53.5 is either true or false. Intermediate probabilities like "two out of three" or "one out of twenty" cannot properly be attached to it. The "reasonable limits" idea simply helps us to avoid making a mathematical statement of probability which would be technically inaccurate. Precise statements of probability in relation to confidence intervals are possible but lie outside the scope of this article.

9 Evidence Concerning Approximations for Standard Deviation, Internal Consistency Reliability, and the Standard Error of Measurement

ROBERT F. MCMORRIS

Computing precise measures for selecting tests and interpreting test scores cannot be attained easily because the formulas for these calculations are complex and the data difficult to obtain. Simplification is achieved through the use of approximation. In this paper McMorris lists various approximations and presents data for judging their accuracy. The approximations are for three common measures used on test scores: the standard deviation (to determine the variability for a set of scores), reliability (to describe a test's accuracy or consistency for a group), and the standard error of measurement (to estimate the amount of error likely in a particular score).

How might these measures be used in selecting or interpreting tests? How does the error involved in using an approximation for a statistic compare with the error of not using the statistic at all? What kinds of "consumers" might appreciate the short-cut methods?

What is the extent of the error involved in approximations for the standard deviation, internal consistency reliability, and the standard error of measurement? Formulas for approximations were proposed by Jenkins—see Diederich

Adapted from a paper by the author entitled, "Evidence on the Quality of Several Approximations for Commonly Used Measurement Statistics", which appeared in the *Journal of Educational Measurement*, 1972, Vol. 9 #2, Summer, pp. 113–122.

(1958), Saupe (1961), and Lord (1957, 1959)— and a modification was proposed by Mason and Odeh (1968). While additional rationales for other formulas have appeared, the number of empirical verifications remains limited. Recently Sabers (1970), Jurs and Hopkins (1971), and Lathrop (1961) have provided findings supporting the use of short-cut approaches for the standard deviation.

METHOD

Data were derived from 85 tests which were item-analyzed by the Computer Center of the State University of New York at Albany. The classroom tests came from a wide variety of academic disciplines and naturally differed considerably not only in content but in length and quality. Thus, the tests provided a severe and realistic test of the approximations.

The various formulas for the approximations and the corresponding exact statistics are presented in Table 1.

The quality of the approximations as estimators of the statistics was described in various ways. The means and standard deviations for the approximations were compared with the same measures for the statistics. The values of the approximations were correlated with those of the statistics, and the relationships shown using scattergrams. Somewhat redundantly, the means and standard deviations for the differences between each approximation and its statistic were also found.

If the value of an approximation is close to that for its corresponding statistic (here the standard deviation, KR20 reliability, or the standard error of measurement), the following results are to be expected:

(1) The means of the approximation and the statistic should be similar, and the mean of the difference between them should be small, both indicating the approximation is not excessively biased.

(2) The standard deviations of the approximation and the statistic should be similar, indicating similar variabilities, and the standard deviation of the differences should be small, indicating the magnitude of the error tends to be small.

(3) The correlation between the approximation and the statistic should be high, indicating that the approximation and the statistic agree in ranking the various tests on this characteristic, e.g., on reliability.

Indications of conditions which relate to the function of the approximations were gained from relating the difference between approximation and statistic to selected test characteristics: average difficulty, number of testees, and number of items. The correlations were computed and also displayed with scattergrams.

For the present paper, approximations for each of the three statistics were computed and compared with the corresponding exact statistics.

TABLE 1. *The Statistics and Their Approximations.*

Label	Formula	Source
SD	$\sqrt{\dfrac{\Sigma x^2}{N-1}}$	
SD1/6	$\dfrac{\Sigma \text{ upper } 1/6 - \Sigma \text{ lower } 1/6}{N/2}$	Jenkins-Diederich
SD6N1	$\dfrac{\Sigma \text{ upper } 1/6 - \Sigma \text{ lower } 1/6}{(N-1)/2}$	Mason and Odeh
SDR/5	range/5	
R	$\text{KR20} = \dfrac{k}{k-1}\left[1 - \dfrac{\Sigma\, pq}{V_t}\right]$	Kuder-Richardson
R21	$\text{KR21} = \dfrac{k}{k-1}\left[1 - \dfrac{kp(1-p)}{V_t}\right]$	Kuder-Richardson
R19K	$1 - \dfrac{.19k}{V_t}$	Saupe
R18K1	$\dfrac{k}{k-1}\left[1 - \dfrac{.18k}{V_t}\right]$	Saupe
R17K1	$\dfrac{k}{k-1}\left[1 - \dfrac{.17k}{V_t}\right]$	Saupe
R16K	$1 - \dfrac{.16k}{V_t}$	Saupe
R23Q	$1 - \dfrac{2k}{23Q^2}$	Saupe
R16R	$1 - \dfrac{.16k}{(\text{SDR}/5)^2}$	McMorris
R1661	$1 - \dfrac{.16k}{(\text{SD}6N1)^2}$	McMorris
SE	$\text{SD}\sqrt{1-R}$	
SE3/7	$3/7\sqrt{k}$	Lord
SE.4	$.4\sqrt{k}$	
$\bar{p}$	$\dfrac{\bar{X}}{k}$	
N	Number of testees	
k	Number of items	

Symbol	Meaning
x	$X - \bar{X}$, deviation from the mean
Σ upper 1/6	sum of the upper 1/6th of the scores
p	proportion of testees answering an item correctly
q	$1 - p$, proportion of testees answering incorrectly
V_t	variance of scores on the total test
Q	semi-interquartile range, quartile deviation

RESULTS

The extent to which the values of the approximations resembled their corresponding statistics is summarized in Table 2.

TABLE 2. *Differences Between Approximations and Statistics Described and Related to Other Test Characteristics.*

Measure[a]	Mean	S.D.	r with Statistic	Differences (Approx.—Stat.) Mean	S.D.	% RMS Error	rs between differences and p	N	k
SD	5.84	2.30							
SD1/6	5.69	2.23	.99	−.15	.19	4	−0.5	.13	−.30
SD6N1	5.79	2.28	.99	−.05	.17	3	−.16	−.09	−.12
SDR/5	5.85	2.41	.90	.02	1.07	18	.09	.61	.02
R	.70	.13							
R21	.60	.19	.98	−.10	.06	17	−.05	−.00	.31
R19K	.62	.18	.94	−.08	.07	15	−.44	.22	.29
R18K1	.65	.17	.92	−.05	.07	12	−.22	.22	.09
R17K1	.67	.16	.91	−.03	.07	11	−.21	.22	.03
R16K	.68	.16	.92	−.02	.06	9	−.19	.24	.04
R23Q	58	.20	.78	−.11	.13	24	−.04	−.11	−.02
R16R	.65	.21	.74	−.04	.14	21	−.09	.59	.10
R1661	.67	.16	.90	−.03	.07	11	−.22	.19	.05
SE	2.92	.75							
SE3/7	3.22	.78	.96	.30	.21	13	.25	−.23	.33
SE.4	2.99	.74	.96	.08	.28	10	−.08	−.24	.19
SK	.57	.48							
p	.69	.09							
N	101.02	105.41							
k	59.40	28.13							

[a] See Table 1 for explanation.

For the *standard deviation* the largest difference in means between an approximation and the statistic was −.15. The approximations utilizing the sums of the upper and lower 1/6ths of the scores were notable in their correlation with the statistic (see also Figure 1)[1] and in the low variability of the differences. The range divided by 5 provided an unbiased but more unpredictable estimate.

---

[1] Explanation of a scattergram may be appreciated by some readers. The results from an approximation for the standard deviation (Y) are compared with the values for the standard deviation itself (X). For this sample of 85 item analyses, the means differed only slightly (the approximation was .05 lower), the standard deviations were virtually the same, and the correlations were almost a perfect 1.000. At the lower left corner of the figure, note that three standard deviations were between 1.660 and 2.086, and the approximations for these three tests all fell within the limits 1.710–2.037. For the five analyses whose standard deviations were between 2.086 and 2.586, four of the approximations were between 2.037 and 2.537 and one was between 2.537 and 3.037, and so on. All the values fell along the diagonal, illustrating the high correlation.

The *reliability* estimates were compared with the results from the Kuder-Richardson Formula #20. The KR21 is an underestimate, as may be shown algebraically but correlates highly with KR20. Saupe (1961) estimated mathematically that his approximations would tend to be closer to KR20 than would KR21. The present data tend to support his contention. The relationship between one of these Saupe approximations and KR20 is displayed in Figure 2. While two short-cut approximations (R23Q and R16R) do more poorly overall than do the Saupe approximations using the variance, the substitution of a 1/6 standard deviation approximation into the traditional standard error formula (R1661) results in quite dependable estimates.

The *standard error of measurement* approximation by Lord (1957, 1959) estimated the results of the standard formula with only slight errors. In addition, when his value of 3/7 (i.e., .43) was replaced by .4, the errors remained small. The correlations of the approximations with the exact statistic were slightly smaller than those reported by Lord for ETS tests, as may be noted visually from Figure 3.

None of the scattergrams of approximations with their statistics suggested non-linearity, i.e., a curve would not summarize the relationship any better than would a straight line.

Errors in approximating were compared with the average difficulty of the test, the number of testees, and the number of items. There was a tendency for the reliability coefficient to be underestimated where tests were difficult or short, and for the standard error of measurement to be overestimated where tests were easy or long. (Both errors tend to be conservative.) The standard deviation approximation using the range (SDR/5) was, of course, highly influenced by sample size: for small numbers of testees the standard deviation was underestimated, for large numbers of testees the standard deviation was overestimated.

The results for the reliability and standard error approximations imply that the Saupe and Lord approximations may be slightly short-cutted to make them more suitable for non-computationally comfortable consumers and for scurrying statisticians.

A judgment at this point: Quickly calculated but probably quite reasonable approximations may be obtained for Kuder-Richardson reliability from R1661 and for the standard error of measurement from SE.4. The standard deviation would likely be well approximated by SD6N1, with gross computational errors detected by using SDR/5.

CONCLUSION

Approximations for the standard deviation, internal consistency reliability, and the standard error of measurement were able to provide good estimates for this set of tests. It appears reasonable to maintain that approximations are adequate for use in practical situations.

FIGURE 1.

Scattergram for the Standard Deviation and an Approximation.

```
11.470
                                                                    4        4
10.537        X = SD            Y = SD6N1
              X = 5.84          Y = 5.79
10.037        s(X) = 2.30       s(Y) = 2.28              2        2
              r = .997
                                                                    0
 9.537
                                              1         1           2
 9.037
                                                   1   1           2
 8.537
                                              1                    1
 8.037
                                         2    1                   3
 7.537
                                    1    5    1                   7
 7.037
                                    4    3                        7
 6.537
                               5    2                             7
 6.037
                          7    1                                  8
 5.537
                     8                                            8
 5.037
           1    11   1                                            13
 4.537
           3                                                      3
 4.037
      3                                                           3
 3.537
 4                                                                4
 3.037
 1    3                                                           4
 2.537
 4                                                                4
 2.037
3                                                                 3
 1.710
      2.086   3.086   4.086   5.086   6.086   7.086   8.086   9.086  10.086  11.086
    1.660  2.586   3.586   4.586   5.586   6.586   7.586   8.586   9.586  10.686
       3    5    3    4    3    4    11   9    7    6    7    8    3    3    1    1    1    2    4         85
```

Figure 2.

Scattergram for Kuder-Richardson 20 and an Approximation.

```
.923
              X = R              Y = R16K                              1    1
.900          X = .70           Y = .68
              s(X) = .13        s(Y) = .16                        5   1    6
.850
                                            1   3   4   1              9
.800
                                        1   5   5                      11
.750
                                    1   6   10  1                      18
.700
                                3   4   4                              11
.650
                        2   1   2   4                    1             10
.600
Y               1           3                                          4
.550
                1   3   2   1                                          7
.500
                2                                                      2
.450
            1                                                          1
.400
                1   1                                                  2
.350
                                                                      0
.300
                                                                      0
.250
        1           1                                                  2
.200
            1                                                          1


    .250    .321    .421    .521    .621    .721    .821    .921
        .271    .371    .471    .571    .671    .771    .871    .940
        1   1   0   2   2   4   5   6   7   15  20  9   9   3   1   85
                                    X
```

FIGURE 3.

Scattergram for the Standard Error of Measurement and an Approximation.

```
5.100     X= SE        Y= SE3/7
          X= 2.92      Y= 3.22                              1       1
5.095     sX= .75      sY= .78
          r= .96                                                    0
4.845
                                          1       2   1            4
4.595
                                                                  0
4.345
                                  2       1   4                   7
4.095
                                  5   1   1                       7
3.845
                          2       1  '2                           5
3.595
                  1       3   4   1                               9
3.345
                  2   6   13  6                                   27
3.095
                  2                                               2
2.845
                  3   2   1                                       6
2.595
          1   3                                                   4
2.345
          2   3                                                   5
2.095
      1   4   1                                                   6
1.845
      1                                                           1
1.595
      1                                                           1
1.400
```

```
        1.540   2.040   2.540   3.040   3.540   4.040   4.540
    1.400   1.790   2.290   2.790   3.290   3.790   4.290   4.600
        3   4   4   6   6   8  21  10   9   3   3   4   2   2      85
                                    X
```

III

DEFINING AND ASSESSING
TEST VALIDITY

Testing experts, although sometimes disagreeing among themselves as to the exact definition of validity, generally concede that
it is one of the most important characteristics of a test. In developing a test or in evaluating an instrument for possible use, questions
about validity should be central. If only fragmentary evidence on
this issue is available, an educator or psychologist will have little
confidence in making descriptive statements or decisions on the
basis of test results.

In order to understand the concept of validity, consideration must
be given to the factors which can influence test scores. The number
and variety of these factors are legion; researchers and practitioners
are aware of the predictable effects of only a small number of their
influences. Especially given the consideration, the concept of validity
is dynamic and complex, and cannot be adequately treated in a sentence or a paragraph. The reader should more fully appreciate this
dynamism and complexity as he reads the articles. As he becomes
more familiar with some of the ideas advanced in these papers, he
should become better able to conceptualize and deal with his own
measurement problems.

This chapter and the previous chapter begin in the same way, with
excerpts from the 1966 revision of the *Technical Recommendations*
(1954, 1955). These *Recommendations*, now termed *Standards*,
have had a great impact upon current thought and practice through
identifying types of validity and reliability, and also in specifying

the type of information deemed essential or desirable in a test manual. The revision is similar in style and content to the original set of recommendations with probably the most obvious change being the condensation of predictive and concurrent validity into one type, termed criterion-related validity. This paper is placed first in the chapter because it provides not only an overview of various types of validity but also a frame of reference for the articles that follow.

The next article contains an evaluation of the above *Standards* directed specifically to educational measurement. Cronbach has listed various questions which may be raised, accompanied by the related types of information helpful to the test interpreter. His addition of the term "educational importance" appears noteworthy now that educators are more openly and typically asking questions concerning accountability.

Specific types of validity are treated in each of the two remaining articles in the chapter. Robert Ebel has provided us with an elaboration of the concept of and a discussion of the problems in assessing content validity. This type of validity frequently seems not only to be misunderstood but also underestimated in importance. While many authors have stated that an achievement test should first be examined for content validity and rejected if this condition is not met, and while Ebel emphasizes the achievement test application, the generality of the content validity topic to the various types of assessment is obvious.

The most controversial type of validity—construct validity—was originally specified in the *Technical Recommendations* (1954). Explanation and extension of the concept of construct validity are provided by Campbell and Fiske, using a special methodological approach as their vehicle. The interested reader is referred to research reports by Bouchard (1968), Dicken (1963), Hicks (1967), and Koppel and Sechrest (1970) for examples of applications of the Campbell-Fiske methodology.

Study of this chapter should allow the reader to establish more relationships when reading later articles in this book. For example, he may wish to recall ideas expressed by the concept of content validity when considering the Taxonomies, goal cards, and criterion-referenced measurement (Articles 14–17), attitude measurement (#24), item selection (#27), and curriculum evaluation (Chapter VII). Criterion-related validity should be recalled when dealing with cultural factors (#25), expectancy tables (#29), limitations of normative data (#31), and the uses for tests (Chapter VIII). Construct validity should be particularly helpful when examining unobtrusive measures (#18), response sets (#19), and creativity measurement (#42).

This chapter, then, proceeds from an overview of validity, including the three standard types of validity, to a modified and enriched treatment of validity in education, to a more complete examination of content validity, and to an explanation of the concept and implementation of construct validity.

NATIONAL COMMITTTEE ON TEST STANDARDS

Of all the questions concerning a test, those related to validity are probably the most important and yet the most difficult to answer. The gathering of reliable evidence bearing on test validity is often expensive and time-consuming. In many instances criteria may be unavailable. This is true primarily because a given test does not possess singular "validity," but will vary in degree of validity, depending upon the situation and intent of the user. The following discussion highlights three major aspects of validity, as determined by a group of test experts. As will be obvious from reading this discussion and the following articles in this section, defining and assessing validity is a very complex task. What validity characteristic would be most important in the development of a test to measure reading comprehension, mental retardation, attitudes toward minority groups, neuroticism, and typing ability?

Validity information indicates the degree to which the test is capable of achieving certain aims. Tests are used for several types of judgment, and for each type of judgment a different type of investigation is required to establish validity. For purposes of describing the uses for three kinds of validity coefficients we may distinguish three of the rather numerous aims of testing:

1. *The test user wishes to determine how an individual performs at present in a universe of situations that the test situation is claimed to represent.* For example, most achievement tests used in schools measure the student's performance on a sample of questions intended to represent a certain phase of educational achievement or certain educational objectives.

2. *The test user wishes to forecast an individual's future standing or to estimate an individual's present standing on some variable of particular significance that is different from the test.* For example, an academic aptitude test may forecast grades, or a brief adjustment inventory may estimate what the outcome would be of a careful psychological examination.

3. *The test user wishes to infer the degree to which the individual possesses some hypothetical trait or quality (construct) presumed to be reflected in the test performance.* For example, he wants to know whether the individual stands high on some proposed abstract trait such as "intelligence" or "creativity" that cannot be directly observed. This may be done to learn something about the individual, or it may be done to study the test itself, to study its relationship to other tests, or to develop psychological theory.

Reprinted and abridged from *Standards for Educational and Psychological Tests and Manuals,* 1966, pp. 12–24. Copyright 1966 by the American Psychological Association and reproduced by permission.

Different types of tests are often used for each of the different aims, but this is not always the case. There is much overlap in types of tests and the purposes for which they are used. Thus, a vocabulary test might be used (1) simply as a measure of present vocabulary, the universe being all the words in the language, (2) as a screening device to discriminate present or potential schizophrenics from brain-damaged individuals, or (3) as a means of making inferences about "intellectual capacity."

To determine how suitable a test is for each of these uses it is necessary to gather appropriate validity information. The kind of information to be gathered depends on the aim or aims of testing rather than on the type of test. The three aspects of validity corresponding to the three aims of testing may be named content validity, criterion-related validity, and construct validity.

A. Content validity is demonstrated by showing how well the content of the test samples the class of situations or subject matter about which conclusions are to be drawn. Content validity is especially important for achievement and proficiency measures and for measures of adjustment or social behavior based on observation in selected situations. The manual should justify the claim that the test content represents the assumed universe of tasks, conditions, or processes. A useful way of looking at this universe of tasks or items is to consider it to comprise a *definition* of the achievement to be measured by the test. In the case of an educational achievement test, the content of the test may be regarded as a definition of one or more educational objectives. The aptitudes, skills, and knowledges required of the student for successful test performance must be precisely the types of aptitudes, skills, and knowledges that the school wishes to develop in the students and to evaluate in terms of test scores. Thus evaluating the content validity of a test for a particular purpose is the same as subjectively recognizing the adequacy of a definition. This process is actually quite similar to the subjective evaluation of the criterion itself. Unless, however, the aim of an achievement test is specifically to substitute for some criterion, its correlation with a criterion is *not* a useful evaluation of the test.

B. Criterion-related validity is demonstrated by comparing the test scores with one or more external variables considered to provide a direct measure of the characteristic or behavior in question. This comparison may take the form of an expectancy table or, most commonly, a correlation relating the test score to a criterion measure. Predictive uses of tests include long-range forecasts of one or more measures of academic achievement, prediction of vocational success, and prediction of reaction to therapy. For such uses the criterion data are collected at a later date than the test data. If however one wishes to know whether a testing procedure can for example take the place of more elaborate procedures for diagnosing personality disorders test and criterion data are gathered concurrently. A test that is related to one or more concurrent criteria will not necessarily predict status on the same criterion at some later date. Whether the criterion data should be collected concurrently with the testing or at a later time depends on whether the test is recommended for prediction or for assessment of present status. One technique useful in interpreting criterion-related validity is the expectancy table. (See article 29 by Wesman for an excellent simplified discussion and illustration of this method.)

C. *Construct validity* is evaluated by investigating what qualities a test measures, i.e., by determining the degree to which certain explanatory concepts or constructs account for performance on the test. To examine construct validity requires a combination of logical and empirical attack. Essentially, studies of construct validity check on the theory underlying the test. The procedure involves three steps. First, the investigator inquires from this theory what hypotheses may we make regarding the behavior of persons with high and low scores? Second, he gathers data to test these hypotheses. Third, in light of the evidence he makes an inference as to whether the theory is adequate to explain the data collected. If the theory fails to account for the data, he should revise the test interpretation, reformulate the theory, or reject the theory altogether. Fresh evidence would be required to demonstrate construct validity for the revised interpretation.

A simple procedure for investigating what a test measures is to correlate it with other tests. We would expect a valid test of numerical reasoning, for example, to correlate more highly with other numerical tests than with clerical perception tests. Another procedure is experimental. If it is hypothesized, for example, that form perception on a certain projective test indicates probable ability to function well under emotional stress, this inference may be checked by placing individuals in an experimental situation producing emotional stress and observing whether their behavior corresponds to the hypothesis.

Construct validity is ordinarily studied when the tester wishes to increase his understanding of the psychological qualities being measured by the test. A validity coefficient relating test to criterion, unless it is established in the context of some theory, yields no information about *why* the correlation is high or low, or about how one might improve the measurement. Construct validity is relevant when the tester accepts no existing measure as a definitive criterion of the quality with which he is concerned (e.g., in measuring a postulated drive such as *need for achievement*), or when a test will be used in so many diverse decisions that no single criterion applies (e.g., in identifying the ability of Peace Corps trainees to adapt to new cultures). Here the traits or qualities underlying test performance are of central importance. It must be remembered, however, that without a study of criterion-related validity a test developed for diagnosis or prediction can be regarded only as experimental.

These three aspects of validity are only conceptually independent, and rarely is only one of them important in a particular situation. A complete study of a test would normally involve information about all types of validity. A first step in the preparation of a predictive (*criterion-related*) instrument may be to consider what *constructs* are likely to provide a basis for selecting or devising an effective test. Sampling from a *content* universe may also be an early step in producing a test whose use for *prediction* is the ultimate concern. Even after satisfactory *prediction* has been established, information regarding *construct* validity may make the test more useful; it may, for example, provide a basis for identifying situations other than the validating situation where the test is appropriate as a predictor. To analyze *construct* validity all the knowledge regarding validity would be brought to bear.

The three concepts of validity are pertinent to all kinds of tests. It is the intended use of the test rather than its nature that determines what kind of evidence is required.

Intelligence or aptitude tests most often use criterion-related validity to show how well they are able to predict academic success in school or college, but the nature of the aptitudes measured is often judged from the content of the items, and the place of the aptitude within the array of human abilities is deduced from correlations with other tests.

For achievement tests content validity is usually of first importance. For example, a testing agency has a group of subject-matter experts devise and select test items that they judge to cover the topics and mental processes relevant to the field represented by the test. Similarly, a teacher judges whether the final test in his course covers situations about which he has been trying to teach his students an understanding. The teacher also judges content when he uses a published test, but he can appropriately investigate criterion-related validity as well by correlating this test with tests he has prepared or with other direct measures of his chief instructional objectives. When the same published achievement test is used for admissions testing, it may reasonably be checked against a later criterion of performance. In any theoretical discussion of what is being measured by the achievement test a consideration of construct validity is required. Whether the score on a science achievement test, for example, reflects reading ability to a significant degree, and whether it measures understanding of scientific method rather than mere recall of facts are both questions about construct validity.

Development of a personality inventory will usually start with the assembly of items covering content the developer considers meaningful. Such inventories are then likely to be interpreted with the aid of theory; any such interpretation calls for evidence of construct validity. In addition a personality inventory must have criterion-related validity if, for example, it is to be used in screening military recruits who may be maladjusted.

Interest measures usually seek to predict vocational or educational criteria, but many of them are also characterized by logical content and constructs. This makes it more likely that they can provide at least a rough prediction for the very many occupations and activities that exist and for which specific evidence of criterion-related validity has not been obtained.

For projective techniques, construct validity is of most importance, although criterion-related validity using criteria collected either concurrently with the testing or afterwards may be pertinent if the instruments are to be used in making diagnostic classifications.

11   *The Validation of Educational Measures*

LEE J. CRONBACH

Because of the kinds of questions that educators are currently asking about their measurements, there has arisen a need to expand and modify the concept of test validity. In the following article Cronbach provides a classification and extension of the concept of validity as originally presented in the Standards for Educational and Psychological Tests and Manuals *(APA, 1966). His comments amplify the psychologically oriented interpretation of construct validity. In addition the reader should find his presentation helpful in understanding criterion-referenced measurement.*

Does the type of information needed depend more on the type of test or on the intended interpretation? How does judging educational importance compare with judging content validity? If an educator maintains that he is measuring reading comprehension, which type of validity information should he seek?

Almost 20 years ago, a group of us were asked by the American Psychological Association to prepare standards for psychological tests. Shortly thereafter, the National Council on Measurement in Education and the American Educational Research Association proposed to set committees to work on standards for *educational* tests. Having two or three sets of standards seemed likely to nullify the whole effort, so Paul Mort, then AERA president, organized a collaborative committee structure. This structure produced the 1954 Technical Recommendations for Psychological Tests, and, in 1955, an achievement-test version. The latter elaborated the recommendations, but did not look educational measurement square in the eye. In retrospect, I cannot say that we were wrong to push the educational problems aside—the committee had quite enough already on its plate. Validity theory for achievement measures probably had to wait until the proposals on aptitude and personality tests were assimilated.

The statement presented here is not a new and competing set of "standards." It supports and perhaps illuminates the existing *Standards* while pointing out crucial questions that no *Standards* and no effort by test publishers alone can cope with. *Validation is the task of the test interpreter.* Others can do no more than offer him material to incorporate into his thinking.

The logic of validation for educational tests is not different from that for psychological tests. Construct validation applies to many achievement tests,

Reprinted and abridged with permission of author and publisher from the *Proceedings of the 1969 Invitational Conference on Testing Problems*, pp. 35–52. Copyright 1970 by Educational Testing Service, Princeton, N.J. Used by permission. All rights reserved.

especially those of higher mental processes. Content validation applies to many psychological measures, notably attitude scales and observations of behavior. How one is to validate depends not on the test but on one's purpose in ̄ ̄g the test. Since virtually no test is confined to a single purpose, it is illogical to speak of test validity. What one has to validate is a proposed interpretation of the test; for any test, some interpretations are reasonably valid and others are not.

One further preliminary remark: The testing movement has given too much attention to comparative interpretations (to individual differences) and too little to absolute, content-referenced measurement. Comparison (competition) is a theme straight out of John Stuart Mill and Charles Darwin. But evaluation of social programs and self-direction by individuals call for absolute judgments. Regarding a training program, what fraction of the graduates can perform the tasks they should? Regarding the student choosing a college major, what are the fields in which he has an active, sustaining interest? To answer such questions, tests must make absolute statements. Comparative ranks are irrelevant; in the ideal situation, everyone earns a high mark. The educator makes many absolute descriptive and predictive interpretations; the traditional, differential validity coefficients are not pertinent to these.

Table 1 outlines the formulation. What evidence is called for, and what judgments, depends on the nature of the interpretation. There is testing for decision making and testing for the purpose of describing a person or group.

TABLE 1. *Summary of Types of Validation*

Focus of investigation	Question asked	Use made of student-response data	Use made of judgment
I. *Soundness of descriptive interpretations*			
Content validity	Do the observations truly sample the universe of tasks the developer intended to measure (or the universe of situations in which he would like to observe)?	Scores on test forms constructed independently may be compared.	To decide whether the tasks (situations) fit the content categories stated in the test specifications. To evaluate the process for content selection, as described in the manual.
Educational importance	Does the test measure an important educational outcome? Does the battery of measures neglect to observe any important outcome?		To compare the test tasks with the educational objectives stated by responsible persons.

TABLE 1. *Summary of Types of Validation* —Continued

Focus of investigation	Question asked	Use made of student-response data	Use made of judgment
Construct validity	Does the test measure the attribute it is said to measure? More specifically: the description of the person in terms of the construct, together with other information about him and the theory surrounding the construct, implies what can be expected of him in various situations; are these implications true?	Scores are compared with measures of behavior in certain other situations. Or, the test is modified experimentally and changes in score are noted.	To select hypotheses for testing. To integrate findings so as to decide whether the differences between persons with high and low scores are consistent with the proposed interpretation. To suggest alternative interpretations of the data.
II. *Usefulness for decision making*			
Validity for selection	Do students selected by the test perform better than unscreened students?	Regression of outcome measure on test score is examined.	To decide whether the criterion fully represents the outcomes desired, including outcomes more distant in time. To decide whether a new situation is enough like the validation situation for the results to generalize.
Validity for placement	Is performance improved when students are allocated to treatments according to their test scores?	Regression slope relating outcome measure to test score for one treatment is compared with that for another treatment.	To decide whether the criterion fully represents the outcomes desired, including outcomes more distant in time. To decide whether a new situation is enough like the validation situation for the results to generalize.

While descriptions ultimately are used for decisions, any one description, such as that given by a beginning-of-year reading test, contributes to a great many decisions by the teacher and perhaps by the pupil. So the descriptive report should convey truthful impressions to the teacher, or to the pupil himself, or to whoever uses it.

DECISION RULES BASED ON TESTS

In this extract, only a little space can be given to the validating of decision rules. Decision making in education is best illustrated in the selection of applicants for advanced training and in the allocation of pupils to curricula or to different instructional schemes.

Validation of a decision rule logically requires an experiment in which, after being tested, persons are allocated to treatments *without regard to the scores* whose usefulness is being validated. The outcomes of the treatment are then appraised. There are usually many outcomes important to the decision maker, and a multidimensional criterion is preferable to a single one.

Every report of validation against a criterion is to be thought of as carrying the warning clause, "Insofar as the criterion is truly representative of the outcome we wish to maximize . . ." The report has to contain a clear description of the criterion and should contain a critique of it by the investigator. The reader must school himself to examine criteria with a hard eye, to convince himself that a test that predicts the stated criterion will also predict the outcome *he* is seeking. The tests that predict one outcome will often not be those that predict another, and prediction formulas that maximize one outcome may reject persons who would be outstanding by another criterion. In selection research one must continually resist the temptation to focus on criteria that are easy to predict. Attention should go to those that are most important.

With regard to selection decisions, modern thought places increased stress on local validation, validation on demographically distinct subgroups, and validity generalization.

A study that predicts school success by a statistical formula has direct significance when the formula is developed in the locale of the proposed application and the situation is sufficiently stable that the findings are representative of what will happen in succeeding years. Only if the supply of applicants and the curriculum remain much the same in character are the findings likely to remain directly applicable. Extrapolation is involved when a validity study is taken as warrant for continuing to use a test a decade later, after circumstances have changed. Far more hazardous extrapolation is involved in taking a published validity study made in a distant institution as warrant for one's local decisions. The legitimacy of an extrapolation to new conditions cannot be judged by statistical means.

It is good practice, where the sample size is sufficient, to treat separately the data for boys and girls, for whites and Negroes, and for subgroups differing markedly in previous preparation. Not infrequently the predictive significance of a score differs from subgroup to subgroup. But complex problems of policy arise in using subgroup statistics. If it were statistically valid to use different tests or different cutting scores for boys than for girls (for example), it would be difficult to convince applicants that sex-linked decision rules were not discriminating unfairly against one sex or the other.

A particularly satisfactory way of organizing input-output data is the "expectancy table," which reports the distribution of outcomes for persons having any particular pretest score. Decision theory requires emphasis not on a validity coefficient but on a regression slope relating the outcome measure to the test score. If the regression slope is great enough, outcomes for selected men are distinctly better than for unselected men, and the test is valid for selection. Its utility depends not just on the correlation between test and criterion, but also on the importance of the decision.

The placement model is the pertinent one when the school is concerned with the consequences of its policies for all the persons under consideration. Let treatments be labeled A and B and express the respective outcomes Y_A and Y_B on a common utility scale, since rational examination of a placement decision is not possible until the outcomes have been expressed in the same units. Again, let X be the predictor. There will be two expectancy tables, one for A and one for B, and corresponding regression functions. The regressions may align in various ways. The utility of the test is to be judged by examining the average outcome among persons distributed into treatments on the basis of test scores against, as a baseline, the outcome among persons who are indiscriminately assigned to the one treatment that is best on the average. A "validity coefficient" indicating that test X predicts success within a treatment *tells nothing about its usefulness for placement.* Comparison of regression slopes is the indispensable information. Placement decisions, I would argue, are more important as a use of tests than selection, but we seem to have no adequate examples of validation of placement procedures. Investigations of aptitude-treatment interactions are required, and the practical difficulties in that kind of research are great. As yet we know next to nothing substantive about which person variables interact with educational treatment variables. Hence, while something can be said regarding the logic of research on placement, actual validation of this kind is still over the horizon. A reasonably extensive discussion of some of the perplexities in research on interaction is given in a report available from ERIC (Cronbach and Snow, 1969).

DESCRIPTIVE INTERPRETATIONS

Three major questions arise regarding descriptive interpretations (see Table 1). 1) Description may be that and almost nothing more. ("James can recognize 80 percent of the words found in freshman textbooks.") The only question is whether the test tasks are a proper sample of the domain referred to. 2) A description may include a value judgment. "James has done well in first-year Spanish" implies that the test is measuring what the listener wants to have taught. A certain printed test in Spanish may be an entirely valid sample of some stated domain, but the domain excludes auditory and oral skills some educators would want to develop. The second validity question is whether the right domain was selected. 3) Descriptions imply predictions and explanations. The interpreter who moves from task language to attribute language invokes constructs. To say that an examinee is anxious, or appreciates painting, or communicates clearly is to suggest what he is expected to do under various circumstances that may arise later. When the description is freighted with implications, the validity question is: Are the implications true?

Content-referenced Interpretations: ■ A content interpretation refers to a universe of tasks or observations. The universe description is an operational definition that restricts the admissible range of instruments, questions, settings, examiners, and so on; even the narrowest definition identifies not a unique operation but a class of operations. An operation is specified when one refers to use of "the Wechsler Block Design materials," but this is a class of instruments; it has thousands of members. The only indispensible requirement in a universe definition is clarity: Reasonable observers must agree as to what falls within the universe and what is excluded. (If the observation is a composite— a test covering several content categories—the requirement applies to the subcategories.)

Content validity has to do with the test as a set of stimuli and as a set of observing operations. The measuring procedure is specified in terms of a class of stimuli, an injunction to the subject that defines his task (what he is to try to do with the stimuli), and an injunction to the observer (rules for observing the performance and reducing it to a score). Judgments about content validity should be restricted to the operational side of testing—that is, to the explicit procedures of measurement. Interpretations regarding the subject's internal processes are to be validated not by judgment but by empirical studies. With regard to the Watson-Glaser Test of Critical Thinking, for example, it is a matter of content validation to have a qualified person judge whether the authors did indeed assemble problems of the sort they called for in their specifications. To ask the judge whether the problems actually elicit "critical thinking" is to solicit his speculations about construct validity.

In principle, validity of the selection of content is to be judged without considering at all the persons to be tested; attention is restricted to the test materials and the universe description. If the content fits the universe definition, the test is content-valid for persons of all kinds. From an absolute point of view the score on a task indicates that the person does or does not possess, in conjunction, *all* the abilities required to perform it successfully. A dictated spelling test is a measure of hearing *and* spelling vocabulary *and* ability to write. In terms of content, however, the spelling test tests ability to spell from dictation. The pupil who is deaf will earn a low score, but that score is a valid report of his inability to spell from dictation.

Professional constructors of achievement tests combine a content outline with a set of response-process categories, such as recall, reasoning, and application of principles. Such a specification has value in broadening the test, but it tends to confuse task operations controlled by the tester with processes presumably used by the subject. The usual content-by-process grid is not a universe specification in our sense. An item *qua* item cannot be matched with a single behavioral process. Finding the answer calls for dozens of processes, from hearing the directions to complex integration of ideas. The shorthand description in terms of a single process can be justified only when one is certain that every person tested can and will carry out all the required processes save one. Even to speak of "required processes," however, is misleading, since the task can perhaps be performed successfully in a variety of ways. In a universe definition, a proper response specification deals with the result a person is asked to produce, not the process(es) by which he succeeds or fails.

Content validity is necessarily limited by the inadequacy of the universe specification, which is usually couched in imprecise, everyday terms and can rarely mention every pertinent aspect of the task. Content is an ill-shaped and undifferentiated mass, hence there is a danger of vagueness in any reference to a content universe. Moreover, while there may be a definable domain of content, there is no existing universe of items. The only items in existence are likely to be those that constitute the so-called sample. It must be acknowledged that writing items to fit a content domain does not closely resemble the drawing of beans from an urn. But the central requirement is only that universe boundaries be well defined; this requirement of operational definition can be met. It is not essential that a universe be denumerable or explicitly catalogued.

What, now, would constitute a rigorous validation of the fit between the operational definition of the universe and the actual test operations? To stimulate thought, one can suggest an experimental validation through duplicate construction. The construction would involve judgment, but the validation would employ completely hard data.

In principle, the rules for selecting test content can be described so fully that there is virtually no uncertainty as to what domain of tasks is to be sampled from. One would ordinarily make a test by a process of item writing, review, tryout, and revision. The experimental verification of a claim of content validity would call for a second team of equally competent writers and reviewers to work independently of the first, according to the same plan. They would be aided by the same definition of relevant content, sampling rules, instructions to reviewers, and specifications for tryout and interpretation of the data as were provided to the first team. In other words, they would work from the same operational definition of admissible procedures. If the universe description and the sampling are ideally refined, the first and second tests will be entirely equivalent. Any person's score will be the same on both tests, within the limits of sampling error. A favorable result, on a suitably broad sample of persons, would strongly suggest that the test content is fully defined by the written statement of the construction rules. An unfavorable result would indicate that the universe definition is too vague or too incomplete to provide a content interpretation of the test.

Test construction is never so logical as this. Ambiguity remains in many definitions of universes, and reviewing of draft items is an art not reducible to rules. No one has ever carried out the two-team study. It is not at all uncommon, however, for the test developer to claim validity by construction, bolstering the claim with a detailed account of the construction process. The test manual may list the textbooks from which content for items was chosen or may display the specifications given to the item writers. The reader is left to judge for himself whether this definition is explicit enough to allow two independent teams to arrive at approximately interchangeable tests.

Content validity is impermanent. The items or tasks in the test reflect social events, job descriptions, accepted beliefs about the world, decisions about what the curriculum should cover, and so on. These change with the passage of time, so that sooner or later the test becomes unrepresentative. The prospective user must be satisfied that a second team following the specified procedure *today* would arrive at a test reasonably like the original.

Correlations have nothing to do with content validation. Nothing in the logic of content validation requires that the universe or the test be homogeneous in content. The topics in the motor vehicle code are diverse: hand signals, right of way, reporting an accident, and so on. To make a decision about an applicant for a license, it is necessary to know whether he would pass a certain proportion of the items belonging to the universe defined by the code. If the items have low correlations (or if they vary in difficulty), it will take a larger sample of items to be confident that the subject's universe score reaches the required level. But, no matter how heterogeneous the universe, with enough items one can estimate the universe score as precisely as desired. Low item intercorrelations do not necessarily imply failure of the test content to fit the definition. Indeed, if the universe is heterogeneous, consistently *high* item intercorrelations imply inadequate sampling.

Correlations between tests are irrelevant to content validity (except in the construction experiment). Some critics are inclined to object to the creation of separate tests or scores for performances that correlate highly. But even if there is a large correlation between, say, a measure of acquaintance with chemical-bond theory and a measure of ability to apply chemical-bond principles, there is justification for keeping the measures separate. First, the absolute level of attainment of one objective might be much higher than that of the other; and this could suggest a need to modify the curriculum. Second, though the items correlate at the end of the instruction currently being given, some new instructional procedure might develop one competence while neglecting to develop the other. Keeping the categories separate in the list of objectives at least reminds all concerned to entertain such a possibility when evaluating the new program. This matter is discussed further in connection with construct validation, where correlations *are* relevant.

EVALUATIVE INTERPRETATIONS ■ When observations at the end of instruction are used to determine how successful some educational activitiy has been, the interpretation embodies value judgments. Hence the validity of an evaluative conclusion depends on the value question: Did the tests appraise the qualities I consider it most important to teach?

That question might elicit a positive answer from one educator and a negative one from another looking at the same tests. A content-valid test cannot satisfy decision makers who hold values unlike those of the test developer. Consequently, an ideally suitable battery for evaluation purposes will include separate measures of all outcomes the users of the information consider important.

The recommendation that the evaluation battery be comprehensive seems to run counter to the concept that an educational test should measure what has been taught. And students think a test "unfair" when it asks about topics not covered in the course. One can agree that it is unjust to let the fate of an individual be determined by a test that, through no fault of his own, he is ill-prepared for. But this only illustrates once more how a test valid for one decision can be invalid for another. Though it is unfair to judge the quality of a teacher's work by a test that does not fit the course of study he was directed to follow, that test may be fair basis for judging the curriculum. If teacher-plus-course-of-study have left the pupil ignorant on some important matter, that is a significant fact about the adequacy of his education.

Sometimes a test can "fit the curriculum" entirely too well. The universe pertinent in summative evaluation is the universe of tasks graduates are expected to perform. To be sure, a curriculum developer who has a restricted objective can use a restricted test to determine how well he achieved *his* end. But if other educators considering adoption of the course desire broader outcomes that go beyond his aims, they will find such restricted studies inadequate.

INTERPRETATIONS EMPLOYING CONSTRUCTS ■ Whenever one classifies situations, persons, or responses, he uses constructs. Every time an educator asks "But what does the instrument really measure?" he is calling for information on construct validity. Constructs help us to interpret both measures used to appraise educational outcomes and measures to forecast response to instruction. The relevance to education of personality constructs such as authoritarianism may be granted readily. It is perhaps less obvious that construct validation is relevant for tests of subject-matter learning. Many phrases used to characterize commonplace educational tests appear to describe mental processes: "scientific reasoning," "reading comprehension," and so on. If such a term is amplified to specify a class of tasks, the interpretation can be limited to content interpretation. Interpreters, however, usually consider processes behind the score. Consider reading comprehension as a trait construct. Suppose that the test presents paragraphs each followed by multiple-choice questions. The paragraphs obviously call for reading and presumably contain the information needed to answer the questions. Can a question about "what the test measures" arise? It can, if any counterinterpretation may reasonably be advanced. At least eight such counterhypotheses have to do with the possible effect on test score of motivation, style of work, speed, and other characteristics of the person. The test may be content-valid, in that it presents reasonable tasks; but perhaps it cannot be validly interpreted as measuring a comprehension skill, distinct from reading speed, vocabulary, and so on.

To validate an interpretation using a construct, one investigates the effect of each disturbing influence pointed out by the counterhypotheses. Construct validation is difficult to explain because so many diverse techniques are required to examine diverse hypotheses and counterhypotheses. Construct validation requires the integration of many studies (Cronbach and Meehl, 1955).

Construct validation begins with the claim that a given test measures a certain construct. This claim is meaningless until the construct is amplified from a label into a set of sentences. When the test interpreter says, "John Jones is high on trait X," he implies many things about Jones. The sentences that generate those implications spell out the meaning of the construct. In principle there is a complete theory surrounding the construct, every link of which is systematically tested in construct validation. While something like this does happen as theory evolves through an endless succession of studies, investigations are far less systematic than this. The test developer (or some later writer) proposes a certain interpretative construct, explains at greater or less length what the construct means, and offers *some* evidence that persons scoring high on the test also exhibit other behavior associated with the construct. The initial report is usually far from convincing; the sophisticated reader will think of alternative ways to account for the test behavior.

If the construct interpretation is taken seriously by the profession, its validity is challenged over and over again. The challenge consists of proposing a counterhypothesis—an alternative construct to account for the test behavior in whole or part. While one could carry out construct validation by a plodding verification of every sentence written about the construct, the work would be interminable. It is the plausible counterinterpretation that directs research toward a possibly vulnerable part of the theory.

Procedures used to examine trait or process interpretations fall into three broad categories: correlational, experimental, and logical. Correlational studies determine how persons who score high on the test differ, in everyday life or in the laboratory, from those low on the test. Several types of correlational studies are mentioned below. The experimental study attempts to alter the person's test performance by some controlled procedure. If it can be shown, for example, that procedures designed to increase a child's confidence raise his score on an information test, this challenges the interpretation of the test as a measure of information alone. A logical analysis of the test content or the scoring rules may disclose disturbing influences in the score. A simple example is the observation that a certain outcome measure is invalid because the test has a low ceiling, so that pupils who do well on the pretest can gain only a few points at most.

CORRELATIONAL STUDIES ■ A construct that can be measured by only one procedure is likely not to be very interesting. When we can invent several diverse procedures whose reports agree well with each other, the construct is significant (Campbell and Fiske, 1959). Thus, if reading comprehension is our construct, we would like to see convergence among tests with multiple-choice response, tests of recall, and tests in which the subject carries out acts for which the test paragraph gives directions. Convergence is shown by correlations across persons within groups, and by correlations across groups, whether the groups are demographic or are the product of experimental manipulations. Indicators of one construct should ordinarily have low correlations with measures interpreted in terms of other constructs. If two tests are very similar in the information they give, it complicates theory to retain two trait names for them.

Among techniques for studying convergence and divergence of indicators is factor analysis. A factor analysis of even a large number of measures of educational outcomes is likely to report only a few factors. This is too often interpreted as implying that the several outcomes "are not really different." Comprehension of physical laws will certainly correlate with ability to reason scientifically because, in a general population, those who have studied science will do better on both types of test. Even if the study is confined to persons who have studied physics, the correlation will remain high because the ablest students will have made greatest progress along both directions. If the high correlation means that there is no distinction between comprehension and reasoning, one could not criticize a curriculum for emphasizing the laws and making no effort to promote reasoning.

At first glance there appears to be a head-on conflict. The curriculum reformer argues that comprehension and reasoning are distinct attainments, and the correlational study proves that whoever is best in one respect is best in the other. The contradiction is resolved by a distinction between a within-group correlation and an across-groups correlation. Within a group completing the same course of study, the two variables correlate. But suppose the class averages for 50 classes are determined, and a correlation across groups is computed from these 50 pairs of values. The curriculum reformer who contends that some teachers neglect to develop reasoning is predicting that this across-groups correlation will be fairly low, that some groups will rank high on comprehension but not on reasoning. Even if the correlation across groups turns out to be high, the reformer has a tenable position to retreat to. If he can design a curriculum that concentrates on scientific reasoning, whose graduates score exceptionally well on the reasoning test while scoring at the norm on the comprehension test, he has proved his point. The high correlation across groups meant only that present curricula are holding the balance between reasoning and comprehension so nearly constant that the best programs (or those drawing the ablest students) get the best results on both dimensions.

CONSTRUCTS AS EDUCATIONAL OBJECTIVES ■ The formal rationale for construct validation sees a construct as defined by a network of relations, all of which are anchored to observables and so are testable. This rationale has been widely accepted in psychology, but its use in education needs further explication. The operationists who want to equate each construct with "one indicator"—rather, with a narrowly defined class of procedures—are advocating that we restrict descriptions to statements of tasks performed or behavior exhibited and are rejecting construct interpretations. Surely, however, the choice of interpretation is the prerogative of the investigator; a type of interpretation productive in one context may be sterile in another.

The writers on curriculum and evaluation who insist that objectives be "defined in terms of behavior" are taking an ultraoperationalist position, though they have not offered a scholarly philosophical analysis of the issue. The person who insists on "behavioral" objectives is denying the appropriateness and usefulness of constructs. The educator who states objectives in terms of constructs (self-confidence, scientific attitude, the habit of suiting one's writing style to his purpose) regards observables as indicators from which the presence of certain dispositions can be inferred. He will not, however, *substitute* "volunteers ideas and answers in class" for "self-confidence." From the construct point of view, behavior such as this is an indicator of confidence, not a definer. No list of specific responses-to-situations, however lengthy, can define the construct, since the construct is intended to apply to situations that will arise in the future and cannot be specified now.

Nearly all current philosophy of science, even the operationism of Bridgman, makes use of constructs embedded in networks. But one still encounters such statements as Ebel's: "If the test we propose to use provides in itself the best available operational definition, the concept of validity does not apply" (Ebel, 1961). But this language gives the game away, for the "best available" definition is presumably not the best conceivable, and "How good is the operation?" remains a meaningful question.

The issue raised by the ultraoperationalists is possibly just a terminological one, since there seem to be few differences of opinion about how tests and test interpretations can and must be used (Hochberg, 1961). There is universal agreement that general propositions embodying descriptive concepts must in the end be verified by means of systematic observation, and that the procedures used to gather these observations must be given an adequate operational description in order to make the report useful.

The person planning instruction or choosing among courses of study has to think in terms of concepts that describe behavior in a broad class of situations. One of the tasks of social science is to seek the right breadth for its concepts, (Nagel, 1961). "Citizenship" is no doubt too broad; "ego-strength" is a good deal better, since it leads one to anticipate different behavior in situations all of which might be thought of as calling for citizenship. One cannot expect, at least in this century, to disentangle ego-strength from interacting traits and situational variables, and so long as each measure is subject to interactive effects, no one measure can be accepted as a standard.

One can retreat to very narrow concepts: citizenship could be broken down at least to the level of "participation in elections" and "obedience to speed laws." This would increase the number of variables beyond the point where they could be investigated, and would leave out of the discussion whatever behavior citizens exhibit in the less standardized aspects of their lives.

The most serious criticism to be made of programs of construct validation is that some of them are haphazard accumulations of data rather than genuine efforts at scientific reasoning. To merely catalogue relations between the test under study and a variety of other variables is to provide a do-it-yourself kit for the reader, who is left to work out his own interpretative theory. Construct validation should start with a reasonably definite statement of the proposed interpretation. That interpretation will suggest important counterhypotheses, and these also will suggest data to collect. Investigations to be used for construct validation, then, should be purposeful rather than haphazard. After collecting his data, the investigator is expected to integrate the hypotheses and findings with each other and to offer a final conclusion as to the soundness of the construct interpretation and the influence of impurities that have been identified.

CONCLUSION

Validation of an instrument calls for an integration of many types of evidence. The varieties of investigation are not alternatives any one of which would be adequate. The person validating a test should give thought to all questions suggested in Table 1, though the relative importance of the questions varies from test to test. The several kinds of study shed light on each other. Thus, criterion-oriented studies generate a theory of individual differences and a theory of tasks and situations. In the light of such constructs, one makes reasonable judgments about the design of new educational situations and the design of new measuring instruments. Since these judgments, in turn, need to be validated, the process of investigation, and therefore the growth of knowledge, never ends.

Responsibility for valid use of a test rests on the person who interprets it. The published research merely provides the interpreter with some facts and concepts. He has to combine these with his other knowledge about the person; he tests and the assignments or adjustment problems that confront them to decide what interpretations are warranted.

12   *Evaluating Content Validity*

....

ROBERT L. EBEL

Content validity has been regarded by measurement experts as being particularly crucial for achievement tests. In fact, without it further consideration of the test is meaningless. It is less obvious that content validity is an important consideration for any type of instrument. The reader is urged to apply the statements made by the author to the type of instrument in which he has the most interest, and to ask himself questions such as: How can the objectivity of content validity assessment be increased? What is included in the "content" besides the subject matter or topics considered? How may content validity be considered as a part of other validity approaches? Should a test be considered an operational definition of the goals of the constructor or user? At what stage in an instructional sequence should evaluation be employed? What are the sources of evidence for content validity?

THE CONCEPT OF CONTENT VALIDITY

It is often said that an educational achievement test possesses content validity to the degree that it samples adequately some clearly specified universe of educational content. This statement lends itself to a common and rather serious misinterpretation. It suggests that the validity of a test is to be judged in terms of its relevance to the materials of instruction rather than the ultimate objectives of instruction. But the validity of an educational achievement test cannot be judged solely, or even principally, in terms of its sampling of the subject matter of a course. Only when the "content" of education is conceived as a set of goals to be attained, rather than as a set of lessons to be studied or as a set of class activities to be carried out, is it educationally useful to seek content validity in a test.

An educational achievement test is one designed to measure the extent of attainment of the ultimate goals of instruction in a particular area by the individuals in a particular group. In passing judgment on the content validity of an educational achievement test one asks, "To what extent does this test require demonstration by the student of the achievements which constitute the objectives of

Reprinted and abridged with permission of author and publisher from an article entitled, "Obtaining and Reporting Evidence on Content Validity," which appeared in *Educational and Psychological Measurement*, 1956, Vol. 16, pp. 269–282.

instruction in this area?" The more directly, completely, and reliably a test measures the attainment of these goals the greater is its content validity.

There is a common and widespread tendency on the part of both teachers and pupils to place primary emphasis on "covering" the subject matter and remembering the materials of instruction, rather than on achieving the objectives of that instruction, i.e., developing abilities for more effective behavior. No subject has ever been introduced into the curriculum that was not in the first instance designed to enable those who studied it to behave more effectively. But teaching procedures are habit forming. The transmission of learning from teachers to scholars, who in their turn become the teachers of other scholars, tends to shift attention away from the ends of instruction, and to focus it on the means.

OPERATIONAL DEFINITIONS OF GOALS

When tests are derived directly from desired behavioral goals, the tests constitute operational definitions of those goals. Such tests are sometimes called "self-defining" tests. This term seems unfortunate, since it suggests that the contents of the test are immune from criticism. A test does not define itself. It defines an educational achievement, and some definitions of that achievement are likely to be more soundly based or more rational than others.

Three objections have been raised to the statement that achievement tests constitute operational definitions of the goals of achievement. The first is that not all of the ultimate goals of education can be measured effectively in a test situation. This is true, and ought to be recognized frankly. An achievement test provides an operational definition of only those goals whose achievement can be observed in test situations. Operational definitions of other goals of achievement must be sought in non-test procedures appropriate for revealing the extent of their achievement.

A second objection is that, since any achievement test constitutes a sample of items from a much larger potential population of items, it provides a very incomplete definition of the goals of achievement. This also is true, but how serious a limitation it is depends on the complexity of the field to be covered by the test and the adequacy of sampling of items in the test. For measurement purposes the particular sample used does constitute the operational definition of achievement. For instructional purposes it is better to regard the hypothetical population of items, from which this particular sample is presumed to have been selected, as constituting a better operational definition of the goals of achievement.

A third objection is that each test constitutes a different operational definition of achievement. The existence of such a multiplicity of definitions, it is argued, is likely to contribute more to confusion than to clarity in thinking. Again there is some truth in this argument. However it discounts the very considerable areas of agreement in the definitions of the same achievement provided by different tests. Further, it implies that agreement on the goals of instruction can be purchased at the price of clarity in the definitions of those goals. This is certainly true, as many vague statements of educational goals attest, but it is a poor bargain. The use of achievement tests as operational definitions of the goals of achievement does not cause disagreements. It simply brings them to light. There is no better way to define many educational goals concretely than to construct tests of the achievement of them.

With these considerations in mind a more precise description of the concept of educational achievement tests as operational definitions of the goals of achievement may be stated. Any educational achievement test may be regarded as a sample of items from a hypothetical population of items which constitutes one operational definition of the testable goals of instruction in the area.

GOALS, CURRICULA, AND TESTS

It is possible to conceive of a neat division of educational labor in which the educational philosopher defines the goals of education, the curriculum maker devises methods for attaining those goals, and the test constructor devises instruments to measure the extent to which they have been attained. But the problems of education are too complex, and our abilities to construct and communicate ideas too limited to make this neat system workable. Each of the specialists needs not only to have his eye on what the other fellow is doing, but needs also to help him do it. This does not mean that education can do without specialists who are philosophers, curriculum builders, or test constructors. What it does mean is that no one of these specialists can stake a claim to one field of operation and insist that all other specialists keep off.

Emphatic, even angry words have been spoken from time to time concerning the harmful influences of tests on education and the evil influences of test makers on the curriculum. Certainly bad tests, or the improper use of good tests, can affect education adversely. Certainly any intended or accidental enforcement of uniformity in educational procedures through a wide-scale testing program cannot be defended. But it is foolish to disregard, and it would be more foolish to abandon, the powerful forces for educational improvement that are available through proper use of good educational achievement tests.

Consider these alternative sequences in the development of an educational program.

FIRST SEQUENCE ■
Step 1. Areas of agreement in desired behavior are identified.
Step 2. Curricula calculated to develop these desired behaviors are designed.
Step 3. Tests are constructed on the basis of the curricula to determine each student's degree of mastery of it.

SECOND SEQUENCE ■
Step 1. Areas of agreement in desired behavior are identified.

Step 2. These behaviors are translated as directly and completely as possible into an extended series of test problems.

Step 3. Curricula are designed to equip students to do as well as possible on problems like those presented in the test.

The first alternative is the one which is commonly followed. The second is equally sound from a logical point of view, and might well in practice prove to be more effective. It is easier to define desirable behavior in terms of test exercises than in terms of curricular procedures. The best of our current educational achievement tests have been derived, not indirectly from curricula, but directly from the ultimately desirable goals of behavior.

QUALITATIVE VS. QUANTITATIVE EVALUATION OF CONTENT VALIDITY

Validity is concerned with the relation between the information the user expects from a test and the information actually supplied by it. There are two bases on which this relationship can be examined, qualitative and quantitative. In using the qualitative basis one asks how closely the behavior apparently called for by the test represents or indicates the desired behavior which constitutes the goal of instruction. At one extreme, a test of competence in shorthand may require behavior identical with the desired behavior. Such a test would be judged highly valid on a qualitative basis. At the other extreme is a test of honesty based on an analysis of handwriting. Since there appears no rational relationship between the behavior called for by the test and the desired behavior, such a test would be judged qualitatively to be low in validity.

Most users of educational achievement tests place considerable faith in the qualitative comparison of the behavior called for by a test with the behavioral goals of instruction. But this process is regarded with considerable mistrust by some specialists in psychological testing. Qualitative examination, they feel, involves personal and highly subjective judgments. Appearances may be deceiving, so that false relationships are accepted as true, and true relationships overlooked. Incidental relationships may be weighted heavily and more fundamental relationships neglected. These specialists discount the importance of content validity, arguing for a more objective, systematic, quantitative approach.

In the quantitative approach the behavior on the test is quantified in the form of a single score. The behavior which the test ought to measure is also quantified, preferably by observing the desired behavior directly and assigning precisely defined scores to various aspects of it. These scores are referred to as criterion scores. A correlation coefficient is then calculated to express the degree of relationship between the test scores and the criterion scores.

On the surface, but on the surface only, this quantitative approach appears to avoid some of the subjective difficulties involved in the qualitative approach. For even in the quantitative approach the selection of acts of behavior to become part of the criterion measure and the assignment of different score values to various manifestations of this behavior involve the exercise of personal, subjective judgment. There are, in fact, added opportunities for error in the quantitative approach, for it involves three steps instead of one. Test behavior must be quantified, desired behavior must be quantified, and the relation between the two must be examined. In the qualitative evaluation of a test, a single, direct comparison is made between test behavior and desired behavior.

The fundamental fact is that one cannot escape from the problem of content validity. If we dodge it in constructing the test, it raises its troublesome head when we seek a criterion. For when one attempts to evaluate the validity of a test indirectly via some quantified criterion measure, he must use the very process he is trying to avoid in order to obtain the criterion measures.

RELATION OF CONTENT VALIDITY TO OTHER TYPES

The nature and importance of content validity may be made clearer by relating it to other types of validity. The degree of *content validity* of a test is a function of the directness, completeness, and reliability with which it measures attainment of the ultimate goals of instruction in a given area. The degree of *concurrent validity* of a test is a function of the correlation between scores on it and scores obtained from an alternative, presumably more valid but less convenient, measurement procedure, *and of the degree of content validity of the alternative procedure.* The degree of *predictive validity* of a test for a given group is a function of the correlation between scores on the test and future measures of the status to be predicted, *and of the content validity of future measures of status.* The degree of *construct validity* of a test is the extent to which a system of hypothetical relationships can be verified on the basis of measures of the construct derived from the test. But this system of relationships always involves measures of observed behavior *which must be defended on the basis of their content validity.* In every case quantitative validation builds on qualitative validation. Statistical validation is not an alternative to subjective validation, but an extension of it. All statistical procedures for validating tests are based ultimately upon common sense agreement concerning what is being measured by a particular measurement process.

OBTAINING EVIDENCE OF CONTENT VALIDITY

The simplest and most direct evidence of content validity is obtained from examination of the test itself by a competent judge. A cursory inspection skimming the test is better than no inspection at all. But if the judge is seriously interested in determining the relationship between what the test asks an examinee to do and what the typical user expects of a test of that sort, he should take the test himself just as a student would do. Only by this means can he give sufficiently close, careful attention to the individual items of the test.

It is true that the judge may not always respond to the items on exactly the same basis as a typical examinee would, and thus may misjudge what a particular item measures. But this does not mean that his judgments of what the test as a whole is measuring are completely untrustworthy. It simply means that he must be competent and work carefully, and that he should if possible check his interpretations against those of other competent judges or typical examinees.

To obtain a summary view of test content it is often helpful to classify the items in broad areas of subject matter and student ability. Areas of content will vary from test to test. In straight subject examinations these areas will ordinarily follow the customary divisions of the subject, as shown in representative textbooks. Even in skills examinations such as reading comprehension the items may be regarded as belonging to different areas of content. Some of the reading passages may be historical, others scientific, others literary prose, and still others poetry.

TYPES OF ABILITY MEASURED

Equally important in judging the content validity of a test is the distribution of items with respect to the types of ability or achievement they require. Many of the items found in educational achievement tests can be classified in one or more of the following broad categories: content detail, vocabulary, fact, generalization, understanding, and application. A content detail item is one of no significance outside the classroom. Its function is to indicate that the examinee has or has not done some particular learning exercises. A vocabulary item is one which requires essential knowledge of the meaning of a particular term for successful response. A factual item is one dealing with an isolated bit of information, frequently a Who? What? When? or Where? type of item. A generalization item is one dealing with a law, principle, general summary, or basic method of procedure. An understanding term is one beginning with the word "Why?", or calling for completions beginning with the word "because." An application item is one which presents a problem to be solved, a decision to be given, or a recommendation to be made in terms of some specifically described situation. Items are classified in these categories, not on the basis of assumed psychological functions involved, but in terms of overt characteristics of the items. While it is seldom possible to classify all of the items in the test with complete confidence that they have been properly classified, the over-all process usually gives a good indication of the emphasis found in the test.

It is sometimes argued that differences in the type of ability called for by a test item are relatively unimportant. A test of factual knowledge was shown in one study to rank pupils in nearly the same order as a test of their problem-solving ability. Other studies have given a contrary indication. Much appears to depend on the character of the previous teaching. If applications are not stressed, pupils may do much better in a test over factual details than on a test involving applications. If applications are stressed, pupils may do equally well on both, since factual knowledge is prerequisite to effective application. Failure to find significant difference in the ranking of a particular group of pupils on different types of test items cannot be accepted as conclusive evidence that the items are measuring identical achievements. In the long run tests which emphasize primarily factual information will tend to direct teaching and learning to the acquisition of factual knowledge. Unless it can be shown, which it has not been and is not likely to be, that pupils who possess factual knowledge can without further emphasis or training achieve desired understanding and make desired applications, emphasis on understanding and applications will be essential in both teaching and testing.

Within both subject-matter and pupil-ability classifications either important or unimportant questions can be asked. The content validity of a test depends on the significance or importance of the questions asked, and on the appropriateness of the balance among various subject-matter and pupil-ability categories. It depends also on the quality of the items themselves. Are they clearly expressed? Is the intended correct answer an adequate answer? Are the distractors plausible, yet not sufficiently defensible to attract many good students? Is the item as a whole of appropriate difficulty?

THE USER AS A JUDGE OF CONTENT VALIDITY

The content validity of a test depends not only on the characteristics of the test itself, but also on the purposes and needs of the user. A test of achievement in first-year high school algebra can be regarded as a generally valid test only to the extent that it measures what good algebra teachers try to teach. It is inevitable that the aims and values of different teachers will differ. It is also obvious that greater weight should be attached to the judgments of certain individuals than to those of others. But it is beyond question that a competent teacher or administrator, clearly aware of appropriate educational goals and familiar with the functions and limitations of various test procedures, can obtain direct evidence concerning the content validity of a test by careful examination of the test itself. Other types of evidence may be useful in judging content validity, but none is more fundamental.

EVIDENCE FROM THE TEST MANUAL

Evidence of content validity may sometimes be obtained by examining the test manual. If the manual presents the test outline, defines the universe of content sampled, summarizes the unique characteristics of the test, and calls attention to the principles guiding the authors and editors of the test in their selection of items, the manual can be extremely helpful in judging the content validity of the test. Since concrete information is more meaningful than abstract, actual items from the test should be used to illustrate the major classifications in the test outline.

In the development of a test, experts are sometimes asked to judge the relationship between the tasks required by the test and the desired behavioral goals. The number of judges used, their competence, and the process they use in evaluating the test help to determine the value of their contributions, and should be reported in the manual. Another factor of great importance, but one which is difficult to assess and report accurately, is the conscientiousness with which they undertook the task of evaluation. In the long run there probably would be greater incentives for the judges to assume responsibility for a careful job if their names were listed on the test booklet or in the manual.

The presentation in test manuals of detailed analyses of the content of a test has sometimes been criticized on the ground that this information tends to encourage teachers to "teach for the test." It cannot be denied that efforts to coach pupils to respond to specific test items is educationally harmful. But it is open to question that a test manual which outlines the contents of the test, or even which indicates the items that fall under each general heading, encourages this practice. Any misguided teacher who regards the final achievement test for her pupils as appropriate lesson material would not be likely to waste time on the manual. As a matter of fact, the manual, in calling attention to the broad categories of items from which the particular items have been drawn, should have the effect of generalizing instruction rather than making it more specific.

VALIDITY AND RELIABILITY

Validity has two aspects, relevance and reliability. What has been said thus far about determining the content validity of a test has been concerned with determining its content relevance. To be valid a test must not only be closely related to the function it is used to measure, but it also must measure that something with reasonable precision. Internal analysis of the data obtained from a single administration of the test under typical conditions to a representative group of examinees can provide adequate evidence concerning the reliability of the test. If item analysis data has been obtained, one of the Kuder-Richardson formulas for reliability is usually most convenient to use. If not, the odds-even coefficient may be more convenient. Either will ordinarily provide quite adequate information on the reliability of the test.

When items are selected empirically on the basis of item analysis data from a particular sample, reliability coefficients should not be computed by rescoring the selected items on the same sample of papers. Nor should the originally obtained indices of discrimination and difficulty be reported as unbiased estimates of these parameters for the selected items. In all cases the reliability coefficient and final item characteristic data should be obtained from a cross-validation sample.

Item analysis data are ordinarily obtained by contrasting the performance of students who scored high on the test with those who scored low. It is possible, and sometimes profitable, to use other sources for the contrasting groups. Two such independently defined groups were used in a recent study which required a test of the grasp of certain concepts in geography. Materials presenting and explaining these concepts were prepared and given to a small group of scholars whose ability to comprehend them was beyond question. Then the test was administered to these scholars. The test was also given to a group of students typical of those to be used later in the main experiment. These students had not had an opportunity to study the explanatory materials. Any item which was not answered correctly by all of the informed experts and which was not missed by all except a chance proportion of the uninformed students was rejected.

In the construction of reading interpretation tests it should be more common practice than it is to administer the test questions independent of the background material. Any item which can be answered correctly by a large proportion of students without reference to the background material can hardly be regarded as a valid test of comprehension of that material.

REPORTING EVIDENCE ON CONTENT VALIDITY

What has been said thus far about obtaining evidence on the content validity of educational achievement tests carries with it in most cases obvious implications for reporting that evidence. Such evidence ought to be reported more fully than is the usual practice. The purpose of reporting this evidence is *not* to convince the test user that the test is valid. It is rather to help him judge whether or not the test is valid for his purposes. The validity of a test is relative to the user and his purposes, as well as to the nature of the group on which it is used.

Test developers can aid test users to judge the content validity of their tests by stating the criteria and principles which guided them in choosing item topics and in writing items, by presenting an outline of the achievements covered by the test, and by indicating which items are intended to measure each of the achievements outlined. They can also aid test users by presenting detailed data on the internal analysis of the test, recognizing that these analyses are likely to be somewhat specific to the population tested.

SUMMARY

This article has dealt mainly with eleven points of view:

1. That the content validity of a test is determined by its relevance to the objectives of instruction rather than by its coverage of the materials of instruction.

2. That good tests of educational achievement provide good operational definitions of the goals of instruction.

3. That tests based on educational goals can directly influence teaching procedures constructively.

4. That there is no essential difference between the rational judgments involved in determining the content relevance of a test and those involved in determining the adequacy of criterion scores.

5. That all types of validity are based ultimately on the content validity of some measurement procedures.

6. That the best evidence of content validity is obtained by detailed, systematic, critical inspection of the test itself.

7. That it is possible to analyze the types of achievement required by the items as well as the content covered by the items in judging content validity.

8. That the test user is more competent than anyone else to judge the relevance of the test to his purposes.

9. That presentation of detailed test specifications and outlines in the test manual helps the user judge its relevance to his purposes.

10. That data from internal analysis of test reliability and item-discriminating power are helpful in judging content validity.

11. That evidence of content validity should be reported more fully than is usually true.

13　*Convergent and Discriminant Validity*

DONALD T. CAMPBELL AND DONALD W. FISKE

Some of the ideas about construct validity found in the first two articles of the chapter are extended in the present article. Campbell and Fiske point out that sometimes we demand high correlations as evidence of construct validity. At other times, however, we wish to discriminate, i.e., to show low correlations where the traits are assumed to be different. Further, we need to assess the importance of the method of measuring traits. The suggested approach for construct validity studies, then, is to measure at least two traits by at least two of the same methods. The various relationships are computed, and are recorded in a table or matrix (multitrait-multimethod matrix). To illustrate, suppose a group was measured by a test battery and also rated by a teacher on verbal

Reprinted and abridged from Donald T. Campbell and Donald W. Fiske, "Convergent and Discriminant Validation by the Multitrait-Multimethod Matrix," *Psychological Bulletin*, 1959, Vol. 56, pp. 81–105. Copyright 1959 by the American Psychological Association and reproduced by permission of the publisher and first-named author.

reasoning, mathematical ability, and clerical speed and accuracy. What would you expect to be the relationships between verbal reasoning and mathematical ability? What would you expect to be the relationships between verbal reasoning and clerical speed and accuracy? Would you expect that verbal reasoning expressed by a test score would correlate more highly with verbal reasoning expressed by a rating or with clerical speed and accuracy assessed by the same test battery? What four criteria suggested by the authors should be used in evaluating the data included in a multitrait-multimethod matrix?

In the cumulative experience with measures of individual differences over the past 50 years, tests have been accepted as valid or discarded as invalid by research experiences of many sorts. The criteria suggested in this paper are all to be found in such cumulative evaluations as well as in recent discussions of validity. These criteria are clarified and implemented when considered jointly in the context of a multitrait-multimethod matrix. Aspects of the validational process receiving particular emphasis are these:

1. Validation is typically *convergent*, a confirmation by independent measurement procedures. Independence of methods is a common denominator among the major types of validity (excepting content validity) insofar as they are to be distinguished from reliability.

2. For the justification of novel trait measures, for the validation of test interpretation, or for the establishment of construct validity, *discriminant* validation as well as convergent validation is required. Tests can be invalidated by too high correlations with other tests from which they were intended to differ.

3. Each test or task employed for measurement purposes is a *trait-method unit*, a union of a particular trait content with measurement procedures not specific to that content. The systematic variance among test scores can be due to responses to the measurement features as well as responses to the trait content.

4. In order to examine discriminant validity, and in order to estimate the relative contributions of trait and method variance, *more than one trait* as well as *more than one method* must be employed in the validation process. In many instances it will be convenient to achieve this through a multitrait-multimethod matrix. Such a matrix presents all of the intercorrelations resulting when each of several traits is measured by each of several methods.

To illustrate the suggested validational process a synthetic example is presented in Table 1. This illustration involves three different traits, each measured by three methods, generating nine separate variables. It will be convenient to have labels for various regions of the matrix, and such have been provided in Table 1. The reliabilities will be spoken of in terms of three *reliability diagonals*, one for each method. The reliabilities could also be designated as the monotrait-monomethod values. Adjacent to each reliability diagonal is the heterotrait-monomethod triangle. The reliability diagonal and the adjacent heterotrait-monomethod triangle make up a monomethod block. A *heteromethod block* is made

TABLE 1. *A Synthetic Multitrait-Multimethod Matrix*

Traits	Method 1 A_1	B_1	C_1	Method 2 A_2	B_2	C_2	Method 3 A_3	B_3	C_3
Method 1 A_1	(.89)								
B_1	.51	(.89)							
C_1	.38	.37	(.76)						
Method 2 A_2	.57	.22	.09	(.93)					
B_2	.22	.57	.10	.68	(.94)				
C_2	.11	.11	.46	.59	.58	(.84)			
Method 3 A_3	.56	.22	.11	.67	.42	.33	(.94)		
B_3	.23	.58	.12	.43	.66	.34	.67	(.92)	
C_3	.11	.11	.45	.34	.32	.58	.58	.60	(.85)

Note—The validity diagonals are the three sets of italicized values. The reliability diagonals are the three sets of values in parentheses. Each heterotrait-monomethod triangle is enclosed by a solid line. Each heterotrait-heteromethod triangle is enclosed by a broken line.

up of a *validity* diagonal (which could also be designated as monotrait-heteromethod values) and the two heterotrait-heteromethod triangles lying on each side of it. Note that these two heterotrait-heteromethod triangles are not identical.[1]

In terms of this diagram four aspects bear upon the question of validity. In the first place, the entries in the validity diagonal should be significantly different from zero and sufficiently large to encourage further examination of validity. This requirement is evidence of convergent validity. Second, a validity diagonal value should be higher than the values lying in its column and row in the heterotrait-heteromethod triangles. That is, a validity value for a variable should be higher than the correlations obtained between that variable and any other variable having neither trait nor method in common. This requirement may seem so minimal and so obvious as to not need stating, yet an inspection of the literature shows that it is frequently not met and may not be met even when the validity coefficients are of substantial size. In Table 1 all of the validity values meet this requirement. A third common-sense desideratum is that a variable correlate higher with an independent effort to measure the same trait than with measures designed to get at difficult traits which happen to employ the same method. For a given variable this involves comparing its values in the validity diagonals with its values in the heterotrait-monomethod triangles. For variables A_1, B_1, and C_1, this requirement is met to some degree. For the other variables A_2, A_3, etc., it is not met and this is probably typical of the usual case in individual differences research, as will be discussed in what follows. A fourth desideratum is that the

---

[1] The reader may profit from sketching Table 1 for himself. It is suggested that he consider only Methods 1 and 2, and that for the correlation coefficients he substitute the italicized labels appearing in the above paragraph. (Editors)

same pattern of trait interrelationship be shown in all of the heterotrait triangles of both the monomethod and heteromethod blocks. The hypothetical data in Table 1 meet this requirement to a very marked degree, in spite of the different general levels of correlation involved in the several heterotrait triangles.[2] The last three criteria provide evidence for discriminant validity.

Before we examine the multitrait-multimethod matrices available in the literature, some explication and justification of this complex of requirements seems in order.

CONVERGENCE OF INDEPENDENT METHODS: THE DISTINCTION BETWEEN RELIABILITY AND VALIDITY ▪ Both reliability and validity concepts require that agreement between measures be demonstrated. A common denominator which most validity concepts share in contradistinction to reliability is that this agreement represents the convergence of independent approaches. The concept of independence is indicated by such phrases as "external variable," "criterion performance," "behavioral criterion" (American Psychological Association, 1954, pp. 13–15) used in connection with concurrent and predictive validity. For construct validity it has been stated thus: "Numerous successful predictions dealing with phenotypically diverse 'criteria' give greater weight to the claim of construct validity than do . . . predictions involving very similar behavior " (Cronbach & Meehl, 1955, p. 295).

Independence is, of course, a matter of degree, and in this sense reliability and validity can be seen as regions on a continuum. Reliability is the agreement between two efforts to measure the same trait through maximally similar methods. Validity is represented in the agreement between two attempts to measure the same trait through maximally different methods. Some evaluation of validity can take place even if the two methods are not entirely independent. In practice, perhaps all that can be hoped for is evidence for relative validity, that is, for common variance specific to a trait, above and beyond shared method variance.

Discriminant validation. While the usual reason for the judgment of invalidity is low correlations in the validity diagonal, tests have also been invalidated because of too high correlations with other tests purporting to measure different things. Such invalidation occurs when values in the heterotrait-heteromethod triangles are as high as those in the validity diagonal, or even where within a monomethod block the heterotrait values are as high as the reliabilities.

When a dimension of personality is hypothesized, when a construct is proposed, the proponent invariably has in mind distinctions between the new dimension and other constructs already in use. One cannot define without implying distinctions, and the verification of these distinctions is an important part of the validational process. In discussions of construct validity it has been expressed in such terms as "from this point of view, a low correlation with athletic ability may be just as

---

[2] For example, the correlation between traits A and B is the highest in each of the triangles. (Editors)

important and encouraging as a high correlation with reading comprehension "
(APA, 1954, p. 17).

THE TEST AS A TRAIT-METHOD UNIT ∎ In any given psychological measuring
device there are certain features or stimuli introduced specifically to represent the
trait that it is intended to measure. There are other features which are characteristic of the method being employed, features which could also be present in
efforts to measure other quite different traits. The test, rating scale, or other
device almost inevitably elicits systematic variance in response due to both
groups or features. To the extent that irrelevant method variance contributes
to the scores obtained, these scores are invalid.

This source of invalidity was first noted in the "halo effects" found in ratings
(E. L. Thorndike, 1920). Studies of individual differences among laboratory
animals resulted in the recognition of "apparatus factors," usually more dominant than psychological process factors. For paper-and-pencil tests, methods
variance has been noted under such terms as "test-form factors" and "response
sets." Cronbach has stated the point particularly clearly: "The assumption is
generally made . . . that what the test measures is determined by the content of
the items. Yet the final score . . . is a composite of effects resulting from the form
of the item used " (Cronbach, 1946, p. 475). "Response sets always lower the
logical validity of a test. . . . Response sets interfere with inferences from test
data " (p. 484).

While E. L. Thorndike (1920) was willing to allege the presence of halo effects
by comparing the obtained high correlations with common sense notions of what
they ought to be (e.g., it was unreasonable that a teacher's intelligence and voice
quality should correlate .63), and while much of the evidence of response set
variance is of the same order, the clear-cut demonstration of the presence of
method variance requires both several traits and several methods. Otherwise,
high correlations between tests might be explained as due either to basic trait
similarity or to shared method variance. In the multitrait-multimethod matrix
the presence of method variance is indicated by the difference in level of correlation between the parallel values of the monomethod block and the heteromethod
blocks, assuming comparable reliabilities among all tests. Thus the contribution
of method variance in Test A_1 of Table 1 is indicated by the elevation of $r_{A_1B_1}$
above $r_{A_1B_2}$, i.e., the difference between .51 and .22, etc.

The distinction between trait and method is of course relative to the test constructor's intent. What is an unwanted response set for one tester may be a trait
for another who wishes to measure acquiescense, willingness to take an extreme
stand, or tendency to attribute socially desirable attributes to oneself (Cronbach,
1946, 1950; Edwards, 1957b).

SOME ILLUSTRATIVE MATRICES ∎ Multitrait-multimethod matrices are rare in the
test and measurement literature. Most frequent are two types of fragment: two
methods and one trait (single isolated values from the validity diagonal, perhaps

accompanied by a reliability or two) and heterotrait-monomethod triangles. Either type of fragment is apt to disguise the inadequacy of our present measurement efforts, particularly in failing to call attention to the preponderant strength of method variance. The evidence of test validity to be presented here is probably poorer than most psychologists would have expected.[3]

TABLE 2. *Intercorrelations and Reliabilities of Four Personality Traits of School Children Measured by Two Different Methods* $(N = 311)$[1]

		Peer Ratings				Association Test			
		A_1	B_1	C_1	D_1	A_2	B_2	C_2	D_2
Peer Ratings									
Courtesy	A_1	(.82)							
Honesty	B_1	.74	(.80)						
Poise	C_1	.63	.65	(.74)					
School Drive	D_1	.76	.78	.65	(.89)				
Association Test									
Courtesy	A_2	.13	.14	.10	.14	(.28)			
Honesty	B_2	.06	.12	.16	.08	.27	(.38)		
Poise	C_2	.01	.08	.10	.02	.19	.37	(.42)	
School Drive	D_2	.12	.15	.14	.16	.27	.32	.18	(.36)

[1] Based on data from Kelley and Krey (1934)

One of the earliest matrices of this kind was provided by Kelley and Krey in 1934. Peer judgments by students provided one method, scores on a word-association test the other. Table 2 presents the data for the four most valid traits of the eight employed. The picture is one of strong method factors, particularly among the peer ratings, and almost total invalidity. For only one of the eight measures, school drive, is the value in the validity diagonal (.16) higher than all of the heterotrait-heteromethod values. The absence of discriminant validity is further indicated by the tendency of the values in the monomethod triangles to approximate the reliabilities.

An early illustration from the animal literature comes from Anderson's (1937) study of drives. Table 3 presents a sample of his data. Once again the highest correlations are found among different constructs from the same method showing the dominance of apparatus or method factors so typical of the whole field of individual differences. The validity diagonal for hunger is higher than the heteroconstruct-heteromethod values. The diagonal value for sex has not been *italicized* as a validity coefficient since the obstruction box measure was pre-sex-opportunity, the activity wheel post-opportunity. Note that the high general level of heterotrait-heteromethod values could be due to either correlation of methods variance between the two methods or to correlated trait variance. On *a priori*

---

[3] Two examples have been selected to illustrate the procedure. (Editors)

TABLE 3. *Intercorrelations and Reliabilities of Drive Measures Obtained by Two Different Methods* $(N = 50)$[1]

		Obstruction Box			Activity Wheel		
		A_1	B_1	C_1	A_2	B_2	C_2
Obstruction Box							
Hunger	A_1	(.58)					
Thirst	B_1	.54	( )				
Sex	C_1	.46	.70	( )			
Activity Wheel							
Hunger	A_2	.48	.31	.37	(.83)		
Thirst	B_2	.35	.33	.43	.87	(.92)	
Post Sex	C_2	.31	.37	.44	.69	.78	( )

[1] Based on data presented by Anderson (1937)

Note—Empty parentheses appear where no appropriate reliability estimates are reported in the original paper.

grounds, however, the methods would seem about as independent as one would be likely to achieve. The predominance of an apparatus factor for the activity wheel is evident from the fact that the correlation between hunger and thirst (.87) is of the same magnitude as their test-retest reliabilities (.83 and .92 respectively).

DISCUSSION

RELATION TO CONSTRUCT VALIDITY ■ While the validational criteria presented are explicit or implicit in the discussions of construct validity (Cronbach & Meehl, 1955; APA, 1954), this paper is primarily concerned with the adequacy of tests as measures of a construct rather than with the adequacy of a construct as determined by the confirmation of theoretically predicted associations with measures of other constructs. We believe that before one can test the relationships between a specific trait and other traits, one must have some confidence in one's measures of that trait. Such confidence can be supported by evidence of convergent and discriminant validation. Stated in different words, any conceptual formulation of a trait will usually include implicitly, the proposition that this trait is a response tendency which can be observed under more than one experimental condition and that this trait can be meaningfully differentiated from other traits. The testing of these two propositions must be prior to the testing of other propositions to prevent the acceptance of erroneous conclusions. For example, a conceptual framework might postulate a large correlation between Traits A and B and no correlation between Traits A and C. If the experimenter then measures A and B by one method (e.g., questionnaire) and C by another method (such as the measurement of overt behavior in a situation test), his findings may be consistent with his hypotheses solely as a function of method variance common to his measures of A and B but not to C.

The requirements of this paper are intended to be as appropriate to the relatively atheoretical efforts typical of the tests and measurements field as to more theoretical efforts. This emphasis on validational criteria appropriate to our present atheoretical level of test construction is not at all incompatible with a recognition of the desirability of increasing the extent to which all aspects of a test and the testing situation are determined by explicit theoretical considerations, as Jessor and Hammond have advocated (Jessor & Hammond, 1957).

RELATION TO OPERATIONALISM ■ Underwood (1957, p. 54) in his effective presentation of the operationalist point of view shows a realistic awareness of the amorphous type of theory with which most psychologists work. He contrasts a psychologist's "literacy" conception with the psychologist's operational definition as represented by his test or other measuring instrument. He recognizes the importance of the literary definition in communicating and generating science. He cautions that the operational definition "may not at all measure the process he wishes to measure; it may measure something quite different." (p. 55) He does not, however, indicate how one would know when one was thus mistaken.

The requirements of the present paper may be seen as an extension of the kind of operationalism Underwood has expressed. The test constructor is asked to generate from his literary conception or private construct not one operational embodiment, but two or more, each as different in research vehicle as possible. Furthermore, he is asked to make explicit the distinction between his new variable and other variables, distinctions which are almost certainly implied in his literary definition. In his very first validational efforts, before he ever rushes into print, he is asked to apply the several methods and several traits jointly. His literary definition, his conception is now best represented in what his independent measures of the trait hold *distinctively* in common. The multitrait-multimethod matrix is, we believe, an important practical first step in avoiding "the danger . . . that the investigator will fall into the trap of thinking that because he went from an artistic or literary conception . . . to the construction of items for a scale to measure it, he has validated his artistic conception." (Underwood, 1957, p. 55) In contrast with the *single operationalism* now dominant in psychology, we are advocating a *multiple operationalism*.

Underwood's presentation and that of this paper as a whole imply moving from concept to operation, a sequence that is frequent in science and perhaps typical. The same point can be made however in inspecting a transition from operation to construct. For any body of data taken from a single operation there is a subinfinity of interpretations possible, a subinfinity of concepts, or combinations of concepts that it could represent.

THE EVALUATION OF A MULTITRAIT-MULTIMETHOD MATRIX ■ The evaluation of the correlation matrix formed by intercorrelating several trait-method units must take into consideration the many factors which are known to affect the magnitude of correlations. A value in the validity diagonal must be assessed in the light of the reliabilities of the two measures involved. Again, the whole approach assumes adequate sampling of individuals: the curtailment of the sample with respect to one or more traits will depress the reliability coefficients and inter-correlations involving these traits. While restrictions of range over all traits produce serious difficulties in the interpretation of a multitrait-multimethod matrix and should be avoided whenever possible, the presence of different degrees of restriction on different traits is the more serious hazard to meaningful interpretation.

Various statistical treatments for multitrait-multimethod matrices might be developed, but we believe that such summary statistics are neither necessary nor appropriate at this time. Psychologists today should be concerned not with evaluating tests as if the tests were fixed and definitive, but rather with developing better tests. We believe that a careful examination of a multitrait-multimethod matrix will indicate to the experimenter what his next steps should be: it will indicate which methods should be discarded or replaced, which concepts need sharper delineation, and which concepts are poorly measured because of excessive or confounding method variance. Validity judgments based on such a matrix must take into account the stage of development of the constructs, the postulated relationships among them, the level of technical refinement of the methods, the relative independence of the methods, and any pertinent characteristics of the sample. We are proposing that the validational process be viewed as an aspect of an ongoing program for improving measuring procedures, and that the "validity coefficients" obtained at any one stage in the process be interpreted in terms of gains over preceding stages and as indicators of where further effort is needed.

THE DESIGN OF A MULTITRAIT-MULTIMETHOD MATRIX ■ The several methods and traits included in a validational matrix should be selected with care. The several methods used to measure each trait should be appropriate to the trait as conceptualized. Although this view will reduce the range of suitable methods, it will rarely restrict the measurement to one operational procedure.

Wherever possible the several methods in one matrix should be completely independent of each other: there should be no prior reason for believing that they share method variance. This requirement is necessary to permit the values in the heteromethod-heterotrait triangles to approach zero. If the nature of the traits rules out such independence of methods, efforts should be made to obtain as much diversity as possible in terms of data sources and classification processes.

Thus, the classes of stimuli, the background situations, or the experimental contexts should be different. Again, the persons providing the observations should have different roles *or* the procedures for scoring should be varied.

Plans for a validational matrix should take into account the difference between the interpretations regarding convergence and discrimination. It is sufficient to demonstrate convergence between two clearly distinct methods which show little overlap in the heterotrait-heteromethod triangles. While agreement between several methods is desirable, convergence between two is a satisfactory minimal requirement. Discriminative validation is not so easily achieved. Just as it is impossible to prove the null hypothesis or that some object does not exist, so one can never establish that a trait as measured is differentiated from all other traits. One can only show that this measure of Trait A has little overlap with those measures of B and C, and no dependable generalization beyond B and C can be made. For example, social poise could probably be readily discriminated from aesthetic interests, but it should also be differentiated from leadership.

Insofar as the traits are related and are expected to correlate with each other, the monomethod correlations will be substantial and heteromethod correlations between traits will also be positive. For ease of interpretation it may be best to include in the matrix at least two traits, and preferably two sets of traits, which are postulated to be independent of each other.

In closing, a word of caution is needed. Many multitrait-multimethod matrices will show no convergent validation: no relationship may be found between two methods of measuring a trait. In this common situation the experimenter should examine the evidence in favor of several alternative propositions: (a) Neither method is adequate for measuring the trait; (b) One of the two methods does not really measure the trait; (When the evidence indicates that a method does not measure the postulated trait it may prove to measure some other trait. High correlations in the heterotrait-heteromethod triangles may provide hints to such possibilities.) (c) The trait is not a functional unity, the response tendencies involved being specific to the non-trait attributes of each test. The failure to demonstrate convergence may lead to conceptual developments rather than to the abandonment of a test.

SUMMARY

This paper advocates a validational process utilizing a matrix of intercorrelations among tests representing at least two traits, each measured by at least two methods. Measures of the same trait should correlate higher with each other than they do with measures of different traits involving separate methods. Ideally, these validity values should also be higher than the correlations among different traits measured by the same method.

Illustrations from the literature show that these desirable conditions as a set are rarely met. Method or apparatus factors make very large contributions to psychological measurements.

The notions of convergence between independent measures of the same trait and discrimination between measures of different traits are compared with previously published formulations, such as construct validity and convergent operationalism. Problems in the application of this validational process are considered.

IV

DESIGNING

MEASUREMENT DEVICES

A test constructor must always begin with an outline of the measuring instrument to be developed. This set of specifications, similar in intent and function to an architect's blueprint, will detail the desired characteristics of the test. It will include indications of the type of reliability considered most important and the method of estimating it. This test design blueprint will summarize the type of validity to be established, with special attention paid to the nature of the criterion. The specifications may also set the number of items, item type to be used (e.g., multiple-choice, rating scale, etc.), nature of administration, and method of scoring. The most important function of the test design, however, is the specification of the behaviors to be measured.

The need to specify these behaviors is as crucial in the development of a classroom achievement test as in any other area of assessment. This is due primarily to the fact that *external* criteria of performance, which might be used for validation purposes, generally do not exist. In one respect an achievement test is self-validating, or more precisely, the test constructor "builds in" validity. In developing a classroom achievement test a paramount concern is the specification of the instructional objectives. Ordinarily, the first step a teacher should take in test development is to review instruction up to that point, while looking carefully at both the content of instruction and the kinds of student behaviors he has attempted to develop.

Most systematic attempts to identify and classify instructional objectives have fallen far short of expectations. One vital reason has been, until the emergence of the *Taxonomy of Educational Objectives*

(Bloom, et al., 1956, Krathwohl, et al., 1964), the lack of a unifying framework tied to learning theory and logically related to actual educational practice. The *Taxonomy* provided a cohesive scheme for organizing teaching and evaluation. This framework could profitably be used to construct, for example, a Table of Specifications for a test covering an entire course of study or a small unit.

The *Taxonomy* is overviewed and expressed in behavioral terms in the first article of the chapter, by Metfessel, Michael and Kirsner. To demonstrate how the *Taxonomy* could be used to frame a Table of Specifications the following illustration from the "Cognitive Domain" has been prepared. It is based on chapters one through four of this book of readings. The hypothetical Table of Specifications is found in Table 1. This two-way grid summarizes the instructional objectives for this four-chapter unit. The selection of content and desired cognitive operations to be dealt with will, of course, vary from instructor to instructor, as will the relative emphases indicated by the percentages. The procedure should lead to systematic measurement, as items for the test will be written in proportions prescribed by the Table. A balanced and valid test should be the result.

TABLE 1. *Hypothetical Table of Specifications for Chapters I–IV of Payne and McMorris' Educational and Psychological Measurement*

DESIRED COGNITIVE OPERATION

Content	Recall of Specifics	Compre-hension	Application	Analysis	Content Total
Procedures of Test Standardization	5%*				5%
Philosophies of Testing	3	7%			10
Types of Reliability	5	3	10%	7%	25
Factors Influencing Reliability	5		5		10
Types of Validity	10	5	5	5	25
Nature of the Criterion	6	4			10
Instructional Objectives	5	10			15
Behavioral Total	39%	29%	20%	12%	100%

*Numbers in cells summarize percent of time spent by instructor developing these skills in class relative to the respective content categories and operations.

The "Affective Domain" of the *Taxonomy* is considered in the second article of the chapter, by Darling. This author challenges us to make effective use of the specifications of affective learning outcomes and suggests ways in which various educational personnel may proceed.

The ultimate in the design of an instructional system would integrate the teaching–learning function with evaluation and feedback activities. One approach and a first step toward this ideal situation is described by Robert Bauernfeind in article 16. His "goal cards" would seem to suggest an excellent way to promote learning by continuous monitoring of student progress. The student can *see* the report of the results of his accomplishments and thereby be immediately rewarded for his efforts.

The advent of any new instructional procedure should invoke a reappraisal of the measurement techniques available to evaluate its effectiveness. Curricular innovations in science, mathematics, and social science have, in fact, caused educators to reevaluate expected student behavior and terms used to describe this behavior. In response to such "new" instructional strategies as mastery learning, performance contracting, and individually prescribed and managed instruction, the concept and methodology of criterion-referenced measurement was developed. Some theoretical, philosophical, and practical implications of this approach to measurement are discussed by Popham and Husek. When objectives change, the measurement techniques employed must of necessity change in order to insure fair and valid evaluation.

There is then, a continuous search for new and more valid ways of measuring. This is of particular concern to the social scientist, educational researcher and measurement specialist because their data sources interact with what it is they are trying to measure. To ask someone "how he feels about school" almost automatically insures a subjective response. What are needed are non-reactive measures. Webb, in an exciting (at least from the standpoint of the quality of the ideas) article, suggests some of these unobtrusive measures.

In the final article of the chapter Lee J. Cronbach presents a summary of research relating to essentially instrument-centered sources of potential measurement error that need to be considered in designing a test. After extensively reviewing the literature, the author concludes that the item format of a test can significantly and adversely influence the resulting scores thereby reducing validity. His recommendations for changes in test construction practice, particularly those relating to the development of correction keys, have constituted a major contribution to the design of measuring instruments.

In summary, various aspects of the test planning process are surveyed in this chapter. The emphasis is on the selection and specification of objectives to be assessed, the ways in which they can be expressed, and their implications for the form the final instrument might take. The reader could profit from a review of Coffman's comments on the nature of "what should be measured" (article 2). In addition potential areas of difficulty in instrument development are reviewed with particular attention paid to objectivity and possible interaction between type of response format and psychological characteristics of the examinee. In instrument development the planning phase is probably the most important. If you don't know where you're going, you're likely to end up somewhere else (Mager, 1962).

14   *Instrumentation of the* Taxonomy of Educational Objectives *in Behavioral Terms*

NEWTON S. METFESSEL, WILLIAM B. MICHAEL, AND DONALD KIRSNER

One criticism sometimes leveled at the Taxonomy of Educational Objectives, *particularly by evaluators, is that it is not couched in behavioral terms. The presence of some latitude in interpreting the various categories of the* Taxonomy *frequently makes the task of curriculum evaluation and test construction difficult. The above authors have made a very practical contribution by identifying infinitives found useful in operationalizing levels in both the cognitive and affective domains.*

In what ways does having objectives stated in behavioral terms facilitate instrument design and development? What are some of the difficulties in attempting to specify all educational objectives in behavioral terms? How might one evaluate the cognitive and affective component of the same objective? *

An educational objective consists of a description of the behaviors of an individual (the learner or examinee) in relation to his processing information embodied in subject matter—that is, what the learner must be capable of doing with certain characteristics or properties of subject matter. The behavioral component, which may be described as a process involved at an appropriate level of the taxonomic classification, is usually expressed in the form of a noun "ability" or a verb of being "able" followed by an infinitive such as the "ability to do" or "able to do". The second component of the objective, which consists of the specific content often found in the formal learning experience (e.g., in the curricular or instructional unit), constitutes a direct object of the verb or infinitive form. The terms "subject matter" or "content" are used in a fairly broad sense, as their level of specificity is highly variable, depending upon the characteristics of the curriculum unit.

INSTRUMENTATION: COGNITIVE DOMAIN

To facilitate the formulation statements of specific behavioral objectives within the framework of Bloom's taxonomy, the writers have included a table (See Table 1) made up of three columns. The first column contains the taxonomic classification identified by both code number and terminology employed in Bloom's (1956) taxonomy. The entries in the second column con-

---

* Reprinted by permission of the publisher, from David A. Payne, *Curriculum Evaluation* (Lexington, Mass.: D. C. Heath and Company, 1974).

Reprinted and abridged with permission of the first author and publisher from an article entitled, "Instrumentation of Bloom's and Krathwohl's Taxonomies for the Writing of Educational Objectives", which appeared in *Psychology in the Schools*, 1969, Vol. 6, pp. 227–231.

112

sist of appropriate infinitives which the teacher or curriculum worker may consult to achieve a precise or preferred wording of the behavior or activity desired. In the third column somewhat general terms relative to subject matter properties are stated. These direct objects, which may be expanded upon to furnish specificity at a desired level, may be permuted with one or more of the infinitive forms to yield the basic structure of an educational objective— activity (process) followed by content (subject matter property). At the discretion of the reader the words "ability" or "able" can be inserted in front of each of the infinitives.

TABLE 1. *Instrumentation of the Taxonomy of Educational Objectives: Cognitive Domain*

Taxonomy Classification	KEY WORDS	
	Examples of Infinitives	Examples of Direct Objects
1.00 Knowledge		
1.10 Knowledge of Specifics		
1.11 Knowledge of Terminology	to define, to distinguish, to acquire, to identify, to recall, to recognize	vocabulary, terms, terminology, meanings(s), definitions, referents, elements
1.12 Knowledge of Specific Facts	to recall, to recognize, to acquire, to identify	facts, factual information, (sources), (names), (dates), (events), (persons), (places), (time periods), properties, examples, phenomena
1.20 Knowledge of Ways and Means of Dealing with Specifics		
1.21 Knowledge of conventions	to recall, to identify, to recognize, to acquire	form(s), conventions, uses, usage, rules, ways, devices, symbols, representations, style(s), format(s)
1.22 Knowledge of Trends Sequences	to recall, to recognize, to acquire, to identify	action(s), processes, movement(s), continuity, development(s), trend(s), sequence(s), causes, relationship(s), forces, influences
1.23 Knowledge of Classification and Categories	to recall, to recognize	area(s), type(s), feature(s), class(es), set(s), division(s), arrangement(s), classification(s), category/categories

Table 1—Continued

	KEY WORDS		
Taxonomy Classification	Examples of Infinitives	Examples of Direct Objects
1.24 Knowledge of Criteria	to recall, to recognize, to acquire, to identify	criteria, basics, elements
1.25 Knowledge of Methodology	to recall, to recognize, to acquire, to identify	methods, techniques, approaches, uses, procedures, treatments
1.30 Knowledge of the Universals and Abstractions in a Field		
1.31 Knowledge of Principles, Generalizations	to recall, to recognize, to acquire, to identify	principle(s), generalization(s), proposition(s), fundamentals, laws, principal elements, implication(s)
1.32 Knowledge of Theories and Structures	to recall, to recognize, to acquire, to identify	theories, bases, interrelations, structure(s), organization(s), formulation(s)
2.00 Comprehension		
2.10 Translation	to translate, to transform, to give in own words, to illustrate, to prepare, to read, to represent, to change, to rephrase, to restate	meaning(s), sample(s), definitions, abstractions, representations, words, phrases
2.20 Interpretation	to interpret, to reorder, to rearrange, to differentiate, to distinguish, to make, to draw, to explain, to demonstrate	relevancies, relationships, essentials, aspects, new view(s), qualifications, conclusions, methods, theories, abstractions
2.30 Extrapolation	to estimate, to infer, to conclude, to predict, to differentiate, to determine, to extend, to interpolate,	consequences, implications, conclusions, factors, ramifications, meanings, corollaries, effects, probabilities
3.00 Application	to apply, to generalize, to relate, to choose, to develop, to organize, to use, to employ, to transfer, to restructure, to classify	principles, laws, conclusions, effects, methods, theories, abstractions, situations, generalizations, processes, phenomena, procedures
4.00 Analysis		
4.10 Analysis of Elements	to distinguish, to detect, to identify, to classify, to discriminate, to recognize, to categorize, to deduce	elements, hypothesis/ hypotheses, conclusions, assumptions, statements, (of fact), statements (of intent), arguments, particulars

Table 1—Continued

Taxonomy Classification	KEY WORDS Examples of Infinitives	Examples of Direct Objects
4.20 Analysis of Relationships	to analyze, to contrast, to compare, to distinguish, to deduce	relationships, interrelations, relevance, relevancies, themes, evidence, fallacies, arguments, cause-effect(s), consistency, consistencies, parts, ideas, assumptions
4.30 Analysis of Organizational Principles	to analyze, to distinguish, to detect, to deduce	form(s), pattern(s), purpose(s), point(s) of view(s), techniques, bias(es), structure(s), theme(s), arrangement(s), organization(s)
5.00 Synthesis		
5.10 Production of a Unique Communication	to write, to tell, to relate, to produce, to constitute, to transmit, to originate, to modify, to document	structure(s), pattern(s), product(s), performance(s), design(s), work(s), communications, effort(s), specifics, composition(s)
5.20 Production of a plan, or Proposed Set of Operations	to propose, to plan to produce, to design, to modify, to specify	plan(s), objectives, specification(s), schematic(s) operations, way(s), solution(s), means
5.30 Derivation of a Set of Abstract Relations	to produce, to derive, to develop, to combine, to organize, to synthesize, to classify, to deduce, to develop, to formulate, to modify	phenomena, taxonomies, concept(s), scheme(s), theories, relationships, abstractions, generalizations, hypothesis/hypotheses, perceptions, ways, discoveries
6.00 Evaluation		
6.10 Judgments in Terms of Internal Evidence	to judge, to argue, to validate, to assess, to decide	accuracy/accuracies, consistency/consistencies, fallacies, reliability, flaws, errors, precision, exactness
6.20 Judgments in Terms of External Criteria	to judge, to argue, to consider, to compare, to contrast, to standardize, to appraise	ends, means, efficiency, economy/economies, utility, alternatives, courses of action, standards, theories, generalizations

Although within a given major process level or sublevel of the taxonomy each infinitive cannot in all instances be meaningfully or idiomatically paired with every direct object listed, many useful permutations of infinitives and direct objects that furnish entirely readable statements are possible. Certainly use of these tables should lead to a substantial gain in the clarity and speed with which teachers and curriculum specialists, as well as those involved in construction of achievement tests, may state curriculum objectives. The writers have found that these tables have been of considerable help to their students, as well as to personnel in public schools who are concerned with writing objectives prior to curriculum development, constructing test items, or to carrying out evaluation studies. Slight modifications can be made with the entries to meet the requirements of specific learning situations.

INSTRUMENTATION: AFFECTIVE DOMAIN

The instrumentation of the Affective Domain (Krathwohl et al, 1964) is the same as that of the Cognitive Domain, to wit, the selection of behaviorally oriented infinitives combined with selected direct objects. (See Table 2.) As in the case of the Cognitive Domain, these are to be conceptualized as examples for the stimulation of other infinitives and objects and, more important, meaningful objectives in a total framework.

TABLE 2. *Instrumentation of the Taxonomy of Educational Objectives: Affective Domain*

Taxonomy Classification	KEY WORDS Examples of Infinitives	Examples of Direct Objects
1.0 Receiving		
1.1 Awareness	to differentiate, to separate, to set apart, to share	sights, sounds, events, designs, arrangements
1.2 Willingness to Receive	to accumulate, to select, to combine, to accept	models, examples, shapes, sizes, meters, cadences
1.3 Controlled or Selected Attention	to select, to posturally respond to, to listen (for), to control	alternatives, answers, rhythms, nuances
2.0 Responding		
2.1 Acquiescence in Responding	to comply (with), to follow, to commend, to approve	directions, instructions, laws, policies, demonstrations
2.2 Willingness to Respond	to volunteer, to discuss, to practice, to play	instruments, games, dramatic works, charades, burlesques
2.3 Satisfaction in Response	to applaud, to acclaim, to spend leisure time in, to augment	speeches, plays, presentations, writings
3.0 Valuing		

Table 2—Continued

Taxonomy Classification	KEY WORDS Examples of Infinitives	Examples of Direct Objects
3.1 Acceptance of a Value	to increase measured proficiency in, to increase numbers of, to relinquish, to specify	group membership(s), artistic production(s), musical productions, personal friendships
3.2 Preference for a Value	to assist, to subsidize, to help, to support	artists, projects, viewpoints, arguments
3.3 Commitment	to deny, to protest, to debate, to argue	deceptions, irrelevancies, abdications, irrationalities
4.0 Organization		
4.1 Conceptualization of a Value	to discuss, to theorize (on), to abstract, to compare	parameters, codes, standards, goals
4.2 Organization of a Value System	to balance, to organize, to define, to formulate	systems, approaches, criteria, limits
5.0 Characterization by Value or Value Complex		
5.1 Generalized Set	to revise, to change, to complete, to require	plans, behavior, methods, effort(s)
5.2 Characterization	to be rated high by peers in, to be rated high by superiors in, and to be rated high by subordinates in and to avoid, to manage, to resolve, to resist	humanitarianism, ethics, integrity, maturity extravagance(s), excesses, conflicts, exorbitancy/ exorbitancies

15   Applications of a Taxonomy of Affective Learning

DAVID W. DARLING

In the previous article summaries of both the Bloom et al. (1956) and Krathwohl et al. (1964) taxonomies were presented. Both the cognitive and affective handbooks are important, but recent developments and movements, particularly in the area of curriculum revision and modification, have brought about an intense reawakening of interest in affective learning outcomes. The desire to be concerned with attitudes, values, and interests raises some important questions for the teacher, curriculum worker, and researcher. It is the author's intent to address some of these questions.

Reprinted with permission of author and publisher (the Association for Supervision and Curriculum Development). Copyright 1965 by the Association for Supervision and Curriculum Development. From an article entitled, "Why a Taxonomy of Affective Learning?" which appeared in *Educational Leadership*, 1965, Vol. 22 (April), pp. 473–475, 522.

What are some ways in which affective objectives can be worked into the school program? What are some of the ways available to measure these kinds of objectives? What is the relationship between cognitive and affective learning? What are some research studies suggested by this article? (The interested reader may also wish to refer to informative articles by Mayhew (1965) and article 24 by Corey in this book.)

Why a taxonomy of affective learning? How does one go about answering such a question? What a task! I submit that this very important question, posed in its present form, cannot be directly answered. It is my intent to develop a rationale which justifies and helps explain the affective taxonomy by exploring the following questions:

1. Are the schools responsible for the development of qualities of character and conscience in learners as expressed in their interests, attitudes, appreciations, values, and emotional sets or biases?

2. Does the taxonomy of affective learning have any practical value in designing and evaluating learning experiences or in curriculum building?

3. Does the affective taxonomy have research potential which will contribute to our growing science of education?

If the answer to the first question is yes, then the affective taxonomy clearly has a contribution to make. The taxonomy represents an intelligent and rational synthesis of much thought and research in psychology and personality theory and gives this synthesis a structure heretofore not visible and hence not communicable. The taxonomy takes the old triad of "interests, attitudes, and values," redefines them in more specific terms (and more categories) and gives a rational ordering to their occurrence.

The reader may recall that there are five levels in the hierarchy of the affective taxonomy: (1) Receiving, (2) Responding, (3) Valuing, (4) Organizing, and (5) Characterization. All the behaviors of Level 1 (Receiving), *i.e., awareness, willingness to receive,* and *selective attention,* are indicators of a progression of interest. Likewise the first step of Level 2 (Responding), *acquiescence in responding,* is the highest level of interest before attitudes are affected. Both interest and attitude are at play when a child exhibits a *willingness to respond* and then derives some *satisfaction from his response* (the two remaining steps in Responding).

Interests, attitudes, and values are all apparent when a child indicates the *acceptance of a value* and then, through his behavior, indicates a *preference for a value.* These behaviors are the first two steps of Level 3. (Valuing). When a child indicates a *commitment* to a value, he has moved beyond mere interest but attitudes and values are still of concern. Also in the attitude-value overlap is the *conceptualization of a value,* a step beyond *commitment,* and the first step of Level 4. (Organizing). Finally, the child (or adult) moves beyond mere attitudes to the highest levels of value formation when he reaches the highest step of Level 4, *organization of a value system*, and then moves through Characterization by *formulating a generalized value set*, and then he is able to relate this set to the larger world in which he lives: there the set becomes the *Characterization of the individual*. The latter two behaviors compose Level 5, (Characterization).

Are not the steps indicated in the taxonomy more specific and indicative of corresponding behaviors than are "interests, attitudes, and values?" Is there not a clear taxonomical progression of behavior that is completely lacking in the triad of "interests, attitudes, and values?" The answers to these questions are obvious. Yet are the schools responsible for the interests, attitudes, and values of students?

Certainly the terms "interests" and "attitudes" appear in the stated objectives of schools often enough to be considered within the province of the school. What about values? If schools are responsible only for "interests" and "attitudes" and not "values," what is the highest step in the taxonomy for which the school has a charge? Can the school ignore the other steps of affective learning indicated in the taxonomy? These questions are left for the reader to ponder.

PRACTICAL UTILITY

It will be some time before any definitive answers to question 2 are forthcoming; the affective taxonomy is too new for any conclusive argument. The writers of the taxonomy are hopeful that the domain will permit curriculum workers to produce a systematic and comprehensive set of affective objectives which are stated clearly and in specific terms. The writers of the taxonomy are also hopeful that the taxonomy will aid in refining methods of measurement in this area and will provide a common vocabulary which will assist the communication process among people working in education. The writers of the taxonomy say little or nothing about how the teachers might use the work. The inference is that the taxonomy is for curriculum workers as such. I would like to pose the notion that a portion of the taxonomy is clearly the domain of the teacher and a portion is clearly the domain of the curriculum worker and that there is an area in which both have a concern—the vital link which gives direction to both ends of the affective continuum.

The daily interaction between pupil and teacher continuously involves the behaviors of Receiving and Responding. It is a long term objective of a teacher that the children develop an *acceptance of a value, preference for a value,* and *commitment to a value*. For instance, it takes time for a student to develop an acceptance of reading as something valued; then a preference for reading over some other activity; and finally, a real commitment to reading.

The curriculum worker's task probably *begins* at this Level 3, (Valuing). The curriculum worker should state specifically what the valuing objectives are, *i.e.*, what values a child ought to accept, prefer, and develop a commitment for.

The curriculum worker must then fit the value objectives into the continuum of higher affective objectives (Organizing and Characterization). The top three levels are very complex and can be realized only over a considerable period of time and after endeavors have produced many values that may be ordered and placed into a master configuration which becomes the characterization set of an individual. The vital link is the posing of Valuing objectives by curriculum workers and the achievement of these objectives by learners through activities provided by teachers.

At another level, a thorough knowledge of the taxonomy by persons who prepare materials for instruction, notably textbooks and programmed materials, might give these productions a significantly different flavor. Or stated in a different way, "What kinds of materials are likely to be produced by persons who lack a knowledge of the affective domain?"

Yet perhaps the most significant "practical use" of the taxonomy lies in whether or not it can be used for research purposes; for, if it is to have any long term effect on the curriculum, it must survive the test of researchability. Educators are looking more and more to research findings when deciding what is to be taught, to whom, by whom, and in what kind of environment. Laymen are becoming more aware of research activity in education and are more accepting of decisions "based on research." Cognitive behavior is clearly more observable and amenable to research. Conscious efforts to promote cognitive learning may crowd out conscious efforts to develop affective learning simply because research answers will be available in the former domain.

RESEARCH POTENTIAL

By their own admission, the writers of the two taxonomies (Bloom et al. 1956—cognitive; Krathwohl et al. 1964—affective) indicate that the separation of objectives into cognitive and affective domains is artificial and cite research which shows that cognition and affect can never be completely separated. Nevertheless, the two taxonomies do permit us to classify observably different kinds of behavior. The writers of the taxonomy indicate very intelligently and rationally what relationships they *believe* exist between the categories of the cognitive and affective domains. What is clearly missing is what the two taxonomies may now make possible; that is, a comprehensive controlled study which ferrets out any relationships that may actually exist.

Such questions as the following may now be posed: "Is the relation between growth at the various levels of cognitive and affective learning positive, negative, or zero?" "When a child is engaged in learning *knowledge of terminology* (Level 1.11, cognitive domain), is there a positive, negative, or zero relation with his *willingness to receive* (Level 1.2, affective domain)?" "At what level of the cognitive domain is the *willingness to receive* most positive?" It should be clear that the two domains (cognition and affect) give us a more definite structure in which to determine specific relationships and their nature. Perhaps the two domains have given us a systematic way to begin studying the vast implications of concomitant learnings.

As demonstrated earlier in the article, the research question is of paramount importance. Clearly, the affective taxonomy serves to generate significant and worthwhile questions which need resolving. The question is, can they be resolved? The authors of the taxonomy claim that the central research problem is how to measure affective behavior with greater validity, reliability, and objectivity.

What behavior will serve as evidence that a child is showing *commitment to a value* rather than merely a *preference for a value?* How does a researcher determine when a child is achieving the *conceptualization of a value* which is affective behavior rather than only cognitive conceptualization? There are many big problems to be solved in order that the affective taxonomy be made researchable.

This is the task of researchers. The writers of the taxonomy have done their task. Now it is up to researchers and practitioners to do the necessary changing and refining.

Why a taxonomy of affective learning? The taxonomy can serve as an aid in clarifying the school's responsibility for promoting learning in the affective realm. The taxonomy may provide practical help to teachers and curriculum workers. Finally, it may further the study of education.

If schools are to meet the needs of an ever changing society, the schools must be in a position periodically to change their educational objectives. The two taxonomies lend themselves well to this task because they give visibility, structure, and definition to objectives which represent current thinking. As the purposes of the schools change, so ought the taxonomies *or* their replacements.

16   *Goal Cards and the Measurement of Educational Progress*

ROBERT F. BAUERNFEIND

How do behavioral objectives fit into the design of measurement devices and instructional processes? One approach to the integration of measurement and instruction is suggested by Dr. Bauernfeind in the following essay. The procedure requires each student to demonstrate at least minimum competence for

Reprinted and abridged with permission of the author and publisher from an article entitled, "Goal Cards and Future Developments in Achievement Testing" which appeared in the *Proceedings of the 1965 Invitational Conference on Testing Problems.* Copyright 1966 by Educational Testing Service, Princeton, N.J. Used by permission. All rights reserved.

each of the explicit instructional objectives. Both teacher and student maintain a record of progress. The need for behavioral objectives stated in terms of proficiency is evident to the reader.

Would the suggested procedure encourage a norm-referenced or criterion-referenced approach to test development? Would you or your students give ratings to the use of goal cards similar to the ratings reported in this article?

In the field of achievement testing especially, it is futile to talk about "good tests" or "bad tests" until we have stated clearly what our objectives are. Why are we testing at all? What is it that we want to accomplish?

In his book, *Judging Student Progress*, Professor R. Murray Thomas (1960) takes the approach that testing comes *fourth* in a sequence of four educational events. First, says Thomas, we need to establish an overall philosophy of the educational objectives we believe in. Second, we need to establish specific objectives for instruction such as, "Can multiply 2-digit numbers," "Can discuss the causes of the Civil War," or "Can describe and explain reasons for achievement testing in schools." Third is the matter of teacher methods: How can we help children to acquire these stated objectives? Fourth, and finally, what kinds of tests should we use to see how well we have done?

I would suggest that, as educators, we are much more skilled in educational methods and in testing than we are in establishing a coherent educational philosophy and in stating specific goals for student growth. And still, you and I would probably agree with Thomas when he implies that discussions of teaching methods and testing are futile—probably even stupid—unless we have clearly established what it is we are trying to do.

If educators will state their goals specifically and in behavioral terms, testing specialists can and will devise valid means by which attainment of these goals can be measured. Until such definitions of goals are stated by colleges, by public schools, by private schools, no one—not teachers, not students, not critics, not test builders—can know what it is that constitutes education, and everyone will continue to grope for evaluation in his own way according to his own definitions (Dobbin 1961).

That was John Dobbin's statement of the problem. And I might add, as one who works both in teaching and in commercial test publishing, that Dobbin's points seem painfully correct. Perhaps some of you agree, and perhaps others of you don't.

For those of us who do agree with these points developed by Thomas, Dobbin, and others, there is the question, "All right, but what can we do to bring some order out of this chaos?" It is here that I would discuss the goal-card idea.

GOAL CARDS AS DEVELOPED IN WINNETKA, ILLINOIS ELEMENTARY SCHOOLS

The card shown in Figure 1 is one side of the goal cards developed for the basic Winnetka curriculum in grades 1–8. This particular card shows the specific goals for arithmetic in grade 1 on one side, and grade 2 on the other side. There are other advanced goal cards for the mathematics curriculum up through grade 8; and there are similar series of goal cards for the fields of language arts, science, and social studies—grades 1 through 8.

FIGURE 1. *Sample Goal Card for Elementary Mathematics Students*

Winnetka Public Schools

MATHEMATICS GOAL RECORD CARD 1

Pupil ———————————————— Teacher ——————— Year ———

Check

Can count 10 objects ....
Can read and write numerals to 10 ....
Recognizes number groups up to 5 ....
Recognizes patterns.of objects to 10 ....
Can read and write numerals to 20 ....
Can count objects to 100 ....
Recognizes numbers to 10 ....
Can read and write numerals to 50 ....
Recognizes addition and subtraction symbols ....
*Understands meaning of the inequality signs ....
Can count objects: ....
    by 2's to 20 ....
    by 5's to 100 ....
    by 10's to 100 ....
Recognizes geometric figures:
    triangle ....
    circle ....
    quadrilateral ....
Recognizes coins (1c, 5c, 10c, 25c) ....
Knows addition combinations 10 and under using objects ......
Knows subtraction combinations 10 and under using objects ....
Recognizes addition and subtraction vertically and horizontally ..
*Can construct simple plane figures with straight edge
    and compass ....
Shows understanding of numbers and number combinations
    (check one)
    1. Using concrete objects ....
    2. Beginning to visualize and abstract ....
    3. Makes automatic responses without concrete objects ......
*Can tell time
    1. Hour ....
    2. Half hour ....
    * (Goals starred are not essential for all students)

Comments:

Each child, starting in grade 1, proceeds through the goals indicated on the goal cards for the four content areas, but not necessarily in the sequence given. He may have accomplished all in the grade 1 goals by the end of the first year, or he may not. He may have moved on into a number of the goals of the ensuing year. At the conclusion of the year, the goal cards accompany the child to the next higher grade, where the teacher continues the process of noting successively all completed goals. This permits continuous extension of the goals, sometimes thought of as a scroll rather than a fixed yearly quota of goals to be accomplished.

It should be stressed that these goal cards list the minimum objectives to be attained. In the upper grades, for example, there is a good deal of provision for adding group goals or individual project goals. Youngsters who are far advanced on these minimum goals are encouraged to take on a variety of enrichment experiences. But, for other youngsters, the printed goal cards provide the focal point for learnings in the basic curriculum areas.

While space does not permit a discussion of all of the uses of these goal cards in the Winnetka system, I would like to mention three points: First, all of these printed goal cards are reviewed annually for possible revision. In this way, the Winnetka teachers are actively involved in curriculum development; and the cards, representing a teacher consensus, provide a solid base for compatible instruction from one classroom to another.

Second, we have been impressed with the high degree of pupil involvement developed in the Winnetka program. Beginning in grade 3, children keep their goal cards at their own desks—turning them in for the teacher's check mark when a unit of work has been successfully completed. Beginning in grade 6, the pupils make their own entries on a replica set of goal cards. (The teacher, however, keeps the "official" record on another set of goal cards which remain in the teacher's possession.)

Third, we have been much impressed with the use of these goal cards in parent-teacher conferences. Parents—especially those new to the Winnetka community—have indicated in these conferences that they can see clearly what the school program is all about and how their child is doing. The interpretations can be normative; but more often they are concerned with individual progress —where Johnny was in September, and where he is now—in terms of the skills he has learned to perform.

GOAL CARDS AS DEVELOPED FOR COLLEGE COURSES

Figure 2 shows one of the goal cards developed for a graduate course at Northern Illinois University. I have used this card as an example because it covers a course in testing—specifically, a course in testing for classroom teachers.

On the first day of the course, each student is given one copy of the goal card for his personal use. It is explained that there are 23 broad skills listed on the goal card, and that he will be given credit for the course when he has performed all 23 skills satisfactorily.

FIGURE 2. *(front) Sample Goal Card for College Course in Educational Evaluation*

EDUCATION 510 GOAL CARD

Student's Name

EDUCATION 510 METHODS OF EVALUATION	Satisfactory	Good	Exceptional Ability
1. Can describe and discuss the relationships among educational philosophy, objectives, methods, and evaluation			
2. Can state educational objectives in clear, concise, and measurable form			
3. Can describe and discuss the purposes of educational tests			
4. Can recognize the probable relationships between test behaviors and criterion behaviors			
5. Can explain the strengths and limitations of major types of test questions, especially—			
—True-False Items			
—Multiple-Choice Items			
—Matching Items			
—Completion Items			
—Essay Items			
6. Can write clear and concise test items, especially—			
—True-False Items			
—Multiple-Choice Items			
—Matching Items			
—Completion Items			
—Essay Items			
*7. Can construct a complete classroom examination appropriate to stated objectives			
8. Can identify desirable practices in giving tests to pupils in the classroom			
9. Can identify desirable practices in scoring classroom tests			
10. Can describe and discuss different ways of organizing test-score results			
11. Can describe and discuss different ways of evaluating test-score results			
12. Can describe and discuss different ways of reporting test-score information to students and their parents			
13. Can recognize the relationship between pictorial scattergrams and product-moment coefficients of correlation			
14. Can construct a scattergram as an estimate of correlation between two measures			
15. Can describe and discuss possible procedures for counseling students from scattergram information			

FIGURE 2. (back) *Sample Goal Card for College Course in Educational Evaluation*

16. Can identify the relationships among "reliability," "validity," and "correlation" .... _____   _____   _____

17. Can describe and explain the uses of standardized achievement tests .... _____   _____   _____
18. Can describe and explain the uses of standardized tests of "mental ability" .... _____   _____   _____
19. Can describe and explain the uses of self-report inventories— standardized measures of "personality" and "interests" .. _____   _____   _____
20. Can explain the essential similarities, and the superficial differences, among various methods of reporting results from standardized tests .... _____   _____   _____

*21. Can prepare a critical report on a standardized test .... _____   _____   _____

22. Can describe and discuss alternative ways of evaluating student progress .... _____   _____   _____
23. Can describe and discuss alternative ways of summarizing student progress for students and their parents .... _____   _____   _____

INSTRUCTOR'S COMMENTS:

SIGNED: _____

Instructor

_____

Date

The instructor provides suggested readings and plans class activities designed to help in the accomplishment of the first five goals. After a suitable period of time, a five-part exam is given—one for each of these first five goals.

On his exam paper, for each goal, the student is given three checks for "exceptional" performance, two checks for "good" performance, one check for "satisfactory" performance, or a zero for "not satisfactory." The check-mark credits are recorded by the instructor on his card for each student, and each student also records his check-mark credits on his own goal card. If performance on a given goal was not satisfactory, the student must arrange to take a make-up test on that one goal at a later date.

Meanwhile, the class moves on to the next set of goals; and the check-mark credits will be used later in assigning grades of A, B, C, or Incomplete. (The starred entries on this goal card indicate cumulative skills that are given extra weight when grades are assigned.)

We might pause here a moment to note the structure of the goals shown in Figure 2. Each goal consists of two parts—an area of subject matter and an action verb. Goal 3, for example, is concerned with the purposes of educational tests, and is prefaced with the verbs "Can describe and discuss." This combination of action verbs and subject matter gives clear direction to the learning process, and will later give direction to relevant evaluation techniques.

Having noted these procedures, you might now be interested in some studies of student reactions to the goal-card idea. In the college courses in which goal cards are being used, we administer an attitude questionnaire to the students near the end of the semester. The questionnaire consists of five positive statements about goal cards, and seven negative statements about goal cards—each statement to be rated on a 9-point scale from "agree very much" to "disagree very much." Mean ratings from five different classes using goal cards are shown in Table 1. All five of these classes were comprised of graduate students in education.

TABLE 1. *Mean Ratings of Goal-Card Attitudes for Five Classroom Groups at the Graduate School Level (Ratings can range from 9—"Agree very much" to 1—"Disagree very much")*

	COURSE:	ED. 510		ED. 602		
	SECTION:	A	B	A	B	C
	(N):	(26)	(14)	(10)	(12)	(11)
1. Goal cards help the student to see what is expected of him		8.3	8.4	8.6	8.7	8.3
2. Goal cards help the student in organizing ideas from class discussions		7.6	7.7	6.3	7.8	6.6
3. Goal cards help the student in preparing for examinations		8.1	8.1	8.1	8.3	8.1
4. Goal cards help the student in organizing his text and library readings		6.6	7.1	7.1	8.1	6.8
5. Goal cards help the student in more efficient learning for the course		7.0	7.6	7.9	7.9	7.5
Mean Rating for Five Positive Statements		7.5	7.8	7.6	8.2	7.5
6. Goal cards often seem complicated, confusing		2.1	2.1	2.3	1.5	2.6
7. Goal cards seem to require more time for learning		1.5	1.6	2.5	1.7	2.0
8. Goal cards leave out learnings that often seem important		5.0	4.6	5.0	3.3	3.7
9. Goal cards seem to be too much oriented toward examinations		5.2	4.9	5.1	3.2	4.2
10. Goal cards depend too much on the teacher's subjective opinions		4.0	3.8	3.8	2.7	3.6
11. Goal cards tend to equalize the group, making the students unduly alike in achievement		3.9	2.9	2.7	2.3	2.2
12. Goal cards simply represent another "gimmick" in education		2.4	2.1	2.9	1.9	2.1
Mean Rating for Seven Negative Statements		3.4	3.1	3.5	2.4	2.9

In general, the student attitudes toward the goal-card idea have been highly favorable, as evidenced by the rather consistent pattern of mean ratings in these five replication studies. The mean rating on the five positive statements has been running around 7.5 on the 9-point scale, and the mean rating on the seven negative statements has been running around 3.5 on the 9-point scale. In all five replication studies we have obtained mean ratings above 8.0

on two positive statements:
- Goal cards help the student to see what is expected of him.
- Goal cards help the student in preparing for examinations.

Among the negative statements, the greatest agreement (or criticism) has occurred on these two items:
- Goal cards leave out learnings that often seem important.
- Goal cards seem to be too much oriented toward examinations.

On these last two items, mean ratings have typically been around 4.5, near the midpoint of the 9-point scale.

APPARENT VALUES OF THE GOAL-CARD IDEA

While we still have much to learn about the goal-card idea, our experiences to date suggest six major values in this type of program:

1. Goal cards help the teacher, or a teacher committee, to state specifically the minimum objectives of a given course of instruction—and to state these objectives, not in terms of books-read, chapters-memorized, or lectures-listened to, but rather in terms of what the student can *do* as a result of the course.

2. Goal cards provide a strong base for communication among educators. The check marks on the goal cards should greatly help other teachers to see where the child stands in a given subject. I am talking here about helping substitute teachers, helping the next year's teachers in elementary grades, and helping teachers in other towns whenever pupils transfer from one community to another.

3. Goal cards provide a strong base for communication with the lay public— school board members, parents, and other interested citizens. For better or worse, these people will have a chance to see clearly just what music appreciation, or U.S. history, or grade 9 general science courses are all about. Some of our citizens may even react negatively to some of the specific items on a given goal card. I suggest that this would be a healthy indication that these people have an interest in the product they are paying for.

4. Goal cards provide a strong base for communication with students. In the first day of the course, the students can see the skills they will be required to develop.

5. Goal cards provide a format whereby one can individualize instruction if he wishes. In the Winnetka plan, pupils work on specific goals at their own pace, and then take check-out tests whenever they feel they are ready. Even in more rigid group instructional programs at the high school and college level, goal cards can be used to insist on the accomplishment of minimum standards on the skills listed. If a college student badly misses on a stated objective, the teacher does not then give him a "C" and go on to the next chapter of the text. Rather, the student can be required to do it over—again and again, if necessary —until he *can* perform that skill to the teacher's satisfaction.

6. And finally, the whole idea gives sharp focus to testing. When one has a goal card with clearly stated objectives, the test items are almost written. If the goal says, "Can describe and explain the causes of World War I," the teacher's check-out test might well say, 'Describe and explain the causes of World War I." And similarly, by placing standardized achievement tests alongside their own goal cards, school personnel can much more readily identify the one or two achievement batteries that seem to make the most sense as tests of goals that were to have been accomplished. If the teachers' goals have been carefully worked out, and if they have found a standardized achievement test that corresponds fairly well with their goals, then they have found a "good" achievement test for their school. I say that without even mentioning Kuder-Richardson formulas for reliability, or standard deviations, or even test reviews in the Mental Measurements Yearbooks.

SUMMARY

I have tried to show how the goal-card idea is being used and to suggest ways in which it might be used. The question before us is this: Could these types of goal cards be created for a 5th-grade science course? For an 8th-grade shop or home economics course? For an 11th-grade course in United States history? For a sophomore psychology course at the college level?

In all of these cases, I submit that goal cards *could* be created; and, for the reasons given in this paper, that they would represent a highly useful development.

17   *Implications of Criterion-Referenced Measurement*

W. JAMES POPHAM AND T. R. HUSEK

The design of any measuring instrument must obviously be responsive to the purpose and objectives in developing the device. In performance testing, proficiency or instructional objectives are involved. One may compare the performance of many individuals on a standard set of tasks or evaluate the absolute performance of individual examinees. These two approaches to measurement, norm-referenced and criterion-referenced, are compared in the following article with regard to a number of technical factors and practical questions which might be raised by the user in the field. Score variability, which is so central to classical psychometric theory, is probably the chief factor discriminating these two approaches. In addition to variability the author considers item construc-

Reprinted with permission of the first named author and publisher from the *Journal of Educational Measurement*, 1969, Vol. 6, #1 (Spring), pp. 1–9.

tion, reliability, validity, reporting, and interpretation.
When would a criterion-referenced measure be preferred over a norm-refer-
enced one? What would be some of the difficulties encountered by a teacher
who relied almost exclusively on criterion-referenced measures? What is a
Guttman "reproducable" test, and what are some possible applications of an
instrument of this type?

The question of what score to use as the most meaningful index of a student's performance on a test has been the subject of many discussions over the years. Percentile scores, raw scores, and standard scores of various kinds have been advocated. The arguments have almost always begun with the premise that the test is a given and that the issue is how to obtain the meaningful score. That is, there has been general acceptance of how the test should be constructed and judged. Test theory as explicated in most elementary testing texts has been assumed to represent a commonly held set of values. In recent years some writers (e.g., Cronbach and Gleser, 1965) have begun to question the usefulness of classical test theory for all testing problems. This broadens and complicates the question above; the problem is now not only how to summarize a student's performance on a test, but also how to insure that a test is constructed (and judged) in a manner appropriate to its use, even if its use is not in the classical framework.

One facet of this issue has particular relevance to tests based on instructional objectives. For several years now, particularly since the appearance of Gleser's article (1963) on the subject, measurement and instructional specialists have been drawing distinctions between so-called *norm-referenced* and *criterion-refer-enced* approaches to measurement. But it appears that, other than adding new terms to the technical lexicon, the two constructs have made little difference in measurement practice. Perhaps the reason for this is that few analyses have been made of the practical implications of using criterion-referenced measures. Most of us are familiar with concepts associated with norm-referenced measurement. We grew up with them. A criterion-referenced approach, however, is another matter. What differences, if any, does a criterion-referenced framework make with respect to such operations as test construction and revision, and to such concepts as reliability and validity? This article will examine some of these implications by contrasting criterion-referenced and norm-referenced approaches with respect to such central measurement notions.

THE BASIC DISTINCTION

It is not possible to tell a *norm-referenced test* from a *criterion-referenced* test by looking at it. In fact a *criterion-referenced* test could also be used as a *norm-referenced* test—although the reverse is not so easy to imagine. However, this truth should not be allowed to obscure the extremely important differences between these two approaches to testing.

At the most elementary level, norm-referenced measures are those which are used to ascertain an individual's performance in relationship to the performance of other individuals on the same measuring device. The meaningfulness of the individual score emerges from the comparison. It is because the individual is compared with some normative group that such measures are described as norm-referenced. Most standardized tests of achievement or intellectual ability can be classified as norm-referenced measures.

Criterion-referenced measures are those which are used to ascertain an individual's status with respect to some criterion, i.e., performance standard. It is because the individual is compared with some established criterion, rather than other individuals, that these measures are described as criterion-referenced. The meaningfulness of an individual score is not dependent on comparison with other testees. We want to know what the individual can do, not how he stands in comparison to others. For example, the dog owner who wants to keep his dog in the back yard may give his dog a fence-jumping test. The owner wants to find out how high the dog can jump so that the owner can build a fence high enough to keep the dog in the yard. How the dog compares with other dogs is irrelevant. Another example of a criterion-referenced test would be the Red Cross Senior Lifesaving Test, where an individual must display certain swimming skills to pass the examination irrespective of how well others perform on the test.

Since norm-referenced measures are devised to facilitate comparisons among individuals, it is not surprising that their primary purpose is to make decisions about *individuals*. Which pupil should be counseled to pursue higher education? Which pupils should be advised to attain vocational skills? These are the kinds of questions one seeks to answer through the use of norm-referenced measures, for many decisions regarding an individual can best be made by knowing more about the "competition," that is, by knowing how other, comparable individuals perform.

Criterion-referenced tests are devised to make decisions both about *individuals and treatments*, e.g., instructional programs. In the case of decisions regarding individuals, one might use a criterion-referenced test to determine whether a learner had mastered a criterion skill considered prerequisite to his commencing a new training program. In the case of decisions regarding treatments, one might design a criterion-referenced measure which reflected a set of instructional objectives supposedly achieved by a replicable instructional sequence. By administering the criterion-referenced measure to appropriate learners after they had completed the instructional sequence, one could reach a decision regarding the efficacy of the sequence (treatment).

Although both norm-referenced and criterion-referenced tests are used to make decisions about individuals, there is usually a difference in the two contexts in which such decisions are made. Generally, a norm-referenced measure is employed where a degree of *selectivity* is required by the situation. For example, when there are only limited openings in a company's executive training program, the company is anxious to identify the *best* potential trainees. It is critical in such situations, therefore, that the measure permit *relative* comparisons among individuals. On the other hand, in situations where one is only interested in whether an individual possesses a particular competence, and there are no constraints regarding how many individuals can possess that skill, criterion-referenced measures are suitable. Theoretically, at the close of many instructional programs we might hope that *all* learners would display *maximum* proficiency on measures reflecting the instructional objectives. In this sense, of course, criterion-referenced measures may be considered *absolute* indicators. Thus, both norm-referenced and criterion-referenced tests can be focused on decisions regarding individuals—it is the context within which these decisions are made that really produces the distinction.

Now one could, of course, use norm-referenced measures as well as criterion-referenced measures to make decisions regarding the merits of instructional programs. Certainly, this has been a common practice through the years as educators have evaluated their curriculum efforts on the basis of pupil performance on standardized examinations. But norm-referenced measures were really designed to "spread people out" and, as we shall see, are best suited to that purpose.

With this initial distinction in mind, we shall now examine the implications of the two approaches to measurement, particularly with respect to criterion-referenced measures, for the following topics: variability, item construction, reliability, validity, item analysis, reporting, and interpretation.

VARIABILITY

The issue of variability is at the core of the difference between norm-referenced and criterion-referenced tests. Since the meaningfulness of a norm-referenced score is basically dependent on the relative position of the score in comparison with other scores, the more variability in the scores the better. With a norm-referenced test, we want to be able to tell Jamie from Joey from Frank, and we feel more secure about telling them apart if their scores are very different.

With criterion-referenced tests, variability is irrelevant. The meaning of the score is not dependent on comparison with other scores; it flows directly from the connection between the items and the criterion. It is, of course, true that one almost always gets variant scores on any psychological test; but that variability is not a necessary condition for a good criterion-referenced test.

The subtle and not-so-subtle implications of this central difference in the relevance of variability must permeate any discussion of the two approaches to testing. For example, we all have been told that a test should be reliable and valid. We have all read about test construction and item analysis. The procedures may not always be simple, the formulas may not be trivial; but there are hundreds of books and thousands of articles to guide us. Unfortunately, most of what these "helpmates" outline as "good" things to do are not only irrelevant to criterion-referenced tests, but are actually injurious to their proper development and use. This is true because the treatments of validity, the suggestions about reliability, and the formulas for item analysis are all based on the desirability of variability among scores. The connection may not be obvious but it is always there.

ITEM CONSTRUCTION

The basic difference between item construction in norm-referenced and criterion-referenced frameworks is a matter of "set" on the part of the item writer. Until we reach that automated era when computers can cough forth many items per minute, someone is going to have to construct them. The primary differences in purposes of norm-referenced and criterion-referenced measurement will usually influence the item writer to a considerable degree in at least one very significant way and, possibly to a lesser extent, in a second way as well.

Most important, when a writer constructs items for a norm-referenced test, he wants variability and, as a consequence, makes all sorts of concessions, sometimes subtle, sometimes obvious, to promote variant scores. He disdains items which are "too easy" or "too hard." He tries to increase the allure of wrong answer options. All of this he does to produce variability. Occasionally this overriding criterion may reduce the adequacy of the instrument, for even spurious factors may be incorporated in items just to produce variance.

The criterion-referenced item writer is guided by another goal. His chief rule is to make sure the item is an accurate reflection of the criterion behavior. Difficult or easy, discriminating or indiscriminate, the important thing is to make the item represent the class of behaviors delimited by the criterion. Those who write criterion-referenced items are usually far more attentive to defining the domain of relevant test responses and the situations in which they should be required. This rather fundamental difference in "set" on the part of criterion-referenced and norm-referenced item writers can clearly contribute to differences in the resulting items.

A second difference associated with test construction is that although norm-referenced and criterion-referenced measures which are used to make decisions regarding individuals require that the same test (or an equivalent form) be used with different individuals, criterion-referenced tests used for evaluating programs need not. The concept of item sampling (Cronbach, 1963, see article 34 in Chapter VII; Husek and Sirotnik, 1968) in which different people complete different items (thereby permitting the sampling of more behavior with shorter tests) is highly appropriate for evaluating the adequacy of treatments. Thus, for such situations a number of different test forms, each containing different criterion-referenced items, could be constructed. Individuals nurtured on the concept of "everybody gets the same items" will often overlook this economic, yet powerful shortcut.

Once the test is originally devised, we would like to have procedures available for improving it. In a norm-referenced context we have available the time-honored devices such as item analyses techniques and reliability estimates which can guide us in test refinement operations. With criterion-referenced measures, however, some of these classical constructs must be used differently. The next few sections of this paper will describe the nature of these differences.

RELIABILITY

We all should know that for a single number to be used to describe the performance of a person on a test, the items on that test should all "measure the same thing" to some minimal extent. That is, the test should be internally consistent. This matter is treated in measurement texts in the chapter on reliability.

Now it is obvious that a criterion-referenced test should be internally consistent. If we argue that the items are tied to a criterion, then certainly the items should be quite similar in terms of what they are measuring. But although it may be obvious that a criterion-referenced test should be internally consistent, it is not obvious how to assess the internal consistency. The classical procedures are not appropriate. This is true because they are dependent on score variability. A criterion-referenced test should not be faulted if, when administered after instruction, everyone obtained a perfect score. Yet, that would lead to a zero internal consistency estimate, something measurement books don't recommend.

In fact, even stranger things can happen in practice. It is possible for a criterion-referenced test to have a *negative* internal consistency index and still be a good test. (See Husek and Sirotnik, 1968, for a more extensive treatment of this possibility.)

Thus, the typical indices of internal consistency are not appropriate for criterion-referenced tests. It is not clear what should replace them. Perhaps we need estimates, comparable to the standard internal consistency formulas, which can take larger temporal units into consideration, for example, by considering both a pre-instruction test administration and a post-instruction test administration as part of the same extended phenomenon. Perhaps ingenious indices can be developed which reflect the ability of a test to produce variation from pre-instruction to post-instruction testing and, in these terms, internal consistency—despite score range restrictions. But until that time, those wishing to improve criterion-referenced tests should not be dismayed if the test, because of little score variance, yields a low internal consistency estimate. It is really unwise to apply such estimates.

The foregoing discussion applies only to situations where the test is used to assess a single dimension, such as one instructional objective, as opposed to several dimensions, such as three very disparate objectives. If the objectives are substantially different, the items measuring them should be considered as different tests, not a single all-encompassing measure.

Other aspects of reliability are equally cloudy. Stability might certainly be important for a criterion-referenced test, but in that case, a test-retest correlation coefficient, dependent as it is on variability, is not necessarily the way to assess it. Some kind of confidence interval around the individual score is perhaps a partial solution to this problem.

The reader should not misinterpret the above statements. If a criterion-referenced test has a high average inter-item correlation, this is fine. If the test has a high test-retest correlation, that is also fine. The point is *not* that these indices cannot be used to support the consistency of the test. The point is that a criterion-referenced test could be highly consistent, either internally or temporarily, and yet indices dependent on variability might not reflect that consistency.

VALIDITY

Many of the procedures for assessing the validity of norm-referenced tests are based on correlations and thus on variability. Hence, with validity, as with reliability, the results of the procedures are useful if they are positive, but not necessarily devastating if they are negative.

Criterion-referenced measures are validated primarily in terms of the adequacy with which they represent the criterion. Therefore, content validity approaches are more suited to such tests. A carefully made judgment, based on the test's apparent relevance to the behaviors legitimately inferable from those delimited by the criterion, is the general procedure for validating criterion-referenced measures.

Certainly, for both norm-referenced and criterion-referenced measures a test specialist might employ construct validity strategies to support the confidence he can give to his instruments. For example, we might wish to augment our confidence in a measure we were using as a proximate predictor (e.g., administered at the close of instruction) of some more distant criterion (e.g., occurring many years hence). If positive intercorrelations occur among several proximate predictors (of the same distant criterion) we could add to our understanding of whether a given proximate predictor was doing its job.

ITEM ANALYSIS

Item analysis procedures have traditionally been used with norm-referenced tests to identify those items that were not properly discriminating among individuals taking the test. For instance, in an achievement test an unsatisfactory item would be one which could not properly discriminate between the more and less knowledgeable learners (as reflected by total test performance). Non-discriminating items are usually those which are (a) too easy, (b) too hard, and/or (c) ambiguous.

For criterion-referenced tests the use of discrimination indices must be modified. An item which doesn't discriminate need not be eliminated. If it reflects an important attribute of the criterion, such an item should remain in the test. We might be interested in a "non-discriminating" item's ability to discriminate among *anyone*, e.g., its ability to discriminate between those individuals who have and those who haven't been exposed to instruction. But, just as in the case of reliability estimates, such indices are not currently available.

A positively discriminating item is just as respectable in a criterion-referenced test as it is in a norm-referenced test, but certainly not more so. In fact, the positively discriminating item may point to areas of instruction (if the criterion measure is assessing the effects of instruction) where the program is not succeeding well enough.

However, negatively discriminating items are treated exactly the same way in a criterion-referenced approach as they are in a norm-referenced approach. An item which discriminates negatively is one which, in an instructional context, is answered correctly more often by the less knowledgeable than by the more knowledgeable students. When one discovers a negative discriminator in his pool of criterion-referenced items, he should be suspicious of it and after more careful analysis can usually detect flaws in such an item.

Of course, discrimination indices are little more than warning flags, and one must still use common sense in weighing the worth of an item identified as a negative discriminator. It might be that some deficiencies in the instruction caused the result rather than any fault of the item. Yet, it is more likely that the item is deficient. For example, suppose that the negatively discriminating item was originally generated, along with 19 other items, as a measure of a particular type of criterion behavior. Now in order for the item to yield a negative discrimination index there would first have to be variable subject performance. But in addition, more of those individuals who scored well on the total 20 item test would have to miss the suspect item more frequently than those who scored badly on the total test. Under such circumstances it seems more likely that it is an item deficiency, rather than instructional deficiency, although the latter possibility should be kept in mind.

Is it worth the trouble? Since we are only concerned with the identification of negative discriminators, not non-discriminators, should criterion referenced measures be subjected to item analysis operations? This would seem to depend on the ease with which one can conduct the necessary analyses. As data-processing becomes increasingly automated and less expensive, such analyses would seem warranted in situations where the effort is not immense.

REPORTING AND INTERPRETATION

We use norm-referenced and criterion-referenced tests to make decisions about both individuals and treatments. We need, therefore, to interpret test results properly in order to make the best possible decisions. With respect to norm-referenced measurement the methods of interpreting the results of an individual's test performance are well known. Since we are interested in an individual's performance with respect to the performance of other individuals, we use such group-relative descriptors as percentile rankings or standard scores. Such indices allow us to tell, from a single score, how well the individual performed in relationship to the group.

When interpreting an individual's performance on a criterion-referenced test, however, such group-relative indices are not appropriate. Some criterion-referenced tests yield scores which are essentially "on-off" in nature, that is, the individual has either mastered the criterion or he hasn't. For example, certain examinations in the chemistry laboratory may require a pupil to combine and treat chemical compounds in such a way that they produce hydrogen. In such tests it is sufficient to report whether or not the learner has displayed the desired criterion behavior.

More commonly, however, a range of acceptable performances exists. For example. suppose that an instructional objective had been devised which required a learner to multiply correctly pairs of three digit numbers. We could prepare 20 items composed of randomly selected digits to measure this skill. Because of possible computation errors, the required proficiency level for each successful student might be set at 90 per cent, or better, thereby allowing errors on two of the 20 items. In reporting an individual's performance on a test such as this, one alternative is to once more use an "on-off" approach, namely, either the 90 per cent minimum has been achieved or it hasn't.

Whether we wish to report the degree of less-than-criterion performance should depend *exclusively* on the use we can make of the data. For example, if there are only two courses of action available to the individual, depending on his success or failure with respect to the criterion, then we need only report it as that, success or failure. However, if some differential experiences are to be provided on the basis of the degree of his less-than-criterion performance then one would be interested in how far away he was from the criterion. For instance, if there were two remedial multiplication programs available, one for those very close to criterion and one for those who scored 60 per cent or below on the 20 item examination, then we would report the degree of his performance. The point is that such gradations in reporting are only a function of the alternative courses of action available to the individual after the measurement has been made.

With respect to the evaluation of treatments, it has already been pointed out that norm-referenced measures are not the most suitable devices for such purposes since their emphasis on producing heterogeneous performance sometimes diverts them from adequately reflecting the treatment's intended objectives. In using criterion-referenced measures for purposes of treatment assessment, e.g., testing the merits of a new set of programmed mathematics materials, we have several alternatives. We could simply report the number of individuals who achieve the pre-established criterion. Although such a procedure seems to supply scant data, it has the advantage of making graphically clear the proportion of learners who did not achieve criterion level proficiency. Too often this result is masked through the use of statistical averages.

We could also use traditional descriptive statistics such as means and standard deviations. Because one is often interested in the average performance produced by a treatment, as well as its variability, such statistics are useful. An average "percentage correct," however, is a helpful addition. Sometimes, if the criterion level for an individual has been set as a particular level, it is useful to report the proportion of the group which reached that level. For instance, using 80 per cent as a criterion level, then one might describe a group's performance as 92–80, indicating that 92 per cent of the group had achieved 80 per cent or better on the test. Such reporting, however, overlooks the proportion and degree of the better-than-criterion performance. It would seem, then, that in using criterion-referenced measures to make decisions about treatments, the best course of action would be to employ a number of these schemes to report the group's performance in order to permit more enlightened interpretations.

DIFFERENT KINDS OF CRITERION-REFERENCED TESTS

Up to this point we have discussed criterion-referenced tests as if there were one such animal. Actually, there are two. One could be said to be the ideal case and the other the more typical case.

In the ideal case the items are not only tied to the criterion but, in addition, the test is homogeneous in a very special sense. Everyone who gets the same score on the test has obtained the score in essentially the same manner. The meaning of a score is thus altogether unambiguous. If we know a person's score we know his response pattern; we know within error limits exactly what he can and cannot do. This would be an ideal criterion-referenced test, since it not only eliminates the need for a reference group but also immediately tells us the behavior repertoire of the student for that criterion. This kind of test has been discussed in the literature for some time. Guttman mentioned it as early as 1944 and Tucker elaborated on the concept in 1952.

Unfortunately, this kind of test is still mostly a dream for educational testers. Since we need to know an immense amount about the subject matter of the test, and perhaps even about the reasons why students make certain kinds of responses, these tests at the present time are found only in relatively restricted and formal areas such as mathematics.

The other type of criterion-referenced test is more typical. The items on the test can be thought of as a sample from a potentially large group that might be generated from a criterion. The score on the test is not completely unambiguous; if we know that a student earned a score of 90 per cent correct we do not know which items he missed. However, we do know, if we have constructed our test properly, that of the items defining the criterion behavior the student missed only 10 per cent. And if the test is homogeneous, this tells us a great deal about what the student can do.

The purpose of the foregoing discussion has been to draw distinctions between norm-referenced and criterion-referenced measurement with respect to several key measurement constructs. Because of the recency of its introduction into the field, criterion-referenced measurement received most attention. This should not imply any superiority of one approach over the other. Each has its relatively distinct role to play. The roles are only relatively distinct because one can usually employ a test developed for one purpose in another situation and still derive useful information from it. It seems, however, that there are some psychometric properties of these two types of measurement which render them most appropriate for the purposes for which they were originally designed.

18   *Unobtrusive Measures*

....

EUGENE J. WEBB

Unconventional sources of information have often been disregarded through lack of interest and effort, oversight, and disrespect. The author and his colleagues (Webb, et al., 1966) have provided a delightful overview of some of the variety of data sources that can be tapped for purposes of measurement and evaluation. The clever illustrations contained in the following paper should expand the alternatives available to educators seeking unobtrusive and unbiased measures. In addition, the ideas should provide a rich source of possible ways of implementing the multitrait-multimethod approach to assessing test validity (see article 13 by Campbell and Fiske).

Would you use only a paper and pencil test to estimate honesty or attitude toward cheating? How might a student inadvertantly indicate interest in school or a particular course? In addition to judging sales figures, how could you unobtrusively determine the popularity of this book of readings?

Reprinted and abridged with permission of the author and publisher from an article entitled, "Unconventionality, Triangulation and Inference", which appeared in the *Proceedings of the 1966 Invitational Conference on Testing Problems*. Copyright 1967 by Educational Testing Service. All rights reserved.

Most students today would agree that it is appropriate to draw simultaneously on multiple measures of the same attribute or construct multiple measures hypothesized to overlap in theoretically relevant components, but which do not overlap on measurement errors specific to individual methods (Garner, 1956; Garner, et al., 1956; and Humphreys, 1960). "Multimethod" has usually been defined as multiple scales or behaviors collected under the condition in which the subject knew he was being tested. Humphreys (1960), for example, when talking of multiple measures of reasoning, spoke of "series analogies and classification items." The multiple methods thus have tended to be multiple variants within a *single* measurement class such as the interview.

Every data-gathering class—interviews, questionnaires, observation, performance records, physical evidence—is potentially biased and has specific to it certain validity threats. Ideally we should like to converge data from several data classes, as well as converge with multiple variants within a single class.

The methodological literature warned us early of certain recurrent validity threats, and the evidence has markedly accelerated in the last few years. It has been 30 years, for example, since Lorge (1937) published his paper on response set, and 20 years since Cronbach (1946) published his influential paper on the same topic.

As a guide to locating the strengths and weaknesses of individual data classes —to better work the convergent multiple-methods approach—my colleagues at Northwestern and I have tried to develop a list of sources of research invalidity to be considered with any data class (Webb, et al., 1966). An outline of these sources of invalidity is contained in Table I.

TABLE 1. *Sources of Research Invalidity*

I. *Reactive Measurement Effect*
  1. Awareness of being tested
  2. Role playing
  3. Measurement as change
  4. Response sets

II. *Error from Investigator*
  5. Interviewer effects
  6. Change—fatigue/practice

III. *Varieties of Sampling Error*
  7. Population restriction
  8. Population stability over time
  9. Population stability over areas

IV. *Access to Content*
  10. Restrictions on content
  11. Stability of content over time
  12. Stability of content over areas

V. *Operating Ease and Validity Checks*
  13. Dross rate
  14. Access to descriptive cues
  15. Ability to replicate

To bring under control some of the reactive measurement effect, we might employ data classes which do not require the cooperation of the student or respondent. By supplementing standard interview or pencil-and-paper measures, more dimensionality is introduced.

In a recent paper which described the use of observation methods in the study of racial attitudes, Campbell, Kruskal, and Wallace (1966) studied seating aggregations by race. Two colleges were picked in the Chicago area—one noted for the liberal composition of its student body and the other more associated with a traditional point of view. Going into lecture halls, they observed seating patterns and the clustering of Negro and white students during class. With a new statistical test developed by Kruskal, they were able to demonstrate a greater racial mixture in the more "liberal" college. They also found, however, that the seating mix in the liberal college was significantly less than that expected by chance.

The linkage of secondary records is another way to develop control over reactivity. An example of this approach is DeCharms and Moeller's (1962) study of achievement imagery. They first gathered the number of patents issued by the United States Patent Office from 1800 to 1950. These data (controlled for population) were then matched to achievement imagery found in children's readers for the same period. There was a strong relationship between the level of achievement imagery in their sample of books and the number of patents per million population. Both data series are non-reactive, and although other rival, plausible hypotheses might explain the relationship, it remains as one piece in the inferential puzzle, uncontaminated by awareness of being tested.

For matching of other archival records, we can note Lewis Terman's (1917) study estimating Galton's IQ (not far from 200) and Galton's own early studies of hereditary genius (1870).

Another class of data comes from physical evidence, one example of which is Fredrick Mosteller's creative study of the degree to which different sections of the *International Encyclopedia of the Social Sciences* were read (1955). He estimated usage by noting the wear and tear on separate sections: dirty edges of pages, frequency of dirt smudges, finger markings and underlinings on pages. He sampled different libraries and even used the *Encyclopedia Britannica* as a control.

Thus far, the emphasis has been on data sources and overlapping classes of data. We might also profitably explore the possibility of using multiple samples. Again, this is different from the usual definition of multiple samples. In addition to sampling a number of different classrooms, or groups of students or cities, one may ask if there are different types or categories of samples available for the variable under study. Is there a group of natural outcroppings among occupations, already formed social and interest groups, or people who have common experiences? Can we economically exploit for research purposes the broad spectrum of already formed groups which may be organized along some principle of direct substantive applicability to the investigation?

Professor James Bryan of Northwestern and I have been interested in the use of these "outcropping" groups as a middle-level sampling strategy—one that straddles the elegant but cumbersome national probability sample and the more circumscribed "N = 80 volunteer males from the introductory psychology class" populations.

Because one sometimes doesn't know the universe for a study and because of cost restraints, subjects are most often selected because of proximity. Our subjects are typically drawn from the subject pool of the introductory class, from friends, friends of friends, or those unlucky enough to be members of the same institution as the investigator, be it the school, the hospital, or the prison.

Consider some convenience samples which may supplement conventional groups. Becker, Lerner and Carroll (1964) used caddies loafing about a golf course waiting for jobs as a subject pool. E. E. Smith (1962) suggested firemen in a fire house. They have almost unlimited time available for questioning and offer the very happy situation of a naturally formed, real group, whose members know each other very well. This is a good setting in which to replicate findings derived from experimentally formed groups in laboratories or from natural groups.

Sometimes these convenient aggregates offer a special opportunity to get a high concentration of usable subjects. To study somatotyping among top athletes in different track and field events, Tanner (1964) went to the 1960 Olympic Village at Rome. In an unpublished 1965 study of proposed brand names for new products, in which one of the criteria was relative invulnerability to regional accents, MacNiven sent interviewers to a nearby airport where they asked travellers to read off lists of names while the interviewers noted variable pronunciations.

In trait measurement, one may define altruism by one or by a series of self-report scales. But it may also be profitable to examine extant groups with some face-valid loading on altruism—say, volunteer blood donors, contributors to charitable causes, or even such groups as those who aided Jews in Nazi Germany.

Bryan and Test (1966) have recently reported on a provocative study of the influence of modeling behavior on altruism. Their objective in a field experiment was to see whether or not people stopped to help someone who had a flat tire. The experiment involved two women stranded with flat tires one quarter of a mile apart on a highway and a model, a man who had stopped to help one of them. In one part of the experiment, the traffic passed the woman and the model and then, farther up the highway, passed the other woman. In the other part of the experiment, the traffic passed only one woman and no model.

Other clusters of groups may help to define or locate a particular ability. Occupational categories may be particularly useful here. For studies of superior depth perception there are natural occupational outcroppings such as magnetic core threaders, jugglers, or grand prix automobile drivers.

Each of these groups possesses other attributes, and one might consider the same group of automobile race drivers as a high risk-taking sample and link them with other high risk-taking groups such as sport and military parachute jumpers (Epstein, 1962).

Or, for studies of deviance, there are the self-help deviant groups of Alcoholics Anonymous, Gamblers Anonymous, and prisoners who volunteer for therapy. All presumably share a common characteristic, but the setting of the phenomenon is varied.

As an expansion of this idea, consider Ernest Haggard's exemplary chapter on isolation and personality (1964). Haggard reviewed studies of isolation: How is personality affected by the restraint of habitual body movement in restricted, monotonous, or otherwise unfamiliar environments? Instead of limiting himself to the laboratory experimentation on sensory deprivation, he went abroad to the large literature of "naturally" occurring isolation. There are research findings on interstate truck drivers, pilots flying missions alone at night or at high altitudes, orthopedic patients in iron lungs, and anecdotal reports of prisoners in solitary confinement, shipwrecked sailors and explorers. Haggard reports the commonalities among these widely *differing* groups, which overlapped on the isolation dimension, and which shared common sensory and personality phenomena. He compares, for example, the anecdotal reports of Admiral Byrd (1938) and the scientific investigation of Rohrer (1960) on International Geophysical Year personnel, both of whom found the individual cutting back on information input under isolated conditions—even when a mass of material was available to consume.

As an aside on the nature of isolated man, Haggard quoted Bombard's (Bombard, 1953, p. x) comments on the sinking of the *Titanic:*

> When the first relief ships arrived, three hours after the liner had disappeared, a number of people had either died or gone mad in the lifeboats. Significantly, no child under the age of ten was included among those who had paid for their terror with madness and for their *madness* with *death.* The children were still at the age of reason.

In another isolation investigation, Sells considered many of the same data in his applied study, "A model for the social system for the multiman extended duration space ship" (Sells, undated). Thinking of such long journeys as a Mars shot, Sells assembled data from many isolated groups, both natural and artificial. His analysis was careful and based on theory. He related the findings from different studies to a general model of an isolated social system—evaluating the degree to which results from the individual studies were likely to transfer to a space vehicle setting. Thus, data from submarine and exploration parties were most applicable, while the findings from shipwreck and disaster studies were least likely to transfer. Naroll (1962) has suggested similar procedures to differentially weight data derived from documentary sources of varying credibility, and Stanley (1961) has offered a broader approach for treating data in the general multitrait-multimethod matrix format.

In this paper, I have stressed two main points. One is the utility of different data-gathering techniques applied concurrently to the same problem. The other is the laying of these techniques against multiple samples which are natural outcroppings of a phenomenon.

From E. G. Boring (1966):

. . . The truth is something you get on toward and never to, and the way is filled with ingenuities and excitements. Don't take the straight and narrow path of the stodgy positivists; be gay and optimistic, like Galton, and you will find yourself more toward than you had ever expected.

19   *Response Sets and Test Design*

LEE J. CRONBACH

Cronbach (1946, p. 476) has defined response set as the "tendency causing a person to give different responses to items than he would when the same content is presented in a different form." To illustrate, suppose two individuals who scored the same on a multiple-choice achievement test scored quite differently on a true-false test based on the same content. Similarly, they might have scored identically on a multiple-choice personality test but quite differently when the same items appeared in a checklist form. Assuming these differences were not due to lack of reliability, they may have been due to response sets operating more for one individual than for another. For example, one of the individuals might tend to select "true" when in doubt, and also one might tend to check many items on a checklist.

Professor Cronbach forcefully demonstrates in the following article how the presence of response sets can invalidate or at least sufficiently mask test scores so as to leave them ambiguous or uninterpretable. (See articles by Rorer (1965), Rundquist (1966), and Block (1965) for expanded discussion of this topic.) What are some of the major types of response sets? Under what conditions are they likely to occur? How can we minimize, control, or utilize their influence?

When a person takes an objective test, he may bring to the test a number of

Reprinted and abridged with permission of author and publisher from an article entitled "Further Evidence on Response Sets and Test Design," which appeared in *Educational and Psychological Measurement*, 1950, Vol. 10, pp. 3–31.

test-taking habits which affect his score. Personal ways of responding to test items of a given form (e.g., the tendency to say "agree" when given the alternatives "agree"—"uncertain"—"disagree") are frequently a source of invalidity. In 1946 the writer assembled evidence demonstrating that these "response sets" are present in a wide variety of tests. Since that time much new evidence has come to light, and it is now possible to examine more completely the nature of response sets.

As our earlier report demonstrated, response sets have been identified in tests of ability, attitude, personality, and interest, and in rating scales. Among the most widely found sets are acquiescence (tendency to say "True," "Yes," "Agree," etc.), evasiveness (tendency to say "?," "Indifferent," "Uncertain," etc.), and similar biases in favor of a particular response when certain fixed alternatives are offered. Other sets include the tendency to work for speed rather than accuracy, the tendency to guess when uncertain, the tendency to check many items in a checklist, etc. Response sets become most influential as items become difficult or ambiguous. Individual differences in response sets are consistent throughout a given test, as shown by split-half coefficients. Response sets dilute a test with factors not intended to form part of the test content, and so reduce its logical validity. Response sets tend to reduce the range of individual differences in score.

EVIDENCE THAT RESPONSE SETS EXIST

It is scarcely necessary to marshal further evidence that reliable individual differences in response sets exist. Yet the widespread use of test forms which permit response sets indicates that their existence is not adequately appreciated. It is not only the old tests—Seashore, Bernreuter, Thurstone attitude, Strong— that suffer from response sets. New tests appear continually, especially tests of attitude and personality, whose forms invite response sets. The writer has routinely requested graduate students to analyze their data for response sets whenever their research employed tests with fixed response categories (A-U-D, Yes-No-?, etc.). *Never has such an analysis failed to disclose individual patterns of response, statistically consistent from item to item.*

The most effective simple design to demonstrate response sets is to obtain a score for each person on the suspected response set. Thus, Lorge (1937) tested the existence of "gen-like," or acquiescense on the Strong test, by counting how many items each person marked "Like." The split-half or Kuder-Richardson reliability of the response-set score can then be computed. Table 1 condenses the evidence obtained by this and other techniques, evidence which, together with that previously assembled, shows conclusively that response sets are to be found in a great many tests.

RESPONSE SETS IN MULTIPLE-CHOICE TESTS ■ The only major form of fixed-alternative test which has so far been found relatively free from response sets is

TABLE 1. *Sample Studies Reporting Response Sets*

Investigator and references	Name and nature of test	Response called for	Response set	Finding
Bennett, Seashore, Wesman (1947)	Differential Aptitudes, Clerical	Checking errors	Speed vs. carefulness	Good students may earn falsely low scores due to set to work accurately at slow speed.
Brotherton, Read Pratt (1948)	Questionnaire on word meanings	Checking fixed categories on six-point scale	Definition of terms	Substantial differences in meaning are found from person to person and group to group. Questionnaires involving many, few, several, etc. "are invalid and unreliable."
Guilford (1947)	Tests of plotting, scale reading, etc.	Solving many items, with time limit	Speed vs. carefulness	In one test, reliability of Rights .76, Wrongs .56. But intercorrelation only —.48. Factor analysis shows "carefulness" often the most prominent factor in Wrongs scores.
Lorge (1937)	Strong Vocational Interest Blank	Like, Indifferent, Dislike	Acquiescence, evasiveness	Reliability for number of L's in two testings is .8; for number of I's, .84.
Mathews (1929)	Interests	L-l-i-d-D	Acquiescence	Reliability of tendency to "like" many items is .75–.79. Responses are altered when choices are in order D-d-i-l-L. Responses at extreme left and fourth from left tend to be used. Shift is greatest on items where students have least pronounced views.
Philip (1947)	Judgment of proportion in color mixtures	Absolute judgment on 11-point scale	Tendency to use certain portions of scale	Some individuals scatter their judgments more broadly over the scale than others. Each individual uses certain "foci" along the scale more often than other responses. Stimuli at the foci and ends of the scale are more often judged correctly than others. "Subsidiary cues" have greatest influence when discrimination is difficult.
Wesman (1947 b)	Spelling	Check all misspelled words	Acquiescence	Incorrect spellings correlate higher with total test than correctly spelled items.

the multiple-choice item. In order to determine whether response sets can be extracted from a typical test of this type, the writer has studied the *Henmon-Nelson Test of Mental Ability, Form A,* for Grades 3–8. (The data for this study were supplied by Kenneth Eells.) Thousands of test papers were available, since every child in several grades in a mid-western city had been tested. The sample for this study was chosen indiscriminately from papers of upper-lower and lower-middle-class children. In administering the test experimentally Eells allowed an extended time of 20 minutes beyond the standard time of 30 minutes. Papers not completed even in the extended time were discarded in the present analysis.

The *Henmon-Nelson* is a suitable test for investigating response sets because items were prepared with care, are fairly well arranged as to difficulty, and are designed so that the correct answer appears about equally often in each of the five response-positions. The hypothesis is that some students may persistently tend to select choices early in the group of five. This would raise their scores on items where the correct answer is choice "1" or "2," but lower them on items keyed "4" or "5." The psychological basis for the hypothesis is the possibility that some students read every alternative and discriminate carefully, where some merely read through the item to find a plausible answer, mark it, and go on to the next item.

The procedure was the usual one: to obtain a "bias" score for each individual and determine its reliability. If the score is reliable, the response set is proved to exist. The response-set score for the present hypothesis consists of "number of errors appearing to the left of the correct answer" minus "number of errors to the right of the correct answer." Before rescoring papers for bias, papers of high-scoring pupils (those having a score above 60 out of 90 items correct) were discarded. This was done to increase the likelihood of finding a response set, since response sets have no opportunity to show themselves when the pupil gets most items correct. For a group of 66 papers bias scores ranged from 24 to −12. The person with the bias score 24 had made 39 errors to the left of the true answer, and only 15 errors to the right of the true answer. Such a preponderance is hard to explain as other than a habit of marking items. For the cases studied, however, the split-half reliability of the bias score was only .095, corrected. Such a low correlation indicates that the postulated response set is of no consequence for this group. A second sample of 84 cases having raw scores of 40 or below in extended time (these pupils had IQ's near or below 80) were studied separately, in order to increase the probability of finding a response set. For these pupils the reliability of the bias score was .42, corrected. Evidently for a group of pupils taking a difficult multiple-choice test, reliable response sets can be found. Bias has a slight relation to raw score; the mean raw score for these poor pupils was 24.5 for those with negative bias, and 29 for those with positive bias. For some reason very poor students tended to mark alternatives to the right of the correct answer proportionately more often than slightly better pupils.

An attempt was made to demonstrate such biases as "preference for position 1." No statistical evidence for such sets could be obtained, although an occasional case does suggest that such biases may occur. One boy, for example, in 90 items never marks the fifth choice as correct, and another student places 30 of his marks on position "1."

A second study was made with a modified version of the *Ohio State University Psychological Examination*, using data made available by N. L. Gage and Dora Damrin. The shortened test they used consists of 90 five-choice vocabulary items, unspeeded. This test was administered to unselected juniors and seniors in several high schools. When papers for all 171 pupils were scored for tendency to place answers before rather than after the correct position, the odd-even reliability of the bias score was found to be .20. When only the lowest 65 students (as judged by the total number right on the test) were used as a sample to determine the reliability of the bias score, the reliability rose to .29. This was a group of students for whom the test was extremely difficult; the highest score for the group was 22 right out of 90. It should be noted that this test is normally used for predicting college success among superior high-school students; the highest score in this limited subdivision of our sample is only chance expectation. When an even more restricted sample was used—the lowest 26 cases, all of whom fell below a raw score of 15 items correct—the reliability of the bias score rose to .54. The mean bias score changed as the quality of students became poorer. For the total group the mean bias score was −6.5; for the second group, −7.7; and for the very lowest group, −9.7. Here, also, the poorest students apparently tended particularly often to mark errors to the right of the correct answer.

Both of these studies demonstrate that response sets are a minor factor, since so great a selection of cases was required in order to demonstrate any evidence of bias. Probably other multiple-choice tests where all subjects mark all items suffer little from response sets. Confirming studies on other multiple-choice tests are desirable, but the generally satisfactory experience with forced-choice tests should encourage their continued widespread use.

STABILITY OF RESPONSE SETS

While there is ample evidence that response sets are consistent throughout a single test, it is important to determine whether they are characteristics of the individual stable from time to time, or are transient sets which can only be regarded as errors in testing rather than personality characteristics.

Some evidence that response sets are stable appears in scattered studies. R. L. Thorndike (1938) reports that on a speeded Air Force test scores obtained at the same sitting correlate no more than scores obtained several hours apart. If a speed-accuracy set is operating, it is not a set which shifts from hour to hour. Singer and Young (1941) found that a tendency to rate varied stimuli as "pleasant" was highly stable, correlations as high as .90 being found under certain conditions over time intervals of two weeks.

Whereas these and similar studies tend to stress the stability in response sets, we ordinarily think of mental sets as easily changed by suitable directions. If the response set is viewed as a way of interpreting an ambiguous situation, as when the word "like" is left for the subject to define, any change in directions should redefine the stimulus elements and alter individual response sets. Several studies show that this can be done.

Rubin (1940) several years ago demonstrated the existence of bias in the Seashore Pitch Test. He gave the Revised Test B twice to 245 college students, and found that the group as a whole used 13958 "High" responses and only 10542 "Low" responses, in judging whether the second tone was higher or lower. According to the key, there were actually an equal number of differences in each direction.

In two ingenious studies Rubin then established that temporary sets are a major element in bias. First he gave a "guessing" test, in which subjects imagined a tossed coin, and wrote down the way they imagined it would fall. One group was given directions as follows: "Imagine a coin which has an H for high on one side, and an L for Low on the other side." In the other group this was reversed: "Imagine a coin which has an L for Low on one side, and an H for High on the other side." There was a significant preponderance of the first-mentioned response on the first-guessed item (i.e., the former group tended to say "H"; the second group to say "L"). There was a significant preponderance of the second-named response on the third guess of the series. Rubin then applied the same reversal to the Seashore test directions. Two hundred and seventy-two students were told, "If the second tone is lower than the first tone, print L; if higher, print H." Only 56.8 percent of the errors were lows marked "H," compared to 60.0 percent when much the same group was given the original directions (but note that some bias remained).

A report that altering directions affect response sets is made by Goodfellow (1940). He finds that in psychophysical judgments the predisposition to report a stimulus as absent was reversed when the directions were worded: "Remember that in approximately one-half of the trials the correct answer will be yes."

GENERALITY OF RESPONSE SETS

To some degree, a person shows consistent response sets from situation to situation. When similar situations are presented, response set scores are significantly correlated. But there is no evidence that response sets are consistent over widely different situations, and Singer and Young's evidence indicates that this is not true. But one does not measure response sets alone. Response sets show only when the response to a situation is in some way unclear. Singer and Young point out that habits of using their rating scale are operative only when "affective arousal is weak or absent." Perhaps affective arousal is weak for one person on tones, for another on odors. This would reduce the response-set correlations.

Response sets might be mere incidental sources of error in measurement, or they might reflect deeper personality traits. Evidence from many sources now combines to show that response sets reflect "real" variables.

Johnston (1948) gave the *Bernreuter Inventory* and the *Hunter Attitude Scale* to two groups of teachers. These groups were chosen on the basis of ratings by their principals, so that one group consisted of "autocratic" teachers, and one consisted of teachers who were markedly "democratic" in classroom practice. Johnston found that these groups differed significantly in response sets. On the Bernreuter, the autocratic group gave an average of 52.6 "Yes," 62.3 "No," and 10.8 "?" responses. The three totals for the democratic group were 55.9, 66.8, and 4.7 respectively. There were 42 teachers in the former group, and 43 in the latter. The difference in "tendency to use question marks" (evasion?) was significant. There was a similar difference on the Hunter scale. The mean number of statements marked "Undecided" rather than "Agree" or "Disagree" was 15 in the autocratic group and 10 in the democratic group.

Possible significance of response sets for empirical prediction is suggested by a study which finds that tendency to respond "?" is correlated negatively with success in selling life insurance (Kahn & Hadley, 1949). While the relationship found was not statistically significant, the difference between the mean number of question marks in the good and poor groups (8.4 vs. 12.8) is large enough to suggest further investigation along this line.

IMPROVEMENT OF TEST DESIGN

The heterogeneous bits of evidence pieced together here and in our previous report have established several generalizations.

1. Any objective test form in which the subject marks fixed-response alternatives ("Yes"-"No," "True-False," "a"-"b"-"c," etc.) permits the operation of individual differences in response sets. The influence of response sets in the multiple-choice test is, however, of minor importance.

2. Response sets have the greatest variance in tests which are difficult for the subjects tested, or where the subject is uncertain how to respond.

3. Items having the same ostensible content actually measure more than one trait, if response sets operate in the test. This is true even for tests which, scored as a whole, are "factorially pure."

4. Slight alterations in directions or training in test-taking alter markedly the influence of response sets. But if the situation is not re-structured by the tester, individual differences in response set remain somewhat stable when similar tests are given at different times.

5. Response sets are to a small degree correlated with external variables such as attitudes, interests, and personality. This shows that they are in part a reflection of "real" and stable traits. To this degree, response-set variance may be valid variance in some investigations.

6. Tests are usually constructed to measure a trait defined by the content of the test items. If the form of the items permits response sets, two persons having equal true scores on the content factor will often receive different scores on the

test. Response sets therefore ordinarily dilute the test and lower its validity.

Generalizations (5) and (6) crystallize the paradox response sets present. Some of the response-set variance is potentially useful, some of it is an interference with measurement. The problem for the tester is to capitalize on the effect of response sets where they are helpful to validity, and to eliminate their influence where it is undesirable. It is therefore important to decide which view is to be taken in any given situation.

METHODS OF ELIMINATING RESPONSE-SET VARIANCE ■ The writer concludes that as a general principle the tester should consider response sets an enemy to validity. Therefore, in most tests and certainly in those not intended to measure personality, we should keep response sets from affecting the test score by one of the following methods: designing test items which prevent response sets, altering directions to reduce response sets, or correcting for response sets.

(a) *Test design.* Since response sets are a nuisance, test designers should avoid forms of items which response sets infest. This means that any form of measurement where the subject is allowed to define the situation for himself in any way is to be avoided. (We must make an exception for tests where his way of interpreting the test is treated as a significant variable. But even so, the above analysis suggests limits to the possible validity of tests like the Rorschach which capitalize on ambiguity.)

Item forms using fixed-response categories are particularly open to criticism. The attitude-test pattern, where the subject marks a statement A, a, U, d, or D, according to his degree of agreement, is open to the following response sets: Acquiescence, or tendency to mark "A" and "a" more than "d" and "D"; evasiveness, tendency to mark "U"; and tendency to go to extremes, to mark "A" and "D" more than "a" and "d". Probably not all three of these sets will operate to a significant degree in any given test, but it is better to eliminate the sets at the outset than to spend effort later trying to measure the effect of the sets and root them out. Test designers generally have argued for retaining the five-point scale of judgment, or the more indefinite seven-point, ten-point, or even continuous scales. Such scales are open to marked individual differences in definition of the reference positions, with the more complex scale offering more chance for personal interpretation. The usual argument for the more finely divided scale of judgment on each attitude item is that it is more reliable and that subjects prefer it. If the latter advantage is significant, the finer scale may be retained and scored dichotomously. The argument that the finer scale gives more reliability is not a sound one, since this is precisely what we would expect if all of the added reliable variance were response-set variance and had no relation to beliefs about the attitude-object in question. There is no merit in enhancing test reliability unless validity is enhanced at least proportionately. It is an open question whether a finer scale of judgment gives either a more valid ranking of subjects according to belief, or (what we are beginning to recognize as even more important) scores more saturated with valid variance. With raters trained to interpret the scale uniformly so that response-set variance is removed, the finer scale may be advantageous.

The writer therefore renews his earlier recommendation that the following forms of item be avoided in tests where high validity is more important than speed-of-test construction: true-false, like-indifferent-dislike, same-different, yes-?-no, agree-uncertain-disagree, and mark all correct answers. What does this leave? Foremost, it leaves the forced-choice or best-answer test. Our attempt to find a response set in the multiple-choice test was almost completely unsuccessful. A set was extracted, and with little reliability, when the test was applied to subjects for whom it was unreasonably difficult. Further studies of multiple-choice tests are still in order, but experience to date justifies the assumption that they are generally free from response sets. One confirmation of the argument that forced choices should be used comes from a study by Owens (1947). He found that substituting forced-choice for the "yes-no" response of the conventional neurotic inventory significantly reduced the number of false positives, i.e., it increased empirical validity. The forced choice has long been used successfully in many fields. Tests of mental ability now use it almost to the exclusion of other forms. Spelling, arithmetic, and grammar tests can certainly be cast in "recognize the right (or wrong) choice" form, rather than checklist forms and others open to response sets. Thurstone used it successfully in his paired-comparison approach to attitudes.

Another important consideration is test difficulty, regardless of item form. The influence of response sets rises with difficulty, and therefore measurement of differences between students who find the test difficult is particularly invalid. This is, first, a reason for not using a test on subjects for whom it is quite difficult. Second, however, it suggests basing measurement on scales of adaptable difficulty. Thus, with the Kuhlmann-Anderson mental-test series, one selects the scales which have a difficulty appropriate for the subject, and if the first tests tried prove to be too difficult, the tester can move to an easier set of items to obtain more accurate measurement. Tests of this type, which are common in psychophysics, would be hard to use in group measurement; but experimental trial of such test designs is worth considering.

(b) *Modification of directions.* If in any test we expect a particular response set to arise, we can revise the directions to reduce the ambiguity of the situation. Another way of accomplishing the same end is to give students general training in test-wiseness. For example, if they know that in most true-false tests about half the items are false, they will tend to avoid excessive acquiescence. If they know that the correction formula is based on chance, they will know that the odds are in their favor when they respond to items where they are uncertain.

It appears to the writer that in most tests subjects should be directed to answer all items, even though this tends to increase the random error variance. In many

situations this source of error is less damaging than the constant errors introduced by differences in tendency to guess, checking threshold, or diligence in
searching for correct answers. Wesman (1947a) reports partial evidence that
grammar items, where the subject marks each error he notices in given sentences,
becomes more reliable when the subject is directed to mark every sentence-part
"correct" or "incorrect," rather than just checking the "incorrects" (but evidence
on validity is lacking).

Whisler (1938) raised the question of response-habits in Thurstone-type attitude scales. He found that some subjects marked six or more items in a 22-item
scale, and for them the reliability (parallel-test) of the attitude score was .89.
But for the subjects who marked five or fewer items that they agreed with, the
reliability was .62. Whisler thought that the subjects who checked more items
were more careful in using the scale or that their attitudes were more integrated.
Hancock (1938) followed Whisler with an experimental alteration of directions.
First, he directed subjects to mark all the statements they accepted, then the five
with which they most agreed, and finally the three of that five which they most
strongly accepted. The shift of directions produced some alteration in scores.
Generally, the standard deviation (in scale value) of scores increased when fewer
items were counted. For those with attitudes favorable to an occupation, the
more items they checked, the closer their score was to the indifference position.
Unfortunately, there is not enough evidence in the Hancock report to give a basis
for selecting any particular number of checks as preferable. If the number of
items checked affects the mean, standard deviation, and reliability, there can be
little justification for permitting the number to vary. It appears desirable to
require every subject to mark a fixed number of alternatives, selecting the statements with which he most agrees. Limited experience with this procedure suggests
that the subject should check around one-fourth of the statements.

(c) *Correction for response sets.* When response sets are entering scores on a
test, we may control or correct for the effect by special scoring keys. One widely
used method is the control score. If a "response-set score" can be obtained, we
may identify all cases with extreme response sets and drop such cases from the
sample, admitting that measurement for them is invalid. The most familiar
examples appear in the control scores of the *Minnesota Multiphasic Personality
Inventory.* Many other tests also permit us to derive such scores as bias or
acquiescence, or number of items marked. In some tests it may be acceptable to
report two scores for every subject; all the essential data in the hypothetical
spelling test discussed earlier could be reported in one score "number right" and
a second "number marked as incorrect." But simultaneous consideration of patterns of scores is awkward.

CAPITALIZING ON RESPONSE-SET VARIANCE ▪ If response sets are thought of as
possibly contributing to validity, one may weight the response sets in a way that
maximizes their contribution. Cook and Leeds (1947) correlate each possible
response on an attitude scale for teachers with a criterion, and assign positive or

negative scoring weights accordingly. One item is as follows, where the numbers in parentheses are weights:

	1	2	3	4	5
It is sometimes necessary to break promises to children.	Strongly agree (0)	Agree (4)	Undecided (−1)	Disagree (4)	Strongly disagree (−1)

The criterion used was a dependable estimate of the ability of teachers to establish rapport with children, which the scale was supposed to predict. It will be noted that the scoring weights are "illogical," since there can be no stronger response to "It is sometimes necessary. . . ." than to disagree (response 4), which amounts to saying "It is never necessary." The weights for responses 4 and 5 reflect the difference in response set (not in logically considered opinion) between teachers in the superior and inferior criterion groups. The defense of the Cook-Leeds procedure, and the comparable method used in Strong's Interest Blank, is that it yields considerable validity. The limitation is that invalid variance is weighted just like valid variance. A particular "good" teacher who has a set to respond very emphatically will be penalized by the weights. The majority of "good" teachers, who avoid extreme responses, will be reliably discriminated by the key. One difficulty with the sheer empiricism represented here is that the weights serve their practical purpose but give little insight into the nature of the variables tested. The only basis for extending or improving the test is trial-and-error, developing many more items of all sorts, and trying them to see how the weights come out.

SUMMARY

This paper summarizes extensive evidence demonstrating that such response sets as bias in favor of a particular alternative, tendency to guess, working for speed rather than accuracy, and the like operate in conventional objective tests. Not only are such sets wide-spread, but they reduce the validity of test scores. The response set can be altered readily by alteration of the directions or by coaching. Some studies show that response sets are somewhat correlated from one test to another (but not if the tests differ greatly in content), and that they are correlated with important external variables. While response-set variance may under certain circumstances enhance logical and empirical validity, it appears that its general effect is to reduce the saturation of the test and to limit its possible validity.

The following recommendations for practice, most of which were previously suggested, are reinforced by the present findings:

1. Response sets should be avoided with the occasional exception of some tests measuring carefulness or other personality traits which are psychologically similar to response sets.

2. The forced-choice, paired-comparison, or "do-guess" multiple-choice test should be given preference over other forms of test item.

3. When a form of item is used in which response sets are possible,

   (a) Directions should be worded so as to reduce ambiguity and to force every student to respond with the same set.

   (b) The test should not be given to a group of students for whom it is quite difficult.

   (c) A response-set score should be obtained and used to identify subjects whose scores are probably invalid.

4. Where response sets are present, attempts should be made to correct for or to capitalize on the response set by an appropriate empirical procedure.

In view of the overwhelming evidence that many common item forms invite response sets, and in view of the probability that these sets interfere with accurate measurement, it will rarely be wise to build new tests around item forms such as A-U-D, Yes-No-?, and "check all correct answers." It is to be hoped that the tests forthcoming in the future will be designed to increase their saturation with the factors the test is seeking to measure.

V

DEVELOPMENT
AND EVALUATION OF
MEASURING INSTRUMENTS

Up to this point the papers in this volume have progressed from a discussion of the purposes of measurement through both theoretical and practical considerations of reliability and validity to consideration of test design. At this point we turn our attention to the difficult task of item writing and evaluation. The word "difficult" is used intentionally, as even the most experienced item writer may produce only a few relatively flawless items in a full day's work. In addition to possession of considerable knowledge and skill in the technical aspects of item writing, the test constructor must be thoroughly grounded in the subject matter or behavior to be measured.

The first article in this chapter, by Max Engelhart, provides some valuable guidelines for writing, administering, and evaluating various types of objective paper-and-pencil achievement test questions. He not only considers the traditional item types such as true-false, multiple-choice, and matching exercises, but also presents some interesting variations. Item forms that can be useful in getting at cause-and-effect reasoning and other higher order cognitive skills as application, extrapolation, and interpolation are illustrated.

In the next three articles empirical estimates of the effects of various factors on item or test scores are reported. These articles illustrate the type of research being conducted in an effort to understand influences on scores. This understanding becomes necessary as we increase our efforts to measure both the performances of groups (see Chapter VII: Curriculum Evaluation) and the criterion-referenced performance of an individual (see the paper by Popham and Husek in Chapter IV). McMorris, Brown, and Pruzek examined the effects of cue, grammar, and length faults in multiple-choice items. Marso studied the effects of arranging multiple-choice items according to item difficulty, similarity of content, and order of class presentation. Marshall and Powers investigated the effects of composition errors and handwriting quality on the evaluation of essay questions. While these studies, even combined with other studies cited in the relevant reviews of literature, do not provide unequivocal answers to all practical and technical measurement questions, they do provide some useful suggestions. In addition they provide guides for possibly fruitful research. To illustrate, a follow-up of Marso's article might test younger students with sufficient time and then again with severe time pressure. With the studies presented here we are reducing some of the idiosyncratic groping associated with devising measures.

Corey extends our concern for instrument development to the affective domain, step-by-stepping through a procedure to measure attitudes, helping the reader to implement the type of measurement referred to in the previous chapter by Darling, and providing an alternative (or supplement) to Webb's unobtrusive approach shown in that same chapter.

When writing and refining a test the developer desires to produce a test of only relevant variables. Hopefully the test will not penalize a student by using inappropriate content, misleading wording, or other irrelevant factors. The authors of the final three papers in this chapter emphasize different aspects of the problem area that such irrelevancies create.

Anastasi considers the testing of culturally different groups. She discusses the cultural basis for items, and recommends the retention of items relevant to the criterion and the rejection of irrelevant items. (The reader may also wish to refer to papers on testing the disadvantaged by Deutsch, et al. in Chapter VIII and by Clements, et al. in Chapter VI.)

The case study presented by Foreman speaks eloquently for the careful analysis of a test by a classroom teacher. Foreman demonstrates how a test and its directions may be refined, thereby reducing some of the irrelevancies and producing a more precise measuring instrument.

The article by Cox contains evidence on possible sources of bias in test composition. When statistics alone become the criterion of item inclusion or exclusion for a test, the test is likely to lose content validity. Cox shows that even the sex make-up of the item analysis group could upset the content balance of the test.

The concern in this chapter is with writing, revising, and selecting stimuli for measuring instruments. First, authors present guidelines for writing items, then estimate the effects of various guidelines through experimental studies, and then specify an approach for developing attitude measures. The authors of the final three papers are concerned with analyzing instruments and items: one with the cultural component in items, one with the revision of a test by a teacher, and one with the biases likely to result from mechanically selecting items according to their statistics.

A final word: What can be more central to testing than constructing and selecting the stimuli? (Don't answer that question, just enjoy the chapter!)

20   *Suggestions for Writing Achievement Test Exercises*

....

MAX D. ENGELHART

The production of a valid test item is both an art and a science. The scientific aspects involve technical knowledge and skills regarding item structure and format, discrimination, difficulty, and reliability. Art comes into play in integrating the scientific, the verbal, and practical aspects of the total operation.

The largest single population of test makers is teachers. They obviously should be well versed in both the art and science of test construction. Unfortunately, many are deficient in both. The guidelines for writing "objective" type test items presented by Dr. Engelhart in the following paper should and hopefully will find wide audience among educators at all levels.

Attempting to write a sample item illustrating each of the exercise types discussed by the author would be an aid to the comprehension of the material of the following article.

Extended discussions of item writing may be found in any number of basic texts on educational measurement (Ahmann & Glock, 1971a & b; Davis, 1964; Ebel, 1972; Gronlund, 1971; Nunnally, 1971; Payne, 1968, 1974; Stanley & Hopkins, 1972; Thorndike, 1971; Thorndike & Hagen, 1969).

The production of locally constructed achievement tests can be greatly facilitated by making available to the participating teachers directions for the writing of test exercises. Unless the instructions are quite explicit, teachers tend to produce exercises which are faulty. Many teachers have difficulty in phrasing adequate directions for a series of exercises. Some teachers are likely to forget that the standard answer sheet limits the number of answers to a given exercise to no more than five. Few teachers realize that it is possible to use a variety of forms. Hence it is desirable to provide teachers with samples of various forms, along with the directions necessary for the writing of exercises of these types. The rest of this

Reprinted and abridged with permission of author and publisher from an article entitled, "Suggestions for Writing Achievement Test Exercises to Be Used in Tests Scored on the Electric Scoring Machine," which appeared in *Educational and Psychological Measurement*, 1947, Vol. 7, pp. 357–374.

article describes the kind of material which may be given to teachers as a means of directing and stimulating the production of achievement test exercises.

GENERAL DIRECTIONS FOR WRITING ACHIEVEMENT EXERCISES

The exercises used in tests must conform to certain patterns so that the students will have no difficulty in recording their answers. Generally, no exercise or test item should have more than five answers including correct and incorrect ones. Each exercise number on the answer sheet is followed by lettered spaces for only five answers. It is possible to write exercises having more than one answer of the five correct, but this practice is not recommended. Where certain series of exercises call for more than one correct answer to each exercise, students are stimulated to mark in the same way in other series of exercises where only one answer per exercise is expected. The practice of asking for more than one answer complicates scoring whether the score is simply to be the number right or the number right minus some fraction of the number wrong. While it is desirable to prepare exercises similar to the types described in later paragraphs, this does not mean that measurement is restricted to the recall of isolated facts. The content of achievement exercises has more influence than their form on the nature of the responses made by the students. Abilities other than mere memory are tested when the content is to some extent novel and when the selection of the correct answer requires discrimination. On the other hand, measurement of memory abilities is justified when the content relates to important facts, concepts, or principles.

In the production of objective exercises serious thought should be given to the planning of the distribution of exercises of various types in order to secure both representative sampling of the subject matter of the course and of a variety of abilities. While it is possible to weight different series of exercises differently in machine scoring, it is much easier to secure appropriate weighting by having the numbers of items or exercises pertaining to each division of subject matter proportional to the importance of the subject matter division. If the general organization of the test as a whole is to follow that of the course, a variety of abilities may be tested within each series of exercises. For example, certain exercises of a series of multiple-answer exercises may require no more than the ability to remember the term defined by the introductory part of each exercise. Other exercises in the same series may require the functioning of abilities transcending memory, if the content of the exercises is to some extent novel. While the introduction of novel content is essential if more than the memory of facts is to be tested, the novel content should be such that the student is able to determine the correct answer by means of thinking about facts he has had an opportunity to learn. This may be illustrated by an example from the field of physics. Suppose that the students have studied Archimedes' Principle that a body is buoyed up by a force equal to the weight of the fluid displaced. Suppose further that the applications of this principle have largely or exclusively been with respect to bodies floating or immersed in liquids. Presume also that the students have learned at some time during the course that both liquids and gases are fluids and that gases, particularly, become less dense as they become warmer. Then the students have had the opportunity to acquire the facts needed in answering a novel and thought-provoking multiple-choice exercise based on the question: "Assuming that the temperature of the gas in a dirigible balloon remains constant, will the balloon go up more rapidly in warm air or in cold air?"

Discriminative thinking is promoted by presenting the student with plausible and somewhat related incorrect answers as well as by the use of novel content or by the presenting of more or less familiar content in unanticipated ways. Discriminative thinking is also promoted by preparing a series of related exercises.

SUGGESTIONS FOR WRITING OBJECTIVE TEST EXERCISES

TRUE-FALSE ITEMS ■ When constructing true-false exercises, avoid writing obviously trivial or meaningless ones. Avoid making broad generalizations which are obviously true or false, i.e., avoid writing statements involving such terms as "always," "never," "none," "only," "all," and "every." Such terms are permissible, however, in intrinsically difficult statements, for example, "All persons born in the United States are citizens of the United States" and "All amphibia live in fresh water." Avoid items that are partly true and partly false, for example, "Cases in equity are sometimes tried by a judge and sometimes by a jury." Avoid items which express opinionated views, unless the purpose is to test the knowledge of the source of an option, as for example, "According to Keynes, government spending is an excellent means of combating depressions." In items designed to measure the knowledge of an important concept or principle, avoid unnecessary technical terms or obscure minutiae. Avoid the writing of unusually long and involved statements. Such statements are more often true than false and test-wise students realize that this is the case. The principles just mentioned also apply to other types of objective exercises. Directions similar to the following should precede each series of true-false statements in the completed test:

After each item number on the answer sheet, blacken *one* lettered space to indicate that the statement is

A. true.

B. false.

True-false exercises may be written on cards, one exercise to a card. The truth or falsity of the exercise should be indicated. Writing exercises on separate cards facilitates the rejection of poor exercises. It is also the best way to proceed if it is the intent to accumulate a file of exercises for future use. If the exercises pertain to a particular chapter of a text or a unit of a syllabus, it is desirable to specify on the card the chapter or unit to which the exercise pertains in order to facilitate checking the accuracy of the phraseology of the exercise and the correctness of the key. The method also facilitates representative sampling of the content of the course.

MULTIPLE-CHOICE ITEMS ■ To reduce the influence of guessing, four or five alternatives should be given. One of the answers should be definitely correct and the others *should be plausible* although incorrect. Avoid consistently writing correct answers which are longer than incorrect ones. The incorrect answers may be similar in form to the correct answers, opposite in meaning to the correct answers, or slightly less precise or complete than the correct answers. (In the latter cases students may be asked to mark the "best" answer.) The exercises should not be unusually long or complex. The answers may be single words or brief phrases, but unless the exercise begins with a question, *each answer must complete the introductory sentence grammatically.*

Where the answers to a multiple-choice exercise are longer than single words or very brief phrases, it is desirable to list the answers. Note that each answer of the first exercise grammatically completes the sentence with which the exercise began. In the following examples note also the difference in style where the "item stem" is a question. Both methods of writing are equally desirable.

1. The fatigue of muscle is due primarily to
    A. the overuse of the individual muscle fibers.
    B. the production of lactic acid within the muscle cells.
    C. excessive carbon dioxide production.
    D. a limitation of the oxygen supply.
    E. a limitation of the food supply.
2. The United States Government under the Articles of Confederation was most successful in meeting which of the following problems?
    A. The raising of money to pay our debts to France and Holland.
    B. The regulation of trade between the states.
    C. The organization of the Northwest Territory.
    D. The alleviation of social discontent.
    E. The making of commercial treaties with foreign nations.

Where multiple-choice exercises are problems in mathematics, or are exercises with numerical answers as in chemistry and in physics, it is an effective device to use the phrase "None of the above answers" as answer E. Occasionally this phrase should represent the correct answer. It should not be used as an incorrect answer, however, if the correct answer listed as an A, B, C, or D answer is an approximation. In this case a student could argue that the exercise has two correct answers.

The following directions might precede each series of multiple-choice exercises in the completed test:

> After each item number on the answer sheet, blacken *one* lettered space to indicate the *best* answer.

(If the exercises can be given a "correct" answer, substitute the word "correct" for "best" in the directions above.)

MATCHING ITEMS ▪ If using a standard IBM answer sheet, each exercise may consist of three definitions to be matched with three terms included in a list of five. The definitions should concern terms that are likely to be confused by the student whose knowledge is not precise. Furthermore, the two extra terms should be good distracters. Similar exercises may pertain to content other than definitions and the terms may be names of places, personages, formulas, or other brief answers. To promote discriminative thinking all of the items in each group of three should pertain to related concepts. Usually the items of a given group should be drawn from the same chapter or unit of subject matter. If these suggestions are followed, repeated use of the exercises is facilitated. An example is given below:

Outcome	*Battle*
3. This victory ended an attempt to cut off New England from the rest of the colonies and was a major factor in the obtaining of the alliance with France.	A. Bunker Hill
	B. Yorktown
	C. Saratoga
	D. Monmouth
4. After Washington's retreat from New York, hope was renewed in the American cause by this victory.	E. Trenton
5. This victory involved a feint toward New York followed by strategy which resulted in a large body of enemy troops being cut off from help by either land or sea.	

Each group of three numbered items should be set off as indicated above. The entire series should be preceded by directions like the following:

After each number on the answer sheet, blacken *one* lettered space to indicate the term at the right to which the item refers.

KEY-LIST ITEMS ▪ There must be not more than five categories in an exercise, but the number of items may vary. The categories should be in some way related to each other, for if one category is unrelated to the others, the items which pertain to it are too easily identified. The numbered items may be phrases or complete sentences. In a given series all of the items should be similar in construction. To facilitate repeated use, all of the items should pertain to the same chapter in a text, to related chapters, or in general to related subject matter. Several examples of key-list exercises are given below. In each case only a few samples of items are listed below each set of directions. All of the types of categories are applicable to a variety of subject-matter fields.

For each of the items 6 through 9, blacken *one* lettered space to indicate that the item is true of
    A. the Monroe Doctrine.
    B. the Open Door Policy.

C. both the Monroe Doctrine and the Open Door Policy.
D. neither the Monroe Doctrine nor the Open Door Policy.
6. By adopting this policy the United States sought to safeguard important interests of the American people.
7. According to this policy the interests of the United States take precedence over those of any European country.
8. Violation of this policy occasioned the enunciation of the "Stimson Doctrine."
9. Our traditional policy of freedom of the seas is basic to this policy.

For each of the items 10 through 12, blacken *one* lettered space to indicate that the statement is
A. true, and is supported by the reason given.
B. true, but not because of the reason given.
C. false.
10. *Everyman* is classified as a morality play, because it deals with material drawn from the *Bible*.
11. The play is essentially an allegory concerning the way to salvation, because the characters are chiefly personifications of human qualities and the plot is an account of how Everyman makes his peace with God.
12. The author describes a systematized and predictable arrangement of the ways of God, because the steps necessary for the salvation of Everyman are clearly defined and commonly accepted.

For each of the following paired items (13–15), blacken *one* lettered space to indicate that the *first* item is
A. greater than the second.
B. less than the second.
C. equal to the second.

13. Amount of energy released in external respiration. . . . . Amount of energy released in internal respiration.
14. Amount of time the ventricles of the heart are contracted. . . . . Amount of time the auricles of the heart are contracted.
15. The rate at which blood pressure falls as the blood passes through the capillaries. . . . . The rate at which blood pressure falls as the blood passes through the veins.

Exercises of the type illustrated below are useful in measuring how well students handle correlated or cause-and-effect relationships. In writing such items where the relationship is definitely cause and effect, the cause should be given first.

For each of the following paired items (16–18), blacken *one* lettered space to indicate that an increase in the first thing is normally associated with,
A. an increase in the second.
B. a decrease in the second.
C. no related change in the second.
16. Amount of carbonates dissolved in the water of a river.
     Number of clams in the river.
17. Temperature of the environment of a mammal.
     Body temperature of the mammal.

18. Number of lemming in an arctic area.
     Number of caribou in the same area.

One means of presenting students with exercises which require reflective thinking rather than memory alone is to set up hypothetical situations which differ from the situations encountered during instruction. The exercises given below illustrate such a series. The facts required in answering these exercises correctly were a part of the regular instruction in physical science.

You have acquired some knowledge of the earth and its motions as they really exist. In this exercise you are to identify the effects of some wholly imaginary conditions. For each of the items 19–22, blacken *one* lettered space to indicate that the item would be true *if* the
  A. orbit of the earth were a circle rather than an ellipse.
  B. orbit of the moon were exactly in the same plane as the orbit of the earth.
  C. axis of the earth were not inclined.
  D. earth had half its present diameter, but retained its present mass.
  E. earth were a perfect sphere.
  (Assume only one of the above imaginary conditions occurs at a time.)
19. All the solar days would be of equal length.
20. Objects would weigh four times as much as they do now.
21. The celestial equator and the ecliptic would be identical.
22. An eclipse of the sun would occur each month.

Exercises Pertaining to Quoted Material ■ The following directions are useful in writing key-list exercises which pertain to quoted material (a paragraph or two, or even a table or a graph).

Basing your judgments solely on the data summarized above, blacken *one* lettered space to indicate that the item is
  A. definitely true.
  B. probably true.
  C. impossible to prove or disprove from the data given.
  D. probably false.
  E. definitely false.

Probably-true statements are justifiable interpolations, extrapolations, or predictions from the information or data given. They may represent legitimate generalizations from information describing a sample, or deductions with respect to a sample where the information pertains to things in general. For example, if the selection pertains to industrial conditions characteristic of the war years, a statement to be marked "B" may describe a trend or condition in a single industry analogous to the general trend or condition, although the particular industry is not mentioned in the selection. Similarly, a statement to be marked "D" may describe a trend for a particular industry opposite to that of the general trend described in the selection. Such exercises may be scored not only to determine the general accuracy of the students in interpreting data, but also to identify students who have tendencies to be overcautious, to go beyond the data, or to make crude errors of judgment. For example, the overcautious student marks A items B or C, and E items D or C. Conversely, the student who tends to go beyond the data, or overgeneralize marks B items A, D items E, and C items by some letter other than C.

Exercises of this type are very appropriate in achievement tests. Since the facts needed in thinking are presented in the quoted material, it seems legitimate to attribute differences in the scores of the students to differences in their ability to think in the subject-matter field. Where the quoted material is novel, or is on a level above that encountered in the course, the scores may be useful as predictions of future success in advanced courses in the same field. Since course marks should be predictions of future success rather than rewards for time spent in class, achievement tests used in determining final marks may well contain a considerable proportion of such exercises.

Exercises Involving Diagrams or Pictures ▪ If there are no more than five pictures or things to be labeled in a diagram, the pictures or parts may be labeled A, B, C, D, and E, and the directions preceding the items may be written: "After each item number on the answer sheet, blacken the *one* lettered space which designates the part of the diagram (or the picture) to which the items correctly refers." Since the categories are inherent in the diagram or pictures, no further directions are needed. The directions, the diagram or pictures, and the statements which constitute the test items should all be on the same page of the test booklet or on a facing page.

The following directions are useful where comparisons are to be made between two diagrams or pictures, for example, reproductions of paintings representing different styles of art. In this instance the pictures may be labeled with Roman numerals.

After each item number on the answer sheet, blacken *one* lettered space to indicate that the item is true of
A. picture I.
B. picture II.
C. both pictures.
D. neither picture.

Where more than five parts of a diagram or locations on a map need to be identified, it is usually preferable to write exercises of the multiple-choice rather than the key-list type. Each exercise may begin with a reference to one of the diagram symbols, for example, "The symbol 'I' refers to (A......, B......, C......, etc.)." In this case the order of the exercises should be the order of the symbols in the diagram. In some cases one can use the answer sheet or exercise numbers as diagram or map symbols. For example, suppose that a map exercise involves locations of battlefields of the Civil War. Number 23 on the map may be in the location of Gettysburg. The corresponding exercise, given on the same page or on a facing page, and in a series of similar exercises may simply be:

23. A. Antietam, B. Gettysburg, C. Chancellorsville, D. Bull Run, E. Petersburg.

The directions for such a series of exercises may be phrased: "After the number on the answer sheet which corresponds to each map or exercise number, blacken the *one* lettered space which designates the correct answer."

In certain fields it is effective to use small diagrams labeled A, B, C, D, and E as answers to ordinary multiple-choice exercises. For example: "Which of the following curves best represents the distribution of intelligence test scores of a large group of 12-year-old children?" "Which of the following symbols represents a cold front on a weather map?" "Which of the following tools should be used to . . . . . ?" An effective E answer is "None of the above . . . . . ." which, if used in several of such exercises, should be the correct answer at least once.

CRITICAL EXAMINATION OF THE ITEMS

After exercises have been written they should be carefully checked for accuracy of phraseology and correctness of the key. It is very desirable to have other teachers of the subject evaluate the exercises with respect to fairness, freedom from ambiguities, and elimination of the too obviously incorrect answers. It is an excellent practice in seeking helpful criticism to have other teachers attempt to key the exercises. When teachers respond differently to an exercise, faults may be encountered of which the writer of the exercise was unaware.

The suggestions contained in this paper should assist teachers in becoming more expert in the art of writing exercises for achievement tests. Critical evaluation of exercises by teachers is suggested above. An examination staff can promote such evaluation by undertaking informal and formal analyses, i.e., by scrutinizing both content and statistical item analysis data. (See the articles by Foreman and Cox later in this chapter for expanded discussion of item analysis techniques.)

The item analysis data pertaining to individual exercises may be recorded on the original cards containing the test items, or they may be recorded adjacent to each item in a keyed test booklet. The percents of correct response are particularly useful to teachers in evaluating attainment of objectives. Both the percents of correct response and the item discrimination indices are useful in identifying faulty exercises. A combination of scholarly writing of exercises, painstaking criticism and editing prior to first use, and thoughtful interpretation of item analysis data cannot help but result in the production of superior achievement tests.

21 Effects of Violating Item Construction Principles

ROBERT F. MCMORRIS, JAMES A. BROWN, AND ROBERT M. PRUZEK

*How potent are the various "rules" of item writing? While doing some of
the "don'ts", such as including grammatical clues to the best answer, would
appear to be silly and lower the evaluation of a test's quality, how seriously
would the test results be affected? One approach to gathering evidence for
answering the question is illustrated in the experiment by McMorris, Brown,
and Pruzek. They added violations of rules to a set of items and administered
the items in both fault-free and violated versions. Did the faults make a difference? Which characteristic of the test was most affected: item difficulty, validity, or reliability? What are the implications of these results for criterion-
referenced measurement, as discussed by Popham and Husek (see article 17)?
What are the implications for exercise construction in National Assessment, as
discussed by Merwin and Womer, on the basis of the information contained in
their article in Chapter VII.*

Numerous rules for constructing multiple-choice items are found in educational measurement texts, yet these rules have little empirical support. The purpose of the present study is to evaluate experimentally the effects of violating
selected item construction principles.

Williamson and Hopkins (1967) compared the effects on validity and reliability of a "none-of-these" option versus a homogeneous fifth option, and
found no significant differences. The National Assessment staff (Merwin and
Womer, 1969) found that the addition of an "I don't know" option increased
exercise difficulty, although not as much as when the exercise was rewritten
in recall format. Chase (1964) estimated the word-count ratio at which
extra-length correct options would induce a set to select these options, and then
showed that practice on short-option, easy items would alter this set. Items
with positive stems have been found to be easier than those with negative stems
(Terranova, 1969). Further, items were easier when there were a minimum
number of changes in stem mode (positive versus negative stems), but reliability seemed unaffected. In addition, interest in the construct of "test-
wiseness" may generate evidence concerning item construction principles (cf.
Alker, Carlson, and Hermann, 1969; Gibb, 1964; Millman, Bishop, and Ebel,
1965; Slakter, Koehler, and Hampton, 1970; Wahlstrom and Boersma, 1968).

Reprinted and abridged from a paper delivered at the annual convention of the National
Council on Measurement in Education and the American Educational Research Association,
Minneapolis, Minn., March 1970. Also appeared as article with same title in the *Journal of
Educational Measurement*, 1972, Vol. 9, #4, Winter, pp. 287–295.

The previous study most directly relevant to the present research was performed by Dunn and Goldstein (1959) who rewrote items from the Army Basic Military Subjects Tests to include violations of item construction principles. The violations were (1) the use of cues, such as repeating a word from the stem in a correct option; (2) grammatical inconsistencies between the stem and the incorrect options; and (3) extra length correct options. Also, question vs. incomplete statement formats were compared, with the question lead arbitrarily designated as the fault. One-quarter of the items were designated to be fault-free, one-half the items contained one fault, and one-quarter contained two faults. The items were administered to a large sample of Army enlistees. Essentially no differences in validity or reliability could be ascribed to the violations, but the faulted items were easier.

In the present study additional evidence concerning the violation of these same three item-writing principles is presented. Whereas Dunn and Goldstein examined responses of soldiers to combat-related subject-matter, the present investigators dealt with the responses of secondary school students to social studies items. Moreover, the methodology of this study was designed to answer more directly the major questions about how item faults influence responses. An American history test was constructed so that half the items were apparently free of item-writing errors. Each of the rest of the items included one of three different intentional violations of item-writing rules. The three types of violations investigated were *cue*, where a word or phrase in the stem provided a cue to the correct option, which was at least somewhat irrelevant to the content; *grammar*, where the correct option was the only one grammatically consistent with the stem; and *length*, where the correct option was longer than any of the incorrect options.

As noted above, the purpose of this study was to evaluate experimentally the effects of the violations of these three item-construction principles. The first objective was to examine the extent to which manipulated violations were reflected in item and subtest scores. The second objective was to estimate the effects of these violations upon estimates of item difficulty, reliability, and predictive validity.

METHODOLOGY

INSTRUMENTATION ■ Items for the experimental test were based on the syllabus categories for the revised New York State curriculum in eleventh-grade social studies. Most of these multiple-choice items were developed by the investigators primarily from items from three sources: the New York State Education Department's Bureau of Elementary and Secondary Educational Testing; Stull, Anderson, and Lindquist (1964); and Harcourt Brace and World, Inc. (1961). The items received criticism from a history professor, several high school social studies teachers, and students in a graduate class in social studies education.

Two pilot forms of different lengths were administered to the 278 students in Regents sections of eleventh-grade social studies in a local suburban school. (The two forms were alternated within each classroom to help insure comparability of the samples responding to each form.) The pilot data were item-analyzed to remove apparent content and item-writing faults, to estimate item difficulties, and to help determine the most appropriate length for the final forms.

Faults were then added to items originally free of item-writing faults and whose difficulty indices in the pilot forms were between 25 and 85%. That is, the items were intentionally contaminated by adding to each item one of the following faults described above: a cue, a grammatical inconsistency, or extra length for the keyed option. Illustrative items appear in Table 1. The investigators attempted to include only realistic and reasonably subtle faults. The resulting experimental instrument contained items matched on content and

TABLE 1. *Illustrative Items in Faulted and Clean Versions*

Type of Fault	Items
Cue	4. In the latter part of the 18th century, a liberal immigration policy [which would lead to a supply of cheap labor], was generally opposed by A Eastern manufacturers. B land speculators. *C labor unions. D railroad companies.
Grammar	13. The Gadsden Purchase rounded out the continental United States by *A adding parts of what is now Arizona and New Mexico. B establish(ing) the boundary between Maine and Canada. C extend(ing) the northern boundary of the United States. D set(ting) the boundary at Puget Sound.
Length	31. For the Northern states, the most objectionable part of the Compromise of 1850 was the A admission of California as a state. B assumption of the national debt of Texas. C extension of popular sovereignity in Utah. *D inclusion of a Fugitive Slave Law [requiring cooperation and enforcement by the states].

*Note.—Insertions made in a clean version of an item to contaminate it are shown by brackets. Deletions from the clean version of an item to convert it to a faulted version are shown by parentheses.

stratified according to difficulty index (25–44%, 45–64%, 65–84%) and type of fault (cue, grammar, length). Of the nine cells, defined by the difficulty and type-of-fault dimensions, six contained two pairs of items in both their original ("clean") and faulted versions. For the remaining three cells, balanced over columns and rows, three pairs of items were included in order that the two final forms be comprised of 42 items each, the greatest number judged to produce essentially a power test within the limitation of a 40-minute period.

Various restrictions resulted in two forms which were as identical as possible except for the faults. As already noted, the items were paired according to content, difficulty, and type of fault. For each form the clean version of one item and the faulted version of the paired item were included. Therefore, each item appeared on both forms, in its clean version on one form and its faulted version on the other. The items were ordered identically for the two forms. Half the items on each form were clean and the other half faulted, with the three faults being equally represented.

The scores on the *Comprehensive Examination in Social Studies* were used as the external criterion for achievement. This New York State Regents Examination is given to eleventh grade social studies students, and is a three hour examination consisting of multiple-choice and essay items.

A verbal ability instrument, the *Quick Word Test* (Level 1, Form Bₘ), was selected as a reliable indicator of general verbal ability which requires very little time to administer. This test was employed to provide evidence concerning the relationship of test-wiseness and intelligence.

SAMPLE ■ The experimental forms were administered to 494 students from two area suburban schools; students in all those eleventh-grade social studies sections preparing for the Regents examination were involved in the study.[1]

Again, the two forms were alternated within each classroom.

ANALYSIS ■ The effects of the violations were first studied by an approach to studying differences described elsewhere (McMorris, Brown, and Pruzek, 1970). The extent of the difference due to each type of fault was estimated.

Data was also analyzed to estimate the effects of the violations upon estimates of item difficulty, internal consistency, reliability, and predictive validity. Difficulty indices were compared for each item in its contaminated vs. its clean versions. For the reliability and validity comparison each form was considered as being composed of two subtests, one contaminated and the other clean. Reliability coefficients (Kuder-Richardson 20s) and correlations with the Regents and *Quick Word Test* were contrasted for the subtests.

---

[1] In schools such as this approximately three-quarters of the students, including the college-bound, are in Regents sections. Because of a scheduling problem 87 of the students at one of the schools did not take the *Quick Word Test*; also the papers for another 12 students had to be excluded for various reasons. However, this loss of cases for one of the variables affected only the precision with which one of the secondary questions could be answered.

RESULTS

The items tended to become easier when the faults were added. The mean differences were 9.4, 7.2, and 3.4% for cue, grammar, and length faults respectively. (Further, these differences were judged to generalize; none of the three confidence intervals spanned zero at the 95% level.)

The differences in item difficulties between the faulted and clean versions may be further examined. The increments of "easiness" for individual items ranged from −6 to 34, with a mean of 6.6. A summary of the mean differences according to type of violation and pilot test item difficulty appears in Table 2. Consistent with the previous table, the greatest increments were for cues and grammar. Also, items of medium difficulty on the pilot test displayed the largest differences for all types of violations.

TABLE 2. *Mean Differences in Item Difficulty Indices between Contaminated and Clean Versions*

Fault	Item Difficulty Level[a]			Weighted Mean
	Easy	Medium	Difficult	
cue	6.5	12.7	6.8	9.4
grammar	3.5	11.8	8.2	7.2
length	3.0	6.5	1.7	3.4

Note.—Each cell mean is expressed as a percent based on either 4 or 6 items, where each item was tested in two versions. The percent correctly answering the clean version was subtracted from the percent correctly answering the contaminated version.
[a] These levels are based on pilot data.

Means and standard deviations are given in Table 3 for the (interspersed) clean and contaminated 21-item half-tests, the difference score between the halves, the Regents, and the *Quick Word Test*. (Since no consistent or sizable sex effects were evident, this classification for data was generally not used in our analysis.) Attempts to insure comparability of the forms (A & B) and of the groups taking the forms were quite successful, although the group taking Form B may have been slightly more capable, judging from their slightly higher means on all the tests.

TABLE 3. *Test Score Means and Standard Deviations*

Test Score	Means		Standard Deviations	
	Form A	Form B	Form A	Form B
Clean (X_c)	11.59	11.76	3.49	3.42
Faulted (X_f)	12.80	13.29	3.52	3.69
$X_f — X_c$	1.21	1.53	3.08	3.08
NYS Regents	76.82	78.10	10.29	9.33
Quick Word	70.78	71.65	11.66	12.54

Comparisons may be made between the half-tests for reliability and validity coefficients by referring to Table 4. The reliability coefficients appear in parentheses in the principal diagonal. Correlations with both achievement (Regents) and intelligence (*Quick Word*) criteria are included in the table. There were essentially no differences in these coefficients due to the contaminations. The relationships for the group which took Form A and the one which took Form B were very similar.

TABLE 4. Correlation Coefficients

Variable	Sex	School	Regents	Quick Word	Clean	Faulted	$X_f - X_c$
Sex		02	06	04	−14	−10	05
School	−11		−07	14	06	−02	−09
Regents	00	02		50	54	58	05
Quick Word	−00	03	47	(88)	40	48	07
Clean (X_c)	−13	08	51	50	(61)	61	−43
Faulted (X_f)	−22	07	47	49	63	(66)	45
$X_f - X_c$	−11	−01	−01	02	−36	50	(04)

[a] Decimals are omitted.
[b] Coefficients above and to the right of the diagonal are for Form A, those below and to the left from Form B. The reliability coefficients on the diagonal are alternate forms (Quick Word) and average Kuder-Richardson 20s (Clean and Faulted), with the difference score reliability ($X_f - X_c$) estimated using the average Kuder-Richardson.
[c] N for Form A = 245 (N for Quick Word rs = 198)
N for Form B = 249 (N for Quick Word rs = 197)

The correlations with sex and school were low, as were the correlations of the difference score ($X_f - X_c$) with itself and with other variables.

DISCUSSION

In general, faults did make the items easier with the largest effects in this study occurring for cue and grammar contaminations. Point estimates were given for the differences in item difficulty due to faults, and confidence intervals supported the contention that these non-zero estimates are not likely to have been due to capriciousness in the allocation of test forms to respondents. Statistical information for the present study can not be used to go beyond the secondary school social studies domain or the particular faults that were selected. Yet since Dunn and Goldstein (1959) obtained similar results in their study of faults for quite different tests and respondents, the investigators believe that the present results are likely to generalize to a number of other situations. In other words, although the ordering of magnitudes of effects for faults in other situations could not be clearly predicted, one would at least expect the faults to make the items easier.

While the insertion of the contaminations tended to make the items easier, the validity and reliability coefficients were essentially unaltered. Perhaps, as noted by Dunn and Goldstein, there were various combinations of compensating variables, where the insertion of faults caused changes which balanced one another. Such compensating variables could have been common to both studies, or have even been idiosyncratic features of the items or the external variables. Another explanation may be that reliability and validity coefficients are not affected because these indices are not sensitive to small changes in means such as those noted in this study.

Testing students on appropriate content is not the same as testing with content-free (or "nonsense") items. Respondents who know the answer to a particular question because they know the content are probably not influenced by a contamination; most people will answer on the basis of some relevant information, not solely on the basis of a set, a fault, or other essentially extraneous information. The realistic test items used for these two studies, as opposed to tests using nonsense items, do confound the effects of faults with knowledge of content. However, these realistic test items do allow for a greater duplication of the practical situation, and therefore provide information more relevant to typical testing.

Knowledge of the content may also be considered with regard to the relationship of intelligence and "test-wiseness" for the individual. In the present study a difference score was computed for each individual by subtracting the score on the supposedly fault-free items from the score on the contaminated items. Such a difference should reflect the extent to which contaminations were used by the individual, and might therefore indicate a type of "test-wiseness". But as noted above, the person who knows the content very well would be relatively unaffected by the errors, and his difference score would be quite small. Also, we would expect a strong linear relationship between achievement and intelligence. Therefore, the more intelligent students may not need the help that contaminations seem to offer in making test items easier. Unfortunately, assessing the relationship of intelligence and "test-wiseness" defined this way is limited because of the unreliability of the faulted-clean difference for individuals.

Perhaps an appropriate way to think of the increment in easiness due to the faults is an assessment of the degree of "test-wiseness" of the students as a group. It would be interesting to compare such indices of "test-wiseness" for different populations of students and different subject-matter domains, especially if populations of respondents were to be differentiated on the basis of age, grade level, SES, and the like. It may be noted that this estimate of "test-wiseness" is considerably more reliable than the "test-wiseness" estimate for individuals referred to previously in the discussion.

Whatever one's specific conjectures as to the reasons for these findings, it seems reasonable that item-writing faults are neither extremely potent, nor nil, in their effects on item scores, and conventional validity and reliability coefficients may tend not to be much affected by these types of faults.

RONALD N. MARSO

Does student test performance depend on whether items are arranged according to item difficulty, similarity of content, order of class presentation, or none of the above? Dr. Marso conducted two experiments to provide evidence to help answer this question.

Judging from his results and from other results to which he refers, is the speediness of a test important in making a tentative answer to this question? Could you speculate as to types of students (age, ability, personality, etc.) for which the arrangement of items might be relatively important?

Writers of test and measurement textbooks continue to advise teachers that item arrangement is an important variable to be considered when devising classroom examinations. Item arrangement suggestions vary from arranging by item type, arranging by related topics or concepts, arranging in order of ascending difficulty, arranging in accord with order of presentation of the material in the class, to arranging by some combination of the above criteria (Gronlund, 1971; Noll, 1965). Few of these suggestions have been validated through empirical procedures, and some suggestions seem not to pass even logical scrutiny.

For example, teachers are advised to arrange items in ascending order of difficulty for motivational reasons. Although this is a sound or even necessary advice for certain speed and standardized tests, it should be questioned on a logical basis when related to a series of classroom examinations. Perhaps an average or slow student would become less motivated (and perhaps more anxious) to attempt more items when he begins to experience difficulty as a result of having learned from past experience that all subsequent items become even more difficult.

Much of the experimental data that does exist regarding item arrangements does not seem to be applicable to or derived from the administration of teacher-devised tests. For example, Brenner (1964) and Sax and Cromack (1966) found that item arrangement significantly influenced test performance, but this relationship appeared when the examinations were administered as speed tests rather than power tests. The latter researchers found that a significant relationship between item difficulty arrangements and student performance existed only when the students were allowed 30 minutes of testing time on a 70-item test. This relationship was not significant when testing time was increased to

Reprinted and abridged from Ronald N. Marso, Test Item Arrangement, Testing Time, and Performance, *Journal of Educational Measurement*, 1970, Vol. 7, pp. 113–118.

48 minutes, thus indicating that, under typical classroom testing procedures, item difficulty arrangements are not related to student performance. In addition, when noting these results one would wonder if the relationship between item arrangements and student performance would have appeared even under the rigid time limits if the scores had been adjusted for items omitted due to the rigid time restrictions. In other words perhaps the Sax and Cromack results indicate only that students spend more time on difficult test items and thus, under rigid speed conditions with the most difficult items being placed first they simply have an opportunity to attempt fewer items. However, this is only speculation as Sax and Cromack did not report information regarding the number of items attempted by the subjects in their study. But more to the point, it is a rather commonly accepted fact that speed does not contribute to valid predictions of most types of classroom achievement (Ebel, 1965). Therefore, one must be careful when applying item arrangement generalizations to classroom testing procedures when these generalizations have not been derived from conditions typical of these procedures.

Two researchers (Smouse & Munz, 1968; Munz & Smouse, 1968) did investigate the relationships among three item arrangements, test anxiety, and student performance on a final examination given in an introductory psychology course. In the first of two experiments these researchers arranged the 100 items on the examination randomly, hard-to-easy, and easy-to-hard; and in addition one group of students received anxiety provoking information prior to the examination. In the second experiment the subjects were given the same examination and item arrangements after being grouped according to type of test anxiety (facilitators, debilitators, nonaffects, and high-affecteds) with those students with intermediate scores evidently being eliminated as only 120 subjects were used from an original sample of 181 subjects. The results from both of these experiments indicated that the item arrangements were not related to student performance on the examination although some rather difficult to explain interactions between test anxiety types and item arrangements appeared in the results of the second experiment. These interactions might have been the result of sampling procedures (subject self-selection and small cell size); however, until this is clarified it suggests that researchers should control for test anxiety when studying the effect of item arrangements.

In an effort to study further the relationship between various item arrangements and student performance, two experiments were conducted to test the following hypotheses: (a) item arrangement based upon item difficulty will not influence student performance or required testing time when tests are administered as power tests; (b) item arrangements based upon similarity of content covered or in order of class presentation will not influence student performance or required testing time when tests are administered as power tests; and (c) the item arrangement factor will not interact with the test anxiety factor.

EXPERIMENT ONE

PROCEDURE ■ In an effort to devise a test with both a sufficient range of item difficulty and with a sufficient number of items to investigate the relationship between item difficulty and performance, two forms of the Quick Word Test (QWT) were administered to 59 students enrolled in two sections of an introductory educational psychology class at Bowling Green State University. These two forms of the QWT (Borgatta & Corsini, 1964), Form Am Level 2 and Form Bm Level 1, yielded an item pool of 200 4-alternative multiple-choice vocabulary items. After completing item analysis procedures of performance on this item pool, 139 items were selected on the basis of difficulty to maximize the item difficulty range on the experimental device. The range of difficulty for these 139 items varied from zero to 100%. These items were arranged in three different formats which were then randomly assigned to a second group of 122 students also enrolled in the same introductory educational psychology course. The item arrangement formats were designated as R (randomly arranged), DE (arranged in descending order of difficulty), and ED (arranged in ascending order of difficulty). These forms were administered as power tests, although each subject's testing time in minutes was recorded as he turned in his test form. In addition each student was given a combination of test anxiety scales identified by Carrier and Jewel (1966) and was classified as upper, middle, or lower one-third relative to the total sample on the basis of these scores. The test anxiety scales were administered several days before the experimental device and not in conjunction with any type of evaluative device.

FINDINGS ■ The students with high degrees of measured test anxiety performed less well on the three different forms of the test but the different item arrangement formats did not influence student performance on the test. Neither item arrangement nor test anxiety was significantly related to the amount of time the students spent on the exam. The cell means for these two analyses are presented on Table 1.

TABLE 1. *Cell Means for the Analyses Completed on the 139 Item Vocabulary Test*

	Time as Dependent Variable Anxiety				Achievement Score as Dependent Variable Anxiety			
	Hi	Ave	Low			Hi	Ave	Low	
R[1]	34.1	33.7	35.2	34.4	R[1]	72.6	78.0	86.6	79.4
DE[2]	26.7	30.5	36.5	31.8	DE[2]	70.5	82.0	80.5	78.1
ED[3]	34.9	32.1	33.6	33.5	ED[3]	77.4	72.7	87.4	78.6
	32.5	32.0	35.2			73.9	77.1	84.7	

[1] Random item arrangement
[2] Items arranged in descending order of difficulty
[3] Items arranged in ascending order of difficulty
(Ns for the cells ranged from 10 to 16.)

DISCUSSION ■ The data obtained from this experiment would seem to indicate that, even when a rather lengthy examination (139 items) with a diverse range in item difficulties (0–100%) is administered as a power or achievement test, arranging items according to difficulty has little or no effect upon either required testing time or upon student performance on the examination. In addition the data indicate that students with greater or less measured test anxiety do not appear to perform differently when item difficulty arrangements are varied. The students classified as having greater test anxiety did perform less well on the exams as other research has revealed. However, the test anxiety levels factor did not appear to interact with the variations in item presentation.

EXPERIMENT TWO

PROCEDURE ■ In an effort to study similarity in content material as an item arrangement procedure, 156 students enrolled in four sections of the same introductory educational psychology course were randomly given one of three different comprehensive final examination item formats. The 103 4-alternative multiple-choice items were presented in random order, in accord with the order of topic presentation during the course with items covering similar concepts or material presented together, or in converse order with topics presented during the course but with items covering similar content together.

FINDINGS ■ Varying the presentation of the items on the test did not significantly influence the students' time taking the test and that students classified as having high, moderate, or low test anxiety did not expend significantly different amounts of time taking the examination.

These tests indicate that the item presentation formats did not influence student performance on the final examination nor did this factor interact with the levels of test anxiety.

The cell means for the analyses completed in this experiment are presented on Table 2.

TABLE 2. *Cell Means for the Analyses Completed on the 103 Item Final Examination*

	Time as Dependent Variable Anxiety					Achievement Score as Dependent Variable Anxiety			
	Hi	Ave	Low			Hi	Ave	Low	
A₁	67.0	62.4	63.5	64.5	A₁	68.6	74.0	73.6	71.8
A₂	74.8	63.7	72.5	69.3	A₂	68.6	68.7	78.3	71.7
A₃	71.7	67.4	72.4	70.5	A₃	65.4	68.8	74.8	69.5
	70.5	64.5	69.1			67.4	70.3	74.4	

A₁ = Random item arrangement
A₂ = Items arranged by content and as presented in class
A₃ = Items arranged by content and opposite to order presented in class

CONCLUSION AND DISCUSSION

In conclusion these experimental results suggest that, even on relatively lengthy examinations which are administered as a classroom or power test, one need not be greatly concerned with arranging test items by difficulty, in order of class presentation, or by similarity of content covered at least in terms of influencing required testing time or student performance. However, on a logical versus an empirical basis, one might still advise a teacher to place a few easy items at the beginning of a test to possibly ease initial test anxiety; but any additional time spent on arranging items by difficulty or content might more profitably be spent on improving teacher-devised tests in other ways.

Generalizations from the results of these experiments must be tempered by additional research as the sample consisted of only college students enrolled in an introductory educational psychology course, as only a limited number of item arrangements were studied, and as no effort was made to investigate the effect of item arrangements upon test reliability and validity. However, as neither the existing empirical data nor logical scrutiny would seem to warrant the practice, it would seem advisable for test and measurement instructors to reconsider if not discontinue suggesting these item arrangement procedures for teacher devised examinations until other data can be obtained from more encompassing studies.

23 *Writing Neatness, Composition Errors, and Essay Grades*

JON C. MARSHALL AND JERRY M. POWERS

Could you answer—or score—an essay item and not wonder about the effects of such variables as writing neatness and composition errors on the rating? Even if raters wish to disregard such extraneous variables, are they likely to be able to do so? Drs. Marshall and Powers have conducted a series of studies to estimate the effects of selected variables on essay grades. One of their studies is reported in the following article. For which variable (writing neatness or composition errors) were the results as you would have expected? What would be the probable effect of using a more structured essay for such a study?

Reprinted and abridged with permission of the first-named author and publisher from *Journal of Educational Measurement*, 1969, Vol. 6, pp. 97–101.

Few concerns in educational measurement have a longer history than those of the effects of reader idiosyncrasies on grades assigned to essays. Marks assigned to essays reflect factors extraneous to the purpose of the exam (Klein & Hart, 1968; Stalnaker, 1951). The effects of these factors were noted in early studies by Edgeworth (1888 and 1890) and Starch and Elliott (1912, 1913a, and 1913b), and since then have been pointed to by measurement specialists as shortcomings of essay exams.

Paper characteristics such as handwriting quality and composition errors are usually apparent to teachers, but in differing degrees, and thus they could logically be factors affecting the grades of an essay exam. With somewhat conflicting results, these factors have been reported to relate significantly to grades assigned to essays (Chase, 1967; Klein & Hart, 1968; Marshall, 1967; Scannell & Marshall, 1966). The relative influence of these characteristics on essay grades has varied considerably among the reported literature.

The purpose of this study was to present further evidence on this issue. Toward this end, the effects of handwriting neatness, composition errors, and their interaction on grades assigned by prospective teachers to an essay exam were analyzed.

PROCEDURE

The general plan for this study was similar to that used for two earlier studies reported by Scannell and Marshall (1966) and Marshall (1967). The same essay exam was used for the three studies. It was based on a question provided by a teacher of American history in Grade 12. The question was: "Was the Civil War avoidable? Take a stand. Support your position in terms of the social, political, and economic events and conditions preceding the War Between the States as discussed in this course." A student's answer which had been assigned a grade of A was supplied by the teacher. This answer was modified by several educators so that it was about B quality. This was supported by the two earlier studies in which 132 prospective teachers and 100 American history teachers assigned mean grades of about B − and B, respectively, to the typed form containing no composition errors. The exact quality of the response is of little consequence as long as a ceiling is not imposed by a perfect or near perfect response.

After the content had been adjusted, the essay was edited so that no gross writing flaws appeared. Then 12 forms of the essay were constructed which contained various numbers of spelling, grammar, or punctuation errors. Twelve high school English teachers participated in this phase of development, with each requested to identify composition errors typical of high school students.

In the Marshall (1967) study, 13 forms of the essay, identical in content but differing in the types and number of composition errors, were graded by 700

American history teachers. They were instructed to grade the exam on the content of the answer. The results indicated an inverse trend between the number of composition errors and the grade assigned to the essay exam. Of particular importance was that the differences between the form lacking in gross composition errors and the forms containing errors were significant for the forms containing 12 or more spelling errors and those containing 12 or more grammatical errors. It was concluded that teachers are influenced by composition quality on essay exams even when they attempt to grade solely on content.

Based on these earlier results, the investigators decided to examine the interaction of handwriting neatness with only the extreme composition error forms: no errors, 18 spelling errors, and 18 grammar errors. These three forms comprised 3 of the 13 forms used in the previous study. The spelling form contained 18 errors evenly scattered throughout the essay. These errors consisted of misspellings such as "Thorecally," "Arstocracy," "Thretened," "Tenshun," "Permated," and "Presidentsy." The grammar form contained 18 errors in verb form, verb tense, use of pronouns, and the like scattered throughout the essay.

Four different writing categories were identified for this study. The first of these was a clean, typewritten copy. The remaining categories represented three levels of hand-writing neatness: neatly written, easy-to-read essay; fairly neatly written, fairly easy-to-read essay; and poorly written, difficult-to-read essay. The nine handwritten forms were written in black ink by three high school boys, with each writer preparing copies of the three error forms. Therefore, the three error forms at each neatness level were prepared by the same individual. These handwritten forms were copied from their respective typewritten forms. Thus, what appeared to be equivalent neatness forms were prepared for each of the error forms.

The 12 forms of the essay response (four categories of writing by three types of errors) were graded by 420 prospective teachers enrolled in undergraduate history of American education and educational psychology classes at the University of Missouri—St. Louis. The essays were graded by the prospective teachers during regular class periods. The essays were sequentially ordered before administering to the readers to guard against systematic bias associated with a class or within a class. The administration took approximately 20 minutes of class time.

Each reader was given a research packet which included one of the 12 examination forms and a complete set of directions. These directions contained: (*a*) a statement indicating that the grades were to be based only upon the content of the answer; (*b*) the complete essay question; (*c*) an outline indicating the content that an outstanding response would contain; and (*d*) a description of the 9-point grading scale to be used, where nine equals "outstanding," seven equals "good," etc. The directions were highly detailed and explicitly stated that the essay was to be graded on content only. In part, the directions stated,

"Grade this examination on *content alone relative to the accompanying content outline* and *what might be expected of a high school senior.* Disregard *everything* but the factors relevant to the content outline."

RESULTS

The means and standard deviations of grades assigned to the 12 essay forms are presented in Table 1. Differences among treatment means were significant for both composition errors and writing. The interaction effect between them was not significant.[1]

TABLE 1. *Means and Standard Deviations of Grades Assigned to the Twelve Forms of the Essay*[a]

Type of Composition Errors		Writing Neatness				Type Means
		typed	neat	fair	poor	
No Errors	Mean	5.86	6.06	5.46	5.43	5.70
	S.D.	1.63	1.53	1.46	1.71	1.61
Spelling	Mean	5.31	5.46	4.63	5.40	5.20
	S.D.	1.43	1.53	1.46	1.53	1.59
Grammar	Mean	4.29	5.46	4.97	4.91	4.91
	S.D.	1.68	1.42	1.66	1.59	1.65
Writing Neatness Means	Mean	5.15	5.66	5.02	5.25	5.27
	S.D.	1.71	1.62	1.57	1.63	1.65

[a] Based on a nine-category scale in which a grade of C equals 5. N = 35 per cell.

The scores assigned to the three error forms and those assigned to the four writing forms were also compared. For writing forms, only the difference between the mean score assigned to the neat handwritten essay (5.66) and the mean score assigned to the fair handwritten one (5.02) was statistically significant (p less than .05). The means for both the spelling and grammar forms were significantly lower than the mean for the no errors form (p less than .05). No other significant differences were found.

DISCUSSION

The results of this study indicate that prospective teachers are influenced by

---

[1] There would have been an interaction if the grades for certain level(s) of writing neatness when combined with certain type(s) of composition errors had been different from what would have been predicted from the appropriate means for neatness and composition errors. For example, there would have been more of an interaction if the mean for the treatment of neat writing combined with spelling errors (here 5.46) was much lower than expected from the mean for all neat writing treatments (5.66) and the mean for the treatments involving spelling errors (5.20). (Eds.)

the quality of composition and the writing neatness of an essay response, even when they are given explicit directions to grade on content alone in accordance with an outline of desired content.

The differences found in this study between composition forms were consistent with those reported in the earlier studies. Since composition errors did not interact significantly with writing, no further discussion on this factor will be presented.

It is interesting to note the relative effects of the various writing forms. The highest mean grade was assigned to the *neat, easy-to-read, handwritten* essay. The mean grade assigned to the fair handwritten essay was the only one significantly lower than this value. The rank order of the writing form means was from highest to lowest: neat handwritten essay, poor handwritten essay, typewritten essay, and fair handwritten essay. The relative positions in this hierarchy of the latter three forms are somewhat surprising in that it might have been expected that a good typewritten paper would serve to the advantage of the examinee and a poor handwritten paper would serve to his disadvantage. Whether the failure of the study to support this hypothesis was an artifact of the somewhat unusual grading situation, or whether it was a reflection of the actual effects of writing neatness on essay grades is open to conjecture.

24   *Measuring Attitudes in the Classroom*

STEPHEN M. COREY

To what extent are educators aware of the attitudes of their students? While educators have definite ideas of desired changes in students' attitudes, they tend to have little relevant information at the end of the school term, let alone at the beginning. Dr. Corey briefly discusses attitude measurement and illustrates a procedure which may be used by a teacher. What would be other illustrations of attitudes amenable to being measured with this approach? What are some of the benefits of having students participate in constructing the scale? What are some of the advantages and disadvantages of Corey's approach compared with that of Webb's as described in the previous chapter?

Elaboration of this topic can be found in books by Edwards (1957) and Oppenheim (1966).

Many recent publications have stressed the importance of giving instruction in attitudes, new values, and points of view to elementary school pupils. One of

Reprinted and abridged with permission of the author and publisher from *Elementary School Journal*, 1943, Vol. 43, pp. 457–461.

the limitations that trouble most teachers who concern themselves with changing the attitudes of their pupils is their inability to know when the attitudes have been changed. Rather effective methods have been developed for measuring learning that involve the acquisition of facts and knowledge, and much progress has been made within the past few years in appraising learning that results in the ability to use knowledge, apply principles, and make inferences. The tests that relate to attitudinal growth, however, leave much to be desired. There is an extensive research literature on the subject, but most of the articles written are not published in journals which come to the attention of classroom teachers.

DEFINITION OF AN ATTITUDE

An attitude may be defined as an emotionally colored predisposition to behave antagonistically or protagonistically, sympathetically or unsympathetically, with respect to any referent, whether it be a person, a group of persons, an institution, a practice, an object, or an idea. Those referents with respect to which our attitudes are protagonistic are values. When our attitudes toward certain referents are antagonistic, those referents are aversions. We tend to have positive or negative attitudes toward almost everything we experience, but the intensity of the attitude, in many cases, is so mild as to make us relatively unaware of any "feeling" about the referent.

DIFFICULTY OF MEASURING ATTITUDES

At the present time strenuous efforts are being made by the press, the radio, and innumerable organized groups, including the schools, to develop and change the attitudes of children and of adults. To determine whether or not real changes have occurred is very difficult, especially when one is forced to resort to paper-and-pencil tests. There is often a wide discrepancy between an attitude as it is reflected in the overt behavior of children and an attitude as it is reported by them on some opinion questionnaire. The writer (Corey, 1937) for example, found that scores on a highly reliable attitude scale measuring opinion were not at all related to actual behavior.

This discrepancy between publicly professed attitudes and actual behavior is greatest, of course, when the behavior in question is likely to lead to censure of some sort. This problem complicates greatly the interpretation of all public-opinion polls on crucial and highly emotionalized issues, and it is on just such issues that we stand in greatest need of knowing what public opinion is.

A TECHNIQUE FOR MEASURING ATTITUDES

Be that as it may be, the following suggestions for obtaining, by the use of quick paper-and-pencil tests, some notion of the attitudes of elementary school children in a class toward any practice or institution or object may have utility. Not only does the technique provide a method for deriving an attitude scale of a simple sort from the population being studied, but it also serves to stimulate discussion. The suggestions made are elaborated at length in several technical articles. (e.g., Thurstone, 1928). The procedure is applicable in the upper elementary school grades and higher.

STEP 1. COLLECTING ATTITUDINAL 'STATEMENTS ■ A teacher who has decided to attempt to bring about a change in the attitude of children toward "Honesty on Examinations" might proceed by first asking each pupil in the class to write down three or four simple statements which represent various attitudes toward cheating. For orientation, illustrations such as the following might be mentioned.

> Cheating is as bad as stealing.
> If a test isn't fair, cheating is all right.
> I won't copy, but I often let someone else look on my paper.
> A little cheating on daily tests doesn't hurt.

In a class of 25–35 children, assuming that the question is one of some concern to them, this simple procedure of collecting attitudinal statements should result in approximately a hundred more or less different opinions about classroom cheating. In order to obtain even a longer list (and this request will be greeted with enthusiasm by most of the children), the pupils might be asked to get similar statements from their parents and friends. This interviewing frequently helps to clarify the children's concept of the referent under consideration and, too, results in the accumulation of a wider variety of attitudinal statements.

STEP 2. SELECTING THE STATEMENTS ■ The 150 or 200 attitudinal statements obtained from the children and their acquaintances are then examined carefully by the teacher, who eliminates obvious duplications and expressions of fact rather than opinion. Wang (1932) has suggested, among others, these criteria (paraphrased and illustrated by the writer) for the selection of good statements to be included in attitude scales.

1. The statement must be debatable; facts or universal truths are out of place.
Poor.—Cheating is against the rules of the school.
Better.—There should be a school rule against cheating.
2. The attitude statement should not be susceptible to more than one interpretation.
Poor.—Teachers would be surprised at the amount of cheating that goes on around here.
3. So-called "double-barreled" statements should be avoided.
Poor.—Cheating is bad, but on an unfair test everyone cheats.

4. Short statements are preferable.

5. Technical terms should be avoided.

The statements which remain after this culling are then mimeographed or duplicated in some other fashion, and the children in the class are asked to check with a plus sign all statements which they believe represent opinions favoring cheating in examinations and with a minus sign all statements which they believe represent opinions opposed to such cheating. This procedure, of course, is the acid test of ambiguity of statement for the population involved and normally results in discussion. By a showing of hands if time is short, or by actual tabulation if there is sufficient time, the teacher can then record the number of plus and minus signs for each of the statements. A rather large number of statements will turn out to be ambiguous in the sense that many of the children will believe the statement favors classroom cheating, while another large group will believe the statement represents an antagonistic opinion. These ambiguous statements can be eliminated. Almost any quantitative criterion can be used, but the writer has found that there is some merit in retaining all statements on which approximately 80 percent of the pupils are in agreement regarding the attitudinal implications of the statements.

STEP 3. ADMINISTERING THE QUESTIONNAIRE ■ The selected statements can be presented to the pupils for reaction in several ways. If time and money are at a premium, the statements can be dictated without seriously interfering with the effectiveness of the testing technique. It is better, of course, to have the statements mimeographed. They can be presented with directions such as these:

This is not a test in the sense that any particular statement is either right or wrong. All these sentences represent opinions that some people hold about cheating on tests. Indicate whether you agree or disagree with the statement by putting a plus sign before all the opinions with which you agree and a minus sign before those with which you disagree. If you are uncertain, use a question mark. After you have gone through the entire list, go back and draw a circle around the minus signs where you disagree very strongly.

It is best not to encourage much discussion at this stage because some of the children are too ready to change their reactions to make them harmonize with group judgments. Some advantage might be gained by having the pupils respond anonomously or even by having them indicate not their own opinion but that of a majority of their classmates.

STEP 4. SCORING THE QUESTIONNAIRE ■ The papers can be scored by the pupils or by the teacher. The former method is quite satisfactory if a very clear statement is made of the scoring directions. It is convenient to score questionnaires in such a way that a high score always means a favorable attitude toward the practice or institution involved, while a low score represents an antagonistic or unfavorable attitude. The first step in the scoring procedure is to go over all the statements and underline those which, in the opinion of most of the pupils (Step 2), favor classroom cheating. The reason for this procedure is that the statements favoring and those opposing the referent are scored differently.

The following scoring values are used for the statements favoring cheating: A plus sign with a circle around it yields five points; a plus sign, four points; a question mark, three points; a minus sign, two points; and a minus sign with a circle around it, one point. Thus, when a person disagrees very strongly with a statement which favors classroom cheating, he earns only one point, whereas, if he agrees very strongly with this same statement, he gets five points.

Those statements which oppose cheating are scored in just the opposite fashion. A plus sign with a circle around it yields one point; a plus sign, two points, etc. In other words, the person who disagrees violently with a statement which opposes cheating actually has a very favorable attitude toward such a practice.

If the questionnaire includes 50 items, the maximum score, which indicates a most favorable attitude toward whatever idea, or practice, or institution, or condition is being considered, would be 250. A score implying indifference would be in the neighborhood of 150, or three points on the average for each statement. Very low scores would indicate antagonistic attitudes, with the minimum score being 50.

ADVANTAGES OF USING ATTITUDE SCALES

When a distribution of attitudinal scores for a group is available, many interesting relationships can be investigated. Some light can be cast on the relation to attitude of sex, intelligence, parents' occupation and educational status, as well as a number of other factors. The most significant inquiries, however, have to do with changes in attitude. Scales such as those described above can be used more than once if the time interval is at least several weeks. Anonymous reactions would not preclude study of group change.

The use of rough-and-ready methods such as this to get some preliminary estimate of the attitudes that children have toward an issue makes it possible for a teacher to determine, after a period of instruction, whether or not the children's learning experiences have brought about a change, at least in their verbal opinions. The chances are that very little effective attitudinal instruction will take place unless teachers have some such approximate method of finding out the effectiveness of the learning activities in which the children engage.

25   *Some Implications of Cultural Factors for Test Construction*

ANNE ANASTASI

Should we retain test items that distinguish cultural or other groups? This is an old question that recently has received extensive legal consideration, thereby demonstrating the heightened concern for providing opportunities for disadvantaged and minority groups. Anastasi provides several ideas to consider on this issue. Can you illustrate situations in which the addition or deletion of particular types of items would increase validity? Would decrease it? Would leave it unchanged? Try extending Anastasi's arguments and your own illustrations to questions of content or construct validity.

Every psychological test is a sample of behavior. As such, psychological tests will—and should—reflect any factors that influence behavior. It is obvious that every psychological test is constructed within a specific cultural framework. Most tests are validated against practical criteria dictated by the particular culture. School achievement and vocational success are two familiar examples of such criteria.

In the construction of certain tests, special consideration has been given to cultural group differences in the selection of test items. The practices followed with regard to items showing significant group differences may be illustrated, first, with reference to sex differences. Insofar as the two sexes represent subcultures with distinct mores in our society, sex differences in item performance may be regarded as cultural differentials. The Stanford-Binet is probably one of the clearest examples of a test in which sex differences were deliberately eliminated from total scores. This was accomplished in part by dropping items that yielded a significant sex difference in percent passing. It is interesting to note, however, that it did not prove feasible to discard all such items, but that a number of remaining items that significantly favored one sex were balanced by items favoring the other sex. The opposite procedure was followed in the construction of the Terman-Miles Interest-Attitude Analysis (Terman and Miles, 1936), as well as in other similar personality tests designed to yield a Masculinity-Femininity Index. In these cases, it was just those items with large and significant sex differences in frequency of response that were retained.

Reprinted and abridged with permission of the author and publisher from the *Proceedings of the 1949 Invitational Conference on Testing Problems*, Educational Testing Service, Princeton, N.J., 1950, pp. 13–17. All rights reserved.

Another type of group difference that has been considered in the selection of test items is illustrated by the so-called culture-free tests,[1] such as the Leiter International Performance Scale (Leiter, 1940) and the R. B. Cattell's Culture-Free Intelligence Test (Cattell, 1940; Cattell, Feingold, and Sarasen, 1940). In these tests, a systematic attempt is made to include only content that is universally familiar in all cultures. In actual practice, of course, such tests fall considerably short of this goal. Moreover, the term "culture-common" would probably be more accurate than "culture-free," since at best, performance on such items is free from cultural differences, but not from cultural influences.

As a last example, let us consider socioeconomic level as a basis for the evaluation of test items. One of the objectives of the extensive research project conducted by Haggard, Davis, and Havighurst (Haggard, Davis, and Havighurst, 1948; Davis and Havighurst, 1948) is to eliminate from intelligence tests those items that differentiate significantly between children of high and low socioeconomic status. On the other side of the picture, we find the work of Harrison Gough (1948) in the construction of the Social Status Scale of the Minnesota Multiphasic Personality Inventory. In this scale, only those items were retained that showed significant differences in frequency of response between individuals in two contrasted social groups.

It is apparent that different investigators have treated the problem of cultural differences in test scores in opposite ways. An obvious answer is that the procedure depends upon the purpose of the test. But such an answer may evade the real issue. Perhaps it is the purpose of the tests which should be more carefully examined. There seems to be some practical justification for constructing a test out of items that show the maximum group differentiation. With such a test, we can determine more clearly the degree to which an individual is behaviorally identified with a particular group. It is difficult to see, however, under what conditions we should want to study individual differences in just those items in which socioeconomic or other cultural group differences are lacking. What will the resulting test be a measure of? Criteria are themselves correlated with socioeconomic and other cultural conditions. The validity of a test for such criteria would probably be lowered by eliminating the "cultural differentials." If cultural factors are important determiners of behavior, why eliminate their influence from tests designed to sample and predict such behavior?

To be sure, a test *may* be invalidated by the presence of uncontrolled cultural factors. But this would occur only when the given cultural factor affects the test without affecting the criterion. It is a question of the *breadth* of the influence affecting the test score. For example, the inclusion of questions dealing with a fairy tale familiar to children in one cultural group and not in another

---

[1] Culture-free has been replaced by the more modest term culture-fair. (Eds.)

would probably lower the validity of the test for most criteria. On the other hand, if one social group does more poorly on certain items because of poor facility in the use of English, the inclusion of these items would probably not reduce the validity of the test. In this case, the same factor that lowered the test score would also handicap the individual in his educational and vocational progress, as well as in many other aspects of daily living. In like manner, slow work habits, emotional instability, poor motivation, lack of interest in abstract matters, and many other conditions that may affect test scores are also likely to influence a relatively broad area of criterion behavior.

Whether or not an item is retained in a test should depend ultimately upon its correlation with a criterion. Tests cannot be constructed in a vacuum. They must be designed to meet specific needs. These needs should be defined in advance and should determine the choice of criterion. This would seem to be self-evident, but it is sometimes forgotten in the course of discussions about tests. Some statements made regarding tests imply a belief that tests are designed to measure a spooky, mysterious "thing" which resides in the individual and which has been designated by such terms as "Intelligence," "Ability Level," or "Innate Potentiality." The assumption seems to be that such "intelligence" has been merely overlaid with a concealing cloak of culture. All we would thus need to do would be to strip off the cloak and the person's "true" ability would stand revealed. My only reaction to such a viewpoint is to say that, if we are going to function within the domain of science, we must have operational definitions of tests. The only way I know of obtaining such operational definitions is in terms of the criteria against which the test was validated. This is true whether a so-called practical criterion is employed or whether the criterion itself is defined in terms of other tests, as in factorial validity. Any procedure, such as the discarding of certain items, that raises the correlation of the test with the criterion, enables us to give a more precise operational definition of the test. But we cannot discard items merely on the basis of some principle which has been laid down *a priori,* such as the rule that items showing significant group differences must be eliminated. If this procedure should lower the validity coefficient of the test, it could have neither practical nor theoretical justification.

It is also pertinent to inquire what would happen if we were to carry such a procedure to its logical conclusion. If we start eliminating items that differentiate subgroups of the population, where shall we stop? We could with equal justification proceed to rule out items showing socioeconomic differences, sex differences, differences among ethnic minority groups, and educational differences. Any items in which college graduates excell elementary school graduates could, for example, be discarded on this basis. Nor should we retain items that differentiate among broader groups, such as national cultures, or between preliterate and more advanced cultures. If we do all this, I should like to ask only two questions in conclusion. First, what will be left? Secondly, in terms of any criterion we may wish to predict, what will be the validity of this minute residue?

26   *Improving a Teacher-Made Test: A Case Study*

EARL FOREMAN

The following article presents in a rather nontechnical manner the logical sequence of procedures used in developing a test. A common-sense approach to test development is indicated throughout the study. Obviously a considerable amount of time went into constructing and refining the instrument described in this paper. Considering the kinds and significance of the evaluations that are likely to be made on the basis of a classroom test, the effort would seem to be justified. What effect did the revision of the directions for taking the test have on reliability? How did the item response data lead to test revisions? What effect did the item analysis have on reliability?

The writer desired to construct a test in the area of literature comprehension at the seventh-grade level. After careful consideration, certain objectives were selected for measurement. Table 1 shows these objectives and the number of times each objective was included among the test items.

The purpose was to measure the skills named as many times and through as wide a variety of devices as was possible in a reasonably timed test. Literary selections were chosen from various sources, and in certain cases the writer composed selections to test specific abilities. The items were arranged roughly in progressive order from simple to difficult. Since the object was to measure depth of comprehension without regard to rate, no time limit was set for the test. As a "dry-run" trial the test was administered individually to children at various levels and to adults, one of whom was an English instructor. Through this device surface defects, such as ambiguities in language and structural obscurities, were discovered and eliminated before the actual administration of the test.

The test in final form consisted of ten sections. Each part contained one literary selection followed by certain statements concerning the selection. By restricting the number of selections, the writer was able to measure, within samples of broader continuity, a factor which seemed of considerable importance in the

Reprinted and abridged with permission of the publisher (the University of Chicago Press) from an article entitled, "Improving the Reliability of a Teacher-Made Test", which appeared in the *School Review*, 1950 (May), Vol. 58, pp. 285–290.

TABLE 1. *Objectives Selected to Be Measured in a Literature-Comprehension Test*

Objective	Number of Times Included
1. Understanding of the situation portrayed	6
2. Understanding of the underlying cause and result of the situation	3
3. Understanding of the author's intent	6
4. Understanding of the moral or lesson, if any	4
5. Understanding of the meaning of specific lines	4
6. Understanding of the meaning of specific words	16
7. Understanding of the meaning of words or phrases used differently in separate contexts	7
8. Critical determination of good and lesser literature	2
9. Ability to compare and analyze central thoughts	2
10. Ability to discover in selections accepted life values or criteria and to distinguish them from values not generally accepted	2

evaluation of most of the skills listed.

For various statistical purposes the first edition of the test was administered to both seventh- and eighth-grade pupils. A total population of ninety pupils took the test—forty-four in Grade VII and forty-six in Grade VIII. As was to be expected, this first administration revealed obvious faults. Among these perhaps the most serious was a low reliability coefficient of .52 as calculated by the Kuder-Richardson Method.

REVISING THE TEST

REVISION OF THE DIRECTIONS ■ The decision was made to revise the test in an effort to increase the reliability. One of the more commonly known devices, that of lengthening the test, was rejected as being impractical in this case and, furthermore, as being a statistical rather than an evidential technique. Instead, attention was directed toward adjustment and revision within the test as it was then constructed.

Upon careful consideration the question arose regarding the pupil's ability to understand the directions given in the test and the difficulty he might experience in indicating his response choices on the test form. It was decided to revise the directions only and to determine what effect this would have on the reliability of the test.

One fault appeared to lie in the method by which the pupil was asked to indicate his answers. In the first edition each literary selection was followed by groups of statements about the selection. One statement in each group was true. The statements were lettered, and corresponding letters were printed at the right margin of the form. The pupil was directed to cross out the letter at the right which corresponded to the letter in front of the true statement. An example taken from the test is given below.

Item 1. In this poem the author is:
  a) Telling a story
  b) Talking nonsense
  c) Describing a scene
  d) Pointing out a moral   a b c d

It seemed unsound psychologically to ask the pupils to cross out a correct-response indication. In addition, he was asked to transfer his attention from the statements to groups of letters placed elsewhere. It should be remembered that this test was constructed for seventh-grade children who, for the greater part, were not "test-wise" in such matters as the use of separate answer sheets. The new directions simplified the answering procedure by asking the pupil to encircle the letter in front of the true statement in each group. This eliminated the attention split and called for a positive response.

In the original administration of the test no introduction was given either by the administrator or within the test form. The pupil was presented immediately with the first selection. In an effort to make clear exactly what the pupil was to do, the revised form included a preface, which presented explanatory samples similar to the material in the test. Directions, marking procedures, and format exactly duplicated the test content. Three groups of statements were presented with each sample selection. In the first group the correct response was indicated. In the second group the pupil was told which was the true statement and was directed to encircle the letter in front of it. In the third group the pupil was asked to determine the correct statement and to indicate it in the proper manner. During the administration of the test the pupils and the administrator read the preface together, and the administrator made sure the pupils understood the directions before proceeding with the test.

Other directions were modified in the attempt to clarify for the child what was to be done. In one section of the test, for example, two literary selections were used instead of one. A short paragraph was introduced in the revised form to indicate to the pupil the departure from the usual form. The mortality on one of the last sections of the test had been high in the first administration. While some of this difficulty was acceptable and was probably due to the complexities presented in the section, it was thought that confusion might be partially due to obscure directions. The directions were, therefore, reworded, and a longer example was included which closely approximated the material in the section. In the original edition the last section had required two answers. The directions were revised so that only one answer needed to be indicated. This revision was accomplished without diminishing in any way the measuring value of the item.

No changes were made in the actual test material. Literary selections, statements, wording of items, and arrangements of items were reprinted exactly as they had appeared in the previous edition. Although certain items obviously needed revision or deletion, the object on this particular administration was to determine the effect of the revision of directions on the reliability. The Kuder-Richardson technique was applied to the scores of the second administration, and the calculations yielded a reliability coefficient of .78. Since no changes had been made other than in directions, the conclusion was reached that for this population the revision of directions was probably responsible for the increased reliability.

REVISION OF THE TEST ITEMS ■ The second attempt to increase the reliability was made through revising the test items. Item analyses had been made on both administrations of the test. An examination revealed that several items should be altered or discarded completely. The difficulty of determining in advance what sorts of changes in items will bring about desired results is illustrated in the following example, of which the results of revision were not significantly successful. One of the first selections presented the story of the fox, the crow, and the piece of cheese. An item concerning the fable follows.

Item 2. The moral in this story is:
    a) Beware of foxes
    b) Use any method you can to get food when you are hungry
    c) Beware of flattery
    d) Don't try to sing if you know you can't

The statement identified by the letter c is, of course, the correct response. However, 29 percent of the pupils in the first administration and 22 percent of the pupils in the second administration had indicated statement d as their choice. It was possible either that the word "flattery" was unfamiliar to many children at the seventh-grade level or that statement d too nearly approached a reasonable solution for the child. An effort to discriminate more closely was made by changing both statements. Statement c in the new form read, "Beware of too much praise." Statement d read, "If you sing, you may lose your food." The results on this item in three administrations of the test are given in Table 2.

For this small population the revision of the item had no significant effect. The revision of a second item was more successful. This selection was a poem in five stanzas. The fourth verse of each stanza indicated that the reader was to complete the thought of the stanza in any manner he chose. This is to say, the poet had written what was actually nonsense verse, concluding each stanza with such a remark as, "Anything you choose to say!" An item following the selection appears below.

Item 3. The poet who wrote this selection:
    a) Is telling a story
    b) Thinks that your ideas are better than his
    c) Is getting you to imagine the story yourself

On the first administration 45 percent of the pupils indicated the correct answer, c. However, 47 percent indicated statement a as the correct response. On the second administration 30 percent of the pupils indicated statement *a* as their choice. Examination of the selection revealed the fact that statement *a* might be considered correct, since the poem actually was a little story although it was incomplete. Statement *a* was changed to read "The poet . . . has no idea of how to write a poem." Results of the three administrations on this item are also shown in Table 2.

For this population, revision of the statement eliminated the persistent indication of what had been previously considered a false response. The overbalance

TABLE 2. *Pupil Responses to Two Statements Appearing in Three Editions of a Literature-Comprehension Test*

Statement and Edition of Test	Number of Pupils	Percent of Pupils Indicating Each Choice as Correct			
		a)	b)	c)	d)
Item 2:					
Edition I	44	9	9	53	29
Edition II	46	7	14	57	22
Edition III	54	12	12	54	22
Item 3:					
Edition I	44	47	6	45	. .
Edition II	46	30	4	60	. .
Edition III	54	4	4	92	. .

of correct responses on the last edition, although this selection is near the less difficult end of the scale, probably calls for some consideration of an increase in the over-all difficulty of the particular group of statements.

Various other item revisions were made. One group of statements concerning a selection in the middle range of difficulty showed a correct response of only 17 percent on the first administration and 9 percent on the second administration. The other two groups of statements concerning the same selection yielded correct responses ranging from 55 percent to 67 percent in the two administrations. While it was expected and entirely acceptable that considerable variation would occur within the groups in any one section, such a wide differential was felt to be a violation of the consistency of the instrument. The entire group of statements under question was discarded, and a new set on a simpler level was devised. The third administration resulted in a correct response of 72 percent.

One of the literary selections was an excerpt from an essay by Emerson. Certain words were incorrectly substituted, other words were misspelled, and various errors were introduced. The pupils were to indicate the errors. Results on the first two administrations were so poor that it appeared that this section of the test was too difficult for any of the seventh-grade pupils tested. The extreme difficulty was traced in part to the original article, which, it was decided, was probably too abstract for Grade VII even in its correct form. A simpler article was written which retained the same number and types of errors. The results of the administration of this item were more satisfactory. While still difficult enough to discriminate, the scoring results were evened out so as to approach more closely the curve of the entire test.

Statistical treatment of the results of the third edition of the entire test yielded a reliability coefficient by the Kuder-Richardson method of .82. While this figure is still not high, the various revisions had resulted in an overall increase of .30 in reliability. Further revision is indicated, and of course administration of the test to larger populations will yield more reliable data.

27   Item Selection Techniques and the Evaluation of Instructional Objectives

RICHARD C. COX

Test experts agree that for a classroom test to be considered valid there must exist a high degree of correspondence between the instructional objectives and the test items. Evaluation of the items must involve both thoughtful and subjective evaluation by a subject-matter expert, as well as statistical data bearing on item difficulty (how many examinees respond correctly) and discrimination (does the item correlate with a logical criterion, usually total test score). A tremendous variety of item analysis techniques have been devised (see, for example, Davis, 1951 and 1952 and Henrysson, 1971). The following procedures described by Cox are representative of the usual methods employed by classroom teachers and commercial test publishers.

If we rely solely on statistical data in the selection of items, what kinds of biases might be introduced into the final test? How does the type of behavior measured with the test item (Taxonomy classification) interact with difficulty and discrimination?

The initial planning of an educational achievement test involves the identification of the subject-matter content and the instructional objectives to be tested. A two-way table of specifications is often utilized at this stage of test construction to insure that these two aspects of test construction are represented.

The *Taxonomy of Educational Objectives* (Bloom, 1956) can be used to classify

Reprinted and abridged with permission of author and publisher from the *Journal of Educational Measurement*, 1965, Vol. 2, pp. 181–185.

test items. To accurately classify a test item it is necessary to know or assume the learning experiences which have preceded the administration of the test. It has been demonstrated that such a classification of test items into the major categories of the Taxonomy can be accomplished with a considerable degree of reliability.

The usual procedure in objective test construction is to prepare a larger pool of test items than will be used in the final form of the instrument. This large pool of items is administered to a tryout group to obtain statistical information to aid in the selection of items for the final test form. When the test is designed to rank subjects on some specified characteristics, item-discriminating power is often used as the criterion for selection of items.

Using the Taxonomy it is possible to classify the items in the original item pool according to the instructional objectives they are designed to measure. If the final form of the evaluation instrument is to validly measure the objectives identified in the original item pool, the method of item selection should not appreciably alter the taxonomical structure of the original item pool. If the item selection procedure biases the final test form by disproportionate selection of items measuring certain instructional objectives, the final form of the test will not validly evaluate the objectives measured by the total test pool. It is the purpose of this study to evaluate the effect of statistical item selection on the structure of the final evaluation instrument as compared with the structure of the original item pool.

PROCEDURE

The item pool used in this study was comprised of 379 four- and five-option multiple-choice items used in an introductory college-level natural science course. The 379 items were classified using the categories of the Taxonomy. Three judges worked independently on this classification using the examples presented in the Taxonomy and in Nelson (1961). There was agreement on the classification of approximately 85 percent of the items. The classification of the remaining items was established after consultation with the subject-matter expert. The total pool of 379 items was classified as follows: Knowledge 108 (27%), Comprehension 110 (29%), Application 91 (24%), and Analysis 76 (20%). None of the items were classified in the Synthesis and Evaluation categories.

Samples of 1,000 males and 1,000 females were selected at random from the 3,150 students who had taken the natural science examinations. The mean score was 235.86 for males and 233.70 for females.

The upper and lower 270 subjects (27 percent) in each distribution were used to compute indices of item difficulty and discrimination. The index of difficulty for a particular item was determined by the percentage of subjects in the upper and lower 27 percent of the total test scores who passed the item. No correction for guessing was employed. The difference and Davis indices were used as item discrimination coefficients.

The average difficulty level of items for males was 62.10 and for females 61.79. The test items were, on the average, slightly easier for males as reflected previously in the mean test scores. The average Difference index for males was 20.28 and for females 21.34. The average Davis index for males was 15.66 and for females 17.04. The difference indices are higher on the average than the Davis indices since the Difference index tends to assign higher values to middle difficulty items than does the Davis index. The higher average values for females also reflects difficulty levels.

To simulate the assembly of a final test form the 100 items with the highest Davis indices were selected from the total item pool. The procedure was repeated using the difference indices as the criteria for item selection. The procedures were followed for both male and female groups. There was approximately 80 percent overlap of common items selected by the two techniques.

RESULTS

Table 1 presents the average difficulty and discrimination indices computed on

TABLE 1. *Average Difficulty and Discrimination Indices by Taxonomical Category for Total Item Pool*

Taxonomical Category	Difficulty Index		Davis Index		Difference Index	
	Male	Female	Male	Female	Male	Female
Knowledge	65.98	66.39	15.25	16.83	19.28	20.18
Comprehension	63.74	63.45	17.16	18.08	22.32	23.22
Application	59.18	58.37	15.24	17.08	19.98	21.31
Analysis	58.04	57.29	14.54	15.79	19.01	20.21

the total item pool for the male and female groups.

The values of the average difficulty and discrimination indices differ with taxonomical category. The average difficulty levels increase with increasing complexity of taxonomical category. Knowledge items are easiest while Analysis items are the most difficult for both males and females.

The average discrimination indices also follow a similar pattern for males and females. In general, Comprehension items are the most discriminating while Analysis items are least discriminating.

After the 100 item tests were selected, the percentage of items classified in each taxonomical category was compiled. These values are presented in Table 2 along with the comparable percentages for the total item pool. Chi-square tests for the comparison of observed and theoretical frequencies were computed for each of the first four columns in Table 2 against the percentages in the total item pool. All chi-square values were significant at the .01 level.

TABLE 2. *Percentage of Most Discriminating Items Classified in Taxonomical Categories by Sex*

Taxonomical Categories	Males		Females		Total Item Pool
	Items Selected by:		Items Selected by:		
	Davis Index	Difference Index	Davis Index	Difference Index	
Knowledge	24	22	24	20	27
Comprehension	38	40	29	36	29
Application	18	21	31	27	24
Analysis	20	17	16	17	20
Total	100	100	100	100	100

The tests composed of the most discriminating items are not representative of the total item pool from which they were selected. These tests would not adequately measure the instructional objectives measured by the total item pool. In general, less emphasis is given to Knowledge and Analysis items and more emphasis to Comprehension items than is the case in the original item pool.

The chi-square test was also used to compare the percentage of items in each category for the male versus female groups. This was done separately for the Davis and Difference indices. Again, chi-square values were significant at the .01 level. These results are especially interesting since approximately 70 percent of the items selected were the same for the male and female groups.

CONCLUSIONS

The major conclusions of this study are as follows:

1. Statistical selection of items from the total item pool has a biasing effect on the selected tests. The proportion of items in the selected tests which measure certain instructional objectives is unlike the proportion of items in the total item pool which measures the same objectives. The selected tests are not representative of the total item pool in this respect.

2. Statistical selection of items from the total item pool operates differentially for male and female groups. When the statistical data obtained from the female tryout group is used to select tests from the total item pool, the results differ from those obtained using the male tryout group. The structure of the selected tests as indicated by the taxonomical structure of the items differs for the male and female groups.

IMPLICATIONS

The practice of statistical selection of items for the final form of an evaluation instrument is seriously questioned by the results of this study. Statistical item selection alone is not sufficient; other variables should be considered.

It has been shown that in the test pool the average discrimination values differ for the four major categories of items classified according to the instructional objective being measured. This should indicate to the test constructor that selection of items from the item pool on the basis of these discrimination indices will be biased in favor of the group of items which contains the highest average discrimination values. This suggests the possibility of selecting the most discriminating items within a particular taxonomical category rather than selecting the most discriminating items from the total item pool. The discrimination index would be computed using only those items in that particular category to obtain items which correlate well with other items in that category. In the planning stages the test constructor should specify the number of items measuring each instructional objective to be included in the final form of the test. The items for the item pool would be written accordingly. Then, within each category a specified number of items would be selected for inclusion in the final form of the test.

This study has also indicated that the sex make-up of the tryout groups has an effect on the statistical item selection. It is a well-known principle that the tryout groups should be essentially similar to the groups for which the test is to be used. The results of this study clearly indicate that the sex make-up of the tryout group makes a difference in the selection of certain types of items for inclusion in the final test form. If, for example, Application items discriminate better for females than for males, then a test constructed using discrimination indices based on a female tryout group will include more Application items than will a test constructed using data for a male tryout group. If the proportion of males and females in the group or groups for which the test is intended is not similar to the proportion of males and females in the tryout group, the test would not validly measure the instructional objectives specified in the planning stage. This could be a critical consideration in the construction or use of a test with an all-male or female group. The test constructor might consider the possibility of computing item discrimination indices separately by sex as well as by taxonomical category and selecting items for the final form of the test accordingly.

VI

INTERPRETING TEST SCORES

The inclusion of a single chapter on interpreting test scores is to some extent misleading, as adequate consideration of all relevant factors involved in test interpretation would necessitate a very lengthy and complex treatment. In trying to give meaning to a particular test score, the interpreter must draw upon his knowledge of the background of the examiner(s), examinee(s), validity, and reliability as they relate to both the particular test with which he is concerned and to testing in general. He must keep in mind the purposes for which the test is being used, such as the decisions which are to be made. He should consider the great variety of factors which influence test scores, be they cognitive, affective or physical. Even without delving into the kinds of information and approaches which would be supplied by various researchers and theorists, it can obviously be seen that a list of vital data necessary for a specific test interpretation would be lengthy.

Nevertheless, the interpretation of test scores deserves separate, deliberate consideration, as evidenced, for example, by the widespread reception of Howard Lyman's (1971) text, *Test Scores and What They Mean*. Certain cautions and certain techniques in the interpretive chain demand emphasis and, indeed, are prerequisites for the practice of test interpretation. Often tests are blamed when the user is the unsophisticated link.

Let us hint briefly at the necessity of and types of information for interpretation. An illustration outside the field of testing will be used. Suppose you ask a man from Outer Myskania, "How long did you attend college?" and he replies, "Seventeen ercs." You probably have added little to your knowledge. Some kind of a base is needed for interpreting this statement: as examples, the number of ercs which equals a year, the amount of time in college typical for the residents of the country, and historically the average amount of time spent in college.

Communication is the key to effective test interpretation. Communication of relevant test results and interpretations to the examinee is imperative, and is also of great consequence to significant others in the examinee's life, (e.g., parents, who are concerned with decision making). In the first article of this chapter, James Ricks presents valuable guidelines and specific suggestions for transmitting test results to pupils and parents. These common sense suggestions should prove helpful to anyone engaged in test interpretation of individuals or groups.

Often we wish to estimate how an individual might perform in the future. Probably the most comprehensible procedure for relating predicator and criterion is the construction of expectancy tables. Alexander Wesman presents a discussion of (1) how such tables can be used to make such decisions for individuals and groups, (2) how they can be used to select individuals for particular purposes, and (3) some of the limitations of using these kinds of tables.

In the third article of the chapter, Clements, Duncan, and Taylor point out several social-psychological factors on the part of both counselor and counselee that can influence evaluation of interview and test results.

Hazardous types of test interpretations are indicated by Junius Davis in the fourth paper. He addresses specifically the problem of using *Scholastic Aptitude Test* norms for college decisions, although the generalizations to other situations are easily recognized. The probability of making some of the unjustified types of statements which the author notes could be decreased with the help of expectancy tables.

In the final article of the chapter, a paper by Frank Womer, the importance of establishing goals for testing programs and the proper use of test results are stressed, and the two topics are meaningfully integrated. He considers ten common misconceptions and misuses of test results, thereby helping us to avoid making certain misinterpretations.

The student, after digesting the many ideas in this set of readings, should appreciate the variety of sins that are committed in the name of test interpretation. He should be aware of the many techniques available to assist in test interpretation—specifically expectancy tables, norm tables, standard scores, percentile ranks, and the many psycho-social variables that interact with test performance and therefore should be considered in the interpretations of the resulting scores. If there is one word which characterizes the problem in deriving meaning from test scores it is "interaction": the interaction of examiner, testing environment, test materials, present and past condition of examinee, nature of decision to be made, and decision-maker.

28   *On Telling Parents About Test Results*

....

JAMES H. RICKS, JR.

With increasing frequency parents are requesting that the results of school testing programs be communicated to them. Indeed in some areas courts have ruled that a child's school records, which typically contain test scores, must be open to his parents.

School personnel are often hard pressed to find the most efficient and understandable techniques by which this request might be met. The following article presents some non-technical and common-sense suggestions that might be used in interpreting test scores.

Like any other organization dealing with people, a school has many confidences to keep. School administrators, teachers, and especially guidance workers inevitably come to know items of private information. A gossip who carelessly passes such information around abuses his position and his relationship with his students. It is both right and important that some kinds of information be kept in confidence.

What about test results? Do they belong in the category of secrets, to be seen only by professional eyes and mentioned only in whispers? Or is their proper function best served when they become common knowledge in the school and its community? (In some towns, names and scores have been listed in the local newspaper, much like the results of an athletic contest.)

We think neither extreme is a good rule. Sometimes there is reason to make group data—figures such as the average and the range from high to low—generally public. Seldom should individual results be published except for the happy announcement of a prize won, a scholarship awarded, and the like. But short of general publication, school guidance workers face a particularly important question: Should parents be told their children's test results?

Hard questions often are hard because they deal with genuinely complicated problems. Simple "solutions" to such questions are likely to be a trap rather than an aid if their effect is to divert our attention from the difficulties we truly face. Simple rules or principles, on the other hand, can be of real help as one

Reprinted with permission of the publisher from *Test Service Bulletin No. 54*, published by the Psychological Corporations, 1959 (December), pp. 1–4.

tackles complex problems and situations. This article will present some rules that we have found useful in facing questions such as—"What should I say when a mother wants to know her son's IQ?" "Should we send aptitude test profiles home with the children?" "We feel that parents in our school ought to know the results of the achievement tests we give, but then it's hard to explain the discrepancies between these and the teachers' grades."

No single procedure, obviously, can be appropriate for every kind of test. Nor for every kind of parent. To Mr. Jones, a well-adjusted and well-educated father, a report of his daughter's test scores may enhance his understanding of her capacities and of what the school has been giving her. To Mr. Green, a somewhat insecure and less knowledgeable man, the identical information may spark an explosion damaging to both child and school. And the counselor or teacher often has no sure way of knowing which kind of parent he will be reporting to.

Two principles and one verbal technique seem to us to provide a sound basis for communicating the information obtained from testing. The two "commandments" are absolutely interdependent—without the second the first is empty, and without the first the second is pointless.

The first: PARENTS HAVE THE RIGHT TO KNOW WHATEVER THE SCHOOL KNOWS ABOUT THE ABILITIES, THE PERFORMANCE, AND THE PROBLEMS OF THEIR CHILDREN.

The second: THE SCHOOL HAS THE OBLIGATION TO SEE THAT IT COMMUNICATES UNDERSTANDABLE AND USABLE KNOWLEDGE. Whether by written report or by individual conference, the school must make sure it is giving real information—not just the illusion of information that bare numbers or canned interpretations often afford. And the information must be in terms that parents can absorb and use.

Few educators will dispute the first principle. It is in parents that the final responsibility for the upbringing and education of the children must lie. This responsibility requires access to all available information bearing on educational and vocational decisions to be made for and by the child. The school is the agent to which parents have delegated part of the educational process—but the responsibility has been delegated, not abdicated. Thoughtful parents do not take these responsibilities and rights lightly.

The parents' right to know, then, we regard as indisputable. But, to know what?

Suppose that as a result of judicious testings the school knows that Sally has mastered social studies and general science better than many in her ninth grade class, but that few do as poorly as she in math. In English usage she stands about in the middle, but her reading level is barely up to the lower border of the students who successfully complete college preparatory work in her high school. The best prediction that can be made of her probable scores on the College Boards three years hence is that they will fall in the range which makes her eligible for the two-year community college, but not for the university. She grasps mechanical concepts better than most boys, far better than most girls. Looking over the test results and her records, her experienced teacher recognizes that good habits and neatness of work have earned Sally grades somewhat better than would be expected from her test scores.

All of these are things Sally's parents should know. Will they know them if they are given the numbers—Sally's IQ score, percentiles for two reading scores, percentiles on another set of norms for several aptitude tests, and grade-placement figures on an achievement battery?

Telling someone something he does not understand does not increase his knowledge (at least not his correct and usable knowledge—we are reminded of the guide's observation about the tenderfoot, "It ain't so much what he don't know, it's what he knows that ain't so that gits him in trouble."). Transmitting genuine knowledge requires attention to content, language, and audience. We have already referred to some of the characteristics of parents as an audience. Let's look at the other two elements.

Content means that to begin with we must ourselves know what we are trying to get across.

We need to know just what evidence there is to show that these test results deserve any consideration at all. We need equally to know the margins and probabilities of error in predictions based on tests. If we don't know both what the scores mean and how much confidence may properly be placed in them, we are in trouble at the start—neither our own use of the information nor our transmission of it to others will be very good.

Content—what we are going to say—and language—how we are going to put it—are inseparable when we undertake to tell somebody something. In giving information about test results, we need to think about the general content and language we shall use and also about the specific terms we shall use.

To illustrate the general content-and-language planning, a guidance director may decide that he wants first to get across a sense of both the values and the weaknesses of test scores. One excellent device for his purpose would be an expectancy table or chart. Such a chart can make it clear to persons without training in statistics that test results are useful predictors and that the predictions will not always be precise. Local studies in one's school or community are of greatest interest. But the guidance director who lacks local data may still find illustrative tables from other places helpful in preparing parents and students to use test results in a sensible way.

Specific terms used in expressing test results vary considerably in the problems they pose. Consider, for example, the different kinds of numbers in which test results may be reported.

IQ's are regarded as numbers that should rarely if ever be reported as such to students or to their parents. The reason is that an IQ is likely to be seen as a fixed characteristic of the person tested, as somehow something more than the test score it really represents. The effect, too often, is that of a final conclusion about the individual rather than that of a piece of information useful in further thinking and planning. Few things interfere more effectively with real understanding than indiscriminate reporting of IQ scores to parents. Grade-placement scores or standard scores of various kinds are less likely to cause trouble than IQ scores are. Still, they may substitute an illusion of communication for real communication. Standard scores have no more meaning to most parents than raw scores unless there is opportunity for extensive explanations. Grade placements seem so simple and straightforward that serious misunderstandings may result from their use. As noted in a very helpful pamphlet (Katz, 1958), a sixth-grade pupil with grade-placement scores of 10.0 for reading and 8.5 for arithmetic does not necessarily rank higher in reading than he does in arithmetic when compared to the other sixth-graders. (Both scores may be at the 95th percentile for his class—arithmetic progress much more than reading progress tends to be dependent on what has been taught, and thus to spread over a narrower range at any one grade.)

Percentiles probably are the safest and most informative numbers to use provided their two essential characteristics are made clear: (1) that they refer not to percent of questions answered correctly but to percent of people whose performance the student has equaled or surpassed, and (2) who specifically are the people with whom the student is being compared. The second point—a definite description of the comparison or "norm" group— is especially important in making the meaning of test results clear.

Much more can be said about the kinds of numbers used to convey test score information. But a more fundamental question remains—are any numbers necessary?

We intend nothing so foolish as suggesting a ban on the use of numbers in reporting test results. But we have been struck repeatedly by the fact that some of the very best counselors and many of the best-written reports present numerical data only incidentally or not at all.

Along with the two "commandments" at the beginning of this article, we mentioned a verbal technique. Generally we dislike formulas for writing or speaking. This one, however, seems to have advantages that outweigh the risks attending its suggestion. It's just a few words: "YOU SCORE LIKE PEOPLE WHO . . ." Or, to a parent, "Your son (or daughter) scores like students who . . ."

The sentence, of course, requires completion. The completion depends on the test or other instrument, the reason for testing, and the person to whom the report is being given. Some sample completions:

YOU SCORE LIKE

". . . people who don't find selling insurance a very satisfactory choice. Three out of four who score as you do and become insurance salesmen leave the job for something else in less than a year."

". . . people who are pretty good at office work, fast and accurate enough to hold a job and do it well."

". . . students who find getting into liberal arts college and getting a B.A.

degree something they can attain only with extra hard work. On the other hand, they find a year or two of technical school interesting and they probably do well in the jobs to which that leads."

". . . students who are disappointed later if they don't begin a language in the ninth grade and plan to take some more math and science. It's easier to head toward business later if you still want to than to go from the commercial course into a good college."

". . . students who don't often—only about one out of four—manage to earn a C average their freshman year at State."

". . . students who have more than average difficulty passing in arithmetic —you (or, to a parent, he) may need some extra help on this in the next few years."

Many more samples will come readily to mind. The most important thing to note is that a satisfactory report combines two kinds of information:

1) the test results of the individual person, and
2) something known about the test or battery and its relationship to the subsequent performance of others who have taken it.

Also, a satisfactory completion puts the school or the counselor out on a limb, at least a little. Some variant of "That's not so!" or, more politely, "How do you know?" will be the reaction in some cases, probably less frequently voiced than it is felt.

Well, let's face it. The decision to use a test at all is a step out on a limb. Some limbs are broad and solid and the climber need feel little or no anxiety. Some are so frail that they offer only hazard, with the bait of an improbable reward. We climb out on some limbs of medium safety because there is evidence of a real chance that they will help us, and those whom we test, toward a worthwhile goal.

The words of the formula need not actually be used in each case. Sometimes percentiles, grade placement scores, or a profile may be what the parents should receive. But it is well to try first mentally stating the meaning of the results in the language suggested above. If this proves difficult or discomforting, a warning signal is on—reporting the numbers is likely not to be constructive in the case at hand!

The audience of parents to which our test-based information is to be transmitted includes an enormous range and variety of minds and emotions. Some are ready and able to absorb what we have to say. Reaching others may be as hopeless as reaching TV watchers with an AM radio broadcast. Still others may hear what we say, but clothe the message with their own special needs, ideas, and predilections.

The habit of using the formula and of thinking a bit about what answer to give if the response is a challenging or doubting one puts the interpreter of test scores in the strongest position he can occupy. In the case of achievement tests it requires him to understand why and how the particular test or battery was chosen as appropriate for his school and his purpose. In the case of aptitude (including scholastic aptitude or intelligence) tests it requires him to examine the evidence offered in the test manual and research studies to back up the test's claim to usefulness. And it reminds him always that it is in the end his thinking, his weighing of the evidence, his soundness and helpfulness as an educator or counselor that is exposed for judgment—not the sometimes wistful ideas of the test author or publisher.

The school—or the counselor—is exposed for judgment when telling parents about the abilities and performances of their children. The parents have the right to know. And knowledge in terms they can understand and absorb is what the school must give.

29   Expectancy Tables — A Way of Interpreting Test Validity

ALEXANDER G. WESMAN

The results of test validation studies are usually reported as correlation coefficients. These coefficients, although meaningful, are too abstract for some test users. One method devised to facilitate the interpretation of test validity is the development and application of expectancy tables (Bittner & Wilder, 1946). In the following non-technical presentation Dr. Wesman demonstrates the selection and use of expectancy tables for individual and group predictions of success. The article concludes with a summary of questions and answers about some of the limitations encountered in the development and use of such tables. A more technical discussion of the topic can be found in an article by Schrader (1965).

How might the use of expectancy tables prove valuable for (a) a classroom teacher, (b) a college admissions officer, and (c) a clinical or counseling psychologist?

"What does a correlation coefficient of .50 mean?" "How can I best interpret to the teachers in my school the meaning of validity coefficients?" "How can I demonstrate to my boss that the tests we are using are successful, when he doesn't understand statistical terminology?" These questions inevitably come up in the experience of any serious test user or consultant. Statistically adequate replies are not sufficient (nor are they often appropriate) to meet the

Reprinted with permission of the publisher (The Psychological Corporation) from *Test Service Bulletin*, No. 38 (December), 1949, pp. 11–15.

problems posed by these queries. A device is needed which can simply and directly reveal the relationships between test scores and performance measures to those who lack the necessary background to understand even the more commonplace statistical terms such as correlation, standard deviation, and variance.

It is easy to sit back in one's chair and insist that anyone who works with tests should have a thorough grounding in basic statistics. This is a laudable philosophy—one can only agree, "Yes, it would be nice." As a matter of practical fact, the success or failure of many test programs depends on our ability to communicate understanding of test results to colleagues who are statistically untrained—to teachers who will use the results in their classrooms or vote for the continuation or rejection of programs in the schools; to superiors in industry who will or will not budget funds for personnel selection through tests; to labor union representatives who question the use of tests by management. These people cannot be sent to the university for a statistics course. They must be informed of the meaning of test results in *their* language, not the language of the technician.

This article deals with a device which can do much to meet this need—the expectancy table.

The expectancy table is not new, it has been known and used in the test field for more than a quarter of a century. But it has not been as widely known or used as it deserves. In the course of developing newer and more complex statistical techniques for the construction and analysis of tests and test batteries, we have too far neglected the communication of understanding to the less initiated. It is to be hoped that this neglect will be recognized and remedied.

An expectancy table is merely a grid (see Figure 1) containing a number of cells. Along the side are indicated the test score intervals; along the top are placed the course grades which have been awarded, the production record or supervisor's rating, the scores on an end-of-term achievement test, or whatever other criterion of success is desired. For each individual we place a tally which shows, vertically, his test score and, horizontally, his rank on the criterion. (Thus, in Figure 1, a student scoring 62 on the Sentences section of the *DAT Language Usage* test and earning a B in Rhetoric would be plotted in the bold-outlined cell.) When the tallying has been completed, the tallies in each cell are added, and this number is recorded in the cell. The numbers in each row of cells are then added and the sum is recorded at the right of each row; the numbers in each column are added and the sum is recorded at the bottom of each column.[1] We now have our basic data for an expectancy table, which may be organized in several ways depending on our primary interest.

---

[1] If a check on the accuracy of the additions is desired, the sums in the right hand margin may be added, and the numbers at the bottom of the columns may be added. These two totals should be equal to each other, and should also equal the original number of cases we started to plot.

SCORES ON D.A.T. SENTENCES TEST	GRADES IN RHETORIC					Totals
	F	D	C	B	A	
80–89					| (1)	1
70–79				| (1)	|||| (4)	5
60–69		||| (3)	++++ ++++ |||| (14)	++++ (5)	22
50–59			++++ |||| (9)	++++ ||| (8)	++++| (6)	23
40–49		||| (3)	++++ ++++ ||| (13)	++++	(6)		22
30–39	| (1)	||| (3)	++++ |||| (9)	||| (3)		16
20–29	| (1)	|||| (4)	||| (3)			8
10–19		|| (2)				2
0–9		| (1)				1
	2	13	37	32	16	100

FIGURE 1. *Expectancy grid showing how students' grades in Rhetoric and previously-earned scores on the* DAT *Sentences Test are tallied in appropriate cells. (Data from Kansas State Teachers College; grade of F = failure, no grade of E given; N = 100 freshman girls; mean test score = 48.58, S.D. = 15.2, r = .71).*

MAKING PREDICTIONS FOR INDIVIDUAL STUDENTS

Suppose that we wish to answer the question, "What is the probability that a student with a given test score will succeed in a specified course?" Table 1 presents the data organized to answer this question.

Each cell frequency has been converted to a percent based on the total number of tallies in its row. The table then reads: Of the 22 freshman girls who took a course in Rhetoric and had scored between 60 and 69 on the Sentences test, 23% (5 girls) earned a grade of A, 63% (14 girls) earned a B, and 14% (3 girls) earned a C. Not one of the girls whose score was in this group received a grade lower than C in Rhetoric. One might predict then that girls who take this course in future terms, and who have attained scores of 60 to 69 on the *DAT Sentences* test, will probably be better than average students, since all

TABLE 1. *Expectancy table prepared from the grid in* FIGURE 1. (*The left-hand table summarizes the frequencies as they appear in the original grid. The right-hand table shows these frequencies converted into per cents.*)

Total No.	Number receiving each grade					Test Scores	Per cent receiving each grade					Total Per cent
	F	D	C	B	A		F	D	C	B	A	
1					1	80–89					100	100
5				1	4	70–79				20	80	100
22			3	14	5	60–69			14	63	23	100
23			9	8	6	50–59			39	35	26	100
22		3	13	6		40–49		14	59	27		100
16	1	3	9	3		30–39	6	19	56	19		100
8	1	4	3			20–29	13	50	37			100
2		2				10–19		100				100
1		1				0–9		100				100
100	2	13	37	32	16							

but 14% earned grades of A and B. Interpretations may be made in the same way for other test scores and individuals.

USING EXPECTANCY TABLES FOR SELECTION PURPOSES

Suppose that the question is posed from a different standpoint. "How can we pick out our best applicants?" Starting with a grid just as we did before, but computing the percentages by columns rather than rows, we prepare our expectancy table to answer this question directly. Table 2 shows such a table for 52 employed stenographers who took the *Seashore-Bennett Stenographic Proficiency Test.* Their test scores are shown at the left, their ratings on stenographic ability at the top. The right-hand column then reads: Of the eleven

TABLE 2. *Expectancy table showing the number and per cent of stenographers of various rated abilities who came from specified score groups on the* S-B Stenographic Proficiency Test. (*N = 52, mean score = 15.4, S.D. = 2.9, r = .61; score is average per letter for five letters*).

Number in each score group receiving each rating on stenographic ability				Stenographic Proficiency Test Scores	Per cent in each score group receiving each rating on stenographic ability			
Below Average	Average	Above Average	Excellent		Below Average	Average	Above Average	Excellent
	4	6	7	18–19		17	40	64
	2	2	4	16–17		9	13	36
	10	5		14–15		44	33	
	4	1		12–13		17	7	
2	2	1		10–11	67	9	7	
1	1			8–9	33	4		
3	23	15	11		100	100	100	100

stenographers rated excellent, 64% (7 girls) scored 18-19 on the test and the remaining 36% (4 girls) scored 16-17. None of the girls rated excellent scored below 16 on the *Stenographic Proficiency test*. We can therefore expect our future excellent stenographers to come from those scoring 16 and higher on the test. Note that the expectancy table does *not* predict that all those who achieve scores of 16 or better will prove excellent. Some of them may be those rated above average or only average. It predicts that most of those who will later prove excellent will probably have come out of this high-scoring group.

MAKING ESTIMATES OF AVERAGE PERFORMANCES

A similar approach, primarily diagrammatic in form, may be used to answer the question, "What is the probability that an office worker will attain an average rating or higher?" Again starting from a basic grid such as is shown in Figure 1, we prepare a graph which is focused entirely at the single category: average and above. For each score group, we calculate the percent of that group which has received ratings of average or better. The data in Table 3 are based on 65 office workers who had previously taken the *General Clerical Test*. The material in Table 3 is read as follows: of the 11 office workers who scored between 50 and 99 on the *General Clerical Test*, 6 of them (55%) later received supervisory ratings of average or better; of the 31 workers who scored between 100 and 149 on this test, 23 (74%) earned ratings of average or better than average, etc. A glance at the diagram indicates the chances that an applicant with a given score will earn a satisfactory rating as an office worker in this company. One who scores over 200 on the test is almost twice as likely to be satisfactory as one who scores below 100.

TABLE 3. *Expectancy table and graph showing per cent expected to rate average or better in office clerical tasks on the basis of scores on the* General Clerical Test. *(N = 65, mean score = 136.1, S.D. = 39.1, r_{bis} = .31).*

General Clerical Test Scores	No. in score group	No. rated average or better	% rated average or better						
200-up	5	5	100						
150-199	18	15	83						
100-149	31	23	74						
50-99	11	6	55						
Total	65			0% 20% 40% 60% 80% 100%					

QUESTIONS AND ANSWERS ABOUT THE LIMITATION OF EXPECTANCY TABLES

The *advantages* of the expectancy table will be self-evident to those who have the problem of interpreting test predictions to teachers and parents, business superiors, and applicants for employment. As is true of most aids, there are *limitations* of which the user of expectancy tables should be aware. Some of these, together with questions which have been asked concerning such tables, are noted below.

Q. Is there any set number of test score groups, or criterion categories, which is most desirable?

A. No. Expectancy tables may consist of as few as four cells (two score groups along the left-hand margin, and two criterion ratings—e.g., pass vs. fail—along the top), or as many as the data will permit. The optimum number is that which best serves the purpose—which best summarizes the relationship we wish to illustrate. The tables used above as illustrations have deliberately been prepared with different numbers of cells, score groups, and criterion categories. Each of the tables might equally well have been prepared in some other way. One guiding principle is to make the number of cells proportional to the number of individuals; the fewer the individuals, the fewer the number of cells.

Q. How does the expectancy table differ from a scatter diagram used for computation of a correlation coefficient?

A. The basic data appearing on the grid from which the expectancy table is prepared are the same as those in a scatter diagram. In fact, a correlation chart can be used to plot these data. The chief difference is in the handling of the data. The expectancy table organizes the material for interpretation of an *individual's chances of success*. The validity coefficient summarizes such data for an *entire group* in one mathematical figure. The expectancy table makes apparent the details of the data at various parts of the distributions; the coefficient, being a kind of average, obscures those details just as any averaging does.

Q. How much confidence may we place in the predictions made on the basis of expectancy tables?

A. The reliability of any statistical measure varies directly with the number of individuals on which the measure is based. Since each cell is likely to contain relatively few cases, the confidence to which we are entitled is less than for measures based on larger numbers of cases. One should recall that the average score of a class is a more stable figure than the score of any individual student. The lesser reliability of individual cell entries (or per cents) is a real limitation of the expectancy table technique, and one of which the user should always be conscious. The limitation is not so great as to vitiate the usefulness of the device. The coefficients computed in most school and industrial situations also fall short of ideal levels of reliability. The lesser reliability of the figures in any expectancy table is frequently compensated for by the clearer interpretation they permit. It should also be remarked that larger frequencies in each cell, and consequently greater permissible confidence in our predictions, may be obtained by lumping together adjacent score groups or criterion ratings. For example, if in Table 2 our score intervals had been plotted as 8–13 and 14–19, and our ratings as average and below vs. above average and excellent, the results would be Table 4, in which the cells have greater frequencies than do those of Table 2. Of course, this also obscures some of the relationships. The user will have to decide which is more important in a given situation.

TABLE 4. *Expectancy table reducing the number of cells in* TABLE 2 *from twenty-four to four.*

Average and Below Average	Excellent and Above Average	Stenographic Proficiency Test Scores	% Average and Below Average	% Excellent and Above Average
16	24	14–19	62	92
10	2	8–13	38	8
26	26		100	100

Q. Can expectancy charts be inferred directly from correlation coefficients?

A. This suggestion is more likely to come from colleagues who are mainly teachers of counselors and personnel men than from those who are actually on the "firing line" and have to deal with real classes and employees. Theoretically, knowing a correlation coefficient one can prepare the scatter diagram (and therefore the expectancy table) which it summarizes. A practical difficulty is that one can do so only when a large number of cases is involved—far larger than one ordinarily finds in a school and industrial situation. With the smaller numbers of cases usually available (50, 100, 150 or even 200), irregularities in the distributions do not permit such inference. Two quite different irregular scatter diagrams may result in the same validity coefficient.

Many users of expectancy tables *will* wish to combine the virtues of such tables with those of validity coefficients by using the same scatter diagram as a basis for both approaches. This tactic is, of course, eminently acceptable.

Q. Do we have to compute per cents for each cell in the expectancy tables, or can we see relationships without doing so?

A. The computation of per cents is useful primarily *as* a way of rendering the figures in each row or column comparable. If we wish to say that John's chances of making good in a course or on a job are 73 out of 100, while Fred's chances are only 33 out of 100, the computation of per cents is necessary. If we are satisfied with knowing that a person's chances are 10 out of 13, or are 23 to 7 in his favor, the frequencies alone may be entirely adequate. Whether frequencies or per cents are used is a matter of individual preference and individual success in communicating the meaning of the data to others.

Q. Is the expectancy table susceptible to other uses than predicting chances of success?

A. One of the most valuable uses of an expectancy table (and of a scatter diagram) is that it helps identify the individuals for whom our predictions of success have gone astray, or those who do not conform to the usual ability patterns. By investigating the personal characteristics and backgrounds of such deviate individuals, we often find clues to unrecognized factors predictive of success or failure in a course or job. For example, by noting over several years those freshmen whose academic performances were much better, or much worse, than was predicted from their scores, one college dean was able to identify several facts which would modify his future predictions—e.g., boys from high school X had particularly good study habits, those from school Y were unusually test-wise, etc. By pointing out instances in which prediction missed the expectancy table permitted going back to the individual—always a healthy step in appraisal of people or programs.

In short, the expectancy table is a tool, and one of potentially considerable value. Like any tool, its usefulness depends on the extent to which it is understood and on the ingenuity and skill of its user. Properly understood, it represents an excellent medium for interpretation and communication of the meaning of test results.

30 Toward Effective Evaluation of the Culturally Deprived

HUBERT M. CLEMENTS, JACK A. DUNCAN, AND WALLACE M. TAYLOR

The process of evaluation as it occurs in a counseling setting is given detailed treatment in the following article. The authors consider five factors which can significantly influence the effectiveness of evaluation. These factors are:

Reprinted with permission of the first named author and publisher (the American Personnel and Guidance Association) from the *Personnel and Guidance Journal*, 1969, Vol. 47 (May), pp. 891–896.

(1) counselor attitude, (2) counselee attitude, (3) method of evaluation and their weaknesses, (4) counselor-counselee value system, and (5) lack of understanding of the purpose of evaluation. One of the more important messages communicated in this paper is that value systems of either counselor and/or counselee can dictate the results of both subjective (interview) and objective (test) evaluations and interpretations.

In what ways might the language used by the counselor influence rapport during test interpretation? What are some ways in which counselor and counselee attitude toward their reasons for coming together could help or hinder the effectiveness of the session(s)? What are some implications of this article for (1) test selection and (2) introduction of the examinee to the purpose(s) of testing?

There exists in the minds of many Americans a stereotype of the rapidly growing segment of our population commonly referred to as the lower socioeconomic strata or the culturally deprived. This group is also variously referred to as the "socioeconomically deprived," the "socially and culturally disadvantaged," the "chronically poor," the "poverty-stricken," and so on. These are the people who are handicapped by depressed social and economic status.

> In many instances they are further handicapped by ethnic and cultural *caste* status. . . . These people are the bearers of cultural attitudes alien to those which are dominant in the broader communities they now inhabit, and their children come to school disadvantaged to the degree that their culture has failed to provide them with the experiences that are "normal" to the kinds of children the schools are used to teaching (Gordon & Wilkerson, 1966, p. 2).

Unfortunately, this segment of our society is generally viewed in a negative manner. Harrington (1963) points out that the middle-class American frequently thinks of the poor as lazy people who just do not want to get ahead, and Riessman (1962, p. 25) comments that those who exist at this level in our society are also popularly visualized by other members of our society as uncontrolled, aggressive, sexually promiscuous, primitive, and insensitive.

> The 1965 Washington Invitational Institute on "Rehabilitation Counseling and the Poverty Field" summarized that . . . people in the poverty group are not viewed as persons with specific remediable problems, but rather as incapable, unwilling and uncooperative individuals who created the situation in which they live. Society does not feel sorry for them and has assumed little obligation for them. Society tends to impose the burden of guilt on the poor, rather than indict itself. Actually, the poor have been dropped from the mainstream by society through circumstances over which they have had little control (Cohen, Gregory, & Pelosi, 1966, p. 31).

These attitudes constitute perhaps the greatest barrier the counselor must overcome in working toward effective evaluations of individuals within this group.

COUNSELOR ATTITUDE IN EVALUATION

The primary factor that must be given consideration in the area of evaluation with this group is that of the counselor's attitude toward these counselees. The attitude of the lay middle-class American has been stated above, and since counselors are largely middle-class in their orientation, they, too, often hold the same attitude as the lay public. Reissman (1962) cautions that such a view of the lower class predisposes one to be pessimistic and cynical regarding these individuals. Often the counselor who holds this stereotyped image enters the counseling relationship with a condescending attitude and with expectations that the counselee must do poorly. The frequent result of this fact is a failure of the counselor and counselee to communicate effectively. It is at these times that the counselor sees himself as the victim of the inevitable failure that awaits those seeking to help those who do not want help.

In many cases, however, these failures are blamed on the counselees because of their "lack of motivation to cooperate." Thus, counselors borrow an attitude of the culturally deprived—fatalism. They say, "I am bound to fail," and they justify the failure by placing the blame on someone or something other than themselves. This self-fulfilling prophecy of failure obviously affects the counselor's objective evaluation of the culturally deprived.

COUNSELEE ATTITUDE IN EVALUATION

While it is true that many of the barriers to effective counseling and evaluation with the culturally deprived are related to the counselor and his function, it must be recognized that there are also numerous counselee-related obstacles. The primary obstacle related to the counselee in the evaluative process is the counselee's attitude. For example, since these counselees are not usually attracted to the middle-class value of high achievement, they may not give their full cooperation and maximum effort when being evaluated. Cohen, et al., state that "a composite picture of a client from a poverty population will probably show an unmotivated, distrustful person unwilling or unable to avail himself of the services to be" (Cohen, et al., 1966, p. 50).

Havighurst underscored the significance of this point with the following observations:

> When the middle class child comes to a test, he has been taught to do his very best on it. . . . To the average lower class child, on the other hand, a test is just another place to be punished, to have one's weaknesses shown up, to be reminded that one is at the tail end of the procession. Hence, this child soon learns to accept the inevitable and to get it over with as quickly as possible . . . (1951, p. 22).

COUNSELOR-COUNSELEE VALUES IN EVALUATION

The counselor must have a complete understanding of the dynamics which are operative in the evaluation process. Invariably, the "middle-class-oriented" counselor and the culturally deprived counselee internalize different social class values which manifest themselves in terms of aspirational levels, beliefs, and expectations. Sherif and Sherif (1965) believe that this dissonance between the middle-class value structure of the counselor and lower-class value structure of the counselee produces an artificiality in the counselor-client relationship. It follows that with this dissonance between the value structures there exists also a like dissonance in the perceptions that each group has of the evaluative process.

The counselor expects a cooperative counselee who is willing to invest of himself in the evaluative process. The counselee with his lack of sophistication in these matters expects the counselor to do something for him. Previous negative experiences with authority figures coupled with the counselor's reluctance to do something for him cause the counselee to see the counselor as another outsider who did not live up to his expectations. The counselor perceives this lack of commitment to the evaluative process as an unwillingness to cooperate, a lack of concern, or some similar negative reaction. Consequently, the relationship ends in failure.

Truax, Wargo, and Silber (1966) found that some counselors did provide low levels of counseling relationships to certain groups of clients against whom they were prejudiced and, therefore, had poor outcomes. They also found that when selected counselors provided high levels of therapeutic conditions such as accurate empathy and non-possessive warmth, then counseling with the culturally disadvantaged proved significantly effective. Thus, if these prejudices of the evaluative process can be overcome, the possibilities for success in subsequent counseling contacts and functions are greatly enhanced.

Deutsch (1963) noted that differences in language associated with social class tend to increase with the age of the child. Thus, as deprived children mature, they fall further and further behind middle-class children in language variables measured. Consequently, even simple testing instructions become difficult for the disadvantaged counselee to comprehend. And follow-up test interpretation and counseling sessions are equally difficult to conduct.

METHODS OF EVALUATION

In addition to attitudes and values involved in evaluation, there is also the matter of procedures and techniques which, when inappropriately implemented, may also have a deleterious effect. For the purpose of this paper, these procedures and techniques will be presented as non-standardized and standardized methods of evaluation.

NON-STANDARDIZED METHODS OF EVALUATION ■ Non-standardized methods of evaluation are often of greater importance than are standardized methods, because they may enable the counselor to ascertain the functional capabilities of the culturally deprived counselee more accurately than would be possible with existing standardized measures which tend to discriminate against lower-class individuals. Gordon states that teachers, counselors, and psychotherapists often place an "exaggerated emphasis on the predictive value of the classification and quantification of psychological appraisal data and . . . neglect qualitative appraisal data as a basis for planning and intervention" (1964, p. 277). He also views the culturally deprived individual as a product of the interaction between organism and environment and believes that effective planning for the culturally deprived must be predicated upon knowledge and understanding of the specific and detailed character of the individual and his experience. This knowledge and understanding "can only result from qualitative appraisal, descriptively reported and leading not simply to diagnosis and classification, but to prescription and treatment appropriate . . ." (p. 280) to the individual.

Non-standardized data are essential for effective evaluation. But in securing the non-standardized data, the counselor must conscientiously strive to prevent their distortion by his own biases and previous experiences. However, the lack of adequate data, or a *failure to recognize* the significance of the demographic and biographical data which are available, further complicates the evaluative process. But the counselor's efforts to incorporate into his thinking such non-standardized data about the counselee as home environment, achievements, relative success in interpersonal relationships, attitudes, aspirations, and interests will enable him to understand and interpret the results of the evaluative process more meaningfully.

Standardized Methods of Evaluation ■ Standardized methods of sampling an individual's behavior which now exist cannot provide the counselor with all of the necessary data for adequately appraising either the culturally deprived or the nonculturally deprived counselee. However, the counselor's efforts to be objective in collecting data regarding counselees can be improved when available standardized measures are used. When using these standardized tests and inventories, the counselor must exercise caution since these measures are not equally applicable to all subcultural groups within the total population.

In their publication, *Guidelines for Testing Minority Group Children*, the Work Group of the Society for the Study of Social Issues (APA, 1964) stated:

> Standardized tests currently in use present three principal difficulties when they are used with the disadvantaged minority groups: (1) they may not provide reliable differentiation in the range of the minority group scores, (2) their predictive validity for minority groups may be quite different from that for the standardization and validation groups, and (3) the validity of their interpretation is strongly dependent upon an adequate understanding of the social and cultural background of the group in question (1964, p. 130).

Therefore, the counselor who is working with a culturally deprived individual must exercise caution even when using the most highly regarded standardized measures. An interpretation of a prediction based on test results which may be invalid or unreliable because of cultural influences can have deleterious effects on the counselee—counselor relationship, but misinterpretation of valid and reliable test results can be just as damaging.

Achievement batteries, intelligence tests, interest inventories, and, in many cases, personality inventories are the most common types of standardized evaluative instruments administered and employed by counselors in working with counselees. And, since it is a generally accepted fact that all standardized evaluative instruments contain some cultural bias, counselors must not delude themselves into interpreting these scores in a vacuum.

For example, Riessman (1932) pointed to inadequate perceptual styles and habits of coping with the demands of academic efficiency by the culturally deprived. The hierarchy presented for these skills showed physical behavior superior to visual behavior which, in turn, was superior to aural behavior. In brief, children of poverty have not attained proper methods of listening and speaking which are basic standards for success in middle-class society.

In the area on intelligence assessment, Herrick, after surveying existing research findings, concluded that there was almost unanimous agreement in the research which showed that ". . . there are significant differences in intelligence test performance of children and youth from different socio-economic backgrounds with children from the higher levels always securing the higher intelligence test scores" (1951, p. 12). The typical mean difference between the scores of children of professionals and the scores of children of unskilled laborers is usually 15 to 25 IQ points. More recent surveys by Tyler (1956), Anastasi (1958), and Cronbach (1960) have concurred with this report by Herrick. Tyler concluded that ". . . the relationship of IQ to socio-economic level is one of the best documented facts in mental history" (1956, p. 137).

In his discussion of interest inventories, Cronbach (1960) points out that these instruments have been found to be of little value when working with individuals who are considering unskilled work situations since "there probably are no special patterns of interest characteristic of the unskilled occupations" (p. 424). Interest inventories can, however, be of considerable value when working with individuals entering the professions or skilled occupations. Therefore, counselors working with counselees whose backgrounds differ significantly from those on which the inventories were standardized must maintain a constant vigil in using these instruments lest they become too complacent and credit these inventories with more than they are designed to reveal.

The effect of cultural deprivation on personality test responses is not conclusive. Auld (1952) in his study of the influence of social class on personality test responses found that only in about one third of the studies were appreciable differences found; however, in those studies that showed differences, the middleclass subjects got more favorable scores than did the lower-class subjects. In essence, in using personality inventories, the counselor must be cognizant of the fact that the results sometimes indicate some divergent personality patterns influenced by cultural differences, which should not be interpreted to be indicative of a personality disorder.

It has been suggested that most standardized measures, including projective personality instruments, tend to favor middle-class individuals. This middle-class test bias may be a result both of poor rapport between the middle-class examiner and the lower-class examinee as well as biased test content. Previous negative experiences with testing, poor rapport, and the absence of a clearly understood and meaningful purpose for the testing may result in poor cooperation and a minimum of effort from the counselee. In fact, Riessman (1962) concluded that "the attitude of the examinee toward the test situation and the examiner was apparently more important than the content of the test items" (p. 53).

CONCLUSION

Evaluation has always been an inseparable concomitant of the educational process. Each student is regularly assessed in many areas, i.e., as to his scholarship, citizenship, deportment, attitude, aptitude, interest, and personality. The purpose of this paper has been to focus attention on some of the factors which operate to invalidate or distort the results of both objective and subjective evaluations of students and, in particular, counselees from the lower socioeconomic segment of our population.

The incongruence between the value systems of the middle-class counselor and the culturally deprived counselee is perhaps the most significant factor leading to inaccurate evaluation. This factor demonstrates itself in all forms of evaluation. Non-standardized evaluations are adversely affected by inaccurate and/or inadequate information about the culturally impoverished counselee. Test weaknesses, counselee rejection of tests, poor rapport between the counselor and counselee, lack of a clearly understood purpose for testing, inadequate forms, and inadequate interpretation of test results are some of the factors which reduces the accuracy and meaningfulness of standardized evaluation.

While it is true that standardized methods of evaluation have definite weaknesses, they can point objectively toward the evaluation of the counselee. However, the counselor should beware lest he ascribe objectivity to the standardized device which it does not possess. Helmstadter pointed out that

> . . . no test, scale, or other device can be thought of as yielding an absolutely true measure of intelligence, aptitude, knowledge, interest, attitude, or personality. These instruments are tools which enable us to describe, diagnose, and predict the behavior of a unique and complete individual with a greater degree of accuracy than is possible with subjective data alone (1964, p. 223).

The usefulness of a particular test with regard to the culturally deprived counselee, or to any other counselee for that matter, is largely dependent upon the knowledge and sense of responsibility of the counselor as well as the validity and reliability of the test.

Since evaluation is an integral part of the counseling process, the information acquired through testing may enhance many phases of social, educational, and vocational counseling. However, the counselor who permits himself to be lulled into a sense of security by normative data, which may not be valid with a particular counselee, not only restricts his own effectiveness as a counselor but also places himself in a position that is ethically questionable. This is particularly true in working with culturally deprived counselees.

The evaluative process, if it is to serve its intended purposes, must be subjected to constant scrutiny. This would tend to assure that the individual counselee, regardless of his socioeconomic status and his level of cultural assimilation, receives information about himself which is both valid and meaningful and, in turn, would aid in overcoming the barriers to effective evaluation.

31   *Non-Apparent Limitations of Normative Data*

JUNIUS A. DAVIS

How often we fail to realize the limitations of a set of data. We may make certain inferences without noting that the information is somewhat irrelevant. The misuse of normative data is one example, and Dr. Davis in the following article notes certain limitations of such data and some potential sources of illegitimate interpretation. These limitations are generally relevant to the use of test-norms information as used in the college selection process. The problems to which the author addresses himself will be of special concern to guidance personnel, but others involved with higher education, including students, should also gain informative insights.

Is it safe to judge the quality of an institution by the quality of its freshmen? Why might norms for an institution become outdated in a short time? How does the desire and the capability of the interpreter affect the type of information which he presents?

Recent emphasis on testing at state, regional, and national levels, and hope nourished by leaders in the professional organizations and state and federal

Reprinted and abridged from an article appearing in *Personnel and Guidance Journal*, 1959, Vol. 37, pp. 656–659, with permission of the author and publisher.

agencies seem to guarantee not only an increase in testing activity, but also a wealth of research data which may make test scores more useful in counseling. It may be expected that normative data on more geographic areas and more institutions will be available than ever before. As colleges become generally more selective, there will be less fear about releasing normative data; as more college officials find good normative data to be of real value in dealing with admissions and guidance problems, an increased number of institutions will make these data available to off-campus colleagues.

With regard to pre-college counseling, this seems to promise that long-sought goals are in sight. We have suffered through advising college-oriented youth with the knowledge that colleges do differ tremendously in competitiveness; yet we have had to guess the climate of intellectual ability from rumor and the degree of severity of admission policy statements in the catalog.

In the University System of Georgia, after a year of sifting data on the 16 tax-supported colleges, it has been found that College Board test scores are related to grades. A variety of comparable data for each of the colleges has been assembled, and every counselor in the high schools of Georgia may now be provided with norms for entering freshmen in these institutions. With institutional averages on the College Board SAT ranging from 250 to 550, there has been great temptation to do so, for it would seem that such would be in the best interests of all.

However, the range of experience which the 16 colleges have provided also demonstrates that accurate normative descriptions in themselves may be quite misleading, even dangerously so.

A FIRST FALLACY

An error which the most sophisticated and well-meaning counselor may make is that of too ready generalization from test scores to assumptions about the merits of the college. Non-guidance personnel in colleges have feared that the naive, upon seeing a panorama of test data on a range of colleges, may jump to the conclusion that intellectual quality of entering freshmen is somehow synonymous with the quality of the institution. Some counselors may scan the data and write off the lower-level colleges as too mediocre for consideration by anyone in a serious frame of mind. The fallacy here is that the quality of a college can be determined only in terms of *growth* of students along societal value lines, not by what students were upon entrance. It is reasonable to assume that some colleges with brilliant freshmen release four years later brilliant seniors who have grown little in the interim beyond what normal maturation elsewhere would have afforded. Thus, to avoid this error the counselor must not only continuously examine the variety of institutions against variety of college aspirants, but he must also retain his searching curiosity into the significant but sometimes subjective elements which signal a strong learning environment, regardless of position of college on the intellectual totem pole.

TEST SCORES AND GRADES

A second limiting characteristic of conventional normative data is not as apparent but is far more likely to mislead counselors or their counselees. Let us say that we have found from normative tables that a given counselee ranks at the 97th percentile on a given intelligence test at College A, at the 70th percentile at College B, and the 45th percentile at College C. On the basis of this information most counselors would seek some effective way of letting the counselee feel he would be in the most advantageous competitive position at College A, where he stands in the top 3 percent of his class. Yet, if there is no relationship between the test score and grades at College A, standing in the top 3 percent is of no advantage.

ATTRITION PHILOSOPHY

A third limitation of conventional normative data may become readily apparent from comparisons of several colleges. Let us take three actual liberal arts colleges in Georgia which are such that a high school senior reasonably might be attracted to all three. Let us say our subject has a College Board SAT-V score of 400, which at College A is at the 80th percentile of entering freshmen, at College B the 70th percentile, and at College C the 74th percentile. At each college the relationship between SAT-V scores and grades is about the same (in the high .40's). On the basis of this information, most counselors would seek good ways of leading the counselee to believe that his chances for success are about equal, or are slightly better at College A than at Colleges B and C. *Yet, an analysis of grades of fall-quarter students at these three colleges shows this is not true.* At these three colleges 54 percent of freshmen with the given SAT-V score of 400 made satisfactory grades their first quarter at College B, 73 percent of the same group achieved the same level or better at College C, *while only 42 percent of freshmen with SAT-V scores of 400 made satisfactory grades at College A.* Thus, in actuality the odds against satisfactory work would be highest at the college at which our counselee looked best among entering freshmen.

The reason for this has to do with differential attrition rates. Of all entering freshmen, College A gave satisfactory first-quarter grades to only 32 percent of the class, while Colleges B and C gave 41 and 63 percent of entering freshmen satisfactory fall-quarter averages. The level of entering freshmen on tests of intelligence or achievement gives no indication, in itself, of the philosophy of the college in regard to what its faculty regards as reasonable proportions of academic failures. Some colleges with low institutional averages on intelligence tests for entering freshmen may deal sternly with all students and permit only a small proportion of beginners to graduate. There need to be orderly ways of dealing with this problem, or great misinformation of potential harm to the college and the applicant can accrue. The answer may lie in the preparation of probability tables showing survival expectancies for persons with different test scores, rather than the percentile rank of various scores as in our conventional norms.

A DOUBLE VARIABLE

The fourth limitation is as dangerous as the others and may be just as difficult to detect from conventional normative descriptions. Let us consider the actual facts concerning one well-known Georgia institution of national standing, and those concerning a small state junior college offering solace in the form of efforts toward effective remedial teaching for applicants fearful of starting college in the big league. At both institutions the high school average had been found to be a good predictor of grades. At both institutions the average entering freshman averaged about B in high school. At both institutions about 50 percent of the entering freshmen had unsatisfactory fall-quarter averages, and at each, 50 percent of students with B high school averages did unsatisfactory academic work. The counselor avoiding some of the limitations of norm tables by using such probability data might "validly" infer that the little junior college would provide just as difficult and competitive an environment as the big league institution for a counselee with a B high school average.

For the colleges in the example (these institutions do exist), our counselor is falling into an easy error which the normative tables or probability data do not expose. All counselees with B averages do *not* have equal chances of survival at either college. In terms of high school record one might stand average at either institution; yet the big institution attracts students not only with good high school records but also with high test scores, while the little college has always attracted students with good records but low test scores. Thus, students with B high school averages at one college had College Board SAT scores averaging about 525, while similar students at the little school had SAT averages of about 380. In technical terms we make the assumption when using norm tables that our counselee may legitimately be considered to be a member of the same population as that reflected by the norms sample, and this does not always hold. Advising the counselee on the basis of one datum alone, such as a single-test score, may ignore other factors related to the spectrum of traits which are important in academic performance. Normative or probability tables on one class of variable alone can divert attention from other important characteristics of students in a given college group.

THE UNEXPECTED VARIABLE

A fifth limitation may become increasingly important in the next few years of tightening college admissions practices. Let us consider a table of norms for College X, based on last year's freshman class, readied quickly for use in the current year. A College Board SAT score of 525 places an applicant in the top fifth of the normative distribution. We send seven seniors at or above this level to College X with our blessings, only to learn that all find the going is too rough for easy survival. College X turns out to be an institution in which the admissions office has sustained in a single year a 40 percent increase in applications and the loss of a dormitory by fire. Thus, the SAT was grasped as a tool for exclusion of applicants, and although a score of 525 was equivalent to the 80th percentile in 1957, it is below the 50th percentile for the class entering in 1958. The faculty at College X suspected a better class in 1958 but could not break away from rules of thumb like "the bottom 10 percent on the final exam in Biology 101 shall fail." The limitations from temporal variation, like limburger cheese, grow stronger with age. Even good local norms can become outdated rather quickly.

DIFFERENT COLLEGE CULTURES

A sixth limitation may grow out of the convincing discoveries made about the usefulness of complete and versatile statistical data. We find our delighted and persevering counselor now a knight in statistical armor, replete with probability tables, multiple regression equations, and armed to the teeth with errors of estimate and the multiple discriminant function. His counselee can get the best varied facts on his probability for survival at a number of colleges.

The counselee may take the statistically safest course of action only to find himself at a school unknown to him three months before, which offers no curricula of interest, and with social and extracurricular patterns the antithesis of what he had hoped to find. The counselee had excellent facts dispensed to him, but the counselor's enthusiasm for the impressive welter of statistical data made these seem to be the only facts worth considering.

USING TECHNICAL DATA

Some counselors feel that the information-imparting aspect of counseling is relatively unimportant and, in fact, incompatible with the crucial clarification of feeling function. In this therapeutic frame of reference test data of any kind are generally held to be relatively unimportant. Other workers of more statistical bent will continue to seek varied but generally highly technical ways of presenting test data in such form as to make their limitations apparent; yet, too often these researchers speak a strange tongue unintelligible to all but their own sect.

Counselors must certainly be able to go beyond the ability to define "percentile" in writing or to know that intelligence tests generally are good predictors of grades. Enough has been learned about validity studies to permit, in the academic situation at least, a potential wealth of tremendously useful data. Counselors must be capable of recognizing the finer technical aspects of the data with which they work to capitalize on these findings, and they must then be versatile and communicative enough to translate the concepts for the counselee, who seldom will have had courses in the statistics of inference.

32   *Tests: Misconception, Misuse, and Overuse*

FRANK B. WOMER

Placing a reliable and valid test in the hands of an untrained and ignorant test interpreter can have serious and unfortunate consequences. If sound procedures for developing and evaluating a testing program are not followed, some of the misuses of tests and test data discussed by Womer in the following article may result. Several recommendations are implicit in the article. Development of an effective testing program requires highly trained, intelligent, and motivated personnel. It is very often the case that an in-service training program in test administration and interpretation should be undertaken concurrently with the establishment of the testing program. Students as well as faculty need to be informed as to the purposes of the program by specifying the ways in which the results will be used.

We are in a boom period of standardized testing in elementary and secondary schools. Millions of tests are administered each year to pupils at all grade levels —achievement tests, mental ability tests, aptitude tests, and interest inventories, as well as several other types of tests and inventories. Some of these tests are given for college scholarship purposes and some for college admissions purposes. Title V of the National Defense Education Act has stimulated, and in some instances required additions to testing programs at the secondary level. In general, however, these external influences account for a relatively small percentage of the total standardized testing undertaken by a school system.

There are at least two factors which have had a greater impact upon the amount of testing done in the schools than NDEA or college requirements. First, there has been and continues to be a natural growth of standardized testing at all grade levels. Second, the rapid growth of the guidance movement has meant a corresponding rapid growth in testing. This latter influence may well be the most influential one operating, for in many schools the testing program is developed by and operated by guidance personnel.

Inauguration or expansion of a testing program is relatively easy. Decisions made one day can be implemented within a week or two. The only time lag is that

---

Reprinted with permission of author from the *Michigan Journal of Secondary Education*, 1961, Vol. 2, pp. 153–161.

of the United States mail in delivering orders for tests and getting test materials from the publisher to the school. Machine methods for test scoring have reduced and, in many cases, eliminated objections that a testing program is a burden upon individual teachers. The school budget and allocation of time for testing are the only real problems to face if an administrator or faculty decides to enlarge the testing program. Thus it is relatively easy to test.

The values of standardized testing, however, cannot be dismissed so quickly. Such values are dependent upon two processes: (1) establishment of proper goals of testing and the development of a testing program to meet those goals, and (2) proper use of test results. Both of these processes are essential to the operation of a successful testing program. Most educators feel, and rightfully so, that the major weakness of testing today is in the area of test use.

Many writers have made this point, and most school administrators are acutely aware of the fact that the ultimate criterion for judging the effectiveness of their testing programs is the correct use of test results. Accumulating test scores in cumulative files is not evidence of test use. Correct use depends upon getting test results into the hands of counselors, teachers, administrators, pupils, and parents and of being sure that each consumer of these results is made knowledgeable enough to interpret them. In this latter statement—"made knowledgeable enough to interpret them"—lies the key to proper test use.

There are a number of ways that test scores are misused or overused and there are a number of misconceptions about tests and test scores that are common enough to warrant special attention. While one could think of innumerable examples of specific errors in test interpretation, the purpose of this article is to point up some of the more common mistakes in order to help increase the knowledgeable use of test results. Ten points have been selected for discussion; others could have been added.

CATEGORIZING A PUPIL AT A SPECIFIC LEVEL OF ACHIEVEMENT OR ABILITY

One of the most common mistakes made by persons unskilled in interpreting test results is the assumption of perfect reliability of a test score. Too often it is assumed that an IQ of 105 represents performance definitely superior to that represented by an IQ of 104 and definitely inferior to that represented by 106. Too often we fail to realize that a test score is best interpreted as a good estimate of the general level of performance, and that it will vary from test to test and from time to time. Test users must accept the concept of variability of test scores over time and over tests. The assessment of human traits and abilities is not at the same level of accuracy as that found in a physics laboratory. It probably is closer to the level of accuracy found in the predictions of weather, in which temperature predictions are generally within a few degrees of actual temperatures, but in which differences of ten or more degrees are common enough to be remembered vividly by critics.

Another aspect of this assumption of greater accuracy than actually prevails is the use of a single estimate (test score) to predict human performance. It is generally wise to insist on having two or three reading scores, or two or three aptitude scores, before putting much confidence in them. This is a direct result of the unreliability present in all test scores. If a pupil receives percentiles of 35 and of 40 on arithmetic tests given in two different years, one can have greater confidence that his level of achievement in arithmetic is in the average range than if only one of these scores is available.

CONFUSION OF NORMS AND STANDARDS

Norms are test scores which tell us the level of performance attained by an average or typical group of pupils. Standards represent human judgments of the level of performance that "should be" attained by a group of pupils. A test user should not assume that "typical" pupil performance is automatically the "proper" level of performance for pupils in a particular school system. It is reasonable, of course, to assume that pupils in many school systems will tend to perform at a level close to the level of test norms. In others, however, it is reasonable to assume that pupils will perform at a higher level or at a lower level.

One occasionally finds a test user who completely fails to grasp the conception of what a test norm is. Since a test norm represents "typical" performance, then of necessity half of the pupils in a typical or average group will have scores at or below the average score. If a teacher of a typical group of pupils finds that 40 percent of his pupils are below grade level in reading, he is to be congratulated. In the norm group for whatever test is being used, 50 percent of all the pupils were at or below grade level. The assumption that all pupils in a class should be at grade level is patently impossible, unless one knows that the poorest achieving pupil in one's class is in the top 50 percent of all pupils his own age or grade.

ASSUMPTION THAT TEST SCORES PREDICT SUCCESS OR FAILURE FOR INDIVIDUAL PUPILS

One way that test results often are overused is based on the assumption that a particular score or series of scores does in fact predict success or failure with unfailing accuracy. It is well established that students who succeed in colleges of engineering generally make high scores on numerical ability tests. Yet it is not correct to conclude from such data that Johnny, with a 50th percentile rank on a test of numerical ability, will not succeed in an engineering course. It is correct to conclude that of every one hundred students with numerical ability scores the same as Johnny's only a small percentage will succeed in an engineering curriculum. The test score does provide information of a probability type; it enables a student or parent or counselor to know the odds for success or failure. It is a well-known fact that long shots occasionally win the Kentucky Derby, but year in, year out the favorites generally win.

It is not unusual for two counselors to look at the same test scores for an individual pupil and to come to somewhat different conclusions. For this reason it is well to face the fact that while test scores do provide information that can be helpful in decision making, the decisions for courses of action are made by human beings, not by the scores.

Added to this overuse of test scores is the failure of some people to utilize all pertinent data available about a student when test scores are known. To allow test scores to outweigh all other judgmental data is a misuse of these scores; to ignore test scores in favor of other judgmental data also is a misuse of these scores.

DETERMINATION OF VOCATIONAL GOALS

"Mary's scores from a clerical speed and accuracy test and from a spelling test are only average. Therefore, Mary should not consider secretarial work as a career possibility." Or, "Since Jim's interest profile shows high scores in 'Scientific' and 'Social Service' he should elect a pre-med course in college." How often can vocational counseling be summed up in just such simple statements? It is so easy to make the jump from test score to occupation, and it seems so logical that this type of interpretation should be accurate. Unfortunately, the predictive validity of test scores in high school for success in specific occupations is not good enough to permit such interpretations. Most evidence of the predictive efficiency of test scores relates those scores to academic curricula. We can say with a fair degree of accuracy that certain patterns of test scores predict fairly well in different curricula. That is the type of validity data that is generally available.

The use of test scores in vocational counseling should tend to open doors of possible occupations rather than close them. Again, presenting the relationship between test scores and occupational areas on a probability basis can be helpful, and is certainly more accurate than making the assumption that certain test scores assure success in one field and failure in another.

ASSUMPTION THAT INTELLIGENCE AND ACHIEVEMENT ARE SEPARATE AND DISTINCT

Here are two sample questions from standardized tests:
1. Extraneous
   a. extra   b. foreign   c. transparent   d. noisy

2. Make *indelible* means
   a. indistinct   b. permanent   c. purple   d. identical

Both are vocabulary items. One of them is taken from a widely used intelligence test (*California Test of Mental Maturity*) and the other from a widely used achievement battery (*Iowa Tests of Educational Development*). Vocabulary items measure the learned meanings of words; vocabulary items are our best single measure of general intelligence or scholastic aptitude. Arithmetic items and general information items are also found in both achievement tests and intelligence tests. It is true, of course, that some items suitable for an intelligence test (number series, verbal analogies) are not good measures of achievement. It also is true that many direct measures of achievement (capitalization, punctuation, spelling) are not good measures of intellectual potential.

There is considerable overlap between standardized tests of achievement and standardized intelligence tests. One of the important differences between the two is the way the results are used. When analyzing achievement test scores one is generally considering past performance, what has been accomplished. When analyzing intelligence test scores one is generally looking forward to the future, predicting performance.

It is well to keep in mind the fact that intelligence is inferred from achievement. We have no direct measures of intelligence completely divorced from achievement.

ASSUMPTION THAT INTERESTS AND APTITUDES ARE SYNONYMOUS

Probably few users of standardized tests would acknowledge a belief in clearly different domains. Yet how many users of standardized interest inventories can truthfully say that they have never made the jump from a high percentile score in "Persuasive" to the suggestion that Bill probably could succeed in sales activities? To say that Bill seems to be interested in many of the same things that are of interest to people who work in occupations that require influencing other people may be accurate. But to say that Bill will likely succeed in one of these occupations is to make the unwarranted jump from interest to aptitude.

There is evidence that interests and aptitudes are correlated, but not at a level that allows us to predict one from the other with a high degree of accuracy. This is not to say that interest inventories are useless, but their use might well center on their motivational attributes, on their power to stimulate pupil concern over long-range planning.

MISCONCEPTION OF THE MEANINGS OF CERTAIN TYPES OF DERIVED SCORES

Students of education have been and are continuing to be taught that an intelligence quotient is obtained by dividing mental age by chronological age, and that mental age is determined by the test performance of students at different age levels. Yet, as a matter of fact, very few of the IQ's to be found in the cumulative folders of elementary and secondary schools today are quotient scores at all. IQ's are standard scores, just as are z scores, T scores, stanines, College Board scores, and others for almost every widely used intelligence test.

It is true that IQ's originally were quotient scores. But, primarily for statistical reasons, the deviation IQ was developed some years ago and has since met with almost universal adoption. Even the Stanford-Binet test switched to a deviation IQ in 1959. The change from a quotient score to a standard score has not necessitated any drastic change in interpretation. Yet it seems to the writer that test users would be well advised to stop paying lip service to a type of score that no longer exists, and to become familiar with standard scores, the type of scores actually being used with our intelligence tests.

The grade-placement or grade-equivalent score is another type of derived score that is frequently misinterpreted or overused. All too often it is assumed that a grade-placement score is an indication of the grade to which a pupil should be assigned. It does not provide that type of information; it simply tells a user whether a pupil is doing high, average, or low quality work. A percentile rank also provides the same assessment of level of work, yet avoids the danger of overinterpretation. If one wishes to compare a pupil's achievement on two different tests in an achievement battery (e.g., reading level versus arithmetic level), a grade-equivalent score may lead one to an important misinterpretation. Because of the variability (standard deviation) of grade-placement scores from test to test it is possible for a sixth-grade pupil to be at the 90th percentile in both reading and arithmetic, yet receive grade-placement scores of 8.8 in reading and 8.0 in arithmetic.[1] If a teacher sees only the grade placement scores of 8.8 and 8.0 he may assume superiority in reading, whereas the two scores represent equivalent performance. For test-by-test comparisons in elementary-level achievement batteries, percentile scores should be used.

GRADING OR PROMOTING PUPILS

Standardized achievement tests are designed with certain purposes in mind. In general, test authors attempt to identify those skills and understandings that are common to most educational programs. They look for the common denominators; they make no attempt to cover those unique aspects of content that a particular school system may incorporate in its curricula offering. They cannot attempt to reflect a particular teacher's goals for his own pupils. Thus, while achievement test results represent very useful assessment of certain skills and understandings that are common to many classrooms, they should not be used to replace a teacher's own assessment devices.

In many schools standardized achievement tests are given toward the beginning of the school year. They are used to look ahead rather than to look back, to diagnose rather than to evaluate or grade. In those schools that use standardized achievement tests at the end of the year, it may be interesting for a teacher to

---

[1] *Iowa Tests of Basic Skills,* end-of-year percentile norms for sixth-grade pupils.

compare the results with his own judgments. It is not wise for the test results to be used to replace his judgments, in either grading or promotion.

JUDGING EFFECTIVENESS OF INSTRUCTION

Just as standardized tests are not designed to be used for grading pupils, they are not designed to be used for grading teachers. Many of the outcomes of class-room instruction cannot be programmed in standardized tests. Those that can be programmed in tests may not be meaningful because of different emphases, different content, and different grade placement in a particular school.

Of special concern is the attitude engendered in teachers in a school attempting to assess instruction through achievement tests. When test results are used to judge teachers, teachers soon learn to teach for the tests.

It is interesting to note that in some instances teachers even feel compelled to "teach for" ability tests. They somehow feel that it isn't respectable to turn in a set of IQ scores for filing in a cumulative record unless all or almost all of them are at least 100. Such a feeling, of course, is based on a misconception of the meaning of intelligence. A teacher may be cutting his own throat with such high scores, for if his pupils all are above average in ability, they may be expected to show equally high achievement levels.

COMPARING RESULTS FROM DIFFERENT TESTS

There is a very natural tendency for test users to assume that a language usage score from one test is directly comparable to a language usage score from another test, that an IQ from one test means the same thing as an IQ from another. When making such assumptions one tends to forget two very important charac-teristics of standardized tests:

1. Test authors do not build their tests on the same specifications, following the same blueprints. Each one develops his own specifications for test construc-tion. There usually is considerable overlap between the plans for a language usage test developed by one author, and the plans developed by another. How-ever, there is never a complete overlap. Scores from two tests measuring the same attribute vary to a certain extent because the test designs vary.

2. The norms for different tests are based upon different groups of pupils. Each test author aims at securing a truly random population of pupils for use in standardizing his test. Each author falls somewhat short of his goal. While it is correct to assume that test norms for two different arithmetic tests are based on groups with considerable overlap in achievement, it is not correct to assume 100 percent overlap.

Thus, two IQ's derived from two different intelligence tests are not exactly equivalent. It has been demonstrated that IQ's can vary as much as 5 or 10 points between different tests for no other reason than that they are different tests.

Sometimes one hears this objection: "But how can IQ's be different from different tests? I thought that all good intelligence tests correlated well with each other." It is true that the correlation between different intelligence tests are generally sizable, and many times are almost as high as the reliability of the separate tests. Such correlations do not guarantee comparability of norms. Such correlations simply say that pupils taking the different tests will tend to get scores putting them in the same relative rank order but not with the same scores. For example, suppose one were to take a set of IQ's (or any other test score) and add 50 points to each score. The correlation between the original IQ's and the new scores would be perfect, yet the two sets of scores would be 50 points apart.

As was mentioned earlier, we are in the middle of a boom period of testing. If the users of tests do a good job of interpreting the results for the improvement of our understanding of boys and girls and for the improvement of instruction, the boom will level off on a satisfactory plateau of test use. If the users of test results fall into the various misuses, overuses, and misconceptions that are possible, the boom will most certainly be followed by a "bust."

It is the thesis of this article that the consumers of test scores must be thoroughly conversant with proper methods of test use and must studiously avoid misuses, overuses, and misconceptions.

"A little knowledge is a dangerous thing."

VII

CURRICULUM EVALUATION

Revitalized interest in the teaching-learning process in American education during the past twenty-five years or so has resulted in, among other things, a phlethora of new curricula. The impetus given curriculum development has come from both subject matter scholars and educational researchers. From the former because of the discovery of new knowledge and insights into how their disciplines are structured. From the latter because of new insights into the learning process as it relates to the organization and presentation of knowledge. The development of any "new" curriculum has associated with it problems of evaluation. The evaluation of over-all effectiveness, cost, type of variables influencing effectiveness, and relevance are a few of the areas in need of assessment. Evaluation techniques previously adequate for assessing the effectiveness of small units of material are significantly less applicable when imposed on larger chunks of information, the learning of which is highly complex, involves prerequisite learnings, and sequential behaviors, or on whole programs.

The following statement summarizes what contemporary curriculum evaluation is all about.

Curriculum evaluation can be viewed as a process of collection and processing data pertaining to an educational program, on the basis of which decision can be made about that program. The data are of two kinds: (1) objective description of goals, environments, personnel, methods and content, and immediate and long range outcomes; and (2) recorded personal judgments of the quality and appropriateness of goals, inputs and outcomes. The data—in both raw and analyzed form—can be used either to delineate and resolve problems in educational programs being developed or to answer absolute and comparative questions about established programs (Taylor and Maguire, 1966).

This broad general description allows the form of a final curriculum evaluation plan to take on any shape dictated by its requirements. A number of models have been suggested which attempt to anticipate this final evaluation design (e.g., Provus, 1971; Stake, 1967; and Stufflebeam, 1968).

There are a number of emphases that differentiate curriculum evaluation from other applications of evaluative procedures. These emphases are concerned with the following areas.

1. *Content of Goals*—The objectives of curriculum evaluation tend to be more process and behavior oriented than concerned with subject matter content.

2. *Breadth of Objectives*—Not only are the objectives different in content, but a greater range of phenomena are involved.

3. *Complexity of Outcomes*—Changes in the requirements for living and education, and the increased knowledge we now possess about the teaching-learning process dovetail into objectives which are quite complex from the standpoint of cognitive and performance criteria. The interface of cognitive, affective and psychomotor variables further complicates our ability to see what must be evaluated.

4. *Focus of Total Evaluation Effort*—There is a definite trend toward a shift from individual learner to total program. This trend is perhaps what distinguishes current thinking about curriculum evaluation from Tyler's (1942) approach.

5. *Context of Evaluation*—Curriculum evaluation should occur in a naturalistic setting. It is in the real-life setting with all its unpredictable contingencies and uncontrolled variables that education takes place. If we teach in that setting we must evaluate in that setting.

Those interested in further readings concerned with curriculum evaluation are referred to the following sources: Stufflebeam, et al., 1970; Payne, 1974; Tyler, 1969; Grobman, 1968; Suchman, 1967; Wittrock and Wiley, 1970; and Wick and Beggs, 1971.

The four articles of this chapter can only suggest the value and complexity of curriculum evaluation models and methodologies. The chapter begins with an article by an authority primarily concerned with curriculum. In it Frymier laments the discrete operation of the planning, implementation, and evaluation phases of education. He pleads for us to integrate these activities and to ask more relevant questions and continuously generate appropriate data and feed it back into the system.

In what has now become a classic presentation, Professor Cronbach alerts us, in the second article of the chapter, to many valuable uses of measurement and evaluation data aimed at improving the teaching-learning situation. Advocating an "absolute" approach to evaluation, the author recommends application of a variety of curriculum studies—process, proficiency, attitude, and follow-up.

Two types of evaluation have been distinguished by Scriven (1967). One type, summative evaluation, is concerned with assessing the final impact and effectiveness of a unit or curriculum. An end-of-course evaluation would be illustrative. The second type of evaluation, formative, described by Dick in the third paper of this chapter, is focused on generating and feeding back data hopefully useful in revising and improving the instructional product, be it a programmed text, unit in French history, laboratory demonstration, or any instructional product or process. In a sense Dick has here operationalized some of Cronbach's suggestions in the previous article.

The chapter closes with a description of the background and initial read-out of results stemming from the monumental effort to assess the gross impact of American education. Merwin and Womer, both former staff directors of the National Assessment of Educational Progress project, describe (1) how the data are gathered, (2) the tremendous scope of the undertaking, (3) the potential value of the data, and (4) some sample exercises with summaries of performances from the first national data collection.

The practice of curriculum evaluation extends from the classroom to the Capitol. Hopefully the data gathered will positively influence decision making. Unfortunately, the potential input from evaluation activities has not been realized. The use of such data needs to be planned for and systematically integrated into the decision making process. After studying the following set of articles the reader should be able to see how and why evaluation data, particularly when used formatively, can be used to improve instructional programs. Finally, he should gain some understanding of large-scale evaluation programs by following the development of the National Assessment of Educational Progress.

33   *Curriculum Assessment: Problems and Possibilities*

JACK R. FRYMIER

The intimate relationship between curriculum development and evaluation is again stressed in this article. It makes simple sense that if you do not ask the appropriate questions you will get the wrong answers or, at the very least, the right answers to the wrong questions. Perhaps, and unfortunately, American educators and evaluators are prone to ask questions related to efficiency rather than effectiveness.

Surely the quality of a curriculum package should not be judged on the basis of the frequency of its use. The most widely used package is not necessarily the best.

Many factors in addition to adoption statistics and cost need to be considered, the most important being the nature of local educational objectives and the characteristics of teachers and student body.

Frymier's analogy between planning, doing, and assessing in government and in education—both social activities—is well drawn.

Is it more important to ask if a new curriculum is effective or to ask if it is better than the existing one? Why? In what way is the effectiveness of instruction more important than efficiency? How can the application of measurement methods help to answer these questions? *

Every model for curriculum development includes the concept of assessment or evaluation. From the theoretical point of view, evaluation plays an important part in improving program in several ways. Purposes can be selected, for example, on the basis of good data about the nature of society or the nature of the learner. Or, content, experiences, organization, and methodology can be set forth in testable form.

For instance, rather than assuming that any particular selection of content or sequence of experiences or methodological approaches or organizational stratagems is effective, responsible leaders in curriculum development can hypothesize about these things, then put their hypotheses to empirical test. Over a period of time such evaluative and assessment techniques should enable curriculum workers to make steady progress in terms of improving program.

Two major developments have forced the concepts of assessment and evaluation into special prominence. Talk of national assessment in education, on the one hand, and the requirement for evaluation built into the Elementary and Secondary Education Act program, on the other, are forcing curriculum workers to reexamine these notions as they apply to curriculum development today.

Any view of the educational scene suggests that programs are changing dramatically. At no time in the history of American schools have curricular changes been so widespread or so intensive as in the past decade. Modifications of course content, organizational structures, methodological approaches, evaluation procedures, and even purposes themselves have been instituted. Unless one is willing to accept change for its own sake, however, he is forced to ask:

*Reprinted by permission of the publisher, from David A. Payne: *Curriculum Evaluation* (Lexington, Mass.: D. C. Heath and Company, 1974).

Reprinted with permission of the Association for Supervision and Curriculum Development and Jack R. Frymier. Copyright 1966 by the Association for Supervision and Curriculum Development. From *Educational Leadership*, 1966, Vol. 21 (November), pp. 124–128.

"Are the curriculum changes really significant?" Or to ask in another way, "Do children learn better in the new programs than they did in the old?"

This, of course, may be the wrong question. Some persons maintain that since the old purposes were not themselves appropriate, it is unreasonable to compare the new efforts today in terms of objectives which are actually obsolete. On the other hand, it may very well be that some kind of accumulated curriculum wisdom has been reflected in the decades of activity which have gone into what we generally describe as "conventional program." If this is true, comparisons of new efforts with previously existing programs may be perfectly legitimate.

NEW QUESTIONS NEEDED

The fact is, these questions are academic. Even though changes in curriculum have been extensive, and many of these changes have been positive, few people are satisfied with the state of affairs in American curriculum today. The inadequacies are so obvious that thoughtful curriculum workers are continuously struggling to find new and more powerful ways to improve the program.

This dissatisfaction arises in part because of a kind of gnawing professional perspective which says: "No program is perfect. We must improve." Part of the dissatisfaction, however, stems from the very real fact that inappropriate and ineffective curricula can be found in almost any district or any building without difficulty at all. Too many children hate the very thought of having to learn in school. Too many find school a boring, unexciting place to be. Too many are unsuccessful in acquiring those ways of behaving which seem desirable to those in charge.

Why is this so? Many factors probably account for such a state of affairs today. I would like to suggest two. In my opinion, we have tended to ask the wrong questions in curriculum, and secondly, assessment has been ineffectively utilized as part of the total educational scheme.

If we ask the wrong questions we always get the wrong answers. In curriculum development we often ask the *frequency* question or the *efficiency* question, for example, rather than the *effectiveness* question. We say, "How many schools are using language laboratories?" or "How many schools have PSSC physics this year?" "How many classrooms are nongraded?" "How many teachers utilize generative grammar or structural linguistics in their language arts programs?"

The assumption underlying these questions is that if more schools are using a particular program, it must be better. Obviously that is the wrong assumption. Frequency is not an appropriate criterion at all.

This fall, for instance, more than half of the youngsters who study physics in our secondary schools will be studying the PSSC physics program, but the proportional enrollment of high school students taking physics has steadily decreased during the same period of time that the new program has come into being. If we assume that the number of programs in use is important, we pose for ourselves the absurd possibility that the time might come when all of the schools would teach a particular course and none of the children would take it, that we would then be doing a perfect job.

Consider another example. Curriculum workers frequently make judgments about program in terms of money. "How much will it cost?" "How efficient will it be?" "Can we afford such an innovation?" These questions presuppose that the basic purpose of education is to save money. No one is willing to agree with that aloud, of course, but the fact remains that if we ask an economic question, we can only get an economic answer. But that is the wrong question.

If schools exist to save money, there are many ways in which expenditures can be reduced. We can lower teachers' salaries, we can increase class size, or we can eliminate expenditures for instructional materials, for instance. These will all save money. The purpose of education is not to save money, though. It is to help children learn.

Curriculum workers must always focus upon the effectiveness question. Does the new program, do the new materials, will the new techniques enable students to learn more, better, faster, than some other approach? Does it make a significant difference in the lives and minds of those we teach? If it does, the program is effective. If it does not, the program is ineffective. Whether it costs more money or less or whether it is widespread or is not evident in any other school at all is immaterial. Frequency questions or economic questions simply get in the way. We must learn to ask the effectiveness question every time.

A CONCEPTUAL FLAW

A deeper, more elusive problem affecting program development, however, stems from the fact that education is a social system with a conceptual flaw. Every social system represents a human undertaking designed to fulfill human needs. Government, science, industry, education—these are all illustrations of different kinds of social systems in evidence today. Looked at in terms of systems theory, every effective social system reflects three phases of operation which accomplish separate functions, and these functions enable the system to maintain itself in an ongoing, dynamic, improving way.

Phase one includes the intellectual activities, the planning, policy making, hypothesizing function. Phase two involves the doing, accomplishing, effecting function. Phase three is the evaluating, assessing, reflecting, judgmental function. Taken together, they represent various aspects of social undertakings which are designed to allow the system to accomplish the objectives toward which it is aimed, and at the same time keep changing for the better.

These three phases of any social system are most clearly illustrated in our concept of government. The planning phase is represented by the legislative branch. The doing phase is represented by the executive branch. The evaluating or assessing phase is represented by the judicial branch. In industry, however, the model still holds. Somebody plans, somebody produces, and somebody judges the effectiveness of those activities in a realistic way.

Any careful study of social systems other than education suggests that these three functions have been made relatively discrete and that they are accomplished by different groups, each one of which has power. That is, the Congress is different than the President, and the Supreme Court is different still. The same notion holds at the state and local level, too. From the functional standpoint, our system of government has been conceptualized in such a way that these different functions are accomplished by separate groups.

Another point, however, rests on the fact that social systems in an open society actually depend upon the third phase of the operation to assure improvement and intelligent change. That is, when the courts decide that a particular law is constitutional or unconstitutional or that a particular action by the President either is or is not appropriate, they feed back into the system new data which guarantee that the enterprise will be able to change itself and to improve. In industry the same thing is also true.

Planning and producing a new product or service represent the first and second phases of that social system in operation. Once the product goes on sale, however, evaluation must occur. Judgments are made by those who buy. If the general public buys the product or service, what they really do is feed back into the system new data which tell those responsible for planning and production that they have done the job well. Or, if the product or service becomes available and the public refuses to buy, this too, constitutes corrective feedback. It tells those responsible that something about their operation is not satisfactory and it must be changed. In either event, evaluation plays the critical role of providing corrective feedback to the other parts of the system so that the entire operation can be improved.

ROLE OF FEEDBACK

Two things are important about our discussion thus far. One is that the concept of corrective feedback, which is performed during the evaluation phase of the social systems operation, represents the precise point at which improvement can be assured. Second, in these illustrations it is also evident that the assessment or evaluation effort is best accomplished by a separate group which has appropriate influence of its own. Congress is not allowed to pass judgment on the constitutionality of its own laws, for example, nor are manufacturing companies permitted to have the ultimate say in the worthwhileness or value of the products they produce. These decisions are reserved for other groups.

In other words, feedback is imperative if the system is to operate at the highest possible level of effectiveness; yet, at the same time, it is probably not possible to assume that those who plan or those who implement can also accomplish the evaluation role. The power of evaluation rests in part upon the nature of the feedback information which is generated by the process, but in part upon the fact that the evaluation group has an authority of its own. Said still another way, our system of government and our system of economics, at least, presume that when the evaluation group makes its decision known, the rest of the system will have to pay attention to the feedback. The rest of the system is not free to ignore the data, whether they are positive or negative in form.

Looked at in terms of such a social systems model, education obviously has a conceptual flaw. School boards accomplish the policy making role. Professional persons undertake the effecting, implementing, doing role. But there is no special group whose responsibilities encompass the assessment function in any meaningful way. The general public passes judgment on the effectiveness of schools, of course, but seldom do they have a way of communicating their concerns with precision to assure improvement in schools. They may vote down a bond issue, for instance, but often as not no one really knows what the negative vote means.

On the other hand, advisory councils or curriculum councils often attempt to perform the evaluation role. In the first instance the fact that their activities are advisory—no one has to pay attention to the feedback—illustrates the fact that the system is not assured of information in such a way that it has to improve. Likewise, curriculum councils may very well study a particular problem in program carefully and creatively, only to find that their recommendations go completely ignored. That such recommendations may be accepted and used only serves to reinforce the fact that they may also be ignored. There is no rigor in the system which insists that we utilize the best that we know.

Theoretically, education has this conceptual flaw. There is no aspect of the system which regularly generates evaluative data, nor is there anything in the concept which requires that the system pay attention to the feedback if it should appear.

Do we need curriculum evaluation? Is assessment important? On these questions everyone agrees. Of course! Where should evaluation occur? Who should accomplish the assessment role? How should these persons be selected? How can we assure ourselves that the system will be able to use and profit by the feedback data which are obtained? These are difficult problems.

Several alternatives seem to be available, but what is needed most now is a thoughtful consideration of analyses such as the one presented here, then extensive discussion of both the problems and possibilities which are involved. We may be on the verge of a genuine breakthrough in education, if we can muster the creative genius to explore the implications inherent in a consideration of the real power of assessing carefully everything we do.

LEE J. CRONBACH

The focus of this article is on the ways in which evaluation may be brought into play in answering three basic questions: (1) how can we improve courses, (2) how well is an individual learning, and (3) how effective is the entire educational system? The nature of the answers to these questions will dictate the kind of data collected, and to some extent the way in which they are gathered. It should again be emphasized that, although difficult to assess, attitudes and other so called "affective" outcomes need to be evaluated. Cronbach's comments apply equally well to a traditional or a recently instituted or newly developed curriculum or course of study. The on-going and feedback nature of an effective evaluation system cannot be overemphasized. It is probably true that the most useful evaluation information is that which allows for adjustments and modifications during the developmental stages of course or curriculum development, rather than examining the end product only. See an article by Forehand (1971) for description of such a system.

What are the relative advantages and disadvantages of comparative versus absolute curriculum evaluation studies? Why does the follow-up study come closest to assessing the ultimate contribution of an educational program? What are the inherent difficulties in undertaking such studies? *

The national interest in improving education has generated several highly important projects to improve curricula, particularly at the secondary-school level. In conferences of directors of "course content improvement" programs questions about evaluation are frequently raised. Those who inquire about evaluation have various motives, ranging from sheer scientific curiosity about classroom events to a desire to assure a sponsor that money has been well spent. While the curriculum developers sincerely wish to use the skills of evaluation specialists, I am not certain that they have a clear picture of what evaluation can do and should try to do. And, on the other hand, I am becoming convinced that some techniques and habits of thought of the evaluation specialist are ill suited to current curriculum studies. To serve these studies, what philosophy and methods of evaluation are required? And particularly, how must we depart from the familiar doctrines and rituals of the testing game?

*Reprinted by permission of the publisher, from David A. Payne: *Curriculum Evaluation* (Lexington, Mass.: D. C. Heath and Company, 1974).

Reprinted with permission of author and publisher from the *Teachers College Record*, 1963, Vol. 64, (#8, May), pp. 672–683. This reprinting of the original paper is based on changes suggested and approved by the author in an earlier version of Heath, Robert (Ed.), *New Curricula*, Harper and Row, pp. 231–248.

DECISIONS SERVED BY EVALUATION

To draw attention to its full range of functions, we may define "evaluation" broadly as the *collection and use of information to make decisions about an educational program.* The program may be a set of instructional materials distributed nationally, the instructional activities of a single school, or the educational experiences of a single pupil. Many types of decisions are to be made, and many varieties of information are useful. It becomes immediately apparent that evaluation is a diversified activity and that no one set of principles will suffice for all situations. But measurement specialists have so concentrated upon one process—the preparation of pencil-and-paper achievement tests for assigning scores to individual pupils—that the principles pertinent to that process have somehow become enshrined as *the* principles of evaluation. "Tests," we are told, "should fit the content of the curriculum." Also, "only those evaluation procedures should be used that yield reliable scores." These and other hallowed principles are not entirely appropriate to evaluation for course improvement. Before proceeding to support this contention, I wish to distinguish among purposes of evaluation and to relate them to historical developments in testing and curriculum making.

We may separate three types of decisions for which evaluation is used:

(1) Course improvement: deciding what instructional materials and methods are satisfactory and where change is needed.

(2) Decisions about individuals: identifying the needs of the pupil for the sake of planning his instruction, judging pupil merit for purposes of selection and grouping, acquainting the pupil with his own progress and deficiencies.

Course improvement is set apart by its broad temporal and geographical reference; it involves the modification of recurrently used materials and methods. Developing a standard exercise to overcome a misunderstanding would be course improvement, but deciding whether a certain pupil should work through that exercise would be an individual decision. Administrative regulation likewise is local in effect, whereas an improvement in a course is likely to be pertinent wherever the course is offered.

It was for the sake of course improvement that systematic evaluation was first introduced. When that famous muckraker Joseph Rice gave the same spelling test in a number of American schools, and so gave the first impetus to the educational testing movement, he was interested in evaluating a curriculum. Crusading against the extended spelling drills that then loomed large in the school schedule—"the spelling grind"—Rice collected evidence of their worthlessness so as to provoke curriculum revision. As the testing movement developed, however, it took on a different function.

The greatest expansion of systematic achievement testing occurred in the

920s. At that time, the content of any course was taken pretty much as estab-
ished and beyond criticism save for small shifts of topical emphasis. At the
administrator's direction, standard tests covering the curriculum were given to
assess the efficiency of the teacher or the school system. Such administrative
esting fell into disfavor when used injudiciously and heavyhandedly in the
920s and 1930s. Administrators and accrediting agencies fell back upon de-
criptive features of the school program in judging adequacy. Instead of col-
ecting direct evidence of educational impact, they judged schools in terms of
ize of budget, student-staff ratio, square feet of laboratory space, and the
number of advanced credits accumulated by the teacher. This tide, it appears,
s about to turn. On many university campuses, administrators wanting to
know more about their product are installing "operations research offices."
Testing directed toward quality control seems likely to increase in the lower
chools as well.

After 1930 or thereabouts, tests were given almost exclusively for judgments
about individuals—to select students for advanced training, to assign marks
within a class, and to diagnose individual competences and deficiencies. For
any such decisions, one wants precise and valid comparisons of one individual
with other individuals or with a standard. Much of test theory and test tech-
ology has been concerned with making measurements precise. Important
hough precision is for most decisions about individuals, I shall argue that in
evaluating courses we need not struggle to obtain precise scores for individuals.

While measurers have been well content with the devices used to make scores
precise, they have been less complacent about validity. Prior to 1935, the pupil
was examined mostly on factual knowledge and mastery of fundamental skills.
Tyler's research and writings of that period developed awareness that higher
mental processes are not evoked by simple factual tests, and that instruction
hat promotes factual knowledge may not promote—indeed, may interfere with
—other more important educational outcomes. Tyler, Lindquist, and their
tudents demonstrated that tests can be designed to measure such general edu-
ational outcomes as ability to comprehend scientific method. Whereas a stu-
lent can prepare for a factual test only through a course of study that includes
he facts tested, many different courses of study may promote the same *general*
understandings and attitudes. In evaluating today's new curricula, it will clearly
be important to appraise the student's general educational growth, which cur-
iculum developers say is more important than mastery of the specific lessons
presented. Note, for example, that the Biological Sciences Curriculum Study
ffers three courses with substantially different "subject matter" as alternative
outes to much the same educational ends.

Although some instruments capable of measuring general outcomes were
prepared during the 1930s, they were never very widely employed. The pre-
ailing philosophy of the curriculum, particularly among "progressives," called
or developing a program to fit local requirements, capitalizing on the capacities

and experiences of local pupils. The faith of the 1920s in a "standard" curriculum was replaced by a faith that the best learning experience would result from teacher-pupil planning in each classroom. Since each teacher or each class could choose different content and even different objectives, this philosophy left little place for standard testing. . . .

Many evaluation specialists came to see test development as a strategy for training the teacher in service, so that the process of test making came to be valued more than the test—or the test data—that resulted. The following remarks by Bloom (1961) are representative of a whole school of thought [Also see Tyler, 1951]:

> The criterion for determining the quality of a school and its educational functions would be the extent to which it achieves the objectives it has set for itself. . . . Our experiences suggest that unless the school has translated the objectives into specific and operational definitions, little is likely to be done about the objectives. They remain pious hopes and platitudes. . . . Participation of the teaching staff in selecting as well as constructing evaluation instruments has resulted in improved instruments on one hand and, on the other hand, it has resulted in clarifying the objectives of instruction and in making them real and meaningful to teachers. . . . When teachers have actively participated in defining objectives and in selecting or constructing evaluation instruments, they return to the learning problems with great vigor and remarkable creativity. . . . Teachers who have become committed to a set of educational objectives which they thoroughly understand respond by developing a variety of learning experiences which are as diverse and as complex as the situation requires.

Thus, "evaluation" becomes a local and beneficial teacher-training activity. The benefit is attributed to thinking about what data to collect. Little is said about the actual use of test results; one has the impression that when test-making ends, the test itself is forgotten. Certainly, there is little enthusiasm for refining tests so that they can be used in other schools, for to do so would be to rob those teachers of the benefits of working out their own objectives and instruments

Bloom and Tyler describe both curriculum making and evaluation as integral parts of classroom instruction, which is necessarily decentralized. This outlook is far from that of "course improvement." The current national curriculum studies assume that curriculum making can be centralized. They prepare materials to be used in much the same way by teachers everywhere. It is assumed that having experts draft materials, and revising these after tryout produces better instructional activities than the local teacher would be likely to devise. In this context, it seems wholly appropriate to have most tests prepared by a central staff and to have results returned to that staff to guide further course improvement.

When evaluation is carried out in the service of course improvement, the chief aim is to ascertain what effects the course has—that is, what changes it produces in pupils [editor's italics]. This is not to inquire merely whether the ourse is effective or ineffective. Outcomes of instruction are multidimensional, and a satisfactory investigation will map out the effects of the course along these dimensions separately. To agglomerate many types of post-course performance into a single score is a mistake, because failure to achieve one objective is masked by success in another direction. Moreover, since a composite score embodies (and usually conceals) judgments about the importance of the various outcomes, only a report that treats the outcomes separately can be useful to educators who have different value hierarchies.

The greatest service evaluation can perform is to identify aspects of the course where revision is desirable [editor's italics]. Those responsible for developing course would like to present evidence that their course is effective. They are intrigued by the idea of having an "independent testing agency" render a judgment on their product. But to call in the evaluator only upon the completion of course development, to confirm what has been done, is to offer him a menial role and to make meager use of his services. To be influential in course improvement, evidence must become available midway in curriculum development, not in the home stretch, when the developer is naturally reluctant to tear open a supposedly finished body of materials and techniques. Evaluation, used to improve the course while it is still fluid, contributes more to improvement of education than evaluation used to appraise a product already placed on the market. . . .

Insofar as possible, evaluation should be used to understand how the course produces its effects and what parameters influence its effectiveness. It is important to learn, for example, that the outcome of programmed instruction depends very much upon the attitude of the teacher; indeed, this may be more important than to learn that on the average such instruction produces slightly better or worse results than conventional instruction.

Hopefully, evaluation studies will go beyond reporting on this or that course and help us to understand educational learning. Such insight will, in the end, contribute to the development of all courses rather than just the course under test. In certain of the new curricula, there are data to suggest that aptitude measures correlate much less with end-of-course achievement than they do with achievement on early units (Ferris, 1962). This finding is not well confirmed, but it is highly significant if true. If it is true for the new curricula and only for them, it has one implication; if the same effect appears in traditional courses, it means something else. Either way, it provides food for thought for teachers, counselors, and theorists. Evaluation studies should generate knowledge about the nature of the abilities that constitute educational goals. Twenty years after the Eight-Year Study of the Progressive Education Association, its testing techniques are in good repute, but we still know very little about what these instruments measure. Consider "Application of Principles in Science." Is this in any sense a unitary ability? Or has the able student only mastered certain principles one by one? Is the ability demonstrated on a test of this sort more prognostic of any later achievement than is factual knowledge? Such questions ought to receive substantial attention, although to the makers of any one course they are of only peripheral interest.

The aim to compare one course with another should not dominate plans for evaluation [editor's italics]. To be sure, decision makers have to choose between courses, and any evaluation report will be interpreted in part comparatively. But formally designed experiments, pitting one course against another are rarely definitive enough to justify their cost. Differences between average test scores resulting from different courses are usually small relative to the wide differences among and within classes taking the same course. At best, an experiment never does more than compare the present version of one course with the present version of another. A major effort to bring the losing contender nearer to perfection would be very likely to reverse the verdict of the experiment.

Any failure to equate the classes taking the competing courses will jeopardize the interpretation of an experiment—and such failures are almost inevitable. In testing a drug, we know that valid results cannot be obtained without double-blind control in which the doses for half the subjects are inert placebos; the placebo and the drug look alike, so that neither doctor nor patient knows who is receiving medication. Without this control, the results are useless even when the state of the patient is checked by completely objective indices. In an educational experiment, it is difficult to keep pupils unaware that they are an experimental group. And it is quite impossible to neutralize the biases of the teacher as those of the doctor are neutralized in the double-blind design. It is thus never certain whether any observed advantage is attributable to the educational innovation as such, or to the greater energy that teachers and students put forth when a method is fresh and "experimental." Some have contended that any course, even the most excellent, loses much of its potency as soon as success enthrones it as "the traditional method."

Since group comparisons give equivocal results, I believe that a formal study should be designed primarily to determine the post-course performance of a well described group with respect to many important objectives and side effects. Ours is a problem like that of the engineer examining a new automobile. He can set himself the task of defining its performance characteristics and its dependability. It would be merely distracting to put his question in the form "Is this car better or worse than the competing brand?" Moreover, in an experiment where the treatments compared differ in a dozen respects, no understanding is gained from the fact that the experiment shows a numerical advantage in favor of the new course. No one knows which of the ingredients is responsible for the advantage. More analytic experiments are much more useful than field trials applying markedly dissimilar treatments to different groups.

Small-scale, well controlled studies can profitably be used to compare alternative versions of the same course; in such a study, the differences between treatments are few enough and well enough defined that the results have explanatory value.

The three purposes—course improvement, decisions about individuals, and administrative regulation—call for measurement procedures having somewhat different qualities. When a test will be used to make an administrative judgment on the individual teacher, it is necessary to measure thoroughly and with conspicuous fairness; such testing, if it is to cover more than one outcome, becomes extremely time consuming. In judging a course, however, one can make satisfactory interpretations from data collected on a sampling basis, with no pretense of measuring thoroughly the accomplishments of any one class. A similar point is to be made about testing for decisions about individuals. A test of individuals must be conspicuously fair and extensive enough to provide a dependable score for each person. But if the performance will not influence the fate of the individual, we can ask him to perform tasks for which the course has not directly prepared him, and we can use techniques that would be prohibitively expensive if applied in a manner thorough enough to measure each person reliably.

METHODS OF EVALUATION

Range of Methods —Evaluation is too often visualized as the administration of a formal test, an hour or so in duration, at the close of a course. But there are many other methods for examining pupil performance, and pupil attainment is not the only basis for appraising a course.

It is quite appropriate to ask scholars whether the statements made in the course are consistent with the best contemporary knowledge. This is a sound and even a necessary procedure. One may go on to evaluate the pedagogy of the new course by soliciting opinions, but here there is considerable hazard. If the opinions are based on some preconception about teaching method, the findings will be controversial and very probably misleading. There are no theories of pedagogy so well established that one can say, without tryout, what will prove educative. . . .

One can accept the need for a pragmatic test of the curriculum and still employ opinions as a source of evidence. During the tryout stages of curriculum making, one relies heavily on the teachers' reports of pupil accomplishment—"Here they had trouble"; "This they found dull"; "Here they needed only half as many exercises as were provided," etc. This is behavior observation even though unsystematic, and it is of great value. The reason for shifting to systematic observation is that this is more impartial, more public, and sometimes more penetrating. While I bow to the historian or mathematician as a judge of the technical soundness of course content, I do not agree that the experienced history or mathematics teacher who tries out a course gives the best possible judgment on its effectiveness. Scholars have too often deluded themselves about their effectiveness as teachers—particularly, have they too often accepted parroting of words as evidence of insight—for their unaided judgment to be trusted. Systematic observation is costly, and introduces some delay between the moment of teaching and the feedback of results. Hence, systematic observation will never be the curriculum developer's sole source of evidence. Systematic data collection becomes profitable in the intermediate stages of curriculum development, after the more obvious bugs in early drafts have been dealt with.

The approaches to evaluation include process studies, proficiency measures, attitude measures, and follow-up studies. A process study is concerned with events taking place in the classroom, proficiency and attitude measures with changes observed in pupils, and follow-up studies with the later careers of those who participated in the course.

The follow-up study comes closest to observing ultimate educational contributions, but the completion of such a study is so far removed in time from the initial instruction that it is of minor value in improving the course or explaining its effects. The follow-up study differs strikingly from the other types of evaluation study in one respect. I have already expressed the view that evaluation should be primarily concerned with the effects of the course under study rather than with comparisons of courses. That is to say, I would emphasize departures of attained results from the ideal, differences in apparent effectiveness of different parts of the course, and differences from item to item; all these suggest places where the course could be strengthened. But this view cannot be applied to the follow-up study, which appraises effects of the course as a whole and which has very little meaning unless outcomes can be compared with some sort of base rate. Suppose we find that 65 per cent of the boys graduating from an experimental curriculum enroll as scientific and technical majors in college. We cannot judge whether this is a high or low figure save by comparing it with the rate among boys who have not had the course. In a follow-up study, it is necessary to obtain data on a control group equated at least crudely to the experimental cases on the obvious demographic variables.

Despite the fact that such groups are hard to equate and that follow-up data do not tell much about how to improve the course, such studies should have a place in research on the new curricula, whose national samples provide unusual opportunity for follow-up that can shed light on important questions. One obvious type of follow-up study traces the student's success in a college course founded upon the high-school course. One may examine the student's grades or ask him what topics in the college course he found himself poorly prepared for. It is hoped that some of the new science and mathematics courses will arouse greater interest than usual among girls; whether this hope is well founded can be checked by finding out what majors and what electives these ex-students pursue in college. Career choices likewise merit attention. Some proponents of the new curricula would like to see a greater flow of talent into basic science as distinct from technology, whereas others would regard this as potentially disastrous; but no one would regard facts about this flow as lacking significance.

Attitudes are prominent among the outcomes with which course developers are concerned. Attitudes are meanings or beliefs, not mere expressions of approval or disapproval. One's attitude toward science includes ideas about the matters on which a scientist can be an authority, about the benefits to be obtained from moon shots and studies of monkey mothers, and about depletion of natural resources. Equally important is the match between self-concept and concept of the field: What roles does science offer a person like me? Would I want to marry a scientist? And so on. Each learning activity also contributes to attitudes that reach far beyond any one subject, such as the pupil's sense of his own competence and desire to learn.

Attitudes can be measured in many ways; the choices revealed in follow-up studies, for example, are pertinent evidence. But the measurement usually takes the form of direct or indirect questioning. Interviews, questionnaires, and the like are quite valuable when not trusted blindly. Certainly, we should take seriously any *un*desirable opinion expressed by a substantial proportion of the graduates of a course (e.g., the belief that the scientist speaks with peculiar authority on political and ethical questions, or the belief that mathematics is a finished subject rather than a field for current investigation).

Attitude questionnaires have been much criticized because they are subject to distortion, especially where the student hopes to gain by being less than frank. Particularly if the questions are asked in a context far removed from the experimental course, the returns are likely to be trustworthy. Thus, a general questionnaire administered through homerooms (or required English courses) may include questions about liking for various subjects and activities; these same questions administered by the mathematics teacher would give much less trustworthy data on attitude toward mathematics. While students may give reports more favorable than their true beliefs, this distortion is not likely to be greater one year than another, or greater among students who take an experimental course than among those who do not. In group averages, many distortions balance out. But questionnaires insufficiently valid for individual testing can be used in evaluating curricula, both because the student has little motive to distort and because the evaluator is comparing averages rather than individuals.

For measuring proficiency, techniques are likewise varied. Standardized tests are useful. But for course evaluation it makes sense to assign *different* questions to different students. Giving each student in a population of 500 the same test of 50 questions will provide far less information to the course developer than drawing for each student 50 questions from a pool of, say, 700. The latter plan determines the mean success of about 75 representative students on every one of the 700 items; the former reports on only 50 items (Lord, 1962). Essay tests and open-ended questions, generally too expensive to use for routine evaluation, can profitably be employed to appraise certain abilities. One can go further and observe individuals or groups as they attack a research problem in the laboratory or work through some other complex problem. Since it is necessary to test only a representative sample of pupils, costs are not as serious a consideration as in routine testing. Additional aspects of proficiency testing will be considered below.

Process measures have special value in showing how a course can be improved because they examine what happens during instruction. In the development of programmed instructional materials, for example, records are collected showing how many pupils miss each item presented; any piling up of errors implies a need for better explanation or a more gradual approach to a difficult topic. Immediately after showing a teaching film, one can interview students, perhaps asking them to describe a still photograph taken from the film. Misleading presentations, ideas given insufficient emphasis, and matters left unclear will be identified by such methods. Similar interviews can disclose what pupils take away from a laboratory activity or a discussion. A process study may turn attention to what the teacher does in the classroom. In those curricula that allow choice of topics, for example, it is worthwhile to find out which topics are chosen and how much time is allotted to each. A log of class activities (preferably recorded by a pupil rather than the teacher) will show which of the techniques suggested in a summer institute are actually adopted and which form "part of the new course" only in the developer's fantasies.

MEASUREMENT OF PROFICIENCY

I have indicated that I consider item data to be more important than test scores. The total score may give confidence in a curriculum or give rise to discouragement, but it tells very little about how to produce further improvement. And, as Ferris (1962) has noted, such scores are quite likely to be mis- or overinterpreted. The score on a single item, or a problem that demands several responses in succession, is more likely than the test score to suggest how to alter the presentation. When we accept item scores as useful, we need no longer think of evaluation as a one-shot, end-of-year operation. Proficiency can be measured at any moment, with particular interest attaching to those items most related to the recent lessons. Other items calling for general abilities can profitably be administered repeatedly during the course (perhaps to different random samples of pupils) so that we can begin to learn when and from what experiences change in these abilities comes.

In course evaluation, we need not be much concerned about making measuring instruments fit the curriculum. However startling this declaration may seem, and however contrary to the principles of evaluation for other purposes, this must be our position if we want to know what changes a course produces in the pupil. An ideal evaluation would include measures of all the types of proficiency that might reasonably be desired in the area in question, not just the selected outcomes to which this curriculum directs substantial attention. If you wish only to know how well a curriculum is achieving *its* objectives, you fit the test to the curriculum; but if you wish to know how well the curriculum is serving the national interest, you measure all outcomes that might be worth striving for. One of the new mathematics courses may disavow any attempt to teach numerical trigonometry, and indeed, might discard nearly all computational work. It is still perfectly reasonable to ask how well graduates of the course can compute and can solve right triangles. Even if the course developers went so far as to contend that computational skill is no proper objective of secondary instruction, they will encounter educators and laymen who do not share their view. If it can be shown that students who come through the new course are fairly proficient in computation despite the lack of direct teaching, the doubters will be reassured. If not, the evidence makes clear how much is being sacrificed. Similarly, when the biologists offer alternative courses emphasizing microbiology and ecology, it is fair to ask how well the graduate of one course can understand issues treated in the other. Ideal evaluation in mathematics will collect evidence on all the abilities toward which a mathematics course might reasonably aim; likewise in biology, English, or any other subject.

Ferris states that the ACS Chemistry Test, however well constructed, is inadequate for evaluating the new CBA and CHEM programs because it does not cover their objectives. One can agree with this without regarding the ACS test as inappropriate to use with these courses. It is important that this test not stand *alone*, as the sole evaluation device. It will tell us something worth knowing, namely, just how much "conventional" knowledge the new curriculum does or does not provide. The curriculum developers deliberately planned to sacrifice some of the conventional attainments and have nothing to fear from this measurement, competently interpreted (particularly if data are examined item by item).

The demand that tests be closely matched to the aims of a course reflects awareness that examinations of the usual sort "determine what is taught." If questions are known in advance, students give more attention to learning their answers than to learning other aspects of the course. This is not necessarily detrimental. Wherever it is critically important to master certain content, the knowledge that it will be tested produces a desirable concentration of effort. On the other hand, learning the answer to a set question is by no means the same as acquiring understanding of whatever topic that question represents. There is, therefore, a possible advantage in using "secure" tests for course evaluation. Security is achieved only at a price: One must prepare new tests each year and consequently cannot make before-and-after comparisons with the same items. One would hope that the use of different items with different students, and the fact that there is less incentive to coach when no judgment is to be passed on the pupils and the teachers, would make security a less critical problem.

The distinction between factual tests and tests of higher mental processes, as elaborated for example in the *Taxonomy of Educational Objectives* (Bloom et al., 1956), is of some value in planning tests, although classifying items as measures of knowledge, application, original problem solving, etc., is difficult and often impossible. Whether a given response represents rote recall or reasoning depends upon how the pupil has been taught, not solely upon the question asked. One may, for example, describe a biological environment and ask for predictions regarding the effect of a certain intervention. Students who have never dealt with ecological data will succeed or fail according to their general ability to reason about complex events; those who have studied ecological biology will be more likely to succeed, reasoning from specific principles; and those who have lived in such an ecology or read about it may answer successfully on the basis of memory. We rarely, therefore, will want to test whether a student "knows" or "does not know" certain material. Knowledge is a matter of degree. Two persons may be acquainted with the same facts or principles, but one will be more expert in his understanding, better able to cope with inconsistent data, irrelevant sources of confusion, and apparent exceptions to the principle. To measure intellectual competence is to measure depth, connectedness, and applicability of knowledge.

Too often, test questions are course-specific, stated in such a way that only the person who has been specifically taught to understand what is being asked for can answer the question. Such questions can usually be identified by their use of conventions. Some conventions are commonplace, and we can assume that all the pupils we test will know them. But a biology test that describes a metabolic process with the aid of the $=$ symbol presents difficulties for students who can think through the scientific question about equilibrium but are unfamiliar with the symbol. A trigonometry problem that requires use of a trigonometric table is unreasonable, unless we want to test familiarity with the conventional names of functions. The same problem in numerical trigonometry can be cast in a form clear to the average pupil *entering* high school; if necessary, the tables of functions can be presented along with a comprehensible explanation. So stated, the problem becomes course-independent. It is fair to ask whether graduates of the experimental course can solve such problems, not previously encountered, whereas it is pointless to ask whether they can answer questions whose language is strange to them. To be sure, knowledge of certain terminology is a significant objective of instruction, but for course evaluation, testing of terminology should very likely be separated from testing of other understandings. To appraise understanding of processes and relations, the fair question is one comprehensible to a pupil who has not taken the course. This is not to say that he should know the answer or the procedure to follow in attaining the answer, but he should understand what he is being asked. Such course-independent questions can be used as standard instruments to investigate any instructional program.

Pupils who have not studied a topic will usually be less facile than those who have studied it. Graduates of my hypothetical mathematics course will take longer to solve trigonometry problems than will those who have studied trig. But speed and power should not be confused; in intellectual studies, power is almost always of greater importance. If the course equips the pupil to deal correctly, even though haltingly, with a topic not studied, we can expect him to develop facility later when that topic comes before him frequently. . . .

The chief objective in many of the new curricula seems to be to develop aptitude for mastering new materials in the field. A biology course cannot cover all valuable biological content, but it may reasonably aspire to equip the pupil to understand descriptions of unfamiliar organisms, to comprehend a new theory and the reasoning behind it, and to plan an experiment to test a new hypothesis. This is transfer of learning. It has been insufficiently recognized that there are two types of transfer. The two types shade into one another, being arranged on a continuum of immediacy of effect. We can label the more immediate pole *applicational transfer,* and speak of slower-acting effects as *gains in aptitude* (Ferguson, 1954).

Nearly all educational research on transfer has tested immediate performance on a partly new task. We teach pupils to solve equations in x, and include in the test equations stated in a or z. We teach the principles of ecological balance by referring to forests, and as a transfer test, ask what effect pollution will have on the population of a lake. We describe an experiment not presented in the text, and ask the student to discuss possible interpretations and needed controls. Any of these tests can be administered in a short time. But the more significant type of transfer may be the increased ability to learn in a particular field. There is very likely a considerable difference between the ability to draw conclusions from a neatly finished experiment, and the ability to tease insight out of the disorderly and inconsistent observations that come with continuous laboratory work on a problem. The student who masters a good biology course may become better able to comprehend certain types of theory and data, so that he gains more from a subsequent year of study in ethnology; we do not measure this gain by testing his understanding of short passages in ethnology. There has rarely been an appraisal of ability to work through a problem situation or a complex body of knowledge over a period of days or months. Despite the practical difficulties that attend an attempt to measure the effect of a course on a person's subsequent learning, such "learning to learn" is so important that a serious effort should be made to detect such effects and to understand how they may be fostered.

The techniques of programmed instruction may be adapted to appraise learning ability. One may, for example, test the student's rate of mastery of a self-contained, programmed unit on the physics of heat or some other topic not studied. If the program is truly self-contained, every student can master it, but the one with greater scientific comprehension will hopefully make fewer errors and progress faster. The program can be prepared in several logically complete versions, ranging from one with very small "steps" to one with minimal internal redundancy, on the hypothesis that the better educated student could cope with the less redundant program. Moreover, he might prefer its greater elegance.

CONCLUSION

Old habits of thought and long established techniques are poor guides to the evaluation required for course improvement. Traditionally, educational measurement has been chiefly concerned with producing fair and precise scores for comparing individuals. Educational experimentation has been concerned with comparing score averages of competing courses. But course evaluation calls for description of outcomes. This description should be made on the broadest possible scale, even at the sacrifice of superficial fairness and precision.

Course evaluation should ascertain what changes a course produces and should identify aspects of the course that need revision. The outcomes observed should include general outcomes ranging far beyond the content of the curriculum itself—attitudes, career choices, general understandings and intellectual powers, and aptitude for further learning in the field. Analysis of performance or single items or types of problems is more informative than analysis of composite scores. It is not necessary or desirable to give the same test to all pupils; rather, as many questions as possible should be given, each to a different, moderate sized sample of pupils. Costly techniques, such as interviews and essay tests, can profitably be applied to samples of pupils, whereas testing everyone would be out of the question.

Asking the right questions about educational outcomes can do much to improve educational effectiveness. Even if the right data are collected, however, evaluation will have contributed too little if it only places a seal of approval on certain courses and casts others into disfavor. Evaluation is a fundamental part of curriculum development, not an appendage. Its job is to collect facts the course developer can and will use to do a better job, and facts from which a deeper understanding of the educational process will emerge.

35   *A Methodology for the Formative Evaluation of Instructional Materials*

WALTER DICK

One of the most important uses of measurement data, if not the most important one, is in the improvement of instruction. This objective can be approached in a variety of ways: by examining the instructional process itself, by assessing the learning environment, or by proceeding in a way similar to the one described in the following article. The author describes how the instructional materials—in this case a programmed text in college calculus—were improved through the use of the feedback of evaluation data. His suggestion for implementing a formative evaluation program aimed at producing effective educational materials is valuable. For a detailed explication of the principles underlying formative evaluation the reader is referred to Scriven (1967), and Bloom et al. (1971).

Would formative evaluation procedures apply equally well in the social sciences and in the biological and physical sciences? How can you determine which type of formative evaluation data is the most important? Should "student interest in material" be a significant source of formative evaluation data? In what ways are formative evaluation and research activities similar? How are they dissimilar?

Various articles have evidenced concern for the type of evaluation information which should be provided the users of new curriculum materials, e.g., Hastings (1966), Joint Committee on Programmed Instruction and Teaching Machines (1966), and Tyler, Gagné, & Scriven (1967). However, Bruner (1966) has lamented that too often evaluation activities occur only *after* the instructional materials have been completed.

Cronbach (1963) has clearly drawn the distinction between evaluation activities occurring during the development of the instructional materials (formative evaluation) and those conducted following the completion of the materials (summative evaluation). During the formative stage of curriculum development, evaluation should be continuously planned and executed in order to provide writers with empirical information about the effectiveness of their materials and ways in which it may be improved.

This article describes the procedures and analyses which were integrated and utilized while the author was an evaluation consultant to the Mathematical

Reprinted with permission of the author and publisher from the *Journal of Educational Measurement*, Vol. 5, #2 (Summer), 1968, pp. 99–102.

Association of America's Committee on Educational Media. The Committee had as one of its projects the construction of a programmed instruction text covering approximately one year of calculus instruction at the collegiate level.

METHOD

SUBJECTS ■ Eighty-five students from four colleges and universities used the Calculus Program as the text for their calculus courses. One instructor at each institution participated in the study.

PROCEDURE ■ The following points were conveyed to and accepted by the instructors:

(1) Homework assignments in the program were made in consecutive order from the text in accordance with the listing provided.

(2) A short test was administered at the beginning of the first class after an assignment was due. (There were 51 assignments and associated tests during the year.)

(3) Tests were collected immediately upon completion; another copy of the test was then given to each student. These served on a basis for discussion or for instruction on particular problems.

(4) Answer sheets used by the students while studying the program were also collected. Amount of studying time was recorded by the students on these answer sheets.

These assessments of student performance without the benefit of formal classroom instruction were judged to be the best indication of program effectiveness per se.

The tests, answer sheets, and comments were sent to the author and a folder was prepared for each of the 51 assignments. Each lesson folder contained the following information: (1) item analysis of the end-of-lesson test. (2) a listing of the incorrect answers to the test items, (3) a guide or reference sheet which indicated where in the program book the information relevant to each test item was taught, (4) the error rate for each of the program frames, (5) a sample of the incorrect responses to the frames, (6) student comments about various parts of the assignment, and (7) reviewer and instructor comments.

The lesson folders were provided to the program writers when they began their summer writing. The main task of the writers was not actually to *write* more materials but to *revise* the existing programs. Preceding the summer session, the author met briefly with the writers and project director and demonstrated possible uses of the evaluation data. The method proposed to the writers for using data for the revision of the programmed materials was as follows:

(1) Study the item analysis of the end-of-lesson test to determine those concepts which were most often missed by the students.

(2) Study the incorrect responses to these particular test items to determine

if there was a straightforward misunderstanding of notation, a complete lack of comprehension of the concept, or a variety of errors.

(3) Use the guide to determine those frames in the program which dealt most directly with the concept(s) missed on the test.

(4) Study the student error rates for these frames. If the program frames are quite similar to the test item, and the error is quite low, more practice frames should be provided. If the error rate is quite high, these frames need revision.

(5) Study the sample of incorrect student responses to this segment of the program. These responses should suggest the nature of the learning difficulty and the type of revision needed.

(6) Study the comments of both the students and the program reviewers for further suggestions concerning the problems encountered with these particular frames.

(7) If no frames in the program correspond to a test item missed by a large percentage of the students, consider the addition of frames that will "bridge the gap" between the present learning materials and what would be considered a transfer type item.

RESULTS

The general consensus among the writers was that the frame error rates and reviewer comments were the most informative data. If the error rate became excessive (which depended upon the writer's own point of view), the incorrect responses to the frames and the student comments were studied. Few of the writers studied the results of the end-of-lesson tests or related test item performance with particular frames in the program.

It was clear that none of the writers had followed the suggested sequence through the data. The writers reported that the end-of-lesson tests, which they had *not* constructed, did not completely represent the objectives they themselves would have tested. The writers did indicate an interest in the students' overall impression of each section of the test, e.g., impressions of continuity, readability, etc. They were also interested in knowing more about the ability level of the students who had made specific comments about segments of the program.

It was of interest to the author to note that when the writers were given a hypothetical alternative of gaining information about the program by going through it personally with three or four students vs. gaining statistical data from 40 or 50 students, the latter procedure was much preferred. There seemed to be a greater acceptance of a more limited type of information from a greater number of students (which appears to provide greater generalizability), and an acknowledgement of difficulty of obtaining suitable guinea pig students.

DISCUSSION

Two of the seven types of information provided to the program writers—the frame error rates and the informed reviewer's comments—were widely used. The student's incorrect responses to the frames and their comments about specific frames were occasionally used. The test item data, the listing of the incorrect responses and the guide which related the test items to the text were seldom used.

The ultimate value of the procedures employed in this project can only be determined by the effectiveness of the revised program. However, on the basis of the experience gained with the current project, certain changes and/or emphasis would be suggested:

(1) The writer or writers of particular portions of a program should be responsible for reviewing test items which have been constructed jointly with a test construction specialist. Such items should be utilized to determine if the program has achieved its objectives. If the test items are constructed solely by another person, the subject-matter writers should review such items before they are used in the classroom.

(2) During the initial writing session, the evaluator should spend time explaining, in detail, the data analysis procedures and their rationale. He should then stay with the writers during the revision process to assist in the interpretation of the data. This suggests that the evaluator should not only be knowledgeable in the areas of measurement and data analysis, but should also have a background in learning theory and experience in the construction of learning materials. His interest and support in the revision process should be an asset in the task of program revision.

(3) At least one, and preferably more, of the program reviewers should be experienced program writers. On this project one of the reviewers used the text in his own classroom and, having constructed programs before, was sensitive to the types of comments and suggestions from both himself and his students which would be most useful to the writers.

(4) Information should be gathered on the students' impressions of relatively small portions of the program, e.g., one or two hours of study. This might be supplemented by an indication of the general ability level of students making various comments about specific segments of the learning materials. The writers clearly indicated that they would react differentially depending upon the ability of the student making a comment.

(5) A clear distinction should be made between the role of the evaluator during the formative stage of program development and during the summative stage. The evaluator should be clearly identified as a member of the project team whose job it is to provide the writers with rele-

vant and meaningful data that will be useful to them during the revision process.

(6) The training of specialists in mathematics education, English education, science education, etc., should include concepts dealing with measurement, statistics, and evaluation procedures, so that the role of the formative evaluator may be performed by subject matter specialists.

36   *Toward National Assessment: History and Results*

JACK C. MERWIN AND FRANK B. WOMER

One of the most significant, if not the most significant large-scale evaluations or data-gathering efforts to be mounted during the last several decades is the National Assessment of Educational Project project. (NAEP). Tyler (1966) has described the general philosophy of NAEP as

. . . evaluation which is to assess the educational progress of larger populations in order to provide the public with dependable information to help in the understanding of educational problems and needs and to guide in efforts to develop sound public policy regarding education. This type of assessment is not focused upon individual students, classrooms, schools, or school systems, but furnishes over-all information about educational attainments of large numbers of people.

The potential usefulness of the results of the NAEP has been likened to that of the Gross National Product or Consumer Price Index, particularly as each relates to rational legislative action and allocation of resources.

The controlling organization, begun in 1964 as the Exploratory Committee on Assessing the Progress of Education, eventually dropped the "Exploratory" and now is the National Assessment of Educational Progress, since 1969 a project of the Education Commission of the States.

The first portion of the following article describes some of the early developmental work with NAEP and its over-all design. It is really a kind of biography or anatomy of a large-scale measurement project. The results section, drawn from the report by Frank Womer, describes a typical NAEP exercise report and several generalizations that seem warranted from an initial read-out of the data.

The application of item-sampling (Lord, 1962; Walberg and Welch, 1967) technique is well illustrated (Cronbach, in an earlier article (34) also commented on the technique). Basically, the idea involves breaking up a large group of potential examinees into smaller units and administering a sub-set of the total item pool to each unit, with the option of overlapping some of the units. Rather than administering a 70 item test to 1,000 subjects, it might make more sense and be more economical of student time to administer a set of 10 tests with seven items each to groups of 100 subjects. The validity of the item sampling technique has been verified by several investigators (Cook & Stufflebeam, 1967; Plumlee, 1964).

What are some of the dangers of such an assessment of educational progress? What are some of the ways in which this assessment could be more meaningfully reported? What requirements for Assessment exercises would be appropriate to use in judging test items? *

The Exploratory Committee on Assessing the Progress of Education started its work by holding conferences with educators, curriculum specialists, administrators, and school board members. From these conferences came a number of recommendations concerning characteristics of a national assessment and procedures that the Committee might use in seeking to carry out its work. These recommendations included: (1) The assessment should be developed in cooperation with teachers and tried out in the schools. (2) Even though all important areas cannot be started at once, the initial effort should include more than the three R's. It was suggested that as time goes on the project should include additional important areas and become more comprehensive. (3) Over the years, as educational objectives change, assessment procedures should change, just as the components of the Gross National Product have changed as our patterns of production have changed. (4) The assessment should be under the direction of a private commission and not be a project of Federal or State Governments. Related to this, it was recommended that financial support of the Committee's initial work come from private sources. The Carnegie Corporation and Ford Foundation provided considerable support, virtually all support now comes from the Federal Government.

GENERAL DESIGN OF NATIONAL ASSESSMENT

On the basis of consultations with various groups and subsequent deliberations the Committee decided that its efforts might best proceed within the following guidelines.

1. Age levels will define the groups to be surveyed and it is practical to con-

---

* Reprinted by permission of the publisher, from David A. Payne: *Curriculum Evaluation* (Lexington, Mass.: D. C. Heath and Company, 1974).

This article is a composite of two publications which are reprinted and abridged with permission of the following respective authors and joint copyright holder, the National Council on Measurement in Education. J. C. Merwin, "The Progress of Exploration Toward a National Assessment of Educational Progress." *Journal of Educational Measurement*, 1966, Vol. 3, pp. 5–10, and Frank B. Womer, "National Assessment Says." *Measurement In Education*, 1970, Vol. 2, pp. 1–8.

sider assessment at four age levels: ages 9, 13, 17, and adult. Age 9 was included because by this age children might be expected to have achieved some of the goals of primary education. By age 13, there should be substantial progress in attaining the goals of elementary education. Seventeen-year-olds are normally high school seniors and the last age group still in school in large numbers. Adults (age 26-35) were included to provide a look at the residual of elementary and secondary education as well as a means of identifying areas where there may be a general continuation of development.

2. At each age level three descriptions should be sought. There should be an attempt to identify behaviors that 90%, 50%, and 10% of the age group can exhibit.

3. The instruments and procedures should be aimed at descriptions of what large groups can do.

4. The objectives used as a basis for developing exercises should be considered authentic by scholars, be goals the schools are trying to achieve, and be considered by thoughtful laymen as things desirable for American youth to learn.

5. Originally it was expected that every exercise used must sample an objective set forth for the project and be meaningful to thoughtful laymen. Both cognitive and non-cognitive objectives should be considered, and cover the areas of reading and the language arts, mathematics, science, literature and the fine arts, vocational education, citizenship, social studies, and music.

One of the goals of the Committee is to evolve instruments and procedures that will be acceptable to informed, education-interested laymen. It was considered desirable to involve such laymen at this point by having them review and critique the sets of objectives developed. The first step was to contact a number of individuals and associations with an interest in education and request nominations of thoughtful, public spirited citizens who might be asked to assist in this review. Groups contacted included the National School Boards Association, the Chamber of Commerce, the National Congress of Parents and Teachers, the National Education Association, the National Committee for Support of the Public Schools, the National Catholic Education Association, and many others. Using the various list of nominees, invitations were extended to people to attend one of four regional conferences. An attempt was made to get a balance of people from large cities, suburban areas, and other types of communities. People from various parts of the United States with primary interest in private education, as well as those basically interested in public education, were invited.

Laymen from large cities, suburban areas, and other types of communities comprised working groups, and each group reviewed all sets of objectives under the chairmanship of one of its members.

Reports on the projects were summarized into a booklet containing the objectives and supporting illustrative statements. Panels were asked to judge each objective in terms of the questions: "Is this something important for people to learn today? Is it something I would like to have my children learn?" While each panel was chaired by one of the lay panel members, staff members sat with each panel and had the complete set of contractors reports available for further elaboration and clarification of the objectives as they were discussed.

Most of the objectives developed by the agencies in their work with scholars and teachers were accepted as desirable for American youth by these laymen. There were recommendations for reworking and rewording some of the objectives and these were taken back to the contractors for reconsideration by their scholar-teacher consulting groups. It will come as no surprise that the most difficult area to pin down with any success was social studies. Most of the lay groups, the Technical Advisory Group, and the Exploratory Committee itself felt the need for a more extensive consideration of this very complex area. For this reason a special conference on the objectives for social studies was held. Scholars from various disciplines that contribute to the area of social studies, leading social studies teachers, and professors specializing in social studies education were called together to review and discuss the objectives in hand and make recommendations for further development of objectives.

Since a large portion of the objectives developed by the scholars and teachers in each area were generally accepted by the lay panels, the Committee moved on to the initial steps in exercise development. The Committee turned to test development agencies for help in this phase of the project.

Since the assessment is aimed at describing what groups can do, it is the sampling of the behavior of *groups*, rather than of *individuals*, that enters into reliability considerations. Responses can be pooled across individuals in a group and thus some of the practical considerations of testing individuals become less important. The time spent by each individual can be relatively short, and it is not necessary that all exercises be completed by every participant. In fact, each person in the sample takes only a small portion of the exercises and possibly spends as little as 30 minutes or so on them. Since we are not after a reliable sample of the individual's behavior, there are dimensions of freedom both in the selection of exercises to be taken by any one individual and the length of time to be spent on an exercise. If certain exercises are somewhat time consuming, an increase in sample size will be called for to maintain the desired level of reliability. The Committee asked the contractors to concern themselves primarily with creating the best designed exercises they can produce to sample the behaviors set forth in the objectives.

The Committee has made progress in its consideration of methods of reporting the results of a census, though much work remains to be done on this aspect of the project. It was decided that no report is to be made for individual students, teachers, or school systems and that there will be no scores. Rather, descriptions based on the exercises themselves will be used to report the outcomes. Such descriptions are presently contemplated for a number of sub-populations which may change over the years. Originally it seemed desirable to incorporate four age levels, four types of community—large city (above 200,000), middle size cities (25,000-200,000), urban fringe, and small town-rural (below 25,000)—two socioeconomic levels, four geographical regions (Northeast, Southeast, Central and West), and two sexes in defining the sub-populations.

For example, the first census might identify science problems that can be successfully solved by 40% of the 13-year-old girls in the country and by 60% of the boys of this age. An examination of the results for sub-populations, however, might show that 80% of the girls of this age from the higher socioeconomic level of large midwestern cities can solve this type of problems while only 40% of the boys from the lower socioeconomic level of large midwestern cities have success. In other words, it would indicate that boys in this particular sub-population have operated at a level similar to girls across the nation on this type of exercise while the girls from this other sub-population are more successful, as a group, than boys across the nation.

PRELIMINARY RESULTS

The projected type of report just described was followed in the initial read out of results in the Summer of 1970. For example, it was found that more young adults between the ages of 26 and 35 (9 out of 10) are aware of the fact that the President does not have the right to do anything affecting the United States that he wants to do than are 17-year-olds (8 out of 10), 13-year-olds (7 out of 10), or 9-year-olds (5 out of 10). The question on which these results are based and the results themselves are presented in Exhibit I. It comes from a Citizenship exercise for National Assessment. While most of the young adults in the National Assessment sample could state an acceptable reason for their answer (8 out of 10), the younger age groups did not do as well (only 2 out of 10 of the 9-year-olds). These results suggest that for this specific bit of information there is continuing growth through the school years and even into young adulthood.

EXHIBIT I

A. Does the President have the right to do anything affecting the United States that he wants to do? (Yes, No, I don't know)

B. (If yes) Why? (Part B was not scored; it was asked to insure that respondents understood Part A and to give them a chance to explain their position.)

C. (If no) Why not?
    (If answer to C is vague) Who or what would stop him from doing what he wants?

Acceptable reasons to C (examples): People could stop him; elected officials could stop him; checks and balances system of government; laws stop him; country would be a dictatorship; not the democratic way.

Unacceptable reasons to C (examples): Police or Vice President would stop him; he wouldn't be doing his job; he might do something that could hurt the country; he would be doing what is right; people vote for him not to; he can't do it; everybody, even the President, has some limitations; he just advises us; he can't do everything since he is only one person.

	Results			
Age	9	13	17	Adult
Stated that the President does *not* have the right to do anything affecting the United States that he wants (No to A)	49%	73%	78%	89%
Stated that the President does not have the right and gave an acceptable reason (acceptable reason to C as well as No to A)	18	53	68	80

Perhaps the most striking feature of National Assessment's first reports is that there are no scores or norms—just individual exercises (questions, items) along with the percent choosing or producing each response (p-values), both correct and incorrect, for each exercise. Those who developed the plan for National Assessment felt that the best way to describe what young people know is to present the questions or tasks that they were asked along with information about how well they performed. This directs attention at actual samples of behavior rather than at some summation of behaviors. It allows the reader of the reports to make his own evaluation of each exercise. He can accept the results as meaningful information useful in teaching and/or curriculum evaluation and/or allocation of educational funds., etc. He can reject a question as meaningless or inappropriate if his judgment leads him to that conclusion. The point is that the reader of a report has all the results before him rather than an average or a summary or a conclusion.

Eventually National Assessment will generate its own standards, although not in the same sense as those established for the usual standardized test. Only half or fewer of the exercises administered by National Assessment in a given year are released that year. The others are retained to be used again three or six years hence. At that time it will be possible to compare the results from a second or third assessment with those obtained previously. Then one can see whether change (progress?) is taking place in the knowledges and skills of

young people over time. This is the ultimate goal of National Assessment—
to measure changes in knowledges, skills and attitudes over time.

Since the first results of National Assessment are benchmark data, they provide neither instantaneous "indictments" of American education nor instantaneous "whitewashing." This fact has been of considerable disappointment to
persons who looked upon the project as one which will provide "answers" to all
sorts of educational questions. An information-gathering project is not designed to provide such answers. But it can and should provide decision-makers
with information useful in decision-making.

Even though the ultimate goal of National Assessment is to assess change,
the first results do point to some generalizations of considerable import, as well as
illustrating specific knowledges and skills and attitudes that young people have
and have not attained. The generalizations discussed here are based on total
national results for Science and on partial national results for Citizenship.
Later reports will include comparisons, item by item, for four geographic regions, size and type of community, sex, color (black versus white), and an
educational index of the home.

LEARNING IN SCIENCE AND CITIZENSHIP PROGRESSES REGULARLY THROUGH THE
SCHOOL YEARS ■ The evidence for this statement is based on "overlap" exercises, those administered to more than one age level. Consistently on the overlap exercises 17s did better than 13s and 13s did better than 9s. There were
15 overlaps between 9s and 13s for Science and 17 for Citizenship. All of the
Science overlaps and 13 of the 17 Citizenship overlaps favor the 13s over 9s.
There were 23 overlaps between 13s and 17s for Science and 73 for Citizenship.
All of the Science overlaps and 47 of the 73 for Citizenship overlaps favor the
17s over 13s. Note that the generalization does not take a position as to whether
the schools, or other social organizations, or the family, or any other causal
factor or combination of factors are responsible.

A statement that learning is taking place as young people proceed through
the school years is not exactly revolutionary. Observation and common sense
have indicated as much. But National Assessment documents this generalization
in terms of specific knowledges and skills. Perhaps the greatest utility of this
specific type of information from overlap exercises will be as an aid to understand when growth is taking place in specific skill and knowledge areas.

VARIABILITY IN SCIENCE AND CITIZENSHIP ACHIEVEMENT IS CHARACTERISTIC OF
YOUNG ADULTS AND SEVENTEEN YEAR OLDS ■ There were 58 Science and 57
Citizenship exercises administered to both 17s and adults. Of these, 38 Science
and 10 Citizenship overlaps yielded higher p-values for the correct answer for
17s, while 20 Science and 47 Citizenship overlaps yielded higher p-values for
adults. Because the 17s did better on more Science exercises than the adults
one might be tempted to assume general superiority of the 17s. However, that
would be a hasty and unsupported generalization. Careful examination of the

overlap exercises has led several reviewers to the conclusion that the exercises for which 17s did better tend to be of a different type than the ones for which adults did better.

The generalization that young adults sometimes show greater achievement than 17s in Science and Citizenship may, like the first generalization discussed, seem to many readers to be another bit of "common sense," but documentation of common sense can have its own utility. Documentation can focus attention upon an area of learning in a way that common sense may not. This simple generalization helps to remind us that much learning takes place outside of schools, that "textbook" learning may have limited utility (if textbook implies rote memory primarily), and that if the ultimate goal of education is an enlightened citizenry one needs to examine carefully what knowledge and skills adults truly need to acquire and retain.

THERE ARE MEANINGFUL KNOWLEDGE AND SKILLS AND ATTITUDES IN SCIENCE AND CITIZENSHIPS AT ALL DIFFICULTY LEVELS ■ The impact of this generalization suggests that all young people have acquired meaningful knowledge and skills that relate directly to objectives of instruction in Science and in Citizenship. Most people probably would have paid lip service to this statement prior to any results of National Assessment, but unfortunately too many of us (including we teachers, who should know better) have acted as if we felt that some youngsters were completely devoid of useful skills or knowledges. As National Assessment results are accumulated over the years, it should be possible to develop a picture of what knowledges and skills all 9s, 13s, and 17s have attained. Whether we will be satisfied with that picture is another question, but at least we will know where students stand. This should be of considerable help in planning for group learning experiences, in avoiding knowledge already acquired and in building knowledge not yet acquired.

The results in Exhibit II suggest that society has done a fairly good job in getting young people to indicate lack of bias toward people of other races, *in a paper and pencil situation*. The obvious response to this is that what people say they would be willing to do and what they really do may not be the same. Nevertheless, if young people did not indicate tolerance, there would be little chance for further progress in race relations. To the author the most disturbing aspect of Exhibit II is that almost half (44 percent) of the respondents at each age level did indicate an unwillingness to accept a person of another race in at least one of the five categories.

EXHIBIT II

People feel differently toward people of other races. How willing would you be to have a person of a different race doing these things?

Results *

[For each situation below, the choices were: Willing to, prefer not to]

| | | % willing to Age | | |
		13	17	Adult
A.	Be your dentist or doctor?	81%	74%	75%
B.	Live next door to you?	83	77	67
C.	Represent you in some elected office?	81	82	82
D.	Sit at a table next to yours in a crowded restaurant?	80	90	93
E.	Stay in the same hotel or motel as you?	83	92	89
Willing to for one or more of the above				
two or more . . .		96	97	93
three or more . . .		94	94	90
four or more . . .		89	88	86
all five . . .		56	56	56

*Not administered to the in-school sample in one large western state, one southeastern county and one southwestern city at the request of state or local authorities.

ITEM WRITERS MAY NOT BE GOOD ENOUGH JUDGES OF EXERCISE DIFFICULTY IN CRITERION-REFERENCED SITUATIONS ■ When reporting the results for Science, three categories of correct responses were established: rather few (0-33 percent) good many (34-66 percent) and most (67-100 percent). The original writer's and reviewers' estimates have now been plotted against the actual results. Of 498 comparisons made for Science, 339 (68 percent) were the same whereas 159 (32 percent) were different. Thus, the item writers and reviewers judged difficulty correctly two-thirds of the time and judged incorrectly one-third of the time. In the authors' opinion, this is not outstanding success. This is not to suggest that the particular writers and reviewers for National Assessment were poor judges, since it is not known whether other writers could have done better or whether writers in other subject areas could have done better.

Across the four age groups the percentages of agreement were 70, 65, 70, and 67 for ages 9, 13, 17 and adult. Thus, judgments were quite similar across ages. The writers were correct 80 percent of the time for the easy exercises (the 90s) whereas they were correct only 60 percent of the time for the others (50s and 10s). The need for making statistical checks is obvious. And in the final analysis it is the students that must tell us what they know and don't know, and what they feel or don't feel.

ADULTS SELECT "I DON'T KNOW" MORE FREQUENTLY ON MULTIPLE-CHOICE TESTS THAN STUDENTS ▪ It may be that school-age youngsters are so geared to guessing on multiple-choice exercises (and rightfully so) that many of them never seriously considered the "I don't know" alternative. Adults, who are assessed in their own homes, probably are less concerned about a "score" that they might be achieving than about giving their best response or straight-forwardly admitting a lack of knowledge. Whether it is good or bad that 17s seem to be prone to more guessing than adults is a debatable question.

INITIAL RESULTS PROVIDED MANY SURPRISES ▪ The fact that trained item writers and reviewers were "surprised" with respect to estimated difficulty fully one-third of the time is strong support for this statement. Noneducators probably will be surprised even more. Evidence for this assumption comes from the initial newspaper articles written about National Assessment results. The education writer for the Washington Post was unhappily surprised that, while 70 percent, 91 percent, and 92 percent of the 13s, 17s, and adults respectively knew that the Senate was the second of the two houses of Congress, 17 percent, five percent, and four percent respectively thought that the Supreme Court was the answer. From a psychometric viewpoint, any p-value above 90 percent might seem to be good, but to a Washington reporter anything less than 100 percent on such an item is unthinkable. The same reporter was disturbed that only half of the 17s and adults could solve this problem correctly: A motor boat can travel five miles an hour on a still lake. If this boat travels downstream on a river that is flowing five miles per hour, how long will it take the boat to reach a bridge that is 10 miles downstream?

One reviewer of the National Assessment Science results finished his comments by listing eight pleasant surprises and 10 unpleasant surprises. He was pleased that 89 percent of 17s knew that living dinosaurs have never been seen by man (The Flintstones not withstanding) and was displeased that only 33 percent of 17s and 25 percent of adults knew that doubling the linear dimensions of a cube increases its volume eightfold.

Readers of the National Assessment reports may want to play the same game—estimating what they think students know and can do in specific exercises before looking at the p-values. Another potentially fruitful approach for teachers and curriculum specialists is to look at the p-values of wrong responses as well as of the correct responses. Such analyses have the potential of shedding considerable light on specific misconceptions that are commonly held. For teachers, broad generalizations that may be abstracted from National Assessment results may be of much less interest than specific, item-by-item analyses. Such analyses probably are best done by subject matter specialists.

VIII

SPECIAL PROBLEMS IN TEST USAGE

While each of the previous chapters tended to be concerned with particular issues and activities, the present chapter contains a sampling of articles concerned with a variety of applications of measurement data. The problems with which these authors deal often have had a long history but nevertheless are problems of contemporary importance and interest. These problems range from estimating gains to the mundane matter of assigning grades, to measuring two extreme groups (the culturally deprived on one hand, college students on the other), to appraising creativity.

These are all crucial topics in today's world. To illustrate: Although measuring achievement status is of importance, educational objectives are frequently phrased in terms of growth; basic decisions of extreme importance are often based on faulty grades; the effective use of education as an agency for social and individual advancement is needed at all levels of ability; and creative abilities tend to be difficult to measure and therefore may not receive adequate encouragement. It is with problems such as these that the papers assembled in this chapter are concerned.

An example of an enduring topic is treated in the first two papers. Educators and psychologists consider changes in behavior as indicative of learning, and therefore must concern themselves with the measurement of gains. Diederich notes three reasons why the assessment of gains, which might appear so simple, is in fact difficult to accomplish well. Stake also notes reasons why gains are difficult

271

to assess well. The context of performance contracting, which he uses, is not only very current and demanding, but also provides stimulation for judging anew other evaluation contexts.

The assignment of grades is another perennial problem for the classroom teacher, and like the assessment of gains, involves procedures which may appear simple and exact to the uninitiated. The second paper in this chapter examines in a unique way the matter of grading. The reader should enjoy as well as profit from Palmer's delightful instructions on how not to accomplish the task.

A further topic of importance in the schools is the testing of minority group children. The current concern with the education of minority groups leads thoughtful people to be apprehensive lest decisions made regarding the schooling of the groups are politically or emotionally rather than professionally based. A working group, with Fishman as chairman, has provided professional advice for testing this special class of students. The guidelines of Fishman's group should prove helpful not only in the construction and selection of instruments for special groups of children but in the interpretation of scores that the instruments yield.

Measurement and evaluation can provide information relevant to describing and decision making for both individuals and for groups. By referring to "groups" we do not mean collecting information on several people simultaneously and efficiently for purposes of making statements concerning each individual. Rather, the emphasis is on the group as a whole, as illustrated in the previous chapter on curriculum evaluation and National Assessment. Another purpose, emphasizing the responses of a whole group, is to describe college environments. Menne appraises three types of procedures for describing such environments and illustrates them sufficiently so that you will likely contemplate your own college's academic attitudes, social stimulation, occupational orientation, and so on.

You might also consider the dimension(s) of creativity in your college. In what ways are the students, and the faculty, creative? How is creativity demonstrated in the classroom, in writing, in performing, in politicking, in socializing? What do we mean by creativity? How do we define and measure it? How would we estimate the validity and reliability of our measures? Through the use of the sixth and final article of the chapter Khatena can be our consultant.

The special problems in test usage discussed in these papers, then, include assessing gains, performance contracting, assigning grades, testing minority group children, describing college environments, and measuring creativity.

PAUL B. DIEDERICH

A technique frequently used to secure data for purposes of evaluating teaching effectiveness and learning involves the testing of pupils before and after an educational experience. Intuitively it would seem that a measure of growth, thus made possible, should provide a more equitable base for judging performance than final class standing. Consideration of three major difficulties encountered in using growth scores, pointed out in the following nontechnical discussion, should lead the reader to a clearer perspective of a very complex topic. (For a more comprehensive and technical treatment of the topic, the reader is referred to a volume edited by Harris, 1963.) How can the major difficulties met in using change scores be overcome? Would the effort be justified? In addition to their application to learning situations, where else in the behavioral sciences might the study of change or growth scores prove valuable? [*]

When a teacher gives a published test of almost any skill that develops more or less continuously, such as reading, writing, or arithmetic, at the beginning of the school year and a parallel form of the same test at the end, the average score is practically certain to rise. In addition to the fact that teachers are better at their jobs than most people realize, all the forces of growth are on their side, just as all the recuperative powers of the body are on the side of the physician. If we ever need evidence to confound our critics, we can find it in the difference between initial and final averages on standardized tests.

If it should occur to the critic, however, or even to a friendly inquirer to find out how much the lowest fifth on the initial test had gained, then the middle fifth, and then the highest fifth, he could upset our apple cart. In most cases it would turn out that the students who made the lowest initial scores had gained by far the most, those in the middle had gained less, and those at the top had gained little or nothing. Some of the latter would even appear to have lost ground. The obvious conclusion would be that instruction had been pitched at the level of the least able, the brighter students had not been stimulated and had loafed on the job, and almost all of the average gain to which we pointed with such pride could be attributed to the fact that the bottom of the distribution had been hauled up to about the level of the initial average.

COOPERATIVE STUDY DATA

That this is not a fanciful or unusual situation is shown by the 1954 Final Report of the Cooperative Study of Evaluation in General Education (Dressel & Mayhew,

[*] Reprinted by permission of the publisher, from David A. Payne: *Curriculum Evaluation* (Lexington, Mass.: D. C. Heath and Company, 1974).

Reprinted and abridged with permission of author and publisher (The University of Chicago Press) from the *School Review*, 1956, Vol. 64, pp. 59–63.

1954). The data presented in Table 1 reflects average gains from the beginning to the end of the freshman year for an average of 1,400 students in nine colleges, from the lowest fifth on the pretest up to the highest fifth, on all instruments developed during the Cooperative Study.

Whatever tests or inventories were used, and wherever they were used, students with the lowest initial scores appeared to gain the most; students with the highest initial scores appeared either to have gained least or to have lost ground. This was true not only of cognitive tests but of instruments attempting to measure appreciations, attitudes, and insight into human relations.

TABLE 1. *Average Gains of Students on Post-Tests, Classified According to Pretest Standing*[1]

Test	Low Group	Low Middle Group	Middle Group	High Middle Group	High Group
Critical Thinking in Social Science	6.89	5.48	3.68	4.20	2.26
Science Reasoning and Understanding	6.26	5.16	2.93	2.04	0.31
Humanities Participation Inventory	18.00	5.05	4.94	1.39	−2.07
Analysis of Reading and Writing	5.33	2.89	1.81	1.22	0.25
Critical Thinking	6.68	4.65	3.47	2.60	1.59
Inventory of Beliefs	9.09	5.31	4.65	3.32	1.01
Problems in Human Relations	3.19	1.67	1.31	1.51	−0.36

[1] Adapted from Paul L. Dressel and Lewis B. Mayhew, 1954.

So many students in so many different colleges were tested that the consistent downward trend in the data on gains, from initially lowest to initially highest, cannot be attributed to the population tested. The fact that the same trend is shown by all instruments developed in the study suggests that it cannot be attributed to poor test construction. The colleges participating in the study were selected for the excellence of their general education programs; they could not all have done a poor job of teaching. It is contrary to all teaching experience to suppose that the initially weak students were, in every case, more highly motivated than the initially strong. The data seem unassailable; yet we cannot accept the conclusion that "poor" students regularly learn more than "good" students. Something in the nature of present test construction or of the test-retest situation gives initial low scorers an advantage. What is it?

PROPHECIES DISCREDITED

Unless we can find answers to this question and do something about them, two of our most hopeful prophecies connected with testing are likely to be discredited. The first may be stated in the form of an incomplete sentence: "When testing turns from the measurement of status to the measurement of growth . . ." What will happen is not very clear, but we assume that it is bound to be good. The data just cited suggest that is bound to be bad. By some quirk in the test-retest situation, poor students will uniformly appear to have grown more than have the good students no matter who teaches them or what is tested.

The second prophecy is that when marks are based on growth rather than on final status, the inequities of the present marking system will disappear. So they will, it seems, but only to be replaced by a great inequity: the guaranteed superiority of the least able. The only way in which good students will be able to get good marks will be to select the most obviously absurd answers to all the items on their pretests.

These prospects, we trust, will not come to pass; the good sense of the profession will reject such outrageous conclusions. But at the same time teachers and administrators are likely to reject testing. They cannot put their faith in instruments that lead to absurd conclusions.

The true conclusion emerging from these considerations, I suggest, is that we do not know very much about the measurement of growth. Testing and retesting will have to be put on some different basis before we can find out and truly evaluate how much students have learned. I do not know how this will be done, but I can review three of the most obvious difficulties that will have to be surmounted.

CEILING EFFECT

The first difficulty is that the pretests may have been too easy for the high-scoring students, and their initial scores were so near the maximum possible scores as to leave little room for improvement. We usually discard this hypothesis far too hastily when we find that the highest final score was 90 percent correct and the average went up only from 50 to 60 percent correct. What we overlook is that the maximum attainable score may be a good deal lower than 100 percent correct.

Good tests of such complex skills as reading and writing go beyond matters on which everyone can agree into questions calling for insight, judgment, and taste— the very qualities in which we hope our best students will show their greatest improvement. On such questions, however, it is impossible to secure 100 percent agreement among qualified critics of the test. On the test of Critical Analysis of Reading and Writing used in the Cooperative Study, for example, no item was admitted to the final form of the test on which fewer than eleven out of the thirteen critics agreed. Restricting the test to items on which everyone agreed would have resulted in a very dull test, unlikely to challenge the brighter students. While the standard of agreement seemed strict enough, there were a good many items that only 84 percent of competent English teachers answered correctly. In such a case we should regard 84 percent correct as the maximum attainable score. Many of the students in the highest fifth came perilously close to this figure in the pretest.

Even so, the highest fifth should have been able to show more than the average gain of a quarter of a point that was reported in the study, for the lowest members of this group got only half the items right on the pretest. Some other explanation is needed.

REGRESSION

The most likely explanation of the apparently unfavorable difference in gains is the phenomenon known as "regression." Scores on all objective tests are determined partly by ability and partly by luck. The items presented to the students are only a sample drawn from an almost infinite number of similar questions that might have been asked. The particular sample that happens to be chosen is bound to favor some students more than others. They have had more experience with these kinds of questions or have given more thought to them. But when a different sample is drawn, luck is not likely to favor the same students to the same degree.

Moreover, students are rarely certain in their choice of answers. On a five-choice item they may eliminate one as absurd and two others as common errors of which they have learned to beware. The remaining two appear equally plausible, and they decide by a mental "flip of a coin." The initial high scorers were lucky in their guesses; the initial low scorers were not. On a second test the proportion of chance success may be reversed.

The phenomenon of regression has been studied by the statisticians, and they have provided an easy-to-use formula to predict what final score is to be expected on the basis of any given initial score—to the extent that chance is involved in both. I can explain how the principle works with a minimum of numbers if we imagine the following situation.

A class has been given a test of reading and writing on their first day in school and a parallel form of the same test on the second day. It is parallel in all respects: covers the same type of content with the same types of items, and the mean, standard deviation, and reliability of the second test are all equal to those of the first. The students have had sufficient practice in taking machine-scored objective tests so that marking the answer spaces is not a problem in either test. They are not told their scores on the first test, nor which answers are correct. They learn nothing about reading and writing in the interim. Let us imagine that the average score on the first test is 16; the average of the lowest fifth is 8; of the highest fifth, 24; and the reliability of the tests, as indicated by the correlation between them, is .70. What average scores of the lowest and the highest fifths may be expected on the second test when chance alone is involved?

In such a situation final scores may be predicted by multplying initial differences from the average by the reliability of the tests.[2] Take the difference of the

---

[2] The actual prediction formula is a bit more complicated, but this simplification is valid for the situation described and illustrates the basic principle that is involved.

lowest fifth from the average of the total group: it is —8. Multiply this by the reliability (.70), and you get —5.6. Take 5.6 from the initial average (16), and the predicted score of the lowest fifth on the second test will be 10.4. Since their initial average was 8, they will appear to have gained 2.4 points.

Similarly, take the difference of the highest fifth from the initial average (+8), multiply by the reliability (.70), and you get 5.6. Add this to the initial average (16), and the predicted score of the highest fifth on the second test will be 21.6. Since their initial average was 24, they will appear to have lost 2.4 points.

While the situation we have imagined is artificial, the same chance factors will operate to the same extent when the tests are given at the beginning and end of the school year—provided that the two tests are strictly parallel. In the ordinary course of events, of course, they are not strictly parallel, and then chance differences will be even greater. We usually do not realize the magnitude of the differences in test-retest scores that may be attributed to chance alone. The figures I have cited were very close to the actual figures for the test of Critical Analysis of Reading and Writing used in the Cooperative Study, rounded for the sake of simplicity. We regarded with some horror the finding that the lowest fifth gained 5.33 points while the highest fifth gained only 0.25 points. But when we consider what might be expected to happen on the basis of chance alone, the lowest group should have gained 2.4 points; it actually gained 5.33; therefore it exceeded a chance gain by 2.93 points. The highest group would be expected to lose 2.4 points; it actually gained 0.25 points; therefore the best approximation of the actual gain is 2.65 points.

We can now view the gains of both groups in better perspective. When set against what would have happened by chance, if no learning whatever had taken place, the lowest fifth gained 2.93 points; the highest fifth gained 2.65 points. Such a finding comes closer, although not close enough, to our intuitive judgment of what these two groups probably learned.

Teachers regard such manipulations uneasily. The raw scores seem to be real; the converted scores, hypothetical. But there is nothing fanciful about the phenomenon of regression. It was originally deduced from observations that children of extremely tall parents tend to be shorter and children of extremely short parents tend to be taller than their parents. The formula expressing this principle can be proved as rigorously as any proposition in geometry, and study after study has shown that this principle must be taken into account if the results are to seem reasonable.

Teachers may wonder why fortune uniformly smiles upon the weakest students and frowns upon the strongest in the test-retest situation. It does nothing of the sort. Both groups will "regress" toward the average to precisely the same extent: their distance from the average multiplied by the reliability of the test. The direction of this regression quite naturally has to be upward for low-scoring students and downward for high-scoring students.

My only quarrel with the use of the regression formula is that, if we stop there, we have not gone far enough. We have wiped out the spurious gains and losses that may be attributed to chance, but the usual result is that the weakest and the strongest groups appear to have gained about the same amount. We have good reason to believe that this is not true. What else keeps the initially high students from showing how much more they have learned than the initially low?

UNEQUAL UNITS OF MEASUREMENT

A further explanation of the discrepancy in gains may lie in the way in which objective tests are constructed. In a four-choice test we tend to put in one best answer, one that is likely to deceive all but the elect, one common error that students make, and one absurd answer that I shall refer to as a "booby trap." These four types of answers may not appear in every item, but let us suppose that there are equal numbers of each in the total test. Consider the case of the boy who in the beginning can rule out only half the booby traps and has to choose among the remaining answers by chance. The part of his score that may be attributed to knowledge or skill is one-eighth. But merely by staying awake in class he may learn to rule out all the booby traps and to avoid the most common types of errors that students make, for these will be emphasized most heavily in class. Hence in the final test he will be able to rule out two out of every four responses on the average and will have to choose, by chance, only between the right and the nearly right. The part of his score that may be attributed to knowledge is now 50 percent. He has gone from one-eighth correct to one-half correct —a gain of 38 percentage points—on the basis of minimum ability and minimum effort.

Now consider the student who can do this well in the beginning. He can already rule out booby traps and common errors; the only way he can improve his score is by learning to distinguish best answers from those that are equally plausible and almost as good. These are hard choices. While the poor student can gain 38 points in a test of 100 items by learning to make easy choices, the good student may have a harder time gaining 10 points, for he has much harder problems to cope with.

Unfortunately there is not yet any precise way to translate responses to test items into equal units of growth. Standard scores based on the normal curve are an improvement on percentiles in estimating growth, but they do not solve the problem, because they rest on the assumption that equal gains of raw-score points represent equal increments in ability, and the whole purpose of this section has been to demonstrate that this is not the case. It is harder to get from the mean up to plus one standard deviation than it is to get from minus one standard deviation up to the mean. All the data presented from the Cooperative Study attest that this is not a fanciful or theoretical argument but a fact, for many students were able to do the latter but relatively few were able to do the former.

The only ultimate answer to this question that I can now foresee is to get norms for gains as well as for status, starting from any given initial score. Until such norms are provided, the best we can do as teachers is to become as familiar with records on our tests as our students are with records in sports. It may be that a gain from 30 to 60 percent correct, while creditable, is nothing to get excited about, for almost everyone who starts at 30 percent correct can make it. But a gain from 80 to 85 percent correct on a difficult test may be breathtaking, for no one has ever made it before.

This plan will not settle the metaphysical argument as to whether a gain from stupidity to mediocrity is better than a gain from competence to brilliance, but at least it will not automatically stack the cards in favor of the former.

38   *Testing Hazards in Performance Contracting*

ROBERT E. STAKE

Since schools exist to improve pupil learning, and since learning is shown by a change in behavior, it would seem that an educator should wish to determine whether the pupil has changed. His interest in assessing change increases if money is involved, especially if the amount paid depends upon a specified demonstrated change in pupil behavior. It would seem that since published achievement tests have been refined over a few decades of use, measuring change in achievement would be a simple, straightforward endeavor, accomplished accurately and reported routinely. Unfortunately, this is not the case. In the following article the author considers issues and problems involving tests, test items, and differences between two sets of scores on the same or parallel measures. For this discussion the differences are computed between measures given at different stages of instruction, usually pre and post, although difference scores generally are haunted by difficulties such as unreliability and the regression effect which are discussed here. Important considerations related to the following article are found in the preceding article by Diederich. The "accountability" dimension of this article is also treated in article 5 by Tyler.

What are advantages and disadvantages of using difference scores from a published reading test to decide whether to fund a particular reading program for next year? What do the scores reflect other than treatment effect? (Consider such topics as irrelevant abilities, limitations of the items, and measurement of differences.) How might one improve his evaluations of treatment

Reprinted and abridged with permission of author and publisher from the *Phi Delta Kappan*, 1971, June, 583–589.

effect by using some ideas from Diederich's and Stake's articles, from criterion-referenced testing (see Popham and Husek's article for example), and from elsewhere?

In the first federally sponsored example of performance contracting for the public schools, Dorsett Educational Systems of Norman, Oklahoma, contracted to teach reading, mathematics, and study skills to over 200 poor-performance junior and senior high school students in Texarkana. Commercially available, standardized, general-achievement tests were used to measure performance gains.

Are such tests suitable for measuring specific learnings? To the person little acquainted with educational testing, it appears that performance testing is what educational tests are for. The testing specialist knows better. General achievement tests have been developed to measure correlates of learning, not learning itself.

Such tests are indirect measures of educational gains. They provide correlates of achievement rather than direct evidence of achievement. Correlation of these test scores with general learning is often high, but such scores correlate only moderately with performance on many specific educational tasks. Tests can be built to measure specific competence, but there is relatively little demand for them. Many of those tests (often called criterion-referenced tests) do a poor job of predicting later performance of either a specific or a general nature. General achievement tests predict better. The test developer's basis for improving tests has been to work toward better prediction of later performance rather than better measurement of present performance. Assessment of what a student is now capable of doing is not the purpose of most standardized tests. Errors and hazards abound, especially when these general achievement tests are used for performance contracting. Many of the hazards remain even with the use of criterion-referenced tests or any other performance observation procedures.

One of the hazards in performance contracting is that many high-priority educational objectives—for various reasons and in various ways—will be cast aside while massive attention is given to other high-priority objectives. This hazard is not unrelated to testing but will not be discussed here. This article will identify the major obstacles to gathering direct evidence of performance gain on targeted objectives.

ERRORS OF TESTING

Just as the population census and the bathroom scales have their errors, educational tests have theirs. The technology and theory of testing are highly sophisticated; the sources of error are well known. Looking into the psychometrist's meaning of a theory of testing, one finds a consideration of ways to analyze and label the inaccuracies in test scores. There is a mystique, but there is also simple fact: no one can eliminate test errors. Unfortunately, some errors are large enough to cause wrong decisions about individual children or school district policy.

Some educators and social critics consider the whole idea of educational testing to be a mistake. Unfortunate social consequences of testing, such as the perpetuation of racial discrimination (Goslin, 1970) and pressures to cheat (McGhan, 1970), continue to be discussed. But, as expected, most test specialists believe that the promise in testing outweighs these perils. They refuse responsibility for gross misuse of their instruments and findings and concentrate on reducing the errors in tests and test programs.

Some technical errors in test scores are small and tolerable. But some testing errors are intolerably large. Today's tests can, for example, measure vocabulary word-recognition skills with sufficient accuracy. They cannot, however, adequately measure listening comprehension or the ability to analyze the opposing sides of an argument.

Contemporary test technology is not refined enough to meet all the demands. In performance contracting the first demand is for assessment of performance. Tests do their job well when the performance is highly specific—when, for example, they measure vocabulary word-recognition skills with sufficient accuracy. They cannot, however, adequately measure listening comprehension or the ability to analyze the opposing sides of an argument.

Contemporary test technology is not refined enough to meet all the demands. In performance contracting the first demand is for assessment of performance. Tests do their job well when the performance is highly specific—when, for example, the student is to add two numbers, recognize a misspelled word, or identify the parts of a hydraulic lift. When a teacher wants to measure performances that require more demanding mental processes, such as conceptualizing a writing principle or synthesizing a political argument, performance tests give us less dependable scores (See Bloom, et al., 1956).

UNREACHED POTENTIALS ■ Many educators believe that the most human of human gifts—the emotions, the higher thought processes, interpersonal sensitivity, moral sense—are beyond the reach of psychometric testing. Most test specialists disagree. While recognizing an ever-present error component, they believe that anything can be measured. The credo was framed by E. L. Thorndike in 1918: "Whatever exists at all exists in some amount." Testing men believe it still. They are not so naive as to think that any human gift will manifest itself in a 45-minute paper-and-pencil test. They do believe that, given ample opportunity to activate and observe the examinee, any trait, talent, or learning that manifests itself in behavior can be measured with reasonable accuracy. The total cost of measuring may be 100 times that of administering the usual tests, but they believe it can be done. The final observations may rely on professional judgment, but this could be reliable and validated judgment. A question for most test specialists, then, is not "Can complex educational outcomes be measured?" but "Can complex educational outcomes be measured with the time and personnel and facilities available?"

When it is most important to know whether or not a child is reading at age-level, we call in a reading specialist, who observes his reading habits. She might test him with word recognition, syntactic decoding, and paragraph-comprehension exercises. She would retest where evidence was inconclusive. She would talk to his teachers and his parents. She would arrive at a clinical description—which might be reducible to a statement such as, "Yes, Johnny is reading at or above age-level."

The scores we get from group reading tests can be considered estimates of such an expert judgment. These objective test scores correlate positively with the more valid expert judgments. Such estimates are not direct measurements of what teachers or laymen mean by "ability to read," nor are they suitably accurate for diagnostic purposes. Achievement gains for a sizable number of students will be poorly estimated. It is possible that the errors in group testing are so extensive that—when fully known—businessmen and educators will refuse to accept them as bases for contract reimbursement.

PROFESSIONAL AWARENESS ■ Classroom teachers and school principals have tolerated standardized test errors because they have not been obligated to make crucial decisions on the basis of test scores. Actually, in day-to-day practice they seldom use test scores (Hastings, Runkel, & Damrin, 1961). When they do, they combine them with other knowledge to estimate a child's progress in school and to guide him into an appropriate learning experience. They do not use tests as a basis for assessing the quality of their own teaching.

In performance contracting, the situation is drastically changed; tests are honored as the sole basis for contract reimbursement. The district will pay the contractor for performance improvement. An error in testing means money misspent. Course completion and reimbursement decisions are to be made without reliance on the knowledge and judgment of a professional observer, without asking persons who are closest to the learning (the teacher, the contractor, and the student) whether or not they see evidence of learning. Decisions are to be made entirely by objective and independent testing. Numerous human errors and technical misrepresentations will occur.

WHICH TEST ITEMS?

It is often unrealistic to expect a project director to either find or create paper-and-pencil test items, administrable in an hour to large numbers of students by persons untrained in psychometric observation and standardized diagnostics, objectively scorable, valid for purposes of the performance contract, and readily interpretable. The more complex the training, the more unrealistic the expectation. One compromise is to substitute criterion test items measuring simple behaviors for those measuring the complex behaviors targeted by the training. For example, the director may substitute vocabulary-recognition test items for reading-comprehension items or knowledge of components for the actual dismantling of an engine. The substitution may be reasonable, but the criterion test should be validated against performances directly indicated by the objectives. It almost never has been. Without the validation the educator should be skeptical about what the test measures.

It always is unrealistic to expect that the payoff from instruction will be apparent in the performances of learners at test-taking time (Broudy, 1970). Most tests evoke relatively simple behavior. Ebel (1971) wrote:

> . . . most achievement tests . . . consist primarily of items testing specific elements of knowledge, facts, ideas, explanations, meanings, processes, procedures, relations, consequences, and so on.

He went on to point out that more than simple recall is involved in answering even the simplest vocabulary item.

Much more complex behavior is needed for answering a reading-comprehension item. These items clearly call for more than the literal meanings of the words read. The student must paraphrase and interpret—what we expect readers to be able to do.

These items and ones for problem solving and the higher mental processes do measure high-priority school goals—but growth in such areas is relatively slow. Most contractors will not risk basing reimbursement on the small chance that evidence of growth will be revealed by these criterion tests. Some of the complex objectives of instruction will be underemphasized in the typical performance-contract testing plan.

The success of Texarkana's first performance-contract year is still being debated. Late winter (1969–70) test results looked good (See Andrew & Roberts, 1970; Dyer, 1970; Lennon, 1971), but spring test results were disappointing. Relatively simple performance items had been used. But the "debate" did not get into that. It started when the project's "outside evaluator" ruled that there had been direct coaching on most, if not all, of the criterion test items, which were known by the contractor during the school year. Critics claimed unethical "teaching for the test." The contractor claimed that both teaching and testing had been directed toward the same specific goals, as should be the case in a good performance contract. The issue is not only test choice and ethics; it includes the ultimate purpose of teaching.

TEACHING FOR THE TEST ▪ Educators recognize an important difference between preparation for testing and direct coaching for a test. To prepare an examinee, the teacher teaches within the designated knowledge-skill domain and has the examinee practice good test-taking behavior (for example, don't spend too much time on overly difficult items; guess when you have an inkling though not full knowledge; organize your answer before writing an essay) so that relevant knowledge-skill is not obscured. Direct coaching teaches the examinees how to make correct responses to specific items on the criterion test.

This is an important difference when test items cover only a small sample of the universe of what has been taught or when test scores are correlates, rather than direct measurements, of criterion behavior. It ceases to be important when the test is set up to measure directly and thoroughly that which has been taught. In this case, teaching for the test is exactly what is wanted.

Joselyn (1971) pointed out that the performance contractor and the school should agree in advance on the criterion procedure, though not necessarily on the specific items. To be fair to the contractor, the testing needs to be reasonably close to the teaching. To be fair to parents, the testing needs to be representative of the domain of abilities they are concerned about. A contract to develop reading skills would not be satisfied adequately by gains on a vocabulary test, according to the expectations of most teachers. All parties need to know how similar the testing will be to the actual teaching.

A DISSIMILARITY SCALE ■ Unfortunately, as Anderson (1970) observed, the test specialist has not developed scales for describing the similarity between teaching and testing. This is a grievous failing. Educators have no good way to indicate how closely the tests match the instruction.

There are many ways for criterion questions to be dissimilar. They can depart from the information taught by: (1) syntactic transformation; (2) semantic transformation; (3) change in content or medium; (4) application, considering the particular instance; (5) inference, generalizing from learned instances; and (6) implication, adding last-taught information to generally known information. For examples of some of these transformations, see Table 1. Hively, Patterson, and Page (1968), Bormuth (1970), and Jackson (1970) discussed procedures for using some of these transformations to generate test items.

For any student the appropriateness of these items depends on prior and subsequent learning as well as on the thoroughness of teaching. Which items are appropriate will have to be decided at the scene. The least and most dissimilar items might be quite different in their appropriateness. The reading-comprehension items of any standardized achievement battery are likely to be more dissimilar to the teaching of reading than any of the "dissimilarities" shown in Table 1. Immediate instruction is not properly evaluated by highly dissimilar items, nor is scholarship properly evaluated by highly similar items. Even within the confines of performance contracting, both evaluations are needed.

TABLE 1. *An example of transformations of information taught into test questions.*

Information taught:	Pt. Barrow in the northernmost town in Alaska.
Minimum transformation question:	What is the northernmost town in Alaska?
Semantic-syntactic transformation question:	What distinction does Pt. Barrow have among Alaskan villages?
Context-medium transformation question:	The dots on the adjacent map represent Alaskan cities and towns. One represents Pt. Barrow. Which one?
Implication questions:	What would be unusual about summer sunsets in Pt. Barrow, Alaska?

For the evaluation of instruction, a large number of test items are needed for each objective that—in the opinion of the teachers—directly measures increase in skill or understanding. Items from standardized tests, if used, would be included item by item. For each objective, the item pool would cover all aspects of the objective. A separate sample of items would be drawn for the pretest and posttest for each student, and instructional success would be based on the collective gain of all students.

Creating such a pool of relevant, psychometrically sound test items is a major—but necessary—undertaking (Dorsett indicated the desirability of such an item pool in the original Texarkana proposal). It is a partial safeguard against teaching for the test and against the use of inappropriate criteria to evaluate the success of instruction.

WHAT THE SCORES MEAN ■ At first, performance contracting seemed almost a haven for the misinterpretation of scores. Contracts have ignored (1) the practice effect of pretesting (not discussed here because of space limitations), (2) the origins of grade equivalents, (3) the "learning calendar," (4) the unreliability of gain scores, and (5) regression effects. Achievement may be spurious. Ignoring any one of these five is an invitation to misjudge the worth of the instruction.

GRADE-EQUIVALENT SCORES ■ Standardized achievement tests have the appealing feature of yielding grade-equivalent scores. Each raw score, usually the number of items right, has been translated into a score indicating (for a student population forming a national reference group) the average grade placement of all students who got this raw score. These new scores are called "grade equivalents." Raw scores are not very meaningful to people unacquainted with the particular test; the grade equivalents are widely accepted by teachers and parents. Grade equivalents are common terminology in performance contracts.

Unfortunately, grade equivalents are available from most publishers only for tests, not for test items. Thus the whole test needs to be used, in the way prescribed in its manual, if the grade equivalents are to mean what they are supposed to mean. One problem of using whole tests was discussed in the previous section. Another problem is that the average annual "growth" on most standardized tests is only a few raw-score points. Consider in Table 2 the difference between a grade equivalent of 5.0 and 6.0 within four of the most popular test batteries..

TABLE 2. *Gain in items right needed to advance one grade equivalent on four typical achievement tests.*

	Grade equivalent 5.0	6.0	Needed for an improvement of one grade equivalent
Comprehensive Test of Basic Skills, Level 3: Reading Comprehension	20	23	3 items
Metropolitan Achievement Test, Intermediate Form B: Spelling	24	31	7 items
Iowa Tests of Basic Skills, Test A1: Arithmetic Concepts	10	14	4 items
Stanford Achievement Test, Form W, Intermediate II: Word Meaning	18	26	8 items

Most teachers do not like to have their year's work summarized by so little change in performance. Schools writing performance contracts perhaps should be reluctant to sign contracts for which the distinction between success and failure is so small. But to do so requires the abandonment of grade equivalents.

THE LEARNING CALENDAR ■ For most special instructional programs, criterion tests will be administered at the beginning of and immediately following instruction, often in the first and last weeks of school. A great deal of distraction occurs during those weeks, but other times for pretesting and posttesting have their hazards, too. Recording progress every few weeks during the year is psychometrically preferred, but most teachers are opposed to "all that testing."

Children learn year-round, but the evidence of learning that gets inked on pupil records comes in irregular increments from season to season. Winter is the time of most rapid advancement, summer the least. Summer, in fact, is a period of setback for many youngsters. Beggs and Hieronymus (1968) found punctuation scores to spurt more than a year between October and April but to drop almost half a year between May and September. Discussing their reading test, Gates and MacGinitie wrote (1965):

. . . in most cases, scores will be higher at the end of one grade than at the beginning of the next. That is, there is typically some loss of reading skill during the summer, especially in the lower grades.

The first month or two after students return to school in the fall is the time for getting things organized and restoring scholastic abilities lost during the summer. According to some records, spring instruction competes poorly with other attractions. Thus, the learning year is a lopsided year, a basis sometimes for miscalculation. Consider the results of testing shown in Table 3.

The six-week averages in Table 3 are fictitious, but they represent test performance in many classrooms. The mean growth for the year appears to be 1.3 grade equivalent. No acknowledgement is made that standardized test results in early September were poorer than those for the previous spring. For this example, the previous May mean (not shown) was 5.2. The real gain, then, for the year is 1.1 grade equivalents rather than the apparent 1.3. It would be inappropriate to pay the contractor for a mean gain of 1.3.

TABLE 3. *Learning calendar for a typical fifth-grade class.*

	Month							
	S	O	N	D	J	F	M	A	M
Mean achievement score	5.0	5.3	5.6	5.9		6.2		6.3

Another possible overpayment on the contract can result by holding final testing early and extrapolating the previous per-week growth to the weeks or months that follow. In Texarkana, as in most schools, spring progress was not as good as winter. If an accurate evaluation of contract instructional services is to be made, repeated testing, perhaps a month-by-month record of learning performances, needs to be considered (see Wrightman and Gorth, 1969).

UNRELIABLE GAIN SCORES ■ (See previous article by Diederich for further elaboration of this topic and the one in the following section.) Most performance contracts pay off on an individual student basis. The contractor may be paid for each student who gains more than an otherwise expected amount. This practice is commendable in that it emphasizes the importance of each individual learner and makes the contract easier to understand, but it bases payment on a precarious mark: the gain score.

Just how unreliable is the performance-test gain score? For a typical standardized achievement test with two parallel forms, A and B, we might find the following characteristics reported in the test's technical manual:

> Reliability of Test A = +.84.
> Reliability of Test B = +.84.
> Correlation of Test A with Test B = +.81.

Almost all standardized tests have reliability coefficients at this level. Using the standard formula (see, for example, Thorndike and Hagen, 1969) one finds a disappointing level of reliability for the measurement of improvement:

> Reliability of gain scores (A − B or B − A) = +.16.

The test manual indicates the raw score and grade-equivalent standard deviations. For one widely used test, they are 9.5 items and 2.7 years, respectively. Using these values we can calculate the errors to be expected. On the average, a student's raw score would be in error by 2.5 items, grade equivalent would be in error by 0.72 years, and grade-equivalent gain score would be in error by 1.01 years. The error is indeed large.

Consider what this means for the not unusual contract whereby the student is graduated from the program, and the contractor is paid for his instruction, on any occasion that his performance score rises above a set value. Suppose—with the figures above—the student exists when his improvement is one grade equivalent or more. Suppose also, to make this situation simpler, that there is no intervening training and that the student is not influenced by previous testing. Here are three ways of looking at the same situation.

Suppose that a contract student takes a different parallel form of the criterion test on three successive days immediately following the pretest. The chances are better than 50–50 that on one of these tests the student will gain a year or more in performance and appear to be ready to graduate from the program.

Suppose that three students are tested with a parallel form immediately after the pretest. The chances are better than 50–50 that one of the three students—entirely due to errors of measurement—will gain a year or more and appear ready to graduate.

Suppose that 100 students are admitted to contract instruction and pretested. After a period of time involving no training, they are tested again, and the students gaining a year are graduated. After another period of time, another test and another graduation. After the fourth terminal testing, even though no instruction has occurred, the chances are better than 50–50 that two-thirds of the students will be graduated.

In other words, owing to unreliability, gain scores can appear to reflect learning that actually does not occur.

The unreliability will give an equal number of false impressions of deteriorating performance. These errors (false gains and false losses) will balance out for a large group of students. If penalties for losses are paid by the contractor at the rate bonuses are paid for gains, the contractor will not be overpaid. But according to the way contracts are being written, typified in the examples above, the error in the gain scores does not balance out; it works in favor of the contractor. Measurement errors could be capitalized upon by unscrupulous promoters. Appropriate checks against these errors are built into the better contracts.

Errors in individual gain scores can be reduced by using longer tests. A better way to indicate true gain is to calculate the discrepancy between actual and expected final performances. Expectations can be based on the group as a whole or on an outside control group. Another way is to write the contract on the basis of mean scores for the group of students. (This would have the increased advantage of discouraging the contractor from giving preferential treatment within the project to students who are in a position to make high payoff gains.) Corrections for the unreliability of gain scores are possible, but they are not likely to be considered if the educators and contractors are statistically naive.

REGRESSION EFFECTS ■ Probably the source of the greatest misinterpretation of the effects of remedial instruction is regression effects. Regression effects are easily overlooked but need not be; they are correctable. For any pretest score, the expected regression effect can be calculated. Regression effects make the poorest scorers look better the next time tested. Whether measurements are error-laden or error-free, meaningful or meaningless, when there is differential change between one measurement occasion and another (when there is less-than-perfect correlation), the lowest original scorers will make the greatest gains and the highest original scorers will make the least. On the average, posttest scores will, relative to their corresponding pretest scores, lie in the direction of the mean. This is the regression effect. Lord (1963) discussed this universal phenomenon and various ways to correct for it.

The demand for performance contracts has occurred where conventional instructional programs fail to develop—for a sizable number of students—minimum competence in basic skills. Given a distribution of skill test scores, the lowest-scoring students—the ones most needing assistance—are identified. It is reasonable to suppose that under unchanged instructional programs they would drop even further behind the high-scoring students. If a retest is given, however, after any period of instruction (conventional or special) or of no instruction, these students will no longer be the poorest performers. Some of them will be replaced by others who appear to be most in need of special instruction. Instruction is not the obvious influences here—regression is. The regression effect is not due to test unreliability, but it causes some of the same misinterpretations. The contract should read that instruction will be reimbursed when gain exceeds that attributable to regression effects. The preferred evaluation design would call for control group(s) of similar students to provide a good estimate of the progress the contract students would have made in the absence of the special instruction.

THE SOCIAL PROCESS

The hazards of specific performance testing and performance contracting are more than curricular and psychometric. Social and humanistic challenges should be raised, too. The teacher has a special opportunity and obligation to observe the influence of testing on social behavior.

Performance contracting has the unique ability to put the student in a position of administrative influence. He can make the instruction appear better or worse than it actually is by his performance on tests. Even if he is quite young, the student will know that his good work will benefit the contractor. Sooner or later he is going to know that, if he tests poorly at the beginning, he can benefit himself and the contractor through his later achievement. Bad performances are in his repertoire, and he may be more anxious to make the contractor look bad than to make himself look good. Or he may be under pressure to do well on the posttests. These are pupil-teacher interactions that should be watched carefully. More responsibility for school control possibly should accrue to students, but performance contracts seem a devious way to give it.

To motivate the student to learn and to make him want more contract instruction, many contractors use material or opportunity-to-play rewards. (Dorsett used such merchandise as transistor radios.) Other behavior modification strategies are common. The proponents of such strategies argue that, once behavior has been oriented to appropriate tasks, the students can gradually be shifted from extrinsic rewards to intrinsic. That they can be shifted is probably true; that it will happen without careful, deliberate work by the instructional staff is unlikely. It is not difficult to imagine a performance-contract situation in which the students become even less responsive to the rewards of conventional instruction.

Performance contracting appears to be popular with the current administration in Washington because it encourages private businesses to participate in a traditionally public responsibility. It is popular among some school administrators because it affords new access to federal funds, because it is a way to get new talent working on old problems, and because the administrator can easily blame the outside agency and the government if the contract instruction is unsuccessful. It is unpopular with the American Federation of Teachers because it reduces the control the union has over school operations, and it reduces the teacher's role as a chooser of what learning students need most. Performance contracting is popular among most instructional technologists because it is based on well researched principles of teaching and because it enhances their role in school operations.

The accountability movement as a whole is likely to be a success or failure on such sociopolitical items. The measurement of the performance of performance contracting is an even more hazardous procedure than the measurement of student performances.

SUMMARY

Without yielding to the temptation to undercut new efforts to provide instruction, educators should continue to be apprehensive about evaluating teaching on the basis of performance testing alone. They should know how difficult it is to represent educational goals with statements of objectives and how costly it is to provide suitable criterion testing. They should know that the common-sense interpretation of these results is frequently wrong. Still, many members of the profession think that evaluation controls are extravagant and mystical.

Performance contracting has emerged because people inside and outside the schools are dissatisfied with the instruction some children are getting. Implicit in the contracts is the expectation that available tests can measure the newly promised learning. The standardized test alone cannot measure the specific outcomes of an individual student with sufficient precision.

39   Seven Classic Ways of Grading Dishonestly

ORVILLE PALMER

The applications of measurement data in the process of evaluation or decision-making are many and varied. In the following article important uses and misuses of test data in the assignment of grades are discussed. Sources of data used in the marking process should, of course, not be limited to tests or examinations. Any evidence related to a course, as long as it was gathered to determine if certain instructional objectives had been attained, should be considered legitimate data. Such a suggestion, however, can lead to a troublesome problem. On the one hand, a teacher desires a common basis for the evaluation of his pupils. Such efforts as outside readings or independent research projects might not be considered, as they may have a different meaning for different students. It is also true that the failure to reward "extra effort" is contrary to the known positive relationships between reinforcement, motivation, and learning. Dr. Palmer's discussion underscores a widely known fact but one which is not generally part of a teacher's conscious awareness, namely, that the assignment of grades involves philosophical decisions. Each teacher must determine what data are germane, what proportion of the class will receive As, Bs, etc. The shortcomings of many marking practices highlighted in the following article are well worth considering. In addition, the reader may wish to consider the following questions: (1) What principles should guide the teacher in marking? (2) How can grading practices be improved? (3) How does the assignment of marks relate to the over-all instructional process?

Reprinted and abridged from *The English Journal*, October, 1962, pp. 464–467, with permission of the National Council of Teachers of English and Orville Palmer.

No two marking systems of teachers are quite alike, even as no two teachers are identical. Nevertheless, the major kinds of bad evaluation systems, or quasi-systems, may be identified.

A first, and wholly indefensible way of grading dishonestly is by abdication. Because of inexperience, inadequate training, or overwork, the teacher in effect abdicates his responsibility for grading fairly and creatively. Such a teacher may claim that an adequate testing program would take more time than he can spare, or that test-making is an art for which he has no talent. At the last moment such a teacher will put together a crude, inadequate test, or use anything he can lay his hands on: a workbook unit test, a dog-eared commercial test; or he may assign an essay topic thought up on the spur of the moment. Rather than tailor his tests to his course, he may tailor his course to any available set of tests. But such a teacher clearly knows very little about student evaluation. He shirks real responsibility in the matter, and unfortunately all too often he does nothing to improve his competence.

The second method of grading dishonestly is by means of what can be called "the carrots and clubs" system. In this system, grades may be raised by performing designated added tasks, or lowered by failure to avoid certain prejudices of the teacher. Here we find the teacher who fails every theme that contains a run-on sentence or, say two spelling errors. And here we meet up with bonuses for good behavior and added effort.

In grade school, I suppose, a teacher may properly grade, in part at least, on "attitude and effort." But in high school and college surely the academic grade should be based on academic performance and little else. It is a mistaken and dangerous kindness—or mode of discipline—to do otherwise. I dare say I shall affront more teachers on this point than any other. I can only urge that the line between rewarded good attitude and effort and favoritism is a treacherous one. I can only say that the more blatantly a teacher "buys" good behavior or extra effort, the greater the damage to class morale, to student ethics, and to academic standards. Beyond any question, the more extraneous factors that enter into the marking system, the less meaning an academic grade possesses. Any grade becomes debased coinage to the same degree that it represents nonacademic effort and attainment. By extraneous factors I mean such things as classroom deportment, neatness of penmanship, imaginative covers for reports and similar artwork, extra credit for reading, and the like. Not that any one of these things is bad or even suspect in itself. My point is simply this: everything of an academic nature that the teacher grades—quizzes, themes, oral and written reports, required or volunteer work—should be graded on its merits and nothing else.

There does not exist a teacher who has wholly freed himself of "halo effect," of all those tangibles and intangibles of personal approval or disapproval of students' attitudes and conduct. Teaching is not, and should not be an impersonal, cold-blooded enterprise. To the extent that it is not, however, it becomes increasingly difficult to make evaluation wholly impersonal. Yet I have observed that one excellent measure of a teacher's honesty and rectitude is the respect that students give to grades bestowed by the teacher known for his fairness and scrupulousness in marking.

A third way to grade dishonestly is by default. This teacher gives as little time to tests as possible. In graduate school we find the professor who reluctantly gives a single term-end test. In secondary schools the teacher who hates tests and claims they are meaningless or farcical or an infernal nuisance will give as few of them as possible. Sometimes his students are in a state of near-panic because the base for grades is so narrow a single misstep could spell disaster. Curiously enough, the teacher who hates tests very often also hates reading student themes, and his students consequently write few themes or none. (Such an arrangement is probably the best single guarantee that students will not learn how to write competently.)

The dishonesty lies precisely in the unfair base. Any test, of whatever nature, is but a limited and inadequate sampling of the student's knowledge and achievement. Every test will have its defects of validity and reliability.

A student instinctively knows that the odds for a valid evaluation improve when he takes four tests rather than a single test. He knows that the chances are better that he will be able to demonstrate his skills and understanding—because the base is broader.

The testing zealots furnish a fourth system of grading unwisely. The zealot sets his students to racing with a vengeance—daily quizzes, almost daily written assignments, weekly tests, quarter-term, mid-term, final examinations, reports of all sorts. He grades everything short of classroom posture. At its extreme, in such systems everything becomes an ordeal, the course an endurance contest or a problem in survival.

The zealot's quizzes check whether the students have read their assigned pages of text, whether assigned short stories or novels were read carefully. They are, in short, a policing device. Even notebooks may be called in and graded.

A certain amount of such police work may be necessary, of course. It should, however, stop well short of constant surveillance and the spirit of the police officer administering a lie detector test.

Until the sheer weight of oversize classes or the scythe of Father Time cuts down these teachers, they average up their dozens of minor and major grades, using elaborate formulas of computation and weighting, secure in the belief they have evolved a scientific, fair system of evaluation. Possibly they have, but I would suggest they have paid too high a price for it. The good will, the student rapport, the main purposes of instruction have been lost somewhere in the process.

Changing the rules in mid-game is a fifth way to grade dishonestly. It is always a temptation to a harried or uncertain teacher. It amounts to shifting the grading standards, either up or down, for workbook tests, themes, examinations, and so on. The teacher may start off the course by distributing quantities of low or failing grades to frighten the students into greater effort, then ease his standards later. He may tighten his grading at mid-term to put spurs into the lazy and laggard, to discipline an unruly class, to merely rectify a grading curve that threatens to be top-heavy with As and Bs, and unballasted with failures.

Here, too, we discover the irate teacher who decides to "get tough" about bad spelling or bad grammar. Henceforward it will be an automatic F for every theme with two or more misspelled words, an F for any essay examination with a run-on sentence, and so on.

Strewing with booby traps the field across which the student must march, making a hazard-cluttered obstacle course of every theme—this may or may not eliminate misspelled words and rambling sentences. It can usually be counted on to put frost on the fragile flower of student creativity and enthusiasm, to put greater tension between teacher and student, even to make learning an ordeal.

A sixth kind of dishonesty is displayed by the psychic grader. His is an ingenuous method—it can scarcely be called a system since it is neither structured nor organic. Undoubtedly it is an ultimate variety or extension of halo effect grading. (Halo effect probably constitutes the chief weakness of teacher-made tests and evaluation.)

The psychic teacher may inform you that he, for one, has no need for anything so coarse-meshed as a test to catch his fish in. You are given to understand that he can tell almost immediately in his bones or by means inscrutable to ordinary man who the A students will be, who the B. And he will swear by the distinction between the two. To this teacher tests are superfluous or at best mere window dressing.

A final classic method of grading dishonestly is anchored in a system of impossible perfection. Teachers adhering to this system inform their students, in effect, that an A is out of the question, and that only the most brilliant and industrious can hope for the accolade of a B. Often this teacher can be counted on to fail twice as many students as anyone else in his department. He prides himself on his high standards. And he grumbles at his soft-hearted colleagues' habit of debasing departmental standards by the indiscriminate bestowal of high grades and by a rabbit-hearted reluctance to fail the dullards.

When you challenge their use of one or more of the above systems or ways of grading, some teachers stubbornly and even angrily reply that it is perfectly fair to use any set of rules you like, so long as you have all your students running the same race and abiding by the same set of rules. This of course has a sporting air to it and seems to doff its cap to egalitarian democracy and our American way of life.

The fact remains that such a reply is specious. The students in any high school class are not running one race but several. They are also racing all the other academic classes in their school, and (if college-bound) they are racing all the other students in all the other high schools in the land.

If every teacher makes his own set of rules and answers to no one's conscience but his own, there can only be anarchy in these races. This, in a very real sense, is the state of affairs today.

Of course nothing can be more corrosive of values and goals than the concept of academic courses as "races" in which the winners snatch the A's, the runners-up win the B's, and the also-rans receive only C's and worse. When the grade becomes more important than the learning itself, education itself is subverted.

40   *Guidelines for Testing Minority Group Children*

MARTIN DEUTSCH, JOSHUA A. FISHMAN, LEONARD S. KOGAN,
ROBERT D. NORTH, AND MARTIN WHITMAN

The usefulness of a test depends in part on appropriate and intelligent administration and interpretation. But perhaps even more important is the compatibility of the group or individual to be examined relative to the test content and its standardization population. With the increased public, private, and governmental concern surrounding the social and educational problems of minority groups, the need to reappraise our testing practices becomes mandatory. The following paper, prepared by a work group of the Society for the Psychological Study of Social Issues under the chairmanship of Dr. Joshua Fishman, makes a very important contribution to the reappraisal process. This report highlights some very significant sources of error originating from implicit and explicit cultural bias that must be taken into account in test development and interpretation.

What are some of the sources of error that may influence test reliability that are somewhat unique to minority groups? How might these influences be controlled? Are interest and personality tests more or less susceptible to bias than achievement and aptitude measures? Why? What are the three kinds of factors the authors indicate may influence predictive validity? What are the major sources of error in test interpretation? In general, what are the major implications of this article for test selection?

Responsible educational authorities recognize that it is as unwise to put educational and psychological tests in the hands of untrained and unskilled personnel as it is to permit the automobile or any highly technical and powerful tool to be handled by individuals who are untrained in its use and unaware of the damage that it can cause if improperly used.

The necessity for caution is doubly merited when tests are administered to members of minority groups. Unfortunately, there is no single and readily avail-

Reprinted and abridged with permission of first named author and the publisher (the Society for Psychological Study of Social Issues) from *The Journal of Social Issues*, 1964, Vol. 20, pp. 129–145.

able reference source to which test users can turn in order to become more fully acquainted with the requirements and cautions to be observed in such cases. The purpose of this committee's effort is to provide an introduction to the many considerations germane to selection, use, and interpretation of educational and psychological tests with minority group children, as well as to refer educators and their associates to other more technical discussions of various aspects of the same topic.

The term "minority group" as we are using it here is not primarily a quantitative designation. Rather it is a status designation referring to cultural or social disadvantage. Since many Negro, Indian, lower-class white, and immigrant children have not had most of the usual middle-class opportunities to grow up in home, neighborhood, and school environments that might enable them to utilize their ability and personality potentials fully, they are at a disadvantage in school, and in after-school and out-of-school situations as well. It is because of these disadvantages, reflecting environmental deprivations and experiential atypicalities, that certain children may be referred to as minority group children.

CRITICAL ISSUES IN TESTING MINORITY GROUPS

Standardized tests currently in use present three principal difficulties when they are used with disadvantaged minority groups: (1) they may not provide reliable differentiation in the range of the minority group's scores, (2) their predictive validity for minority groups may be quite different from that for the standardization and validation groups, and (3) the validity of their interpretation is strongly dependent upon an adequate understanding of the social and cultural background of the group in question.

I. RELIABILITY OF DIFFERENTIATION ■ In the literature of educational and psychological testing, relatively little attention has been given to the possible dependence of test reliability upon subcultural differences. It is considered essential for a test publisher to describe the reliability sample (the reference group upon which reliability statements are based) in terms of factors such as age, sex, and grade level composition, and there is a growing tendency on the part of test publishers to report subgroup reliabilities. But to the best of our knowledge, none of the test manuals for the widely used tests give separate reliability data for specific minority groups. Institutions that use tests regularly and routinely for particular minority groups would do well to make their own reliability studies in order to determine whether the tests are reliable enough when used with these groups.

RELIABILITY AFFECTED BY SPREAD OF SCORES ■ In addition to being dependent on test length and the specific procedure used for estimating reliability (e.g., split-half or retest), the reliability coefficient for a particular test is strongly affected by the spread of test scores in the group for which the reliability is established. In general, the greater the spread of scores in the reliability sample, the higher the reliability coefficient. Consequently, if the tester attempts to make differentiations within a group which is more homogeneous than the reference or norm group for which reliability is reported, the actual effectiveness of the test will be found to be lower than the reported reliability coefficient appears to promise. For many tests there is abundant evidence that children from the lower socio-economic levels commonly associated with minority group status tend to have a smaller spread of scores than do children from middle-income families, and such restriction in the distribution of scores tends to lower reliability so far as differentiation of measurement with such groups is concerned.

CHARACTERISTICS OF MINORITY GROUP CHILDREN THAT AFFECT TEST PERFORMANCE ■ Most of the evidence relating to the contention that the majority of educational and psychological tests tend to be more unreliable, i.e., more characterized by what is technically called "error variance," for minority group children, is indirect, being based on studies of social class and socio-economic differences rather than on minority group performance per se. Nevertheless, the particular kinds of minority groups that we have in mind are closely associated with the lower levels of socio-economic status.

For children who come from lower socio-economic levels, what characteristics may be expected to affect test performance in general, and the accuracy or precision of test results in particular? The list of reported characteristics is long, and it is not always consistent from one investigation to another. But at least it may be hypothesized that in contrast to the middle-class child the lower-class child will tend to be less verbal, more fearful of strangers, less self-confident, less motivated toward scholastic and academic achievement, less competitive in the intellectual realm, more "irritable," less conforming to middle-class norms of behavior and conduct, more apt to be bilingual, less exposed to intellectually stimulating materials in the home, less varied in recreational outlets, less knowledgeable about the world outside his immediate neighborhood, and more likely to attend inferior schools.

Some Examples. Can it be doubted that such characteristics—even if only some of them apply to each "deprived" minority group—will indeed be reflected in test taking and test performance? Obviously, the primary effect will be shown in terms of test validity for such children. In many cases, however, the lowering of test validity may be indirectly a result of lowered test reliability. This would be particularly true if such characteristics interfere with the consistency of performance from test to retest for a single examiner or for different examiners. Consider the following examples and probable results:

Example: A Negro child has had little contact with white adults other than as distant and punitive authority figures. *Probable Result:* Such a child might have difficulty in gaining rapport with a white examiner or reacting without emotional upset to his close presence. Even in an individual testing situation he might not respond other than with monosyllables, failing to give adequate answers even when he knows them. The examiner, reacting in terms of his own stereotypes, might also lower the reliability and validity of the test results by assuming that the child's performance will naturally be inferior, and by revealing this attitude to the child.

Example: Children from a particular minority group are given little reason to believe that doing well in the school situation will affect their chance for attaining better jobs and higher income later in life. *Probable Result:* Such children will see little purpose in schooling, dislike school, and will reject anything associated with school. In taking tests their primary objective is to get through as rapidly as possible and escape from what for them might be an uncomfortable situation. Their test performance might, therefore, be characterized by a much greater amount of guessing, skipping, and random responses than is shown by the middle-class child who never doubts the importance of the test, wants to please his teacher and parents, and tries his best.

SPECIAL NORMS OFTEN NEEDED

When the national norms do not provide adequate differentiation at the lower end of the aptitude or ability scale, special norms established locally are often useful. For instance, if a substantial number of underprivileged or foreign-background pupils in a school or school district rank in the lowest 5 percent on the national norms, local norms might serve to provide a special scale within this range. If the score distribution with the first few percentiles of the national norms is mainly a function of chance factors, however, a lower level of the test or an easier type of test is needed for accurate measurement of the low-scoring children.

RESPONSIBILITIES OF TEST USERS ■ The sensitive test user should be alert to reliability considerations in regard to the particular group involved and the intended use of the tests. In assessing reports on test reliability provided by test manuals and other sources, he will not be satisfied with high reliability coefficients alone. He will consider not only the size of the reliability samples, but also the nature and composition of the samples and the procedures used to estimate reliability. He will try to determine whether the standard error of measurement varies with score levels, and whether his testing conditions are similar to those of the reliability samples. He will ask whether the evidence on reliability is relevant to the persons and purposes with which he is concerned. He will know that high reliability does not guarantee validity of the measures for the purpose in hand, but he will realize that low reliability may destroy validity.

The examiner should be well aware that test results are characteristically influenced by cultural and subcultural differentials and that the performance of underprivileged minority group children is often handicapped by what should be test-extraneous preconditions and response patterns. He should not necessarily assume that the child from a minority group family will be as test-sophisticated and motivated to do his best as are the majority of environment-rich, middle-class children.

If the examiner finds—and this will be typical—that the reliability sample does not provide him with information about the reliability of the test for the kind of children he is testing, he should urge that the test results not be taken at face value in connection with critical decisions concerning the children. Very often careful examination of responses to individual test items will indicate to him that the apparent performance of the child is not adequately reflecting the child's actual competence or personality because of certain subcultural group factors.

II. VALIDITY ▪ Of course if an individual's test scores were to be used only to describe his relative standing with respect to a specified norm group, the fact that the individual had a minority group background would not be important. It is when an explanation of his standing is attempted, or when long-range predictions enter the picture (as they usually do) that background factors become important.

For example, no inequity is necessarily involved if a culturally disadvantaged child is simply reported to have an IQ of 84 and a percentile rank of 16 on the national norms for a certain intelligence test. However, if this is interpreted as meaning that the child ranks or will rank no higher in learning ability than does a middle-class, native-born American child of the same IQ, the interpretation might well be erroneous.

FACTORS IMPAIRING TEST VALIDITY ▪ Three kinds of factors may impair a test's predictive validity. First, there are test-related factors—factors or conditions that affect the test scores but which may have relatively little relation to the criterion. Such factors may include test-taking skills, anxiety, motivation, speed, understanding of test instructions, degree of item or format novelty, examiner-examinee rapport, and other general or specific abilities that underlie test performance but which are irrelevant to the criterion. Examples of the operation of such factors are found in the literature describing the problems of white examiners testing Negro children (Dreger and Miller, 1960), of American Indian children taking unfamiliar, timed tests (Klineberg, 1935), and of children of certain disadvantaged groups being exposed for the first time to test-taking procedures (Haggard, 1954).

It should be noted that some test-related factors may not be prejudicial to disadvantaged groups. For example, test-taking anxiety of a disruptive nature (Sarason et al., 1960) may be more prevalent in some middle-class groups than in lower-class groups. In general, however, the bias attributable to test-related factors accrues to the detriment of the culturally disadvantaged groups.

INTEREST AND PERSONALITY INVENTORY SCORES ▪ When standardized interest inventories are used, special caution should be observed in making normative interpretations of the scores of culturally disadvantaged individuals. When a child has not had opportunities to gain satisfaction or rewards from certain pursuits, he is not likely to show interest in these areas. For example, adolescent children in a particular slum neighborhood might rank consistently low in scientific, literary, musical, and artistic interests on the Kuder Preference Record if their home and school environments fail to stimulate them in these areas. With improved cultural opportunities, these children might rapidly develop interests in vocations or avocations related to these areas.

Scores on personality inventories may also have very different significance for minority group members than for the population in general (Auld, 1952). Whenever the inventory items tap areas such as home or social adjustment, motivation, religious beliefs, or social customs, the appropriateness of the national norms for minority groups should be questioned. Local norms for the various minority groups involved might again be very much in order here.

PREDICTING COMPLEX CRITERIA ▪ A second class of factors contributing to low predictive validity is associated with the complexity of criteria. Criteria generally represent "real life" indices of adjustment or achievement and therefore they commonly sample more complex and more variegated behaviors than do the tests. An obvious example is the criterion of school grades. Grades are likely to reflect motivation, classroom behavior, personal appearance, and study habits, as well as intelligence and achievement. Even if a test measured scholastic aptitude sensitively and accurately, its validity for predicting school marks would be attenuated because of the contribution of many other factors to the criterion. It is important, therefore, to recognize the influence of other factors, not measured by the tests, which may contribute to criterion success. Since disadvantaged groups tend to fare poorly on ability and achievement tests, there is particular merit in exploring the background, personality, and motivation of members of such groups for compensatory factors, untapped by the tests, which may be related to criterion performance.

In some instances, such as in making scholarship awards on a statewide or national basis, test scores are used rigidly for screening or cut-off purposes to satisfy demands for objectivity and "impartiality." The culturally disadvantaged child (quite possibly a "diamond-in-the-rough") is often the victim of this automatic and autocratic system. Recourse lies in providing opportunities where the hurdles are less standardized and where a more individualized evaluation of his qualifications for meeting the criterion may prove to be fairer for him.

EFFECTS OF INTERVENING EVENTS ON PREDICTIONS ▪ A third set of contributors to low criterion validity is related to the nature of intervening events and contingencies. This class of conditions is particularly important when the criterion measure is obtained considerably later than the testing—when predictive rather than concurrent validity is at stake. If the time interval between the test administration and the criterial assessment is lengthy, a host of situational, motivational, and maturational changes may occur in the interim. An illness, an inspiring teacher, a shift in aspiration level or in direction of interest, remedial training, an economic misfortune, an emotional crisis, a growth spurt or retrogression in the abilities sampled by the test—any of these changes intervening between the testing and the point or points of criterion assessment may decrease the predictive power of the test.

One of the more consistent findings in research with disadvantaged children is the decline in academic aptitude and achievement test scores of such children with time (Masland, Sarason, and Gladwin, 1958). The decline is, of course, in relation to the performance of advantaged groups or of the general population. It is plausible to assume that this decline represents the cumulative effects of diminished opportunities and decreasing motivation for acquiring academic knowledge and skills. When such cumulative effects are not taken into consideration, the predictive power of academic aptitude and achievement tests is impaired. If it were known in advance that certain individuals or groups would be exposed to deleterious environmental conditions, and if allowances could be made for such contingencies in connection with predictions, the test's criterion validity could be improved.

Looking in another direction, the normative interpretation of the test results cannot reveal how much the status of underprivileged individuals might be changed if their environmental opportunities and incentives for learning and acquiring skills were to be improved significantly.

In situations where minority group members are likely to have to continue competing with others under much the same cultural handicaps that they have faced in the past, normative interpretation of their aptitude and achievement test scores will probably yield a fairly dependable basis for short-term predictive purposes. When special guidance or training is offered to help such individuals overcome their handicaps, however, achievement beyond the normative expectancies may well be obtained, and predictions should be based on expectancies derived specifically from the local situation. In this connection it should be recognized that attempts to appraise human "potential" without defining the milieu in which it will be given an opportunity to materialize are as futile as attempts to specify the horsepower of an engine without knowing how it will be energized.

"CULTURE FAIR" AND "UNFAIR" IN THE TEST AND IN SOCIETY ▪ The fact that a test differentiates between culturally disadvantaged and advantaged groups does not necessarily mean that the test is invalid. "Culturally unfair" tests may be valid predictors of culturally unfair but nevertheless highly important criteria. Educational attainment, to the degree that it reflects social inequities rather than intrinsic merit, might be considered culturally unfair. However, a test must share this bias to qualify as a valid predictor. Making a test culture-fair may decrease its bias, but may also eliminate its criterion validity. The remedy may lie in the elimination of unequal learning opportunities, which may remove the bias in the criterion as well as in the test. This becomes more a matter of social policy and amelioration rather than a psychometric problem, however.

The situation is quite different for a test that differentiates between disadvantaged and advantaged groups even more sharply than does the criterion. The extreme case would be a test that discriminated between disadvantaged and advantaged groups but did not have any validity for the desired criterion. An example of this would be an academic aptitude test that called for the identification of objects, where this task would be particularly difficult for disadvantaged children but would not be a valid predictor of academic achievement. Here, one could justifiably speak of a true "test bias." The test would be spuriously responsive to factors associated with cultural disadvantage but unrelated to the criterion. Such a test would not only be useless for predicting academic achievement but would be stigmatizing as well.

While certain aptitude and ability tests may have excellent criterion validity for some purposes, even the best of them are unlikely to reflect the true *capacity for development* of underprivileged children. For, to the extent that these tests measure factors that are related to academic success, they must tap abilities that have been molded by the cultural setting. Furthermore, the test content, the mode of communication involved in responding to test items, and the motivation needed for making the responses are intrinsically dependent upon the cultural content.

ELIXIR OF "CULTURE-FAIR" TESTS ■ The elixir of the "culture-fair" or "culture-free" test has been pursued through attempts to minimize the educational loading of test content and to reduce the premium on speed of response. However, these efforts have usually resulted in tests that have low validities for academic prediction purposes and little power to uncover hidden potentialities of children who do poorly on the common run of academic aptitude and achievement tests.

In spite of their typical cultural bias, standardized tests should not be sold short as a means for making objective assessments of the traits of minority-group children (italics ours, eds.). Many bright, non-conforming pupils, with backgrounds different from those of their teachers, make favorable showings on achievement tests in contrast to their low classroom marks. These are very often children whose cultural handicaps are most evident in their overt social and interpersonal behavior. Without the intervention of standardized tests, many such children would be stigmatized by the adverse subjective ratings of teachers who tend to reward conformist behavior of middle-class character.

III. TEST INTERPRETATION ■ *The most important consideration of all is one that applies to the use of tests in general—namely, that test results should be interpreted by competently trained and knowledgeable persons wherever important issues or decisions are at stake* (italic ours, eds.). Here, an analogy may be drawn from medical case history information that is entered on a child's record. Certain features of this record, such as the contagious disease history, constitute factual data that are easily understood by school staff members who have not had medical training. But other aspects of the medical records, as well as the constellation of factors that contribute to the child's general state of health, are not readily interpretable by persons outside the medical profession. Consequently, the judgment of a doctor is customarily sought when an over-all evaluation of the child's physical condition is needed for important diagnostic or predictive purposes. So, too, the psychological and educational test records of children should be interpreted by competently trained professional personnel when the test results are to be used as a basis for decisions that are likely to have a major influence on the child's future.

There are several sources of error in test interpretation stemming from a lack of recognition of the special features of culturally disadvantaged groups. One of these may be called the "deviation error." By this is meant the tendency to infer maladjustment or personality difficulty from responses which are deviant from the viewpoint of a majority culture, but which may be typical of a minority group. The results of a test might accurately reflect a child's performance or quality of ideation, but still the results should be interpreted in the light of the child's particular circumstance in life and the range of his experiences. For example, a minister's son whose test responses indicate that he sees all women as prostitutes, and a prostitute's son whose test responses give the same indication may both be accurately characterized in one sense by the test. The two boys may or may not be equally disturbed, however. Clinically, a safer inference might be that the minister's son is the one who is more likely to be seriously disturbed by fantasies involving sex and women.

There is evidence to indicate that members of a tribe that has experienced periodic famine would be likely to give an inordinate number of food responses on the Rorschach. So too might dieting Palm Beach matrons, but their underlying anxiety patterns would be quite different than those of the tribesmen. Or to take still another example, the verbalized self-concept of the son of an unemployed immigrant might have to be interpreted very differently from that of a similar verbalization of a boy from a comfortable, middle-class, native-American home.

A performance IQ that is high in relation to the individual's verbal IQ on the Wechsler scales *may* signify psychopathic tendencies but it also may signify a poverty of educational experience. Perceiving drunken males beating up women on the Thematic Apperception Test may imply a projection of idiosyncratic fantasy or wish, but it may also imply a background of rather realistic observation and experience common to some minority group children.

For children in certain situations, test responses indicating a low degree of motivation or an over-submissive self-image are realistic reflections of their life conditions. If these children were to give responses more typical of the general population, they might well be regarded as subgroup deviants. In short, whether test responses reflect secondary defenses against anxiety or are the direct result of a socialization process has profound diagnostic import, so that knowledge of the social and cultural background of the individual becomes quite significant.

WHAT DOES THE TEST REALLY MEASURE ■ A second type of error, from the viewpoint of construct and content validity, might be called the "simple determinant error." The error consists in thinking of the test content as reflecting some absolute or pure trait, process, factor, or construct, irrespective of the conditions of measurement or of the population being studied. Thus, a fifth-grade achievement test may measure arithmetical knowledge in a middle-class neighborhood where most children are reading up to grade level, but the same test with the same content may be strongly affected by a reading comprehension factor in a lower-class school and therefore may be measuring something quite different than what appears to be indicated by the test scores.

Generally, the test-taking motivation present in a middle-class group allows the responses to test content to reflect the differences in intelligence, achievement, or whatever the test is designed to measure. On the other hand, in a population where test success has much less reward-value and where degree of test-taking effort is much more variable from individual to individual, the test content may tap motivation as well as the trait purportedly being measured.

Caution and knowledge are necessary for understanding and taking into account testing conditions and test-taking behavior when test results are being interpreted for children from varying backgrounds. A child coming from a particular cultural subgroup might have very little motivation to do well in most test situations, but under certain conditions or with special kinds of materials he might have a relatively high level of motivation. As a result, considerable variability might be evident in his test scores from one situation to another, and his scores might be difficult to reconcile and interpret.

How a question is asked is undoubtedly another important factor to consider in interpreting test results. A child might be able to recognize an object, but not be able to name it. Or he might be able to identify a geometric figure, but not be able to reproduce it. Thus, different results might be obtained in a test depending upon whether the child is asked to point to the triangle in a set of geometric figures or whether he is required to draw a triangle.

RESPONSE SETS MAY AFFECT TEST RESULTS ■ In attitude or personality questionnaires, response sets such as the tendency to agree indiscriminately with items or to give socially desirable responses may contribute error variance from the viewpoint of the content of behavior it is desired to sample. To the extent that such sets discriminate between socially advantaged and disadvantaged groups, the target content area may be confounded by specific test format. Thus, a scale of authoritarianism may be found to differentiate among social classes, but if the scale is so keyed that a high score on authoritarianism is obtained from agreement with items, the social class differences may be more reflective of an agreement set rather than an authoritarian tendency. If authoritarian content is logically distinct from agreement content, these two sources of test variance should be kept distinct either through statistical control, by a change in the item format, or by having more than one approach to measurement of the trait in question. From the standpoint of content validity, there is a third type of error. This may be termed the "incompleteness of content coverage" error. This refers to a circumscribed sampling of the content areas in a particular domain. In the area of intelligence, for instance, Guilford (1966) has identified many factors besides the "primary mental abilities" of Thurstone and certainly more than is implied in the unitary concept of intelligence reflected by a single IQ score. As Dreger and Miller (1960) point out, differences in intellectual functioning among various groups cannot be clearly defined or understood until all components of a particular content area have been systematically measured.

Familiarity with the cultural and social background of minority-group children not only helps to avoid under-evaluating the test performance of some children, but also helps to prevent over-evaluating the performance of others. For example, children who have been trained in certain religious observances involving particular vocabularies and objects, or those who have been encouraged to develop particular skills because of their cultural orientations, might conceivably score "spuriously" high on some tests or on particular items. In other words, any special overlap between the subgroup value-system of the child and the performances tapped by the test is likely to be an important determinant of the outcome of the test.

FAILURE BARRIERS MAY BE ENCOUNTERED ■ Failure-inducing barriers are often set up for the minority-group child in a testing situation by requiring him to solve problems with unfamiliar tools, or by asking him to use tools in a manner that is too advanced for him. To draw an analogy, if a medical student were handed a scalpel to lance a wound, and if the student were to do the lancing properly but were to fail to sterilize the instrument first, how should he be scored for his accomplishment? If he had never heard of sterilization, should his skillful performance with the instrument nevertheless be given a "zero" score? Similarly, if a child from a disadvantaged social group shows a considerable degree of verbal facility in oral communication with his peers but does very poorly on tests that stress academic vocabulary, can he justifiably be ranked low in verbal aptitude?

In a broad sense, most intelligence test items tap abilities involving language and symbol systems, although opportunities for developing these abilities vary considerably from one social group to another. One might reasonably expect that a child living in a community that minimizes language skills—or, as depicted by Bernstein (1960), a community that uses a language form that is highly concrete —will earn a score that has a meaning very different from that of the score of a child in a community where language skills are highly developed and replete with abstract symbolism. It is important, therefore, to interpret test results in relation to the range of situations and behaviors found in the environments of specific minority groups.

SOME SUGGESTED REMEDIES ▪ While this analysis of the problems involved in the use and interpretation of tests for minority group children may lead to considerable uneasiness and skepticism about the value of the results for such children, it also points up potential ways of improving the situation. For example, one of these ways might consist of measuring separate skills first, gradually building up to more and more complex items and tests which require the exercise of more than one basic skill at a time. With enough effort and ingenuity, a sizable universe of items might be developed by this procedure. Special attention should also be given to the selection or development of items and tests that maximize criterial differentiations and minimize irrelevant discriminations. If a test is likely to be biased against certain types of minority groups, or if its validity for minority groups has not been ascertained, a distinct caveat to that effect should appear in the manual for the test.

Furthermore, we should depart from too narrow a conception of the purpose and function of testing. We should re-emphasize the concept of the test as an integral component of teaching and training whereby a floor of communication and understanding is established and learning capabilities are measured in repeated and cyclical fashion.

Finally, we should think in terms of making more use of everyday behavior as evidence of the coping abilities and competence of children who do not come from the cultural mainstream. Conventional tests may be fair predictors of academic success in a narrow sense, but when children are being selected for special aid programs or when academic prediction is not the primary concern, other kinds of behavioral evidence are commonly needed to modulate the results and implications of standardized tests.

CONCLUSION ▪ Tests are among the most important evaluative and prognostic tools that educators have at their disposal. How unfortunate, then, that these tools are often used so routinely and mechanically that some educators have stopped thinking about their limitations and their benefits. Since the minority group child is so often handicapped in many ways, his test scores may have meanings different from those of non-minority children, even when they are numerically the same. The task of the conscientious educator is to ponder what lies behind the test scores. Rather than accepting test scores as indicating fixed levels of either performance or potential, educators should plan remedial activities which will free the child from as many of his handicaps as possible. Good schools will employ well-qualified persons to use good tests as one means of accomplishing this task.

In testing the minority group child it is sometimes appropriate to compare his performance with that of advantaged children to determine the magnitude of the deprivation to be overcome. At other times it is appropriate to compare his test performance with that of other disadvantaged children—to determine his relative deprivation in comparison with others who have also been denied good homes, good neighborhoods, good diets, good schools, and good teachers. In most instances it is especially appropriate to compare the child's test performance with his previous test performance. Utilizing the individual child as his own control and using the test norms principally as "bench marks," we are best able to gauge the success of our efforts to move the minority group child forward on the long, hard road of overcoming the deficiencies which have been forced upon him. Many comparisons depend upon tests, but they also depend upon our intelligence, our good will, and our sense of responsibility to make the proper comparison at the proper time and to undertake proper remedial and compensatory action as a result. The misuse of tests with minority group children, or in any situation, is a serious breach of professional ethics. Their proper use is a sign of professional and personal maturity.

41   *Techniques for Evaluating the College Environment*

JOHN W. MENNE

It should be apparent from the comments contained in many of the readings thus far presented that for many purposes evaluation does, or at least should, involve a variety of variables. One general class of variates are those associated with the educational-learning environment. Wittrock (1970) thinks such environmental variables are so important that they hold a central place in his evaluation model. The following article describes three general classes of techniques useful in assessing macro-environments, in this case institutions of higher learning. The author not only describes these techniques but comments on (1) their applicability, and (2) criteria useful in their development. A significant contribution to the environmental assessment literature has recently been made by Stern (1970).

How could you apply these techniques in selecting or classifying college students? How could a prospective college student apply the results in selecting a college? What are some research applications of environmental measures? [*]

Three basic approaches have been used in studying the college environment.

OBJECTIVE INSTITUTIONAL CHARACTERISTICS ■ The first approach is concerned with objective, readily-measured institutional characteristics—number of students, percentage of males, tuition, operating budget per student, number of

[*]Reprinted by permission of the publisher, from David A. Payne: *Curriculum Evaluation* (Lexington, Mass.: D. C. Heath and Company, 1974).

Reprinted and abridged with permission of author and publisher from the *Journal of Educational Measurement*, 1967, Vol. 4, 219–225.

library books, etc. Astin and Holland (1961) appear to be the first to use this approach, and its development has been reported in a series of studies by Astin, (e.g., 1962, 1963, 1965b). Richards *et al.* (1966) have reported a thorough study of the junior colleges using this "objective" method.

In this procedure a large number of readily-measured "objective" variables (33 for Astin, 36 for Richards) are reduced by factor analysis to a smaller number of relatively independent scales or factors which are labeled in a way which, hopefully, communicates the overall meaning of the variables influencing the particular scale or factor. Institutional scores are scaled for a large number (representative sample) of institutions. Astin's procedure has been called the Environmental Assessment Technique (EAT).

SUBJECTIVE STUDENT PERCEPTIONS ■ The second approach is concerned with student perceptions of the institutional environment. Pace and Stern (1958) appear to have originated this approach with the development of the College Characteristics Index (CCI) from which Pace (1963) developed his College and University Environment Scales (CUES). Using a similar approach Hutchins (Hutchins, 1962; Hutchins & Nonneman, 1966) has developed and used an instrument (the Medical School Environment Inventory, MSEI) specifically designed for the study of medical schools, and Fanslow (1966) has developed the College Environment Inventory for Women (CEIW).

In this approach students are asked to respond whether an item does or does not pertain to their institution. The items relate to various aspects of the college environment—e.g., social activities, classroom and extra-classroom performance and procedures, school rules, cultural activities, faculty characteristics. The items then are reduced to a small number of scales, usually by factor analysis. The scales are labeled in such a way as to communicate the overall meaning of the item responses which influenced the particular scale. Again institutional scale scores are derived for a representative sample of U.S. institutions. The scale scores can be profiled.

OBSERVABLE BEHAVIORS ■ The third approach is less developed than the first two. It measures specific observable student behaviors such as time spent in study, number of social activities per week, or attendance at a concert. Astin (1965a) has indicated he is working along this line with his instrument entitled the Inventory of College Activities (ICA), and has reported a study focused on classroom behaviors (Astin, 1965c). A similar study at the University of Massachusetts was reported by Schumer and Stanfield (1966). In this study an inventory of 192 questions pertaining to observable student behaviors was factor analyzed into eight relatively independent factors thought to describe the institutional environment.

Astin (1965a) believes that all three approaches are needed to describe completely the institutional environment. But the only studies so far reported in the literature have investigated the correlations between the scales or factors of various assessment devices and also the relationship of such scores to measures of student personality (McFee, 1961).

EVALUATION OF THE THREE APPROACHES

In any evaluation it is necessary to define the purpose. If it is to *compare* institutions, these intentions would be achieved when there is a relatively stable and accurate set of scale scores available for the majority of our college institutions. The interested person can then look up the rankings of the institutions he wishes to compare. Astin (1965b) has made this type of information available. However this approach may not be sufficiently sensitive to environment changes which do occur. For example Hutchins and Nonneman (1966) have shown that the rankings of the medical institutions on various objective variables tend to remain quite stable, and recent rankings are very similar to rankings going back as far as 1910. New buildings, new budgets, increased faculty or students may change ranking temporarily, but will there be a permanent change in any comparison to other institutions?

On the other hand, an environmental change such as an addition to the library, change in dormitory rules, or a new cultural center can have an immediate effect on the student image or perception of the institution (Pace, 1963). It seems reasonable to suppose that the library addition, rule change, or cultural center will also immediately influence student behaviors. Since almost every institution is expanding, the new changes may not change significantly the inter-institution rankings but may change the campus atmosphere—the perceptions and behaviors of the student.

The institutional assessment may also be intended to provide better information to guidance counselors. This would seem to follow as a practical application of the objective comparison purpose discussed above and Astin (1965b) made explicit this combination of purposes. Thus the "objective" approach benefit seems designed to provide a basis for an objective comparison of institutions, and one application of this comparative data is in guiding students to the appropriate institution.

However, just why should the results of this "objective" approach benefit the counselor? Does he have information about a student which can be used to predict a successful outcome in an institution with such and such ratings on the scales of the "objective" measurement? Further, in using data in guidance, the important fact may not be that school A has 8000 whereas school B has 15,000, but that students at school B perceive their institution as having a friendly and congenial atmosphere whereas the students at school A perceive the atmosphere as impersonal, without group loyalty or involvement. Thus the subjective approaches—the students' image or perception of the environment and the students' behaviors in the environment—must complement the objective approach when the purpose of the study is to provide comparative data for the use of administrators and guidance counselors.

The validity of applying any one of these three methods will depend upon the ultimate purpose in gathering the data. The majority of applications will revolve around the assessment of the effect of some change in the environment. A frequently used paradigm of pre-test–treatment–post-test is employed when environmental manipulations are to be made. The most useful technique to use in the pre and post assessment is probably that derived from Subjective Student Perceptions.

Following are five general criteria which should prove useful in developing perception instruments.

CRITERIA FOR DEVELOPING SUBJECTIVE STUDENT PERCEPTION TECHNIQUES

1. The object studied is the environment, not the students or faculty. The data gathered are furnished by the people in the environment; it is their perceptions of the environment. Yet the perceptions are only the means to get at the object of the study—the environment. A sample of students from various environments would not get at the objectives of the study; but a sample of students from the same environment will yield a measure related to the characteristics of their common environment.

2. The instrument should have a low within-institution variance and high between–institution variance. Students in the same environment should see their common environment in much the same way. If there is a wide variation in the perception of the common environment, it would be questionable whether the instrument was measuring the environment or something else, perhaps a personality factor of the individual student. Also, this criterion requires that the instrument be developed with data from a number of institutions. If the instrument yielded the same scores for dissimilar institutions, it would be questioned just what is being measured—for it is quite unlikely that dissimilar institutions have the same environment. The instrument should also yield approximately the same score when used at one time on various random samples of similarly experienced students in a common environment.

3. The scores should *not* correlate highly with personality characteristics of the raters. The instrument that is picking up personality characteristics is not measuring environments—at least *not only* environments. Likewise we would not expect the instrument that is picking up personality characteristics to yield the desired low within–institution variance unless students having a personality aspect in common have been attracted to the same institution.

4. The instrument should have scales that are relatively few in number, not highly intercorrelated, and understandable. This criterion is concerned with the practical usefulness of the instrument. Obviously any thorough measure of an environment will be multi-dimensional. But if the resulting measures are to provide information for experimental changes—for example, manipulation on the part of administrators—the measures or scales must be readily understandable and verbally communicable, there must not be too many of them, and they should be relatively independent (thus not highly correlated) measures.

Factor analysis often yields factors that are not amenable to verbal explanation and communication. Likewise the factor analyst may reduce dimensionality only to the point where highly independent factors appear. The individual factors resulting may be good measures but the dimensionality remaining (the number of factors) is still much too great to give the administrator the practical information he needs in relatively simple form. Therefore, a compromise is required between the need for a small number of understandable factors and for independent factors. It may be necessary to sacrifice some factor independence in favor of a low number of understandable factors. Thus the factor analytic technique, the reduction in dimensionality, and the rotation must be guided by this criterion.

5. Should the scores correlate with the "objective" measures like school size, budget, and faculty-student ratio? The answer to this reduces to the answer to the question: What is the purpose of these studies? If it is believed that the subjective instrument which correlates highly with certain objective aspects of the environment is a better instrument, then evidence of a high correlation is essential. Yet we previously used an example of school A with 8000 students wherein the environment is perceived as impersonal, without group loyalty or involvement, and of school B with 15,000 students where the environment is perceived as friendly and congenial. School C may be the same size as school A but the students' perceptions of the environment may be more like that of B rather than A. Thus it would not seem that high correlations with objective measures is essential for the perception-type instrument.

On the other hand, correlational studies between various objective variables and scores on a perception-type instrument can be most useful. If the administrator wants to manipulate the environment in a certain way, how does he know just what to manipulate? Moderate correlations between objective variables and perception scale scores would seem to predict that is the objective variable was manipulated, the perception might change. Thus these correlational studies can be most useful in the environmental manipulation paradigm; they could provide information for the administrator as to what aspect of the environment should be manipulated in order to effectively change the environment.

JOE KHATENA

Suppose we were to specify a universe of skills, knowledges, and abilities we considered important and desirable for our students, employees, or colleagues to acquire or develop. It would follow that if we were interested in assessing whether or not their skills, knowledges, or abilities had been acquired we would have to test for them. Comparing what we desire with what we actually test for will provide a crude indication of the validity of both the tests we use and the adequacy of our testing and evaluation program. One ability frequently overlooked in most programs is creativity. Khatena's article should help us identify potentially useful ways of measuring creativity and alert us to some of the special reliability and validity problems encountered in devising and describing creativity measures.

The theoretical model of intellect which Binet used in the construction of his intelligence test has been modified, elaborated and even transformed over the years to give at least three main theoretical positions. The first is the global concept of intelligence which recognizes the existence of verbal, nonverbal or performance intelligence (Wechsler, 1958). The second is the hierarchical structure of human intelligence with the "g" factor in eminence (Vernon, 1950). The third is the multi-dimensional model of the three faces of intellect which denies the first two positions subscribing rather to five intellectual operations which enter into the processing of various content and product categories (Guilford 1956).

It is interesting to note that while Binet (1909) and Spearman (1930) recognized the presence of creative mental functioning, it was Guilford (1956) who saw and gave it an appropriate position in his theoretical model. Although there have been many studies of creative mental functioning prior to Guilford's pronouncements, no one presented it in such a comprehensive framework where divergent thinking is seen in appropriate perspective. This unique contribution effectively set the stage for much of the research in the measurement of creative thinking abilities in the years that followed its initial expression (Guilford 1956).

Foremost among psychometrists and psychologists who ventured forth to construct suitable instruments to measure divergent thinking were Guilford (1959) and Torrance (1962). Although their approaches to the problem have been

Reprinted and abridged with permission of the author and publisher from an article entitled "Some Problems in the Measurement of Creative Behavior," which appeared in the *Journal of Research and Development in Education*, 1971, Vol. 4, #3, pp. 74–82.

quite different (Guilford attempting to measure divergent abilities through a testing format which generally requires the subject to respond to many stimuli, each setting out to measure a specific ability relative to the *Structure-of-Intellect Models,* and Torrance attempting to measure divergent abilities through the presentation of several complex tasks designed to trigger the expression of several creative abilities at once) both give major roles to fluency, flexibility, originality and elaboration. These abilities have been described elsewhere (Guilford, 1967; Torrance, 1962) as the number of responses made, the shifts in thinking which produce responses of different categories, the statistical infrequency of responses, and the adding of detail to the basic idea or thought expressed respectively.

The scrutiny and critical evaluation that followed the inception of measuring the creative thinking abilities have focused attention on the challenging and problematic nature of developing appropriate instruments. These have centered in the main around problems of theoretical rationale, reliability and validity.

DEFINITIONS

Definitions of creativity are multiple and there is no universally accepted definition and method for quantitative evaluation of creativity. This is to be expected since creativity involves rational and irrational elements. In fact, interaction between the rational and irrational is a unique energizing factor in the act of creation. Although various attempts have been made to define creative mental functioning, there are elements operating in the dynamics of such mental functioning which have not and may never be altogether made explicit. Hence any attempt to construct and develop measuring instruments of creative behavior and mental functioning will have to depend upon an inherently discrepant frame of reference. What is essential is the recognition of this flaw with provision for some kind of compensatory control probably in the form of sampling a subject's response universe in several randomly selected situations rather than one, and certainly with several rather than a single instrument.

An important aspect of measuring creative mental functioning is the way credit is to be awarded for creative versus non-creative responses. This is a very real problem especially when it comes to the scoring procedure to be adopted for originality. There is not much of a problem for the award of credit for fluency since this can be done by merely counting the number of responses given. Nor is there much of a problem when it comes to flexibility since by categorizing responses, credit can be awarded for shift in thinking from one category to another with the number of category shifts determining flexibility credit. Credit for elaboration is determined by counting the number of new ideas expressed by details added to the basic idea. The real problem is to decide upon the originality of a response, and this will depend upon how one describes originality and the weight one gives to it in the continuum of creative expression.

How does one set about awarding credit to this creative element and yet not appear arbitrary? Certainly there is a very strong desire to apply subjective judgment to determine creative strength of what is being appraised and this is when Mathew Arnold's concept of *touchstone* as it applies to recognized masterpieces as criteria can be utilized. But this is in itself circular since what decided the creative worth of the criteria was also subjective judgment. The trouble with a subjective procedure is that generally it is not provided for the making of fine discriminations between taste and creative dynamism. Thus, when one is called upon to make an appraisal of the relative worth of a crea-tive product it is the goodness or badness (as determined by the criterion of taste) of the product that one judges rather than the creative energy that gave birth to the product itself.

Generally originality has been equated with newness, novelty, uniqueness or the production of "something no one else would think of." In attempting to gain precision in making this latter essential discrimination, those concerned with measuring creative potential have turned to probability theory for help. Orginality as a facet of creative potential can be determined by using the principle of infrequency so that, for example, credit can be given to a response depending upon how frequently it occurs with zero credit being given to a response which occurs 5% or more of the time, 1 credit if it occurs 4 to 4.99% of the time to 5 credits being given if a response occurs 1% or less of the time. This procedure which provides an objective frame of reference for the individ-ual with references to the population of which he is a member, has now be-come well established as a procedure for the measurement of originality in many tests of creativity (e.g., Torrance, 1962; and Khatena, 1969).

Mednick (1967), and Starkweather (1965), however, have used different approaches to the problem of scoring for originality: a credit of one or zero is awarded depending upon a correct or incorrect associative response being given on Mednick's test of originality (1959), and on Starkweather's test (1965) an originality credit of one is awarded each time the response to a sharp stimuli is different (for that individual). The present scoring procedures seem to have made discrimination between taste and potential to produce the new and unique and so are promising as tools for the quantification of a hitherto difficult to quantify variable, originality.

RELIABILITY

Reliability is a problem peculiar to all measuring instruments, but it is con-siderably greater for instruments that attempt to measure creative functioning.

It is important to consider the problem of standardizing the test instructions given to subjects prior to the presentation of the test stimuli so that all subjects will receive the same instructions. The test administrator or examiner is a variable which can influence respondents' test behavior, thereby affecting reliability data. That is why it is essential that proper preparation be made by the examiner before administering the test, preparation in the form of looking over the directions manual for relevant instructions which may list the materials required for the test. The establishment of rapport is essential to tests of creativity, especially relative to the creation of a non-testing atmosphere to reduce inhibiting factors. In fact, the more aware and knowledgeable the examiner is of the theoretical background and intent of the test the more likely the test will be administered appropriately. For the past several years, Torrance and his students have been experimenting with a variety of warm-up experiences to enhance performance on creativity tests and are trying to standardize them sufficiently for more widespread use.

The reliability of a test is also affected by the accuracy of the scoring. Tests of creativity that call for many possible responses expose the scorer to a greater exercise of subjective judgment in the act of determining appropriate response credits, although reference is made to an objective scoring procedure. Hence it is necessary to check the accuracy of the scoring and continually to obtain interscorer reliability data.

Internal consistency of the test is another problem that needs clarification. It becomes more difficult with tests that call for use of the imagination. It must be remembered that imagination is not always on the wing nor can it be forced to take flight at the proddings and will of stimuli meant to stimulate those elements that spark off the creative experience.

To examine test-retest reliability of such instruments either by using the same or alternate forms of a test is not altogether appropriate either. There is the additional contaminating variable of the time interval and so many extraneous conditions between the first and a second administration of a test of creativity which is well known relative to testing in general.

Respondents themselves contribute to the problem of reliability. There are other variables like emotional and bodily states operating on the individual in the test situation that will affect his creative output. In addition, the motivational level of the respondent will certainly make a difference in the test situation which is an attempt to create conditions resembling creative urgings in real situations. This has led to a highly pertinent observation that the more expensive the energy the greater the motivational level required (Torrance, 1966). The effects of stress and mental health as it effects creative behavior (Torrance, 1965) also bear significant and vital relationships to test reliability data (Torrance, 1966).

It is surprising then that reliability indices have been found to be reasonably high in most instances taking cognizance of the multi-dimensional nature of the problem. Only in this way can instruments that set out to measure so tenuous and almost nebulous an area of mental functioning be regarded in proper perspective and appropriately evaluated.

VALIDITY

Of all the problems appertaining to the construction of a test purporting to measure creative behavior and mental functioning, validity has been the predominant concern of many thinkers in the field; it has been among the central issues discussed in three University of Utah Conferences on the identification of scientific talent (Taylor, 1956, 1958, 1959) and has invited the appraisal, comment and criticism of many researchers (e.g. McNemar, 1964; Yamamoto, 1965; Wallach & Kogan, 1965).

The several dimensions of validity are well known and succinctly clarified by the Joint Committee on "Standards for Educational and Psychological Tests and Manuals" to include content validity, criterion-related validity and construct validity each area of which must be taken into account in the validation of a test if the test is to have any meaning at all (1966) (see article 10 in Chapter III of this volume).

The main problem of *content* validity appears to hinge on the appropriate sampling of stimuli from the stimuli universe and the sub-categories constituting it. So many phenomena enter into the structure and function of the perceptual frames of reference of the creative individual and get involved with the irrational, imaginative and creative energizing forces of mental functioning that it would be foolhardy to minimize the problem of isolating these into their separate components for analysis even in a simulated experience. With the educational achievement test and its close relative the intelligence test, stimuli can be more easily sampled from a better known content universe, whereas the content universe of tests of creative behavior and mental functioning is less familiar and certainly not as clearly defined as would be desired.

This problem of content has been significantly evaluated in terms that consider it ridiculous for anyone to attempt to develop a comprehensive battery of tests of creative thinking that would sample any kind of universe of creative thinking abilities on the grounds that one can behave creatively in an almost infinite number of ways, nor can anyone specify the number and range of test tasks necessary to give a complete assessment of the person's potentialities for creative behavior (Torrance, 1966). More recently, Guilford, in commenting about the complex nature of this problem with particular reference to the content areas of divergent production factors, indicates that with the exception of musical composing and arranging most of these areas can be accounted for (1967).

In selecting tasks for inclusion in batteries of creative thinking tests, two quite divergent positions have been taken by Torrance (1966) and Wallach and Kogan (1965). Torrance has deliberately selected tasks that tap somewhat different types of functioning. In doing this, he has used both theories about the important different kinds of functioning that occur in creative behavior and data from factor analyses. In using the factor analysis data, he selected tasks that loaded on different factors and eliminated tasks too closely related to one another. Wallach and Kogan, on the other hand, have limited their selection of tasks to those requiring association and sought tasks that would yield high intercorrelations with one another. This difference in approaches must be recognized in evaluating the studies that have been made with the Torrance and the Wallach-Kogan instruments.

Stimuli that have been used for tests of creativity have ranged from the verbal to the non-verbal which bring into play the sense of sight, hearing, touch and movement of one form or another in structured and less structured circumstances (e.g., Barron, 1958; Mednick, 1959; Torrance, 1962; Khatena, 1969).

The problem of obtaining suitable *criteria* to validate measures of creative behavior provides no easy solution. Ideally an instrument measuring creative potential should find support in the actual productivity of the individual tested. To this end Guilford recommended at the 1959 University of Utah Conference the initiation of longitudinal studies for the purpose of establishing predictive validity which several years later Yamamoto reiterated as being essentially nonexistent. Recently, however, Torrance and his associates have reported validity studies with periods of seven and eight years intervening between the collection of the prediction and criterion data. In all of these studies validity coefficients of around .50 have been obtained with various indices of creative behavior.

Another approach that could be taken would be to determine in advance creative individuals through their personalities, performances and products, and use these as criteria to find predictive validity for tests of creativity. This approach too was recommended by the Utah conference (Taylor, 1959).

Rhodes' (1961) definition of creativity as involving person, product, process, and press also suggests several approaches to the problem of selecting suitable validation criteria as, for example, personality assessment procedures, biographical inventories, questionnaries, checklists, psychological tests, classroom experiments, experimental manipulation of the environment and the like.

To add to all these problems there are always such problems as determining evaluation criteria, evaluator competence, context of evaluation, appropriate design and methodology, to mention but a few.

With *construct* validity we are handling a very fundamental problem. In fact, the determination of the content of a test has to refer in the first instance to the theoretical framework of the test and hence content validity is contingent upon construct validity. A construct which can be couched in such simple terms as "creativity" is the ability of "making many original contributions" (Joint Committee on Test Standards, American Psychological Association, 1966, p. 23) or in more complex terms as:

> a process of becoming sensitive to problems, deficiencies, gaps in knowledge, missing elements, disharmonies, and so on; identifying the difficult; searching for solutions, making guesses, or formulating hypotheses about the deficiencies; testing and retesting these hypotheses and possibly modifying and retesting them; and finally communicating the results (Torrance, 1966, p. 6).

However, it is essential that a theoretical rationale be formulated as a frame of reference for the construction of a test of creativity.

The approaches to the validation of a construct can be considered not only in terms of what is but also what is not creativity. Studies involving comparison of personality characteristics of persons achieving high and low scores on tests of creativity have been reported as one means of establishing construct validity (Torrance, 1966). The repeated findings of low relationship between intelligence and creativity measures offer yet another approach. Negative relationships between attitudinal rigidity illustrates a third approach to the problem of determining validity (Fleming & Weintraub, 1962). Computations of correlation coefficients with other well established creativity tests based upon similar frames of reference can also be used for this purpose (Yamamoto, 1963).

Other approaches that have been taken to find construct validity pivot around sociometric analyses, psychiatric diagnosis, observation of classroom behavior, job performances, and child-parent relationships. (See Torrance, 1966 for illustrative references and description of a variety of approaches. Eds.)

CONCLUSION

Sound research over the past two decades has answered many thorny problems relative to the construction and development of instruments that set out to measure creative behavior and mental functioning. Studies arising from work in this area have focused on major problems that will be encountered and have outlined several important approaches that can be taken to effect the refinement and development of such instruments. The focus has been on a multidimensional mode of attack on the problems relative to reliability and validity with the need for strict objectivity in the scoring and interpretation procedures emphasized. The quantification of creative behavior has been a major step in a positive direction. However, for a more accurate interpretation of creative behavior there is need for a fuller appreciation of the dynamic functions of the irrational-imaginative components of the creative intellect. How effectively this problem can be dealt with offers yet another direction of research.

But to ignore this would be to simulate the behavior of one of Charles Dickens' famous caricatures, Mrs. General, who swept under the carpet what she did not understand or could not handle and said they did not exist.

IX

EDUCATIONAL AND PSYCHOLOGICAL TESTING IN SOCIAL PERSPECTIVE

Each year seems to bring a considerable volume of intense critical comment concerning educational and psychological testing. We, of course, have a reference to the flood of popular magazine and newspaper coverage of testing problems, as well as such books as *The Brain Watchers* (Gross, 1962), *The Tyranny of Testing* (Hoffman, 1962), and *They Shall Not Pass* (Black, 1963). These publications reflect some real public antipathy, uneasiness, distrust, and ignorance about tests and testing. They are written by the professional and by the layman alike, with occasional words added by hack journalists. Many of the criticisms are justified, most are not. As in the case with many expositions on somewhat technical or social phenomena intended for public consumption, particularly those related to education, the views expressed are often narrowly defined and biased. It is, therefore, hoped that the papers selected for inclusion in this final chapter of the book will provide the reader with a balanced social-psychological view of the present state of the art and science of testing.

Two initial comments are in order. First, the critics of testing have said nothing new. They offer no unique words of wisdom or new insights. They have not exposed any long-forgotten or hidden psychometric skeletons in the tester's closet. Secondly, criticisms are focused on a perhaps unethical or at least ignorant segment of the psychology profession. Often such criticisms represent observations on the self-appointed testers, the small minority of individ-

321

uals who wish to make a quick profit. The unfortunate result, however, is that the public is likely to assume that these same criticisms apply to tests *and* testers in general.

What can be said in support of the "critics"? The potential positive effects of what the critics posit can readily be discerned. First, they reinforce what has long been known about the inadequacy of certain testing practices. Second, their comments should serve to caution both professional and layment against the misuse of tests. Third, they have really joined their voices with those of the professional tester in calling for better training for those individuals who administer, interpret, and use tests. Lastly, they have made a significant contribution by underlining the certain areas in need of research. This last positive result, however, leads directly to a distinct and unfortunate negative influence. Specifically, the critics, both directly by their influence on professional educators and indirectly through parents, may tend to deter schools from participating in the much needed research in testing. Also on the negative side is the fact that the tests, instruments, methods, or devices themselves take the brunt of criticism, when it is all too often the case that it is the *users* who are at fault.

Most observers would agree that the need and responsibility for improving communications between the testing profession and the public are being reawakened and revitalized. Publications by Chauncy and Dobbin (1963), Hawes (1964), and the American Psychological Association (1965) attest to this fact. Continued vigilance on the part of professional and lay groups to expose the quacks and incompetents, pressure for higher standards in the test publishing industry, and more intensive pre-service and in-service training in measurement would seem to be in order.

Several of the issues discussed in the foregoing paragraphs are given expanded treatment in the following articles. The chapter begins with a general policy statement adopted by the American Psychological Association with regard to psychological assessment. The position taken is that the individual being assessed should be protected from incompetency and invasion of his privacy. Protection of the rights of the individual is of utmost concern to professional, layman and governmental personnel.

An articulate and well balanced critique of the current art and science of testing is next presented by sociologist David Goslin. The author begins by considering criticisms of the type of test, how it is used, and assumptions regarding its validity. He concludes by continuing the theme introduced in the previous APA policy statement concerning invasion of privacy. Through this article we see that there are a great many very positive things that can be said about tests and testing.

In the third article some of the critics of testing are taken to task. In particular the basic assumptions and conclusions of Banesh Hoffman, whose book

The Tyranny of Testing (1962) wrought such a furor a decade ago, come in for an evaluation. The reader is urged to seek out Hoffman's criticisms and read the Goslin and Dunnette articles with an open mind, and to evaluate the merits of the respective arguments and points of view.

Concluding this chapter is a cogent paper by Robert L. Ebel. Unlike many commentators on testing, Ebel provides some suggestions for the improvement of testing practices, particularly with regard to the needed communication between the professional and the public. He also presents some enlightening comments on the consequences of *not* testing.

In this final chapter the editors have attempted to present a summary overview of some of what is good, what is bad, and what the problems and potentials are in the application of educational and psychological measurement. If the public is to be helped through the use of tests—and they constitute a powerful force that can be employed to improve the human conditions—they must also be protected from intentional and unintentional misuses. Teachers in particular are in an excellent position to make measurement payoff in the improvement of learning and the learning situation. If we are to assist all individuals to perform at their highest level, achieve all they are capable of achieving, and become and feel all they are capable of becoming and feeling, we must have knowledge of their differential characteristics. Tests can help us gather such information.

43   *Psychological Assessment and Public Policy*

AMERICAN PSYCHOLOGICAL ASSOCIATION

Based on the specialized purposes, methodologies, and requirements of psychological assessment, four policy implications can be derived. These position statements, developed by the Board of Professional Affairs of the American Psychological Association, specify the necessity of protecting those seeking out assessment or being assessed as part of a service, vocational or educational regime from (1) incompetent personnel, (2) outdated, obsolete, and invalid instrumentation, and (3) invasion of privacy. In addition provision should be made for a continuing research and feedback program. The following statement also considers some of the special problems imposed by attempting to measure and evaluate personality.

What legal and professional sanctions are suggested as being necessary by this position statement? What are the implications of the statement for (1) test publishers, (2) professional organizations in the behavioral sciences, and (3) training institutions?

The nature of man and of society makes it necessary that we attempt to assess psychological characteristics. Individual human beings differ from one

---

Reprinted with permission of the publisher and copyright holder, the American Psychological Association, from the *American Psychologist*, 1970, Vol. 25. #3 (March), pp. 264–266.

another in a variety of ways; society requires a variety of diverse contributions from its members. The more accurately we can judge each person's suitability for potential roles consistent with his interests, the more successfully a society will function. Accurate assessment brings benefits to the individual as well by enabling him to locate the particular kinds of situations in which he can function most effectively as he seeks education, employment, medical and psychological services, and fuller personal development.

In attempting to understand others and to predict how they will function under various circumstances, all of us utilize a great variety of assessment methods—observations, careful or casual, interviews, formal or informal, and comments and recommendations based on varying degrees of acquaintance with the person being judged. Specialized psychological assessment techniques have been developed as refinements on these general methods or as supplements to them. What such specialized techniques add is some indication of the validity and usefulness of the information. They also provide some degree of *standardization of conditions* under which observations are made or samples of behavior obtained and, where possible, some *quantification* of the findings. This makes possible systematic comparisons of the individual's characteristics with those of reference or norm groups. But the psychological procedures are similar in many ways to the more informal appraisals of people that constantly go on.

SPECIAL FEATURES OF PSYCHOLOGICAL ASSESSMENT

Because techniques of psychological assessment are *instruments* designed and built for specific tasks, they require specialized knowledge if they are to be used correctly. One cannot choose the most appropriate instrument for a particular purpose or make valid interpretations of the scores or protocols that respondents produce unless he possesses such knowledge. It is much more than a matter of proper administration and scoring procedures. Indeed, for conventional objective tests, little more is needed than adheres to the instructions for administering and scoring. It is the body of research information associated with an instrument that furnishes the basis for decisions about what it does and does not measure or reveal, how accurate or reliable it is under various circumstances, and what special cautions must be observed in its use.

The accumulation of this essential information requires the cooperation of large numbers of persons, persons who are not themselves being assessed for any particular purpose. Millions of men, women, and children, for example, have taken intelligence and achievement tests as participants in research projects designed to establish test validity and develop norms. Persons in all walks of life have filled out interest inventories, attitude scales, and personality questionnaires in order to furnish the data psychologists needed to develop scoring systems and scaling procedures. A test or other standardized assessment instrument represents this total effort, not simply the intentions of its author. It cannot lead to sound inferences about an individual's characteristics unless this research has been done, and the person interpreting the test is familiar with it.

Often a test is used solely as a predictor of probable successful performance, as in selecting candidates for a job or school. In this case the score is treated as if it provides no information on the person's characteristics other than likelihood of success. No interpretations of test performance or inferences about personal characteristics are required for this kind of use. Although a practitioner employing a test for such purposes need not be familiar with the supporting research, the person responsible for prescribing its use should be.

Information derived from instruments used in psychological assessment as well as the instruments themselves become *dated*, and their significance may change markedly over time. A person's score or protocol indicates only his present status, and while it may constitute a basis for predicting future status, such predictions have not turned out to be very accurate except over short periods of time. Although dated or obsolete information should not be used for decision-making purposes, it may be valuable for research and should be retained using adequate coding procedures to protect the identity of the individual. The instruments themselves also require frequent updating to replace obsolete items and stimuli and to insure that norms are representative of the appropriate segments of the population.

A special difficulty in psychological assessment, particularly when used in employment or placement rather than treatment situations, is the problem of faking and response sets. It has been obvious from the beginning to anyone who examines a typical personality inventory or questionnaire that it is quite possible for respondents to falsify their answers. In circumstances where one wishes to make a good impression, this *social desirability* response set may have a considerable effect on the scores from which inferences are to be made. This and other effects of various response sets have been exhaustively studied, and ways of at least partially controlling them have been developed. The appropriate use of techniques for psychological assessment requires a thorough familiarity with this body of research knowledge.

Several policy implications follow from these essential features of psychological assessment. First, the individual assessed should be protected against unwarranted *inferences* by persons not equipped with the requisite background of knowledge. It cannot be expected that psychiatrists, classroom teachers, personnel managers, or heads of government agencies will have this kind of expertise, although some of them may possess it. Normally, therefore, arrangements will need to be worked out for collaboration with psychologists who have specialized in the kinds of assessments being conducted.

Second, the individual assessed should be protected against unfavorable evaluation based on obsolete information. This is a problem not peculiar to psychological assessment methods. An old letter of recommendation may be fully as damaging as a low IQ recorded on one's record, although the quantitative appearance of the latter makes it less apparent, perhaps, that it is no longer relevant. All proposals for data banks and permanent record systems must grapple with this problem and provide appropriate safeguards for verifying the accuracy of the records and for discarding periodically the obsolete information.

Third, the individual must be protected against unnecessary intrusions into his privacy. The assessment procedures used should be intelligently selected for particular purposes. Unnecessary tests should not be administered, and unnecessary questions should not be asked.

Fourth, whatever policies are set up to insure these kinds of protection should be of such a nature as to maintain conditions that will facilitate the research on which new and improved assessment procedures can be based. Flat prohibitions of certain kinds of tests or questions would retard research on the ways in which such tests and questions might be validly used. To require the destruction of all records of test scores and protocols along with the interpretations derived from them would make impossible some very significant kinds of longitudinal research on personality. The objective of whatever policies are adopted should be to protect the right of each individual to be soundly evaluated, realizing that to do this requires a constant effort to improve the techniques by means of which evaluations are made. The proper control is to vest responsibility in the person carrying out the assessment rather than to place arbitrary restrictions on the methods he is permitted to use.

ADDITIONAL PROBLEMS IN PERSONALITY ASSESSMENT

While not differing in principle from the assessment of abilities, the assessment of personality (sometimes called noncognitive) characteristics involves extra complications related to policy issues. In instruments for personality assessment the relationship of the respondent's test behavior to his behavior in life situations is more indirect than it is in the typical ability testing situation, where the items to which he is responding are often samples of the problems he must solve in the world outside the testing room. Whether the instrument for assessing personality requires the individual to answer questions about his attitudes, symptoms, and feelings, or whether it asks him to read meaning into inkblots or tell stories about ambiguous pictures, the psychologist's task of *validating* the instrument is a complex and difficult one. The fact that there is as yet no general agreement about what the most important personality traits are adds to the difficulty.

A special problem that may arise in personality assessment is that some of the item content is drawn from areas of human experience most likely to be regarded as private, so that such assessment techniques are especially likely to raise questions about whether a respondent's right to privacy has been infringed. For a variety of reasons it has seemed necessary or important to include some inquiry into the individual's sexual and religious ideas in instruments designed for personality assessment. Interpretations of these measures are dependent on the context in which they were standardized. If there is too much deviation from the standardized contexts by eliminating items, some distortion might be introduced into interpretations.

In formulating policies to deal with these problems, the basic requirement is the one emphasized in the previous section—that decisions about what assessment procedures are to be used and how they are to be handled should be based on recommendations from persons competent to make them—ordinarily a psychologist with specialized training in assessment. It is the responsibility of organizations and agencies in which assessment is carried on to place such persons in charge of the operations. It is the responsibility of universities and colleges to educate them in such a way that they can carry out this complex task. It is the responsibility of professional societies, such as the American Psychological Association, to formulate standards and ethical codes controlling their activity. Many states have statutory procedures for qualifying psychologists who meet legally established standards of competence and ethical conduct controlling their activity. Legal proscriptions of certain kinds of tests, items, or procedures can only handicap them in their efforts to make sound, relevant judgments about individuals.

The central concept governing what information is to be obtained from a person whose characteristics are to be assessed for a particular purpose is *relevance*. In employment situations, for example, inquiry about family, sexual, or religious matters should be carried on only if its relevance to the employee's fitness for the position in question has been established; in such instances its use may be justifiable. Always, however, relevance must be weighed and justified in terms of socially accepted values and principles.

The right of an individual to decline to be assessed or to refuse to answer questions he considers improper or impertinent has never been and should not be questioned. This right should be pointed out to the examinee in the context of information about the confidentiality of the results. Whenever possible, he should be told who will have access to the information and for what purposes. The burden of proof that assessment techniques are relevant to the situation falls on the professional person responsible for the undertaking. His competence is the foundation on which the whole structure must rest.

44   *Standardized Ability Tests and Testing*

DAVID A. GOSLIN

Standardized educational and psychological tests (see first article in book) have made and will continue to make significant contributions to American life. Criticisms and controversies have periodically indicated that many problems exist. Some of these are long-standing, others have risen due to more recent changes in society. In the following article David Goslin discusses several critical issues that must be met and resolved if the field is to progress and realize its greatest potentials. Among the issues considered are criticisms related to tests themselves, how they are applied, and questions related to validity. There are, of course, criticisms that are somewhat unrelated to the tests themselves. Test sophistication and wiseness, and the influence of tests on examinee self-concept are just two areas in need of exploration. The author closes his essay with a consideration of the always critical question related to testing and test results—invasion of privacy.

Related discussions are to be found in articles by Angoff and Anderson (#1), Womer (#32), and Ebel (#46).

Standardized ability tests have been a source of considerable controversy in recent years. Growing competition for jobs and for all educational opportunities has intensified the search for better ways to evaluate individual abilities and aptitudes and to identify intellectual potential at progressively earlier ages. Standardized tests of various types increasingly are used to identify applicants throughout the educational system, as well as by the military, the civil service, and business and industry (Brim, Goslin, Glass and Goldberg, 1964; Goslin, 1963 and 1967; Goslin, Epstein and Hallock, 1965).

This reliance on results of standardized tests has caused questions to be raised about the validity of the tests used, as well as their effects on those who take them and on the society that uses them to differentiate among its members. (Brim, Neulinger, and Glass, 1965). Thus far, there have been very few, if any, attempts to bring together all of the criticisms that have been leveled against tests, and to place them in an analytical framework that would permit a systematic evaluation of their validty. In this paper the validity of standardized tests is discussed, and major criticisms of tests are summarized within such a framework.

Reprinted with permission of author and publisher (American Association for the Advancement of Science) from *Science*, 1968, Vol. 159, pp. 851–855.

THREE VARIABLES OF CRITICISM

Criticisms of testing relate to three variables: the type of test, how it is used, and assumptions regarding its validity. First, the type of testing being used must be considered. Ability tests may be divided into tests that attempt to measure inherent capabilities, potentials, or abilities acquired over a long time, and tests designed to measure specific achievements.

Intelligence and aptitude tests are implicitly assumed to measure a relatively deep and enduring quality. This quality may be viewed as changeable; however, startling changes are assumed to be rare except under specific conditions, as when extreme cultural deprivation is ameliorated. Intelligence and aptitude tests therefore generate anxiety in people tested. The high cultural value placed on intellectual abilities in our society also makes any instrument which purports to measure general intellectual abilities a source of fascination. For these reasons, such tests have been a major source of controversy and debate.

Although less often perceived as unfair, since they measure skills acquired in a particular area over a short time, achievement tests potentially exert a considerable influence on subject matter and teaching methods, as well as on what skills appear desirable. Among all tests, they are distinctive in that it is easier in the case of an achievement test to see what one is measuring, since the universe of abilities being sampled by the test is theoretically finite and far more easily specified.

The second variable is the use to which the test is put. Test results may be used for selection and placement, or counseling, and sometimes both. A test used to select among a group of candidates for a job, or among applicants for admission to a school, or a test used to assign individuals to specific groups (like tracks in a school) has an essentially predictive function. It is used to predict individual performance with respect to that of the other members of the group.

Tests may also be used as a basis for providing an individual with information about his abilities and aptitudes. This use of tests is theoretically different from that previously mentioned because the information provided to the "counselee" is intended to enable him to decide about his future. In the former case, although the individual sometimes decides for himself (as whether or not to apply), others ultimately decide for him. However, counseling frequently directs the individual to one of several alternatives. In this case, depending on the information and how it is transmitted, the counselor may actually be the decision-maker.

Finally, criticisms may either question the validity of tests or they may have little or nothing to do with whether the test measures what it is supposed to measure. Here we must ask: Is the force of the criticism affected by whether we assume the test to be a valid measure of what it is supposed to measure or not?

CRITICISMS OF THE VALIDITY OF ABILITY TESTS

Several critics have claimed that certain characteristics of tests make them unfair and invalid predicators for certain individuals or groups. These critics have singled out three types of individuals.

First, Hoffmann (1962) and others have claimed that these tests are unfair to deep thinkers. Critics who take this position claim that certain items on standardized tests penalize bright students because they are ambiguously worded or because the alternatives presented include one or more options (scored as incorrect) that the mediocre student passes by, but which the extremely bright student correctly perceives as being possibly correct answers. One cannot dispute the fact that Hoffmann and others have demonstrated clearly the existence of such items on tests that are currently in use.

Although it is not known whether any extremely bright students have actually suffered because of poorly written tests, Hoffmann's point is valid, at least in the abstract. It seems unlikely, however, in our achievement-oriented society, that very many geniuses remain undiscovered, regardless of their performance on standardized tests (or more important, that more geniuses are missed because of standardized tests than would be missed with alternative selection techniques).

Second, any test designed to be given to individuals in our heterogeneous society will discriminate against people with a cultural background different from that of the majority. To take an extreme case, if a pupil cannot read English because Spanish is spoken at home, he is not likely to do well on tests of reading comprehension in English, or, in fact, on any test written in English. Members of any group whose life experiences differ significantly from those on which the test was standardized will also be at a disadvantage.

Partly, this is a problem of standardization. Conceivably, special norms could be developed on any test for every distinctive group likely to take the test, so that both inter- and intragroup comparisons could be made. But another principle is involved. Most standardized tests are designed to predict success of individuals in the broader society, or in the setting in which the individual wishes to gain admission. Thus, tests are doing their job when they discriminate. If facility in English is assumed necessary for success, then a test of that facility is not unfair. In such cases, it can be pointed out that it is not the test which is unfair, but rather the circumstances which have permitted the deprivation to persist. However, any inferences about the general intellectual abilities of members of disadvantaged or other special groups based on test scores should be avoided at early ages.

Finally, tests may be unfair to individuals who lack special skills required for taking standardized tests. For almost everyone, these skills may be assumed to develop as a result of repeated contact with tests. Some individuals, however, take more tests than others. The amount of experience required to make this factor an unimportant influence in test performance is unknown. It might be assumed, however, that tests are unfair to some individuals without the requisite experience with tests. Hence, extensive testing in elementary and junior high school is beneficial, but inequalities may be created when some schools test more frequently than others. The problem is acute for foreigners from countries where tests are not widely used (for example, foreign applicants to American graduate and professional schools).

FACTORS AFFECTING VALIDITY OF TESTS

Standardized ability tests are not perfect predictors of subsequent performance, even in situations that require abilities similar to those required on the test. Highest coefficients of correlation between test scores and measures of subsequent performance are obtained for short-range academic performance (Lavin 1965). For example, scores of standardized tests given in the 12th grade predict first-year college grades fairly well. As the length of time between the test and criterion situation increases, the magnitude of the correlation is reduced. Similarly, as the criterion situation becomes more dissimilar from the test situation, the correlation is reduced. Thus, most existing studies show no correlation between test scores and subsequent occupational success (nor is any correlation shown between academic performance as measured by grades and subsequent occupational success). Because test scores correlate only moderately with long-range academic performance and not at all with postacademic performance, one can raise serious questions about their usefulness and reliability.

Three factors contribute to this lack of correlation. First, it is often difficult to establish clear criteria for successful postacademic performance. Many studies have relied on performance ratings by professional colleagues, fellow workers, or superiors. These are frequently unreliable and are based on other factors, such as personal qualities. Use of objective criteria, such as number of scientific papers published, may be criticized as being superficial.

Second, there is the problem of range restriction. Accurate predictions about the relative performance of individuals are easily made where there are sizable differences between individuals; a high degree of variance in the distribution of abilities measured makes prediction easy. However, where differences among members of the group tested are small, it is difficult to predict later performance of the members of the group relative to one another. Thus, predictions in a homogeneous group, such as college graduates, are risky. The phenomenon of range restriction accounts in large part for the lack of correlation between either test scores or academic performance and occupational success among able students.

Third, one should not assume that there is a linear relation between qualities measured by a standardized test and occupational success. The assumption that intelligence alone determines success is superficial. In fact, many studies have revealed that the relation between intellectual abilities and success in our society is very complicated. For example, although Terman demonstrated clearly that his gifted group as a whole was more successful than less intellectually able groups, he found no relationship between intelligence and later performance within the gifted group (Terman, 1959).

These findings are corroborated by the previously noted lack of correlation between college performance and subsequent nonacademic success and suggest that intellectual abilities may function as a threshold variable in relation to occupational advancement. A minimum level of intelligence is obviously required for most occupations, but once at or above this threshold, individual achievement relative to others in the same field is determined by qualities not measured by tests of intellectual abilities.

It should be noted that fields of endeavor differ not only in basic requirements of intelligence, but also with respect to the amount of difference made by increments over this level in one's chances of achieving success. In other words, qualities other than basic intelligence are more important in some fields than in others. [Incidentally, this does not have to be the case; it just happens that our society works this way at present. One could, for example, imagine a society in which a perfect correlation between intelligence and success could be achieved by assigning all jobs and status in the society on the sole basis of intelligence (Young, 1958).]

There is some controversy about whether ability tests measure innate capabilities (presumed unchangeable) or learning. Few people with any sophistication in psychometrics believe that even intelligence tests measure only innate capabilities. However, there are significant differences in opinion about whether the qualities measured by intelligence tests are more or less influenced by learning than by inherent potential. Assumptions about exactly what the test measures are likely to have an important effect on how test scores are used. If one interprets a child's performance as an indication of what he has learned (as opposed to a result of innate capability), then one is less likely to make long-run predictions about the child's ultimate success on the basis of his test scores (for example, his motivation might increase, and he might do better next time).

One of the most important criticisms of tests is that they contribute to their own validity by functioning as self-fulfilling prophecies. Hypothetically, a child who does well on a test, and, as a consequence of his performance, is placed in an advanced class, or receives special attention from his teachers, or who is admitted to a good university, is more likely to do well than the one whose score was lower. The likelihood that the optimistic prediction made on the basis of a high test score will be fulfilled is therefore increased because the person who scores high receives special advantages, whereas the individual who does poorly is often denied opportunities.

Experimental data from a recent study by Rosenthal and Jacobson (1968) confirm this hypothesis. They gave all of the children in one California elementary school an ordinary intelligence test at the beginning of the school year. They informed the teachers that the test they had given was specially designed to identify children who could be expected to show substantial I.Q. gains during the coming year. In each class, they then selected at random ten children and informed the teachers that these children had done particularly well on the test. This group in each class formed the experimental group, and the remainder of the children in each class served as the control group. An intelligence test given at the end of the school year showed that the experimental groups in grades kindergarten, one, two, and three had made significant gains in I.Q. when compared to the children in the control groups. In addition, teachers rated children in the experimental groups as being superior to those in the control groups in personal qualities, such as cooperativeness, interest in school affairs, and social adjustment. These data reveal that teachers' expectations contributed substantially to the increased test scores of the children in the experimental groups. Here the first test score reported to the teachers became a self-fulfilling prophecy. The implications of this point are far-reaching, especially for policies concerning the use of standardized intelligence tests in the elementary grades.

CRITICISMS INDEPENDENT OF THE VALIDITY OF TESTS

The following criticisms may be hypothesized to hold, whether one argues that tests are valid measures of ability or not. In some cases, the force of the criticism is increased if one assumes tests to be highly valid predictors. These criticisms, therefore, stem from the potential social effects of testing, rather than from questions regarding the accuracy of tests.

Standardized ability tests are used throughout the educational system, and children take such tests at periodic intervals. In addition, the spread of the technology of standardized test construction has led many teachers to make use of objective questions in tests they construct. It has been suggested that continual exposure to multiple-choice items during the elementary and secondary grades tends to result in constriction of children's ability to reason. In particular, it is claimed that emphasis on evaluation techniques in which there is always a right and wrong answer makes it difficult for children to deal with issues on which there is no clear right or wrong answer. Children, it is claimed, are therefore handicapped when they attempt to work through questions involving ethical or philosophical judgments, or when arriving at a decision depends upon identifying the assumptions one is going to begin with.

There is no proof that this is a valid criticism. Colleges claim that incoming students do not write as well as formerly, but there is no way of knowing if the older generation is just complaining about the new one, or, if true, whether it is because proportionally more people are going to college today. Lack of a suitable control group (that is, college students who have not taken standardized tests) makes research on this topic difficult.

When a student takes a college entrance examination or almost any standardized test, not only he, but also his teachers and his school, are being tested, since his performance reflects his training. As a consequence, tests have a potentially significant impact on subject matter and teaching methods. Only a very small minority of teachers interviewed in a recent study (Goslin, Epstein and Hallock, 1965; Goslin, 1967) claimed to spend much time preparing students for standardized tests or indicated that they have ever altered a course because the subject matter covered by a standardized test was different from what they normally taught. Nevertheless, there is some evidence that in many situations standardized tests do exert an influence on what is taught. The well-known New York Regents' examination program is pertinent here. Since both teachers and schools were being evaluated along with students, there was, and still is, considerable pressure to prepare students to take the Regents' achievement examinations. Reports of students being drilled on old copies of the Regents' examinations were common. That tests have had an impact on the curricula in this case cannot be disputed (Brickell, 1962).

Whether or not teachers make special efforts to prepare students for taking particular standardized tests, such tests can have a more general impact on curricula. For example, widely used external examinations, like the College Board achievement tests, may result in pressure on a school system to adopt a new curriculum if the school perceives that the content covered by the test differs significantly from that which is being presented in the school. Thus, standardized tests based on the new mathematics curriculum can be expected to speed the adoption of this curriculum in schools.

It should be noted that such an effect is not necessarily deleterious. Standardized tests may raise school standards as often as they limit innovation and experimentation. This, of course, was the idea behind the Regents' examination program when it was initiated. The problem is striking a balance between raising standards and setting arbitrary limits.

More and more schools, colleges, and testing agencies are giving individuals either their specific score or percentile rank, or a general idea of how they did on standardized tests. Regardless of how such information is transmitted to the examinee, it may be hypothesized that it will affect self-image, motivation, and aspirations in some cases. Users of tests have alternately been criticized for withholding test scores and for indiscriminately giving results. The effect of receiving information about one's abilities will depend on the perceived legitimacy of the source of the information (for example, the pupil's counselor), the perceived accuracy of the test, and the degree to which the test score confirms one's own estimate, including how threatening or rewarding it is. Obviously, individuals make use of many different types of information in arriving at an estimate of their abilities; standardized test scores are only one of many ways in which individuals get information about their capabilities. Data from a national sample of high school students (Brim, Goslin, Glass and Goldberg, 1964) indicate that test scores are of relatively minor importance in shaping self-estimates of ability, in comparison with such things as school grades, comments of peers and parents, and contact with teachers.

Test scores do have a potentially great impact when the individual's self-estimate varies considerably from his test score and when he cannot rationalize his poor performance, or when the score is substantially higher than his estimate. Under such conditions we may expect a shift in self-estimate of ability to affect the individual's aspirations, his motivation, and, secondarily, future personal decisions. We should also consider the consequences for overall aspiration levels in the society of a system in which individuals are classified very early with respect to their abilities and available opportunities for the future.

The use of any single criterion or set of criteria to sort individuals into groups or to decide which individuals will be admitted to a group affects the structure and characteristics of groups so formed. These implications may be examined under the following headings: (i) social structure within groups, (ii) tendencies toward uniformity in the characteristics of group members, and (iii) implications for the society as a whole.

With regard to (i), the current widespread use of standardized tests to allocate students to instructional groups or to tracks within schools causes social differentiation within schools based on qualities measured by standardized tests. Ability groupings reduce social contact between pupils of differing levels of ability (as measured by standardized tests). Research indicates that such differentiation may affect performance levels of low-ability pupils negatively, while not significantly facilitating the performance of high-ability pupils (Yates, 1966). In addition, it is clear that ability grouping impedes the process of acculturation of members of culturally deprived groups, who tend to end up together in the low-ability groups.

As for (ii), the use of any single criterion for forming groups produces a strong tendency toward uniformity in the members of the group. Our elite colleges and universities, for example, have difficulty achieving diversity in the student body while admitting only students of exceptional ability. The problem becomes more acute when standardized tests are heavily relied upon as a measure of intellectual ability.

Concerning (iii), Wolfle has pointed out that the success of modern, complex societies depends in large part on the availability of a talent pool in which a great diversity of abilities and skills is represented (Wolfle, 1960). To create such a talent pool, rewards of social status, prestige, and economic returns must be provided for individuals possessing many different talents. A tendency to rely heavily on standardized tests of a limited set of intellectual skills in the allocation of opportunities for achievement must necessarily reduce the diversity of talent available. Here, we might consider testing more abilities than those measured by current tests. We must also ensure adequate rewards for individuals possessing abilities not measured by tests, but which are important for the successful functioning of the society.

DO TESTS INVADE PRIVACY?

A test is a potential invasion of privacy because personal information is made available to others. Very important values in American society suggest that individuals have the right to decide to whom and under what conditions they will make available to others information about themselves. Correlative to this point, however, is the fact that participation in the society carries with it certain obligations and responsibilities. Further, certain groups clearly have the right to demand information from those who want the privileges of group membership. Thus, no one is likely to object to being given a driving test before being permitted to operate a motor vehicle. Similarly, few people object to the requirement that they must take an entrance test in order to gain admission to a university or college. In each case, the right of a group to information that is relevant to the stated objectives and goals of the group has been established.

Two important questions remain, however. First, under what conditions does a group have the right to ask aspiring members for information that is irrelevant to the purposes and goals of the group? In order to answer this question, it is probably necessary to make a distinction between public and private groups. A private group usually has the right to ask of applicants for membership anything, whether relevant or irrelevant. The applicant then decides whether he wishes to reveal this information. In the case of a group supported by the society as a whole, including all of the potential applicants to the group, the situation is more difficult. Would it be, for example, legitimate for the state to ask individuals to reveal information about their sexual behavior as a requirement for obtaining a driver's license? Most of us would, I think, object to such a requirement on the grounds that it represents an invasion of our privacy that is not justified by the service being rendered. The issue is one of relevance: must the school have such information in order to do its job?

There is, however, a second and more difficult problem in the case of school testing. In each of the cases presented above, the individual retains a choice as to whether he will submit himself to the test or not. Thus, if an individual does not want to take the College Board Scholastic Aptitude Test (SAT), he does not have to. Nor does he have to submit to a driver's test. As a result of his decision, he may have to give up his chances of attending certain colleges or driving an automobile, but the choice in each case is his. But, for the most part, a child does not have a choice about whether he will take tests or not, including standardized tests. A parent might move to another community, in which the school system did not use standardized tests (if he could find one), or he might send his children to a private school that did not administer tests (if he could afford one). For most parents these are not realistic alternatives.

Does this constitute an invasion of privacy? Carried to its extreme, an affirmative answer leads one to the conclusion that children should be permitted to refuse to take all tests, even those given by their teachers in class. Although this sounds absurd, it is not an unreasonable claim. If a child refused to participate in classroom tests, he would fail his courses and would not be promoted, but this would be his (or his parents') decision. The school clearly does have a right to require pupils to demonstrate their proficiency in school subjects before according them advanced status. But does the school also have the right to require pupils to demonstrate their general intellectual ability apart from their proficiency in specific subjects? If a child refused to take an I.Q. test given in school, would he fail his course? Does a school need such information in order to decide whether or not a child should be promoted?

If one concludes that a school has the right to collect information about intellectual abilities of its pupils, does the school also have the right to withhold this information from the pupil and his parents? Conversely, what right do parents and pupils have to know what information the school possesses about them? In at least one case (in New York State), the courts ruled that parents do have the right of access to information on the pupil's permanent record card maintained by the school.

SUMMARY AND CONCLUSIONS

At the outset a distinction was made between criticisms directed at the validity of tests and criticisms not affected by the validity of the tests. It was noted further that all criticisms of tests must take into consideration the type of test and the use to which the test is put.

Criticisms of the validity of tests involved the following issues: (i) tests may be unfair to certain groups and individuals, including the extremely gifted, the culturally disadvantaged, and those who lack experience in taking tests; (ii) tests are not perfect predictors of subsequent performance; (iii) tests may be used in overly rigid ways; (iv) tests may not measure inherent qualities of individuals; and (v) tests may contribute to their own predictive validity by serving as self-fulfilling prophecies.

Criticisms that are more or less independent of test validity included the effects of tests on (i) thinking patterns of those tested frequently; (ii) school curricula; (iii) self-image, motivation, and aspirations; (iv) groups using tests as a criterion for selection or allocation, or both; and (v) privacy. Several concluding remarks are in order:

1. This paper has focused almost entirely on *criticisms* of tests. However,

338 Marvin D. Dunnette

the positive value of standardized tests should not be ignored. Here we must keep in mind what possible alternative measures would be used if standardized tests were abandoned.

2. We must begin thinking about tests in a much broader perspective—one that includes consideration of the social effects of tests as well as their validity and reliability.

3. Finally, an effort should be made to develop rational and systematic policies on the use of tests with the culturally disadvantaged, the dissemination of test results, and the problem of invasion of privacy. Such policies can be formulated only if we are willing to take a long hard look at the role we want testing to play in the society. Standardized tests currently are a cornerstone in the edifice of stratification in American society. It is up to the social scientist to conduct research that will enable policy makers in education, business and industry and government to determine in a consistent and rational way the ultimate shape of this edifice.

45 An Evaluation of Test Critics and Their Assumptions

In previous publications Dr. Banesh Hoffmann has detailed some specific criticisms of tests and testing. The present paper reviews these allegations and presents counter arguments. Among the issues considered are (1) the relationship of creativity, intelligence, and achievement, (2) the presence of ambiguity in and dubious keying of multiple-choice test items, (3) the use of essay exams, (4) the use of statistical techniques in test development and analysis, and (5) the claim that tests constitute an invasion of privacy.

First, let us consider some of the major assumptions made by Hoffmann (1962) in his book, *The Tyranny of Testing*, and consider the relative validity of each. Later, we will comment on some of the broader charges made by other critics and the relative validity of these.

CREATIVITY, INTELLIGENCE, AND ACHIEVEMENT TEST PERFORMANCE

Conveniently, Hoffmann spells out his assumptions on page 150 of his book.

Reprinted and abridged with permission of author and publisher from an article entitled "Critics of Psychological Tests: Basic Assumptions: How Good?" which appeared in *Psychology in the Schools*, 1963, Vol. 1, pp. 63–69.

The first is as follows:

> "The tests deny the creative person a significant opportunity to demonstrate his creativity and favor the shrewd and facile candidate over the one who has something to say."

I personally know of no evidence to suggest that tests stifle the creative person. The major problem with making such a charge or assumption is that little satisfactory research has been done to define the so-called trait of creativeness. The usual procedure has been simply to call people "creative" who happen to score high on so-called "creativity" tests. Recently Robert Thorndike (1963) has analyzed the relative factorial purity of the content of the standard IQ tests and of the so-called creativity or divergent thinking tests. He finds that tests of creativity actually correlate more highly with convergent thinking tests than they do with themselves. Evidence such as this is hardly sufficient to sustain an argument that the so-called trait or behavior which we label "creative" has been successfully measured by tests now available. Unfortunately, the usual approach is to label persons as creative who score high on these factorially, poorly defined "creativity" tests rather than on the basis of any behaviorally defined reference outside the tests themselves.

Hoffmann cites the study by Getzels and Jackson (1962) described in their book, *Creativity and Intelligence.* Unfortunately the Getzels and Jackson study is a particularly poor example of what I have just discussed. In their study Getzels and Jackson define creativity on the basis of scores on a variety of measures of fluency and divergent thinking. In one part of their study they contrast two groups selected on the basis of high scores on IQ tests and creativity tests, respectively. The average IQ of the students selected on the basis of IQ tests was 150 whereas the average IQ of students selected on the basis of the "creativity" tests was only 127. Getzels and Jackson report that these two groups who differ by 23 points in IQ did not differ on standard multiple-choice achievement examinations. Yet Hoffmann says on page 146 of his book:

> In view of the above how much faith can we have in the IQ as an unbiased predictor of scholastic achievement even when the scholastic achievement is measured by multiple-choice methods. Think of the number of gifted students who were penalized in our schools because they lack the IQ knack.

It is difficult for me to understand how Hoffmann can use the data of the Getzels and Jackson study to make such a comment. Just the opposite is, in fact, true: the "low ability" (IQ = 127) students were not penalized on achievement examinations; they scored the same as the "high ability" (IQ = 150) students.

Even so there seems to be a widely held misconception that teachers somehow like the highly "creative" children less well than the highly intelligent children. As a matter of fact, Getzels and Jackson are often cited as evidence and they do state that "the high IQ students are preferred over the average students by their teachers, the creativity students are not." The actual facts as shown by the Getzels and Jackson data are that teachers' preferences were in the same direction for both groups and of very nearly the same magnitude. The difference, however, was not statistically significant for the "creative" children. Thus the reader and the public is left by this cavalier treatment of data with the unjustified impression that the teachers prefer the "high IQ's" to the "high creatives." In my opinion this is irresponsible reporting of research data—reporting that is nicely designed to lead people with an axe to grind (such as Mr. Hoffmann) astray.

MISSING THE "DEEP" STUDENT

Let us consider a second assumption made by Hoffmann. He says:

They penalize the candidate who perceives subtle points unnoticed by less able people including the test makers. They are apt to be superficial and intellectually dishonest with questions made artificially difficult by means of ambiguity because genuinely searching questions did not readily fit into the multiple-choice format.

A comment such as this of course ignores the massive amount of careful research which actually goes into the construction and final validation of a test item. For example, it is well known that distractors are purposely written to "fool" the less able person. We know that information about responses made by persons of different levels of knowledge shows without question that the degree of ambiguity perceived by the examinee is inversely related to his knowledge of the subject matter. In other words, in a good test item the less one knows the more ambiguous does the question appear. In spite of this, Hoffmann states on page 67 "and the more one knows about the subject the more glaring the ambiguities become." Hoffmann, of course, has no evidence to support this assumption.

COMMUNICATION PROBLEMS

A further assumption made by Hoffmann may be stated as follows: "They take account of only the choice of answer and not of quality of thought that lead to the choice," and "They neglect skill and disciplined expressions." Hoffmann apparently feels very strongly that objective examinations fail to assess a mysterious entity which he calls "quality of thought" or that they give little opportunity for "disciplined expression." Naturally, he offers no definitions for these mysterious attributes and he certainly suggests no reliable nor valid way of measuring them. In fact Hoffmann seems diligently to resist all references to the concepts of reliability and validity.

In addition to the fact that Hoffmann fails to define quality of thought or disciplined expression, it is noteworthy that he gives in Chapter 3 a series of very convincing arguments for not using essay examinations to measure so-called quality of thought or disciplined expression. For example, Hoffmann states that it is difficult in writing an essay question to choose a topic which will be fair to all examinees. He further states that even if a topic finally is chosen, it is extremely difficult to determine whether the essay is actually relevant to the question, further that it is difficult to overcome the problem of negative halo due to poor handwriting, poor spelling, or poor punctuation. He brings up the problem of different graders of essay examinations using different standards and he even cites the difficulty of the grader changing his standards as he moves through the examinations which he must grade. Hoffmann concludes that essay exams may be unfair, indeed that they are unfair for the testing of the students.

Thus Hoffmann works himself into a corner by criticizing objective exams because they fail to assess quality of thought or disciplined expression; yet he leaves no alternative for assessing these non-defined entities by any other means (such as by essay exams).

In his discussion of this problem he cites a study by the Educational Testing Service showing that a 90-minute essay test was less good than an objective exam, the English Composition Test, for predicting faculty ratings in English Composition. Faced with this evidence that an essay exam is less worthy, Hoffmann simply argues that these results are silly and that they could not possibly have been obtained. He appears to be using logical analysis in order to overcome or to reject empirical results. Essentially, of course, Hoffmann is simply confusing content with predictive or concurrent validity.

THE IDENTIFICATION OF MERIT

Finally, perhaps the potentially most damaging assumption and the one which would be the most difficult for Hoffmann to sustain has to do with the effect of tests in the identification of individual merit. He states, "They have a pernicious effect on education and the recognition of merit." Furthermore he seems to be concerned about the idea that multiple-choice testing might somehow be "efficient" and he feels that efficiency is bad in and of itself. For example, on page 90 he states,

> Let us not sacrifice too much for the sake of efficiency. In some respects the dictatorship is more efficient than a democracy and the lie detector more efficient and scientific than the jury. The efficient Nazis made medical experiments directly on men and women.

After reading this I find myself very curious about Mr. Hoffmann's stand on fluoridation of water, which certainly must be regarded as one very efficient way of decreasing the incidence of dental caries. However, lest I be charged with arguing in the same manner as I am accusing Mr. Hoffmann of doing, let me hasten to offer something in a more positive vein.

Today, through objective tests we can identify the many abilities of children and for the first time do a good job of mapping the true individuality of each and every child. In other words, tests provide us with the best means available for assessing individuality and discovering and rewarding individual merit. In my opinion this function is undoubtedly the greatest strength of testing and it is an entirely fallacious and unfounded assumption on the part of Hoffmann that tests are instead working against the recognition of individual merit and the wise and humane utilization of human resources. The creative genius of men such as Terman, Thurstone, Guilford and Strong cannot be nullified by a few Hoffmanns, Packards, Grosses, or Whytes.

Hoffmann argues that statistics should not take precedence over rational analysis of an item's content. I would tend to agree with this statement. Even if empirical validity did show that an item was valid, if a wrong answer were keyed, I would not then proceed to use this wrongly keyed answer. Thus, I would say that empirical validity should not necessarily carry the day over content validity and in so saying I am in essential agreement with Hoffmann. Unfortunately, Hoffmann completely ignores the fact that statistical validation of test items is most often an effective means of discovering poor and ambiguous items. Nowhere in his book does Hoffmann mention that item analysis is primarily a means of identifying poorly keyed and ambiguous items.

A common complaint about psychological testing is that it is an invasion of privacy. It is possible that this criticism may have some merit. This is the point, of course, at which it is incumbent upon the users of psychological tests to demonstrate the validity of any items which might otherwise be regarded as an invasion of privacy. A major point usually ignored by critics of psychological testing when they discuss the invasion of privacy is the distinction between institutional and individual decisions. If a firm is using a test to assess candidates and an individual desires employment with that firm, the use of the test is for the purpose of helping the institution to make a hiring decision; the purpose is not to give guidance or to protect the privacy of the individuals being tested. It is true, but perhaps beside the point, that an increase in the accuracy of institutional decisions will, over the long run, be accompanied by an increasing proportion of accurate or "correct" individual decisions.

Finally, it should be noted that the critics very rarely suggest any alternative to psychological testing. Gardner (1961) in his book, *Excellence*, says the following:

> Anyone attacking the usefulness of the tests must suggest workable alternatives. It has been proven over and over again that the alternative methods of evaluating ability are subject to gross errors and capable of producing grave injustices.

I believe that our careful examination of the assumptions by the various critics of psychological testing can lead to only one conclusion: The basic assumptions are erroneous and fallacious; they are based for the most part on lack of information, as apparently is the case for Hoffmann, or more seriously on a refusal to accept the strong evidence showing that individuality can be assessed with accuracy and in such a way as to give better recognition to real merit than has ever before been the case in either our educational or industrial institutions.

46   *The Social Consequences of Educational Testing*

ROBERT L. EBEL

In the following article Dr. Ebel describes the present posture of educational and psychological testing, with respect to both justified and unjustified criticisms by the layman and professional. The author considers four potentially harmful consequences of testing and whether these consequences should legitimately be feared. In discussing means by which these dangers may be eliminated or ameliorated, he also raises the important question of the social consequences of not testing.

Tests have been used increasingly in recent years to make educational assessments. The reasons for this are not hard to discover. Educational tests of aptitude and achievement greatly improve the precision, objectivity, and efficiency of the observations on which educational assessments rest. Tests are not alternatives to observations. At best they represent no more than refined and systematized processes of observation.

But the increasing use of tests has been accompanied by an increasing flow of critical comment. Again the reasons are easy to see. Tests very in quality. None is perfect and some may be quite imperfect. Test scores are sometimes misused. And even if they were flawless and used with the greatest skill, they would probably still be unpopular among those who have reason to fear an impartial assessment of some of their competencies.

Many of the popular articles critical of educational testing that have appeared in recent years do not reflect a very thoughtful, unbiased consideration of its social consequences. Most of them are obvious potboilers for their authors and sensational reader-bait in the eyes of the editors of the journals in which they appear. The writers of some of these articles have paid courteous visits to our offices. They have listened respectfully to our recitals of fact and opinion. They

Reprinted and abridged with permission of author and publisher from the *Proceedings of the 1963 Invitational Conference on Testing Problems.* Educational Testing Service, copyright © 1964, pp. 130–143. (By special arrangement with the American Council on Education) All rights reserved.

have drunk coffee with us and then taken their leave, presumably to reflect on what they have been told, but in any event to write. What appears in print often seems to be only an elaboration and documentation of their initial prejudices and preconceptions, supported by atypical anecdotes and purposefully selected quotations. Educational testing has not fared very well in their hands.

Among the charges of malfeasance and misfeasance that these critics have leveled against the test makers there is one of nonfeasance. Specifically, we are charged with having shown lack of proper concern for the social consequences of our educational testing. These harmful consequences, they have suggested, may be numerous and serious. The more radical among them imply that because of what they suspect about the serious social consequences of educational testing, the whole testing movement ought to be suppressed. The more moderate critics claim that they do not know much about these social consequences. But they also suggest that the test makers don't either, and that it is the test makers who ought to be doing substantial research to find out.

THE ROLE OF RESEARCH

If we were forced to choose between the two alternatives offered by the critics, either the suppression of educational testing or extensive research on its social consequences, we probably would choose the latter without much hesitation. But it is by no means clear that what testing needs most at this point is a large program of research on its social consequences. Let me elaborate.

Research can be extremely useful, but it is far from being a sure-fire process for finding the answers to any kind of a question, particularly a social question that perplexes us. Nor is research the only source of reliable knowledge. In the social sciences, at least, most of what we know for sure has not come out of formal research projects. It has come instead from the integration of a very large number of more or less incidental observations and accounts of human behavior in natural, rather than experimental situations. There are good reasons why research on human behavior tends to be difficult and often unproductive, but that is a story we cannot go into now.

For present purposes, only two points need to be mentioned. The first is that the scarcity of formal research on the social consequences of educational testing should not be taken to mean that there is no reliable knowledge about those consequences, or that those engaged in educational testing have been callously indifferent to its social consequences. The second is that scientific research on human behavior may require commitment to values that are in basic conflict with our democratic concerns for individual welfare. If boys and girls are used as carefully controlled experimental subjects in tough-minded research on social issues that really matter, not all of them will benefit, and some may be disadvantaged seriously. Our society is not yet ready, and perhaps should never become ready to acquiesce in that kind of scientific research.

HARMFUL CONSEQUENCES

Before proceeding further, let us mention specifically a few of the harmful things that critics have suggested educational testing may do:

1. It may place an indelible stamp of intellectual status—superior, mediocre, or inferior—on a child, and thus predetermine his social status as an adult, and possibly also do irreparable harm to his self-esteem and his educational motivation.

2. It may lead to a narrow conception of ability, encourage pursuit of this single goal, and thus tend to reduce the diversity of talent available to society.

3. It may place the testers in a position to control education and determine the destinies of individual human beings, while, incidentally, making the testers themselves rich in the process.

4. It may encourage impersonal, inflexible, mechanistic processes of evaluation and determination, so that essential human freedoms are limited or lost altogether.

These are four of the most frequent and serious tentative indictments. There have been, of course, many other suggesstions of possible harmful social consequences of educational testing. It may emphasize individual competition and success, rather than social cooperation, and thus conflict with the cultivation of democratic ideals of human equality. It may foster conformity rather than creativity. It may involve cultural bias. It may neglect important intangibles. It may, particularly in the case of personality testing, involve unwarranted and offensive invasions of privacy. It may do serious injustice in particular individual cases. It may reward specious test-taking skill, or penalize the lack of it.

PERMANENT STATUS DETERMINATION

Consider first then, the danger that educational testing may place an indelible stamp of inferiority on a child, ruin his self-esteem and educational motivation, and determine his social status as an adult. The kind of educational testing most likely to have these consequences would involve tests purporting to measure a person's permanent general capacity for learning. These are the intelligence tests, and the presumed measures of general capacity for learning they provide are popularly known as IQ's.

Most of us here assembled are well aware of the fact that there is no direct, unequivocal means for measuring permanent general capacity for learning. It is not even clear to many of us that in the state of our current understanding of mental functions and the learning process, any precise and useful meaning can be given to the concept of "permanent general capacity for learning." We know that all intelligence tests now available are direct measures only of achievement in learning, including learning how to learn, and that inferences from scores on those tests to some native capacity for learning are fraught with many hazards and uncertainties.

But many people who are interested in education do not know this. Many of them believe that native intelligence has been clearly identified and is well understood by expert psychologists. They believe that a person's IQ is one of his basic, permanent attributes, and that any good intelligence test will measure it with a high degree of precision. They do not regard an IQ simply as another test score, a score that may vary considerably depending on the particular test used and the particular time when the person was tested.

Whether or not a person's learning is significantly influenced by his predetermined capacity for learning, there is no denying the obvious fact that individual achievements in learning exhibit considerable consistency over time and across tasks. The superior elementary school pupil may become a mediocre secondary school pupil and an inferior college student, but the odds are against it. Early promise is not always fulfilled, but it is more often than not. The A student in mathematics is a better bet than the C student to be an A student in English literature as well, or in social psychology.

On the other hand, early promise is not always followed by late fulfillment. Ordinary students do blossom sometimes into outstanding scholars. And special talents can be cultivated. There is enough variety in the work of the world so that almost anyone can discover some line of endeavor in which he can develop more skill than most of his fellow men.

In a free society that claims to recognize the dignity and worth of every individual, it is better to emphasize the opportunity for choice and the importance of effort than to stress genetic determinism of status and success. It is better to emphasize the diversity of talents and tasks than to stress general excellence or inferiority. It is important to recognize and to reinforce what John Gardner has called "the principle of multiple chances," not only across time but also across tasks.

The concept of fixed general intelligence, or capacity for learning, is a hypothetical concept. At this stage in the development of our understanding of human learning, it is not a necessary hypothesis. Socially, it is not now a useful hypothesis. One of the important things test specialists can do to improve the social consequences of educational testing is to discredit the popular conception of the IQ. Wilhelm Stern, the German psychologist who suggested the concept originally saw how it was being over-generalized and charged one of his students coming to America to "kill the IQ." Perhaps we would be well advised, even at this late date, to renew our efforts to carry out his wishes.

Recent emphasis on the early identification of academic talent involves similar risks of oversimplifying the concept of talent and overemphasizing its predetermined components. If we think of talent mainly as something that is genetically given, we will run our schools quite differently than if we think of it mainly as something that can be educationally developed.

We should judge the value of the tests we use not in terms of how accurately they enable us to predict later achievement, but rather in terms of how much help they give us to increase achievement by motivating and directing the efforts of students and teachers. From this point of view, those concerned with professional education who have resisted schemes for very long-range predictions of aptitude for or success in their professions have acted wisely. Not only is there likely to be much more of dangerous error than of useful truth in such long-range predictions, but also there is implicit in the whole enterprise a deterministic conception of achievement that is not wholly consistent with the educational facts as we know them, and with the basic assumptions of a democratic, free society.

Prediction has to do with the future, and the future ought to be of greater concern to us than the past. I think that a measurement must be related to some other measurements in order to be useful, and that these relationships provide the basis for, and are tested by, predictions. But these relationships also provide a basis in many educational endeavors for managing outcomes—for making happen what we want to happen. And I cannot agree that precision in language or clarity of thought is well served by referring to this process of controlling outcomes as just another instance of prediction. The etymology and common usage of the word "prediction" imply to me the process of foretelling, not of controlling.

The direct, exclusive, immediate purpose of measurement is always description, not either prediction or control. If we know with reasonable accuracy how things now stand (descriptions), and if we also know with reasonable accuracy what leads to what (functional relations), we are in a position to foretell what will happen if we keep hands off (prediction) or to manipulate the variables we can get our hands on to make happen what we want to happen (control). Of course our powers of control are often limited and uncertain, just as our powers of prediction are. But I have not been able to see what useful purpose is served by referring to both the hands-off and the hands-on operations as prediction, as if there were no important difference between them. It is in the light of these semantic considerations that I suggest that tests should be used less as bases for prediction of achievement, and more as means to increase achievement. I think there is a difference, and that it is important educationally.

LIMITED CONCEPTIONS OF ABILITY

Consider next the danger that a single widely used test or test battery for selective admission or scholarship awards may foster an undesirably narrow conception of ability and thus tend to reduce diversity in the talents available to a school or to society.

Here again, it seems, the danger is not wholly imaginary. Basic as verbal and quantitative skills are to many phases of educational achievement, they do not encompass all phases of achievement. The application of a common yardstick of aptitude or achievement to all pupils is operationally much simpler than the use of a diversity of yardsticks, designed to measure different aspects of achievement. But overemphasis on a common test could lead educators to neglect those students whose special talents lie outside the common core.

Those who manage programs for the testing of scholastic aptitude always insist, and properly so, that scores on these tests should not be the sole consideration when decisions are made on admission or the award of scholarships. But the question of whether the testing itself should not be varied from person to person remains. The use of optional tests of achievement permits some variation. Perhaps the range of available options should be made much wider than it is at present to accommodate greater diversity of talents.

The problem of encouraging the development of various kinds of ability is, of course, much broader than the problem of testing. Widespread commitment to general education, with the requirement that all students study identical courses for a substantial part of their programs, may be a much greater deterrent of specialized diversity in the educational product. Perhaps these requirements should be restudied too.

DOMINATION BY THE TESTERS

What of the concern that the growth of educational testing may increase the influence of the test makers until they are in a position to control educational curricula and determine the destinies of students?

Those who know well how tests are made and used in American education know that the tests more often lag than lead curricular change, and that while tests may affect particular episodes in a student's experience, they can hardly ever be said to determine a student's destiny. American education is, after all, a manifold, decentralized, loosely organized enterprise. Whether it restricts student freedom too much or too little is a subject for lively debate. But it does not even come close to determining any student's destiny, not nearly as close as the examination systems in some countries, ancient and modern.

But test makers have, I fear, sometimes given the general public reason to fear that we may be up to no good. I refer to our sometime reluctance to take the layman fully into our confidence, to share fully with him all information about his test scores, the tests from which they were derived, and our interpretations of what they mean.

Secrecy concerning educational tests and test scores has been justified on several grounds. One is that the information is simply too complex for untrained minds to grasp. Now it is true that some pretty elaborate theories can be built around our testing processes. It is also true that we can perform some very fancy statistical manipulations with the scores they yield. But the essential information revealed by the scores on most educational tests is not particularly complex. If we understand it ourselves, we can communicate it clearly to most laymen without serious difficulty. To be quite candid, we are not all that much brighter than they are, much as we may sometimes need the reassurance of thinking so.

Another justification for secrecy is that laymen will misuse test scores. Mothers may compare scores over the back fences. The one whose child scores high spreads the word around. The one whose child scores low may keep the secret, but seek other grounds for urging changes in the teaching staff or in the educational program. Scores of limited meaning may be treated with undue respect and used to repair or to injure the student's self-esteem rather than to contribute to his learning.

Again it is true that test scores can be misused. They have been in the past and they will be in the future. But does this justify secrecy? Can we minimize abuses due to ignorance by withholding knowledge? We do not flatter our fellow citizens when we tell them, in effect, that they are too ignorant, or too lacking in character to be trusted with the knowledge of their children, or of themselves, that we possess.

Seldom acknowledged, but very persuasive as a practical reason for secrecy regarding test scores is that it spares those who use the scores from having to explain and justify the decisions they make. Preference is not and should not always be given to the person whose test score is the higher. But if score information is withheld, the disappointed applicant will assume that it was because of his low score, not because of some other factor. He will not trouble officials with demands for justification of a decision that in some cases might be hard to justify. But all things considered, more is likely to be gained in the long run by revealing the objective evidence used in reaching a decision. Should the other subjective considerations prove too difficult to justify, perhaps they ought not to be used as part of the basis for decision.

If specialists in educational measurement want to be properly understood and trusted by the public they serve, they will do well to shun secrecy and to share with the public as much as it is interested in knowing about the methods they use, the knowledge they gain, and the interpretations they make. This is clearly the trend of opinion in examining boards and public education authorities. Let us do what we can to reinforce the trend. Whatever mental measurements are so esoteric or so dangerous socially that they must be shrouded in secrecy probably should not be made in the first place.

The testers do not control education or the destinies of individual students. By the avoidance of mystery and secrecy they can help to create better public understanding and support.

MECHANISTIC DECISION MAKING

Finally, let us consider briefly the possibility that testing may encourage mechanical decision making, at the expense of essential human freedoms of choice and action.

Those who work with mental tests often say that the purpose of all measurement is prediction. They use regression equations to predict grade-point averages, or contingency tables to predict the chances of various degrees of success. Their procedures may seem to imply not only that human behavior is part of a deterministic system in which the number of relevant variables is manageably small, but also that the proper goals of human behavior are clearly known and universally accepted.

In these circumstances there is some danger that we may forget our own inadequacies and attempt to play God with the lives of other human beings. We may find it convenient to overlook the gross inaccuracies that plague our measurements and the great uncertainties that bedevil our predictions. Betrayed by overconfidence in our own wisdom and virtue, we may project our particular value systems into a pattern of ideal behavior for all men.

If these limitations on our ability to mold human behavior and to direct its development did not exist, we would need to face the issue debated by B. F. Skinner and Carl Rogers before the American Psychological Association some years ago. Shall our knowledge of human behavior be used to design an ideal culture and condition individuals to live happily in it at whatever necessary cost to their own freedom of choice and action?

But the aforementioned limitations do exist. If we ignore them and undertake to manage the lives of others so that those others will qualify as worthy citizens in our own particular vision of utopia, we do justify the concern that one harmful social consequence of educational testing may be mechanistic decision making and the loss of essential human freedoms.

A large proportion of the decisions affecting the welfare and destiny of a person must be made in the midst of overwhelming uncertainties concerning the outcomes to be desired and the best means of achieving such outcomes. That many mistakes will be made seems inevitable. One of the cornerstones of a free society is the belief that in most cases it is better for the person most concerned to make the decision, right or wrong, and to take the responsibility for its consequences, good or bad.

The implications of this for educational testing are clear. Tests should be used as little as possible to impose decisions and courses of action on others. They should be used as much as possible to provide a sounder basis of choice in individual decision making. Tests can be used and ought to be used to support rather than to limit human freedom and responsibility.

CONCLUSION

In summary we have suggested that those who make and use educational tests might do four things to alleviate public concerns over their possibly adverse social consequences:

1. We could emphasize the use of tests to improve status, and de-emphasize their use to determine status.
2. We could broaden the base of achievements tested to recognize and develop the wide variety of talents needed in our society.
3. We could share openly with the persons most directly concerned all that tests have revealed to us about their abilities and prospects.
4. We could decrease the use of tests to impose decisions on others, and instead increase their use as a basis for better personal decision making.

When Paul Dressel read a draft of this paper, he chided me gently on what he considered to be a serious omission. I had failed to discuss the social consequences of *not* testing. What are some of these consequences?

If the use of educational tests were abandoned, the distinctions between competence and incompetence would become more difficult to discern. Dr. Nathan Womack, former president of the National Board of Medical Examiners, has pointed out that only to the degree to which educational institutions can define what they mean by competence and determine the extent to which it has been achieved can they discharge their obligation to deliver competence to the society they serve.

If the use of educational tests were abandoned, the encouragement and reward of individual efforts to learn would be made more difficult. Excellence in programs of education would become less tangible as a goal and less demonstrable as an attainment. Educational opportunities would be extended less on the basis of aptitude and merit and more on the basis of ancestry and influence; social class barriers would become less permeable. Decisions on important issues of curriculum and method would be made less on the basis of solid evidence and more on the basis of prejudice or caprice.

These are some of the social consequences of *not* testing. In our judgment, they are potentially far more harmful than any possible adverse consequences of testing. But it is also our judgment, and has been the theme of this paper, that we can do much to minimize even these possibilities of harmful consequences. Let us, then, use educational tests for the powerful tools they are with energy and skill, but also with wisdom and care.

REFERENCES

ADKINS, DOROTHY C. *Statistics*. Columbus: Charles E. Merrill Books, 1964.

ADKINS, DOROTHY C. Measurement in relation to the educational process. *Educational and Psychological Measurement*, 1958, Vol. 18, pp. 221–240.

AHMANN, J. S., and GLOCK, M. D. *Measuring and evaluating educational achievement.* (Also *Evaluating pupil growth*) Boston: Allyn and Bacon, 1971.

ALKER, H. A., CARLSON, J. A., and HERMANN, M. G. Multiple-choice questions and student characteristics. *Journal of Educational Psychology*, 1969, Vol. 60, pp. 231–243.

AMERICAN PSYCHOLOGICAL ASSOCIATION. Testing and public policy (Special Issue). *American Psychologist*, 1965, Vol. 20, pp. 857–993.

AMERICAN PSYCHOLOGICAL ASSOCIATION. Society for the Study of Social Issues. *Guidelines for testing minority group children.* Washington, D. C.: American Psychological Association, 1964.

AMERICAN PSYCHOLOGICAL ASSOCIATION. *Technical recommendations for psychological tests and diagnostic techniques.* Washington, D. C.: 1954 (Also supplement to *Psychological Bulletin*, 1954, Vol. 51, pp. 1–38).

ANASTASI, ANNE. *Differential psychology.* New York: Macmillan (Third Edition) 1958.

ANDERSON, R. C. Comments on Professor Gagné's paper. Wittrock, M. C. & Wiley, E. (Eds.) *The Evaluation of Instruction.* New York: Holt, Rinehart and Winston, 1970, pp. 126–133.

ANDREW, D. C., and ROBERTS, L. H. Final evaluation report on the Texarkana dropout prevention program. Magnolia, Arkansas: Region VIII, *Education Service Center*, July 20, 1970 (mimeographed).

ASTIN, A. W. The inventory of college activities (ICA): Assessing the college environment through observable events. Paper presented at the Annual Meeting of the American Psychological Association, Chicago, 1965. (a)

ASTIN, A. W. *Who goes where to college.* Chicago: Science Research Associates, 1965. (b)

ASTIN, A. W. Classroom environment in different fields of study. *Journal of Educational Psychology,* 1965, Vol. 56, pp. 275–282. (c)

ASTIN, A. W. Further validation of the *Environmental Assessment Technique. Journal of Educational Psychology,* 1963, Vol. 54, pp. 217–226.

ASTIN, A. W. An empirical characterization of higher educational institutions. *Journal of Educational Psychology,* 1962, Vol. 53, pp. 224–235.

ASTIN, A. W., and HOLLAND, J. L. The environmental assessment technique: A way to measure college environment. *Journal of Educational Psychology,* 1961, Vol. 52, pp. 308–316.

AULD, F., JR. Influence of social class on personality test responses. *Psychological Bulletin,* 1952, Vol. 49, pp. 318–331.

AUSUBEL, D. P. *The psychology of meaningful verbal learning.* New York: Grune & Stratton, 1963.

BARRON, F. The psychology of imagination. *Scientific American,* 1958, Vol. 199, pp. 111–166.

BECKER, S., LERNER, M., and CARROLL, JEAN. Conformity as a function of birth order, payoff, and type of group pressure. *Journal of Abnormal and Social Psychology,* 1964, Vol. 69, pp. 318–323.

BEGGS, D. L., and HIERONYMUS, A. N. Uniformity of growth in the basic skills throughout the school year and during the summer. *Journal of Educational Measurement,* 1968, Summer, pp. 91–97.

BENNETT, G. K., SEASHORE, H. G., and WESMAN, A. G. *Differential aptitude tests,* Manual. New York: Psychological Corporation, 1947.

BEREITER, C., and ENGELMANN, S. *Teaching disadvantaged children in the preschool,* Englewood Cliffs, N. J.: Prentice-Hall, 1966.

BERNSTEIN, B. Language and social class. *British Journal of Sociology,* 1960, Vol. II, pp. 271–276.

BINET, A. *Les idees modernes sur les enfants.* Paris: E. Flamerion, 1909.

BITTNER, R. H., and WILDER, C. E. Expectancy tables: a method of interpreting correlation coefficients. *Journal of Experimental Education,* 1946, Vol. 14, pp. 245–252.

BLACK, HILLEL. *They shall not pass.* New York: William Morrow and Company, 1963.

BLOCK, J. *The challenge of response sets.* New York: Appleton-Century-Crofts, 1965.

BLOMMERS, P., and LINDQUIST, E. F. *Elementary statistical methods in psychology and education.* Boston: Houghton Mifflin Co., 1960.

BLOOM, B. S., HASTINGS, J. T., MADAUS, G. F., *et al. Handbook on formative and summative evaluation of student learning.* New York: McGraw-Hill, 1971.

BLOOM, B. S. Learning for mastery, UCLA, Center for the Study of Evaluation, *Evaluation comment,* May 1968, Vol. 1, Number 2.

BLOOM, B. S. Quality control in education. *Tomorrow's teaching.* Oklahoma City: Frontiers of Science Foundation, 1961. pp. 54–61.

BLOOM, B. S., *et al. Taxonomy of educational objectives. Handbook I: The cognitive domain.* New York: David McKay Co., 1956.

BOMBARD, A. *The voyage of the heretique.* New York: Simon & Schuster, 1953.

BORGATTA, E. F., and CORSINI, R. J. *Quick word test manual.* Chicago: Harcourt Brace Jovanovich, 1964.

BORING, E. G. Personal communication, 1966.

BORMUTH, J. *On the theory of achievement test items.* Chicago: University of Chicago Press, 1970.

BOUCHARD, T. J., JR. Convergent and discriminant validity of the *Adjective Check List* and *Edwards Personal Preference Schedule. Educational and Psychological Measurement,* 1968, Vol. 28, pp. 1165–1171.

BRADLEY, J. I., and MCCLELLAND, J. N. *Basic statistical concepts (a self-instructional text).* Chicago: Scott, Foresman and Co., 1963.

BRENNER, M. H. Test difficulty, reliability and discrimination as functions of item difficulty order. *Journal of Applied Psychology,* 1964, Vol. 48, pp. 98–100.

BRICKELL, H. M. Organizing New York State for educational change: A report to the state commissioner of education. Albany, New York: State Department of Education, 1962.

BRIM, O. G., JR., GOSLIN, D. A., GLASS, D. C., and GOLDBERG, I. *The use of standardized ability tests in American secondary schools.* New York: Russell Sage Foundation, 1964.

BRIM, O. G., JR., NEULINGER, J., and GLASS, D. C. *Experiences and attitudes of American adults concerning standardized intelligence tests.* New York: Russell Sage Foundations, 1965.

BROTHERTON, D. A., READ, J. M., and PRATT, K. C. Indeterminate number concepts II: Application to children to determinate number groups. *Journal of Genetic Psychology,* 1948, Vol. 73, pp. 209–236.

BROUDY, H. S. Can research escape the dogma of behavioral objectives? *School Review,* 1970, November, pp. 43–56.

BRUNER, J. S. *Toward a theory of instruction.* Cambridge, Mass.: Belknap Press, 1966.

BRYAN, J. H., and TEST, MARY ANN. Models and helping. Unpublished paper, Northwestern University, 1966.

BYRD, R. E. *Alone.* New York: Putnam's, 1938.

CAMPBELL, D. T., KRUSKAL, W. H., and WALLACE, W. P. Seating aggregation as an index of attitude. *Sociometry*, 1966, Vol. 29, pp. 1–15.

CAMPBELL, D. T., and FISKE, D. W. Convergent and discriminant validation by the multi-trait, multi-method matrix. *Psychological Bulletin*, 1959, Vol. 56, pp. 81–105.

CARRIER, N. A. and JEWELL, D. O. Efficiency in measuring the effect of anxieties upon academic performance. *Journal of Educational Psychology*, 1966, Vol. 57, pp. 23–26.

CARROLL, J. A. A model for school learning. *Teachers College Record*, 1963, Vol. 64, pp. 723–733.

CATTELL, R. B. A culture-free intelligence test: I. *Journal of Educational Psychology*, 1940, Vol. 3, pp. 161–179.

CATTELL, R. B., FEINGOLD, S. N., and SARASON, S. B. A culture-free intelligence test: II. Evaluation of cultural influence on test performance. *Journal of Educational Psychology*, 1940, Vol. 32, pp. 81–100.

CHASE, C. I. The impact of certain factors in the reading of essay examinations. Paper presented at the Annual Meeting of the American Educational Research Association, New York, February, 1967.

CHASE, C. I. Relative length of option and response set in multiple-choice items, *Educational and Psychological Measurement*, 1964, Vol. 24, pp. 861–866.

CHAUNCEY, H., and DOBBIN, J. E. *Testing: its place in education today.* New York: Harper and Row, 1963.

COFFMAN, W. E. Patterns of growth in basic skills in two elementary school classrooms over a four-year period. *The Seventeenth Yearbook, NCMUE*, 1960, pp. 141–151.

COHEN, J. S., GREGORY, R. J., and PELOSI, J. W. *Vocational rehabilitation and the socially disabled.* Syracuse: Syracuse University Press, 1966.

COOK, D. L., and STUFFLEBEAM, D. L. Estimating test norms from variable size item and examinee samples. *Educational and Psychological Measurement*, 1967, Vol. 27, pp. 601–610. (See same article in *Journal of Educational Measurement*, 1967, Vol. 4, No. 1 (Spring), pp. 27–33).

COOK, W. W., and LEEDS, C. H. Measuring teacher personality. *Educational and Psychological Measurement*, 1947, Vol. 7, pp. 399–410.

COREY, S. M. Professed attitudes and actual behavior. *Journal of Educational Psychology*, 1937, Vol. 28, pp. 271–280.

CRONBACH, L. J., and SNOW, RICHARD E. *Final report: individual differences in learning ability as a function of instructional variables.* Stanford University, 1969. Not available from the authors. May be ordered from ERIC Document Reproduction Service by requesting ED–029–001.

CRONBACH, L. J., and GLESER, G. C. *Psychological tests and personnel decisions.* Urbana: University of Illinois Press. (Second Edition), 1965.

CRONBACH, L. J. Evaluation for course improvement. *Teachers College Record*, 1963, Vol. 64, pp. 672–683.

CRONBACH, L. J., RAJARATNAM, N., and GLESER, GOLDINE C. Theory of generalizability: A liberalization of reliability theory. *British Journal of Statistical Psychology*, 1963, Vol. 16, pp. 137–163.

CRONBACH, L. J. *Essentials of psychological testing*. New York: Harper. (Second Edition), 1960; (Third Edition), 1970.

CRONBACH, L. J., and MEEHL, P. E. Construct validity in psychological tests. *Psychological Bulletin*, 1955, Vol. 52, pp. 281–302.

CRONBACH, L. J. Coefficient alpha and the internal structure of tests. *Psychometrika*, 1951, Vol. 16, pp. 297–334.

CRONBACH, L. J. Further evidence on response sets and test design. *Educational and Psychological Measurement*, 1950, Vol. 10, pp. 3–31.

CRONBACH, L. J. Test "reliability": its meaning and determination. *Psychometrika*, 1947, Vol. 12, pp.1–16.

CRONBACH, L. J. Response sets and test validity. *Educational and psychological Measurement*, 1946, Vol. 6, pp. 475–494.

DAVIS, A., and HAVIGHURST, R. J. The measurement of mental systems (Can intelligence be measured?). *Scientific Monthly*, 1948, Vol. 66, pp. 301–316.

DAVIS, F. B. *Educational measurements and their interpretation*. Belmont, California: Wadsworth Publishing Co., 1964.

DAVIS, F. B. Item analysis in relation to educational and psychological testing. *Psychological Bulletin*, 1952, Vol. 49, pp. 97–121.

DAVIS, F. B. Item selection techniques. In Lindquist, E. F. (Ed.) *Educational Measurement*. Washington, D.C.: American Council on Education, 1951, (Chapter 9), pp. 266–328.

DECHARMS, R., and MOELLER, G. Values expressed in American children's readers: 1800–1950. *Journal of Abnormal and Social Psychology*, 1962, Vol. 64, pp. 136–142.

DEUTSCH, M. The disadvantaged child and the learning process. In Passow, A. H. (Ed.) *Education in depressed areas*. New York: Teachers College, Columbia University, 1963.

DICKEN, C. F. Convergent and discriminant validity of the *California Psychological Inventory*. *Educational and Psychological Measurement*, 1963, Vol. 23, Number 3, pp. 449–459.

DIEDERICH, P. B. Simplified measurement techniques for teachers. In Edith M. Huddleston (Ed.) *Yearbook of the National Council on Measurements Used in Education*, 1958, pp. 24–29.

DOBBIN, J. E. Some New Directions Needed in Testing. Speech given at the American College Personnel Association meeting in Denver, Colorado, March 28, 1961.

DREGER, R., and MILLER, K. Comparative psychological studies of Negroes and whites in the United States. *Psychological Bulletin*, 1960, Vol. 57, pp. 361–402.

DRESSEL, P. L., and MAYHEW, L. B. *General education: Explorations in evaluation.* Washington: American Council on Education, 1954.

DUNN, T. F., and GOLDSTEIN, L. G. Test difficulty, validity, and reliability as functions of selected multiple-choice item construction principles. *Educational and Psychological Measurement,* 1959, Vol. 19, pp. 171–175.

DYER, H. S. Performance contracting: Too simple a solution for difficult problems. *The United Teacher,* November 29, 1970, pp. 19–22.

EBEL, R. L. When information becomes knowledge. *Science,* 1971, January, pp. 130–131.

EBEL, R. L. *Measuring educational achievement.* Englewood Cliffs, N.J.: Prentice-Hall, 1965.

EBEL, R. L. Must all tests be valid? *American Psychologist,* 1961, Vol. 16, pp. 640–647.

EDGEWORTH, F. Y. The element of change in competitive examinations. *Journal of the Royal Statistical Society,* 1890, Vol. 53, pp. 460–473 and pp. 644–663.

EDGEWORTH, F. Y. The statistics of examinations. *Journal of the Royal Statistical Society,* 1888, Vol. 51, pp. 599–635.

EDWARDS, A. L. *Statistical analysis.* New York: Holt, Rinehart, and Winston, Inc. (Third Edition), 1969.

EDWARDS, A. L. *The social desirability variable in personality assessment and research.* New York: The Dryden Press, 1957. (a).

EDWARDS, A. L. *Techniques of attitude scale construction.* New York: Appleton-Century-Crofts, 1957. (b).

EPSTEIN, S. The measurement of drive and conflict in humans: theory and experiment. In *1962 Nebraska Symposium on Motivation.* Lincoln: University of Nebraska Press, pp. 127–206.

FANSLOW, ALYCE M. *Environments in college home economics units as perceived by students.* Unpublished doctoral dissertation, Ames, Iowa: Iowa State University, 1966.

FERGUSON, G. A. On learning and human ability. *Canadian Journal of Psychology,* 1954, Vol. 8, pp. 95–112.

FERRIS, F. L., JR. Testing in the new curriculum: Numerology, tyranny, or common sense? *School Review,* 1962, Vol. 70, pp. 112–131.

FINDLEY, W. G .(Ed.) The Import and Improvement of School Testing Programs. *The Sixty-second Yearbook of the National Society for the Study of Education.* Chicago: University of Chicago Press, 1963.

FLEMING, E. S., and WEINTRAUB, S. Attitudinal rigidity as a measure of creativity in gifted children. *Journal of Educational Psychology,* 1962, Vol. 53, pp. 81–85.

FREEMAN, F. *Theory and practice of psychological testing.* New York: Holt, Rinehart and Winston (Third Edition), 1962.

FURST, E. J. *Constructing evaluation instruments.* New York: Longmans, Green and Co., 1958.

GAGNÉ, R. Learning hierarchies. *Educational Psychologist.* 1968, November, Vol. 6, No. 1.

GAGNÉ, R. *The conditions of learning.* New York: Holt, Rinehart, and Winston, 1965.

GALTON, F. *Hereditary genius,* New York: D. Appleton, 1870.

GARDNER, J. *Excellence.* New York: Harper and Row, 1961.

GARNER, W. R. Context effects and the validity of loudness scales. *Journal of Experimental Psychology,* 1954, Vol. 48, pp. 218–224.

GARNER, W. R., *et al.* Operationism and the concept of perception. *Psychological Review,* 1956, Vol. 53, pp. 149–159.

GATES, A. I., and MACGINITIE, W. H. *Technical manual for the Gates–Mac Ginitie reading tests.* New York: Teachers College Press, Columbia University, 1965, p. 5.

GETZELS, J. W., and JACKSON, P. W. *Creativity and intelligence; explorations with gifted students.* New York: John Wiley & Sons, 1962.

GIBB, B. G. Test-wiseness as secondary cue response, Unpublished doctoral dissertation, Stanford University. Ann Arbor, Michigan: *University Microfilms,* 1964. 64–7643.

GLASER, R. Instructional technology and the measurement of learning outcomes: Some questions. *American Psychologist,* 1963, Vol. 18, pp. 519–521.

GLASS, G. V., and STANLEY, J. C. *Statistical methods in education and psychology.* Englewood Cliffs, N.J.: Prentice-Hall, 1970.

GLASSER, W. *Schools without failure.* New York: Harper & Row, 1969.

GOODFELLOW, L. D. The human element in probability. *Journal of General Psychology,* 1940, Vol. 33, pp. 201–205.

GORDON, E. W., and WILKERSON, D. A. *Compensatory education for the disadvantaged.* New York: College Entrance Examination Board, 1966.

GORDON, E. W. Counseling socially disadvantaged children. In Riessman, F., Cohen, J., and Pearl, A. (Eds.) *Mental health of the poor.* New York: The Free Press, 1964.

GOSLIN, D. A. Ethical and legal aspects of the collection and use of educational information. Paper presented at the Invitational Conference on Testing Problems. New York, October, 1970.

GOSLIN, D. A. *Teachers and testing.* New York: Russell Sage Foundation, 1967.

GOSLIN, D. A., EPSTEIN, R. R., and HALLOCK, B. *Testing in elementary schools.* New York: Russell Sage Foundation, 1965.

GOSLIN, D. A. *The search for ability.* New York: Russell Sage Foundation, 1963.

GOTKIN, L. G., and GOLDSTEIN, L. S. *Descriptive statistics; a programmed textbook* (Two volumes). New York: John Wiley, 1964.

GOUGH, H. G. A new dimension of status: I. Development of a personality scale. *American Sociological Review,* 1948, Vol. 13, pp. 401–409.

GROBMAN, HULDA. *Evaluation activities of curriculum projects.* Monograph no. 2 in AERA Series on Curriculum Evaluation. Chicago: Rand McNally, 1968.

GRONLUND, N. E., *Constructing achievement tests*, Englewood Cliffs, New Jersey: Prentice-Hall. (Second Edition), 1971.

GROSS, M. L. *The brain watchers.* New York: Random House, 1962.

GUILFORD, J. P. *The nature of human intelligence.* New York: McGraw-Hill, 1967.

GUILFORD, J. P. Intelligence 1965 model. *American Psychologist,* 1966, Vol. 21, pp. 20–26.

GUILFORD, J. P. *Fundamental statistics in psychology and education.* New York: McGraw-Hill, (Fourth Edition) 1965.

GUILFORD, J. P. *Personality.* New York: McGraw-Hill, 1959.

GUILFORD, J. P. Structure of intellect. *Psychological Bulletin.* 1956, Vol. 14, pp. 469–479.

GUILFORD, J. P. (Ed.) *Printed Classification Tests.* AAF Aviation Psychology Program Research Reports No. 5, Washington, D.C.: Government Printing Office, 1947.

GUTTMAN, L. A basis for scaling qualitative ideas. *American Sociological Review,* 1944, Vol. 9, pp. 139–150.

HAGGARD, E. A. Isolation and personality. In Worchel, P. and Byrne, D. (Eds.) *Personality change.* New York: Wiley, 1964.

HAGGARD, E. A. Social status and intelligence: an experimental study of certain cultural determinants of measured intelligence. *Genetic Psychology Monographs,* 1954, Vol. 49, pp. 141–186.

HAGGARD, E. A., DAVIS, A., and HAVIGHURST, R. J. Some factors which influence performance of children on intelligence tests. *American Psychologist,* 1948, Vol. 3, pp. 265.

HANCOCK, J. W. An experimental study of limiting response on attitude scales. In H. H. Remmers (Ed.) *Further studies in attitudes, Series III. Studies in higher education,* 1938, Lafayette, Indiana: Purdue University, Vol. 34, pp. 142–148.

HARBINGTON, M. *The other America.* New York: Macmillan, 1963.

HARCOURT BRACE JOVANOVICH, INC., *Metropolitan high school social studies test.* New York: HBJ. (Experimental Edition), 1961.

HARRIS, C. W. (Ed.) *Problems in measuring change.* Madison: University of Wisconsin Press, 1963.

HASTINGS, J. T. Curriculum evaluation: The why of the outcomes. *Journal of Educational Measurement,* 1966, Vol. 3, pp. 27–32.

HASTINGS, J. T., RUNKEL, J., and DAMRIN, DORA E. *Effects on use of tests by teachers trained in a summer institute.* Cooperative Research Project No. 702.

Urbana, Illinois: Bureau of Educational Research, College of Education, University of Illinois, 1961.

HAVIGHURST, R. J. What are the cultural differences which may affect performance on intelligence tests? In Eells, K. W. (Ed.), *Intelligence and cultural differences*. Chicago: University of Chicago Press, 1951.

HAWES, G. R. *Educational testing for the millions*. New York: McGraw-Hill, 1964.

HELMSTADTER, G. C. *Principles of psychological measurement*. New York: Appleton-Century-Crofts, 1964.

HENRYSSON, S. Gathering, analyzing and using data on test items. In Thorndike, R. L. (Ed.) *Educational measurement*. Washington, D.C.: American Council on Education. (Second Edition), 1971, pp. 130–159.

HERRICK, V. E. What is already known about the relation of IQ to cultural background. In Eells, K. W. (Ed.) *Intelligence and cultural differences*. Chicago: University of Chicago Press, 1951.

HICKS, J. M. Comparative validation of attitude measures by the multi-trait, multi-method matrix. *Educational and Psychological Measurement*, 1967, Vol. 27, pp. 985–995.

HIVELY, II, W., PATTERSON, H. L., and PAGE, SARA H. A 'universe-defined' system of arithmetic achievement tests. *Journal of Educational Measurement*. 1968, Winter, pp. 275–290.

HOCHBERG, H. Intervening variables, hypothetical constructs, and metaphysics. In Feigl, H. and Maxwell, G. (Eds.), *Current issues in philosophy of science*. New York: Holt, Rinehart and Winston, 1961, pp. 448–456.

HOFFMAN, B. *The tyranny of testing*. New York: The Crowell-Collier Press, 1962.

HOLT, J. *How children fail*. New York: Pitman, 1968.

HUMPHREYS, L. G. Note on the multi-trait-multi-method matrix. *Psychological Bulletin*, 1960, Vol. 57, pp. 86–88.

HUSEK, T. R., and SIROTNIK, K. Item sampling in educational research: An empirical investigation. Paper presented at the national meetings of the American Educational Research Association, Chicago, February, 1968. Available as NAPS Document 00255 from ASIS National Auxiliary Publications Service, c/o CCM Information Science, Inc., 22 West 34th Street, New York City, 10001. Remit $1.00 for microfiche or $3.00 for photocopies.

HUTCHINS, E. B., and NONNEMAN, A. J. Construct validity of an environmental assessment technique for medical schools. Paper presented at the Annual Meeting of the American Educational Research Association, Chicago, 1966.

HUTCHINS, E. B. The evaluation of environmental determinants. Paper presented at the Annual Meeting of the American Psychological Association, St. Louis, 1962.

JACKSON, P. W. *Life in classrooms.* New York: Holt, Rinehart and Winston, 1968.

JACKSON, R. *Developing criterion-referenced tests.* Princeton, N. J.: ERIC Clearing House on Tests, Measurement, and Evaluation, Educational Testing Service, June, 1970.

JACKSON, R. W., and FERGUSON, S. A. *Studies on the reliability of tests.* Department of Educational Research Bulletin 12. Toronto, Canada: University of Toronto, 1941.

JESSOR, R., and HAMMOND, K. R. Construct validity and the Taylor anxiety scale. *Psychological Bulletin,* 1957, Vol. 54, pp. 161–170.

JOHNSTON, A. M. *The relationship of various factors to autocratic and democratic classroom practices.* Unpublished doctoral dissertation, University of Chicago, 1948.

JOINT COMMITTEE ON PROGRAMMED INSTRUCTION AND TEACHING MACHINES. Recommendations for reporting the effectiveness of programmed instruction materials. *NSPI Journal* March 1966, pp. 3–9.

JOINT COMMITTEE ON TEST STANDARDS OF THE AMERICAN PSYCHOLOGICAL ASSOCIATION, AMERICAN EDUCATIONAL RESEARCH ASSOCIATION AND NATIONAL COUNCIL ON MEASUREMENT IN EDUCATION. *Standards for educational and psychological tests and manuals.* Washington American Psychological Association, 1966.

JOSELYN, E. G. Performance contracting: What it's all about. Paper presented at the Truth and Soul in Teaching Conference of the American Federation of Teachers, Chicago, January, 1971.

JURS, S. G., and HOPKINS, K. D., Jenkins' short-cut formula for standard deviations: Its accuracy with non-normal distributions. Paper presented at the annual meeting of the National Council on Measurement in Education, New York, February 1971.

KAHN, D. F., and HADLEY, J. M. Factors related to life insurance selling. *Journal of Applied Psychology,* 1949, Vol. 23, pp. 132–140.

KATZ, M. *Selecting an achievement test: Principles and procedures.* Princeton: Educational Testing Service, 1958. (Evaluation and Advisory Service Bulletin No. 3).

KELLEY, T. L., and KREY, A. C. *Tests and measurement in the social sciences.* New York: C. Scribner and Sons, 1934.

KELLEY, T. L. Note on the reliability of a test: A reply to Dr. Crum's criticism. *Journal of Educational Psychology,* 1924, Vol. 15, pp. 193–204.

KHATENA, J. Onomatopeia and images: preliminary validity study of a test of originality. *Perceptual and Motor Skills,* 1969, Vol. 28, pp. 335–338.

KLEIN, S. P., and HART, F. M. Chance and systematic factors affecting essay grades. *Journal of Educational Measurement,* 1968, Vol. 5, pp. 197–206.

KLINEBERG, O. *Race differences.* New York: Harper, 1935.

KOPPEL, M. A., and SECHREST, L. A multitrait-multimethod matrix analysis of sense of humor. *Educational and Psychological Measurement,* 1970, Vol. 30, pp. 77–85.

KRATHWOHL, D. R., BLOOM, B. S., and MASIA, B. B. *A taxonomy of educational objectives: Handbook II, the affective domain.* New York: David MacKay Co., 1964.

LATHROP, R. L. A quick—but accurate—approximation to the standard deviation of a distribution. *Journal of Experimental Education,* 1961, Vol. 29, pp. 319–321.

LAVIN, D. E. *The prediction of academic performance.* New York: Russell Sage Foundation, 1965.

LEITER, R. G. *The Leiter international performance scale.* Santa Barbara, California: Santa Barbara State College Press, 1940.

LESSINGER, L. *Every kid a winner: Accountability in education.* N. Y.: Simon and Schuster, 1970.

LENNON, R. T. Accountability and performance contracting. Paper presented at the annual meeting of the American Educational Research Association, New York, February, 1971.

LINDQUIST, E. F. (Ed.) *Educational measurement.* Washington, D.C.: American Council on Education, 1951.

LORD, F. M., and NOVICK, M. R. *Statistical theories of mental test scores.* Reading, Massachusetts: Addison-Wesley, 1968.

LORD, F. M. Elementary models for measuring change. Harris, W. (Ed.) *Problems in Measuring Change.* Madison, Wisconsin: University of Wisconsin Press, 1963, pp. 21–38.

LORD, F. M. Estimating norms by item-sampling. *Educational and Psychological Measurement,* 1962, Vol. 22, pp. 259–267.

LORD, F. M. Tests of the same length do have the same standard error of measurement. *Educational and Psychological Measurement,* 1959, Vol. 19, pp. 233–239.

LORD, F. M. Do tests of the same length have the same standard error of measurement? *Educational and Psychological Measurement,* 1957, Vol. 17, pp. 510–521.

LORGE, I. Gen-like: halo or reality? *Psychological Bulletin,* 1937, Vol. 24, pp. 545–546.

LYMAN, H. B. *Test scores and what they mean.* Englewood Cliffs, New Jersey: Prentice-Hall. (Second Edition), 1971.

MAGER, R. F. *Preparing objectives for programed instruction.* San Francisco: Fearon Publishers, 1962. (Most recent printing titled "Preparing Instructional Objectives.")

MARSHALL, J. C. Composition errors and essay examination grades re-examined. *American Educational Research Journal,* 1967, Vol. 4, pp. 375–385.

MASLAND, R., SARASON, S., and GLADWIN, T. *Mental subnormality*. New York: Basic Books, 1958.

MASON, G. P., and ODEH, R. E. A short-cut formula for standard deviation. *Journal of Educational Measurement*, 1968, Vol. 5, pp. 319–320.

MATHEWS, C. O. The effect of the order of printed response on an interest questionnaire. *Journal of Educational Psychology*, 1929, Vol. 20, pp. 128–134.

MAYHEW, L. B. Measurement of noncognitive objectives. In Berg, H. D. (Ed.) *Evaluation in social studies*. 35th Yearbook of the National Council for the Social Studies. Washington, D. C.: NCSS, 1965, Chapter 6, pp. 115–136.

McCOLLOUGH, CELESTE, and VAN ATTA, L. *Introduction to descriptive statistics and correlation. (A program for self-instruction)*. New York: McGraw-Hill. 1965.

McCOLLOUGH, CELESTE, and VAN ATTA, L. *Statistical concepts. (A program for self-instruction)*. New York: McGraw-Hill, 1963.

McFEE, ANNE. The relation of students' needs to their perceptions of a college environment. *Journal of Educational Psychology*, 1961, Vol. 52, pp. 25–29.

McGHAN, B. R. Accountability as a negative reinforcer. *American Teacher*. 1970, November, p. 13.

McMORRIS, R. F., BROWN, J. A., and PRUZEK, R. M., Experimental Effects of Violating Item Construction Principles. Paper presented at the annual meeting of the National Council on Measurement in Education and the American Educational Research Association, Minneapolis, Minnesota, March 1970.

McNEMAR, Q. Lost: our intelligence? Why? *American Psychologist*. 1964, Vol. 18, pp. 871–882.

McNEMAR, Q. *The revision of the Stanford-Binet scale*. Boston: Houghton-Mifflin Company, 1942.

MEDNICK, S. A., and MEDNICK, MARTHA T. *Remote Associates Test: Examiners Manual*. Boston: Houghton Mifflin, 1967.

MEDNICK, S. A. *Remote Associates Test*. New York: Houghton Mifflin, 1959.

MERWIN, J. C., and WOMER, F. B. Evaluation in assessing the progress of education to provide bases of public understanding and public policy. In Tyler, R. W. (Ed.) *Educational Evaluation: New Roles, New Means*, (the 68th Yearbook of the National Society for the Study of Education) Chicago: NSSE, 1969, pp. 305–334.

MILLMAN, J., BISHOP, C. H., and EBEL, R. L. An analysis of test-wiseness. *Educational and Psychological Measurement*, 1965, Vol. 25, pp. 707–726.

MINIUM, E. W. *Statistical reasoning in psychology and education*. New York: John Wiley, 1970.

MOSTELLER, F. Use as evidenced by an examination of wear and tear on selected sets of ESS. In Davis, K. et al., A study of the need for a new encyclopedia treatment of the social sciences. Unpublished manuscript, 1955, pp. 167–174.

MUNZ, D. C., and SMOUSE, A. D. Interaction effects of item-difficulty sequence and achievement—anxiety reaction on academic performance. *Journal of Educational Psychology*, 1968, Vol. 59, pp. 370–374.

NAGEL, E. *The structure of science*. New York: Harcourt, Brace, and World. 1961, pp. 505–508.

NAROLL, R. *Data quality control*. Glencoe, Ill.: Free Press, 1962.

NELSON, C. H. Evaluation in the natural sciences. In Dressel, P. L. *Evaluation in higher education*. Boston: Houghton-Mifflin Co., 1961.

NOLL, V. H., *Introduction to educational measurement*, Boston: Houghton-Mifflin, 1965.

NUNNALLY, J. C. *Educational measurement and evaluation*. N. Y.: McGraw Hill, 1972.

OPPENHEIM, A. N. *Questionnaire design and attitude measurement*. New York: Basic Books, 1966.

OWENS, W. A. Item form and "false-positive" responses on a neurotic inventory. *Journal of Clinical Psychology*, 1947, Vol. 3, pp. 264–269.

PACE, C. R. *CUES college and university environment scales*. Princeton, New Jersey: Educational Testing Service, 1963.

PACE, C. R., and STERN, G. G. An approach to the measurement of psychological characteristics of college environments. *Journal of Educational Psychology*, 1958, Vol. 59, pp. 269–277.

PAYNE, D. A. *The assessment of learning: Cognitive and affective*. Lexington, Mass.: D. C. Heath, 1974.

PAYNE, D. A. (Ed.) *Curriculum evaluation: Commentaries on purpose-process-product*. Lexington, Mass.: D. C. Heath, 1974.

PAYNE, D. A. *The Specification and Measurement of Learning Outcomes*. Waltham, Mass.: Blaisdell, 1968.

PHILIP, B. R. Generalization and central tendency in the discrimination of a series of stimuli. *Canadian Journal of Psychology*, 1947, Vol. 1, pp. 196–204.

PLUMLEE, LYNNETTE B. Estimating means and standard deviations from partial data—an empirical check on Lord's item sampling technique. *Educational and Psychological Measurement*, 1964, Vol. 24, pp. 623–630.

PROVUS, M. *Discrepancy evaluation*. Berkeley, California: McCuthan Pub. Corp., 1971.

RHODES, M. An analysis of creativity. *Phi Delta Kappan*. 1961, Vol. 42, pp. 305–310.

RICHARDS, J. M., RAND, LORRAINE M., and RAND, L. P. Description of junior colleges. *Journal of Educational Psychology*, 1966, Vol. 57, pp. 207–214.

RIESSMAN, F. *The culturally deprived child*. New York: Harper & Row, 1962.

ROHRER, J. H. Human adjustment to antarctic isolation. Armed Services, Technical Information Agency, Publication AD 246610, Arlington Hall Station, Arlington, Virginia, 1960.

RORER, L. G. The great response-style myth. *Psychological Bulletin*, 1965, Vol. 63, pp. 129–156.

ROSENTHAL, R., and JACOBSON, LENORE. *Pygmalion in the classroom: Self—fulfilling prophecies and teacher expectations.* New York: Holt, Rinehart and Winston, 1968.

RUBIN, H. K. *A constant error in the Seashore test of pitch discrimination.* Unpublished masters' thesis, University of Wisconsin, 1940.

RUNDQUIST, E. A. Item and response characteristic in attitude and personality measurement: A reaction to L. G. Rorer's "The great response-style myth". *Psychological Bulletin*, 1966, Vol. 66, pp. 166–177.

SABERS, D. L. The accuracy of short-cut estimates for standard deviation of raw score distributions on teacher-made tests. Paper presented at the annual meeting of the National Council on Measurement in Education, Minneapolis, March 1970.

SARASON, S., and OTHERS. *Anxiety in elementary school children.* New York: Wiley, 1960.

SAUPE, J. L. Some useful estimates of the Kuder-Richardson Formula Number 20 reliability coefficient. *Educational and Psychological Measurement*, 1961, Vol. 21, pp. 63–71.

SAX, G., and CROMACK, T. R. The effects of various forms of item arrangement on test performance. *Journal of Educational Measurement*, 1966, Vol. 3., pp. 309–311.

SCANNELL, D. P., and MARSHALL, J. C. The effect of selected composition errors on the grades assigned to essay examinations. *American Educational Research Journal*, 1966, Vol. 3, pp. 125–130.

SCHRADER, W. B. A taxonomy of expectancy tables. *Journal of Educational Measurement*, 1965, Vol. 2, pp. 29–35.

SCHUMER, H., and STANFIELD, R. Assessment of student role orientation in college. *Proceedings of the 74th Annual Convention of the American Psychological Association*, 1966, 285–286.

SCRIVEN, M. The methodology of evaluation. In *Perspectives of Curriculum evaluation* (AERA Monograph Series on Curriculum Evaluation, No. 1). Chicago: Rand McNally, 1967.

SELLS, S. B. A model for the social system for the multiman extended duration space ship (NASA report No. 44–009–008), undated.

SHERIF, M., & SHERIF, C. W. *Problems of youth: Transitions to adulthood in a changing world.* Chicago: Aldine, 1965.

SINGER, W. B., and YOUNG, P. T. Studies in affective reaction: III. The specificity of affective reactions. *Journal of General Psychology.* 1941, Vol. 24, pp. 327–341.

SLAKTER, M. J., KOEHLER, R. A., and HAMPTON, S. H. Learning test-wiseness by programmed tests. *Journal of Educational Measurement*, 1970, Vol. 7, pp. 247–254.

SMITH, E. E. Obtaining subjects for research. *American Psychologist*, 1962, Vol. 17, pp. 577–578.

SMOUSE, A. D., and MUNZ, D. C. The effects of anxiety and item difficulty sequence on achievement testing scores. *Journal of Psychology*, 1968, Vol. 68, pp. 181–184.

SNYGG, D. Another look at learning theory. *Educational Psychologist*, 1963, Vol. 1, No. 1 (October).

SPEARMAN, C. *Creative mind.* London: Cambridge University Press, 1930.

STAKE, R. E. The countenance of educational evaluation. *Teachers College Record*, 1967, Vol. 68, pp. 523–540.

STALNAKER, J. M. The essay type examination. In Lindquist, E. F. (Ed.) *Educational Measurement*, Washington, D.C.: American Council of Education, 1951, pp. 495–530.

STANLEY, J. C. Reliability. In Thorndike, R. L. (Ed.) *Educational Measurement*. Washington, D.C.: American Council on Education. (Second Edition), 1971, Chapter 13, pp. 356–442.

STANLEY, J. C. Analysis of unreplicated three-way classification, with applications to rater bias and trait independence. *Psychometrika*, 1961, Volume 26, pp. 205–219.

STANLEY, J. C., and HOPKINS, K. D. *Educational and psychological measurement and evaluation.* Englewood Cliffs, N. J.: Prentice-Hall, Inc., 1972.

STARCH, D., and ELLIOT, E. C. Reliability of grading work in mathematics. *School Review,* 1913, Vol. 21, pp. 254–259. (a)

STARCH, D., and ELLIOT, E. C. Reliability of grading work in history. *School Review*, 1913, Vol. 21, pp. 676–681. (b)

STARCH, D., and ELLIOT, E. C. Reliability of the grading of high school work in English. *School Review*, 1912, Vol. 20, pp. 442–457.

STARKWEATHER, E. K. *An originality test for preschool children.* Stillwater, Oklahoma: Oklahoma State University, 1965 (mimeo).

STERN, G. G. *People in context: Measuring person–environment congruence in education and industry.* New York: John Wiley & Sons, Inc., 1970.

STUFFLEBEAM, D. L., et al. *Educational evaluation and decision making.* (Phi Delta Kappa Commission on Evaluation) Itasca, Illinois: F. E. Peacock Publishers, 1970.

STUFFLEBEAM, D. L. Toward a science of educational evaluation. *Educational Technology*, 1968, Vol. 8, pp. 5–12.

STULL, H., ANDERSON, H. R., and LINDQUIST, E. F., *Selected test items in American History*. Washington, D. C.: National Council for the Social Studies. (Fifth Edition), 1964.

SUCHMAN, E. A. *Evaluative research (principals and practice in public service and social action programs*). New York: Russell Sage Foundation, 1967.

TANNER, J. M. *The physique of the Olympic athlete.* London: Allen and Unwin, 1964.

TAYLOR, C. W. (Ed.) *The Third* (1959) *University of Utah Research Conference on the Identification of Creative Scientific Talent.* Salt Lake City: University of Utah Press, 1959.

TAYLOR, C. W. (Ed.) *The 1957 University of Utah Research Conference on the Identification of Creative Scientific Talent.* Salt Lake City: University of Utah Press, 1958.

TAYLOR, C. W. (Ed.) *The 1955 University of Utah Research Conference on the Identification of Creative Scientific Talent.* Salt Lake City: University of Utah Press, 1956.

TAYLOR, P. A., and MAGUIRE, T. O. A theoretical evaluation model. *Manitoba Journal of Educational Research,* 1966, Vol. 1, pp. 12–17.

TAYLOR, P. A., and MAGUIRE, T. O. Technical recommendations for psychological tests and diagnostic techniques. *Psychological Bulletin Supplement,* 1954, Vol. 51, 2, Part 2, pp. 1–38.

TERMAN, L. M. *The gifted group at mid-life.* Stanford, California: Stanford University Press, 1959.

TERMAN, L. M., and MILES, C. C. *Sex and personality: Studies in masculinity and femininity.* New York: McGraw-Hill, 1936.

TERMAN, L. M. The intelligence quotients of Francis Galton in childhood. *American Journal of Psychology,* 1917, Vol. 28, pp. 209–215.

TERRANOVA, C. The effects of negative stems in multiple-choice test items. Unpublished doctoral dissertation, State University of New York at Buffalo. Ann Arbor, Michigan: University Microfilms. 1969. 69–20, 512.

THOMAS, R. M. *Judging student progress.* New York: David McKay Co. (Second Edition). 1960, pp. 5–15.

THORNDIKE, R. L. (Ed.) *Educational measurement.* Washington, D.C.: American Council on Education. (Second Edition), 1971.

THORNDIKE, R. L. and HAGEN, ELIZABETH. *Measurement and evaluation in psychology and education.* (Third Edition). New York: Wiley, 1969. p. 197.

THORNDIKE, R. L. Reliability. In Lindquist, E. F. (Ed.) *Educational measurement,* Washington: American Council on Education, 1951.

THORNDIKE, R. L. Critical note on the Pressey interest-attitudes test. *Journal of Applied Psychology,* 1938, Vol. 22, pp. 657–658.

THORNDIKE, E. L. A constant error in psychological ratings. *Journal of Applied Psychology,* 1920, Vol. 4, pp. 25–29.

THURSTONE, L. L. The measurement of opinion. *Journal of Abnormal and Social Psychology,* 1928, Vol. 22, pp. 415–430.

TORDA, C. Some observations on the creative process. *Perceptual and Motor Skills,* 1970, Vol. 31, pp. 107–126.

TORRANCE, E. P. *Torrance tests of creative thinking: Norms-technical manual* (*Research edition*). Princeton, New Jersey: Personnel Press, 1966.

TORRANCE, E. P. *Constructive behavior: Personality and mental health.* Belmont, Cal.: Wadsworth, 1965.

TORRANCE, E. P. *Guiding creative talent.* Englewoods Cliffs, N.J. Prentice-Hall, 1962.

TRUAX, C. B., WARGO, D. G., and SILBER, L. D. Effects of high accurate empathy and non-possessive warmth during group psychotherapy upon female institutionalized delinquents. *Journal of Abnormal Psychology*, 1966, Vol. 71, pp. 267–274.

TRYON, R. C. Reliability and behavior domain validity: reformulation and historical critique. *Psychological Bulletin*, 1957, Vol. 54, pp. 229–249.

TUCKER, L. Scales minimizing the importance of reference groups. *In Proceedings of the 1951 invitational conference on testing problems.* Princeton, New Jersey: Educational Testing Service, 1952, pp. 22–28.

TYLER, LEONA E. *The psychology of human differences,* (Second Edition) New York: Appleton-Century-Crofts, 1956.

TYLER, R. W. (Ed.) *Educational evaluation: new roles, new means.* Sixty-eighth Yearbook of the National Society for the Study of Education. Chicago: University of Chicago Press, 1969.

TYLER, R. W. The objectives and plans for a national assessment of educational progress. *Journal of Educational Measurement*, 1966, Vol. 3, pp. 1–4.

TYLER, R. W. The functions of measurement in improving instruction. In Lindquist, E. F. (Ed.) *Educational measurement.* Washington, D. C.: American Council on Education 1951, pp. 47–67.

TYLER, R. W. General statement on evaluation. *Journal of Educational Research*, 1942, Vol. 35, March, pp. 492–501.

TYLER, R. W., GAGNÉ, R. M., and SCRIVEN, M. *Perspectives of curriculum evaluation.* Chicago: Rand McNally, 1967.

UNDERWOOD, B. J. *Psychological research.* New York: Appleton-Century-Crofts, 1957.

VERNON, P. E. *The structure of human abilities.* New York: Wiley, 1950.

WAHLSTROM, M. W., and BOERSMA, F. J. The influence of test-wiseness upon achievement. *Educational and Psychological Measurement*, 1968, Vol. 28, pp. 413–420.

WALBERG, H. J., and WELCH, W. W. A new use of randomization in experimental curriculum evaluation. *School Review*, 1967, Vol. 75, pp. 369–377.

WALLACH, M. A., and KOGAN, N. *Modes of thinking in young children: A study of the creativity-intelligence distinction.* New York: Holt, Rinehart and Winston, 1965.

WANG, C. K. A. Suggested criteria for writing attitude statements. *Journal of Social Psychology*, 1932, Vol. 3, pp. 367–373.

WEBB, E. J. et al. Unobtrusive measures: Nonreactive research in the social sciences. Chicago: Rand McNally, 1966.

WECHSLER, D. The measurement and appraisal of adult intelligence (Fourth Edition) Baltimore: Williams and Wilkins, 1958.

WESMAN, A. G. Active versus blank responses to multiple-choice items. Journal of Educational Psychology, 1947, Vol. 38, pp. 89–95. (a)

WESMAN, A. G. The usefulness of correctly spelled words in a spelling test. Journal of Educational Psychology, 1947, Vol. 37, pp. 242–246. (b)

WHISLER, L. D. Reliability of scores on attitude scales as related to scoring method. In Remmers, H. H. (Ed.), Further studies in attitudes series III. Studies in higher education, 1938, Lafayette, Indiana: Purdue University, Vol. 34, pp. 126–129.

WICK, J. W., and BEGGS, D. L. Evaluation for decision-making in the schools. Boston: Houghton Mifflin, 1971.

WILLIAMSON, M. L., and HOPKINS, K. D. The use of 'None-of-these' versus homogeneous alternatives in multiple-choice tests: Experimental reliability and validity comparisons. Journal of Educational Measurement, 1967, Vol. 4, pp. 53–58.

WITTROCK, M. C. The evaluation of instruction: cause-and-effect relations in naturalistic data. In Wittrock, M. C., and Wiley, D. C. (Eds.) The evaluation of instruction. New York: Holt, Rinehart and Winston, 1970.

WITTROCK, M. C., and WILEY, D. C. (Eds.) The evaluation of instruction. New York: Holt, Rinehart and Winston, 1970.

WOLFLE, D. L. Diversity of talent. American Psychologist, 1960, Vol. 15, pp. 535–545.

WOMER, F. B. Pros and cons of external testing programs. North Central Association Quarterly, 1961, Vol. 36, pp. 201–210.

WRIGHTMAN, L., and GORTH, W. P. CAM: The new look in classroom testing. Trend. 1969, Spring, pp. 56–57.

YAMAMOTO, K. Validation of tests of creative thinking: A review of some studies. Exceptional Children, 1965, Vol. 31, pp. 281–290.

YAMAMOTO, K. Creative writing and school achievement. School and Society, 1963, Vol. 91, pp. 307–308.

YATES, A. Grouping in education. New York: Wiley, 1966.

YOUNG, M. The rise of the meritocracy. London: Thames and Hudson, 1958.

GLOSSARY

ACADEMIC APTITUDE   The combination of native and acquired abilities needed for school work. (See Aptitude.)

ACCOUNTABILITY   Responsibility for certain educational changes or levels of student performance.

ACHIEVEMENT TEST   A test that measures the extent to which a person has "achieved" something—acquired certain information or mastered certain skills, usually as a result of specific instruction or general schooling.

AGE EQUIVALENT   The age for which a given score is the real or estimated average score.

AGE-GRADE TABLE   A table showing the relationship between the chronological ages of pupils and the school grade in which they are classified.

AGE NORM   Values or scores representing typical or average performance for individuals classified according to chronological age.

ADJUSTMENT INVENTORY   Usually a self-report instrument used to uncover personal and social adjustment problems. Term sometimes used synonymously with personality test, mental health analysis, and temperament test.

ALTERNATE-FORM RELIABILITY   A measure of the extent to which two equivalent or parallel forms of a test correlate with each other in measuring whatever they do measure.

ALTERNATIVE   See Distractor.

This glossary based in part on *Test Service Notebook No. 13* published by Harcourt Brace Jovanovich, Inc., and *A Glossary of Measurement Terms* published by California Test Bureau of McGraw-Hill. Excerpts reprinted by special permission.

APTITUDE A combination of abilities and other characteristics, whether native or acquired, known or believed to be indicative of an individual's ability to learn in some particular area. Thus, "musical aptitude" would refer broadly to that combination of physical and mental characteristics, motivational factors, perhaps musical knowledge, and conceivably other characteristics, which is conducive to acquiring proficiency in the musical field. Some exclude motivational factors, including interests, from the content of aptitude, but the more comprehensive use seems preferable.

ARITHMETIC MEAN The sum of a set of scores divided by the number of scores. (Commonly called either average or mean.)

ARTICULATED TESTS A series of tests in which different levels of the test are used for different ages or grades and which have been constructed and standardized so that the same or comparable elements or objectives are measured in the overlapping ranges among the various levels of the test. Well articulated tests have considerable overlapping from level to level in order to test the wide ranges of abilities and achievements in any given grade or class. A well articulated series of test batteries yields the same derived scores on a given grade group when either a lower or higher level of the test is used.

AUDITING The independent examination of an educational effort or performance contract to verify results, check on processes, personnel, and progress, and make a report to an interested external agency. Akin to the financial audit but of educational products and processes.

AVERAGE A general term applied to measures of central tendency. The three most widely used averages are the *arithmetic mean*, the *median*, and the *mode*.

BALANCE The degree to which the proportion of items measuring particular outcomes corresponds to the "ideal test" or that suggested by the table of specifications.

BATTERY A group of several tests standardized on the same population, so that results on the several tests are comparable (integrated norms). Sometimes loosely applied to any group of tests administered together, even though not standardized on the same subjects.

BEHAVIORAL OBJECTIVES Statements of intended educational outcomes in terms of criteria for student performance. Sometimes including conditions under which the behavior is to be observed. Akin to "performance" and "competency" objectives.

CEILING The upper limit of ability that can be measured by a test. Individuals are said to have reached the ceiling of a test when they have abilities that are above the highest performance level at which the test can make reliable discriminations.

CENTILE A value on the scoring scale below which are a given percentage of cases. According to some statisticians, the term centile is often superfluously called percentile. (See Percentile.)

CLASS INTERVAL   The divisions of a frequency distribution bounded by upper and lower score values. (See Frequency Distribution.)

COMPLETION ITEM   A test question calling for the completion (filling in) of a phrase, sentence, etc., from which one or more parts have been omitted. A test question for which one examinee must supply (rather than select) the correct response.

CONCURRENT VALIDITY   See Criterion-related validity, and Predictive Validity.

CONFIDENCE INTERVAL   A set of numbers believed to include the numerical value of that which is being estimated, e.g., given a 68% confidence interval for a true score, one could assert with 68% confidence that the true score falls within the interval. The probability may be considered as an indication of the degree of belief that the value actually falls within the interval, or as an indication of the percentage of correct assertions if the procedure is repeated.

CONSTRUCT VALIDITY   Term related to the psychological qualities a test measures. By both logical and empirical methods the theory underlying the test is validated; must be based on theory and empirical evidence. Examples: correlations of the test score with other test scores, factor analysis, or a study of the effect of speed on test scores. (See Validity.)

CONTENT VALIDITY   General descriptive term which refers to how well the content of the test samples the subject matter, the behaviors, or the situations about which conclusions are to be drawn. Content validity is especially important in an achievement test. Tied to use of table of specifications. Examples of procedures: textbook analysis, description of the universe of items, judgment of the adequacy of the sample, representative illustrations of test content, inter-correlations of sub-scores, opinions of jury of experts. (See Validity.)

CORRECTION FOR GUESSING   A reduction in score for wrong answers, sometimes applied in scoring true-false or multiple-choice questions. Many question the validity or usefulness of this device, which is intended to discourage guessing and to yield more accurate rankings of examinees in terms of their true knowledge. The assumption is made that if an examinee guesses on an objective test, the number of wrong answers resulting will be proportional to the number of alternate responses in each item.

CORRELATION   Relationship or "going-togetherness" between two sets of scores or measures; tendency of scores on one variable to vary concomitantly with the other, as the tendency of students of high IQ to be above average in reading ability. The existence of a strong relationship—i.e., a high correlation—between two variables does not necessarily indicate that one has any causal influence on the other. (See Correlation Coefficient.)

CORRELATION COEFFICIENT (r)   The most commonly used measure of relationship between (paired facts or numbers). Indicates the tendency of two or more variables or attributes to rank themselves or individuals measured on these variables in the same way. It (r) ranges in value from -1.00 for perfect negative relationship through 0.00 for none or pure chance to $+1.00$ for perfect positive relationship, and summarizes the degree of and direction of the relationship. (See Correlation.)

CRITERION   A standard by which a test may be judged or evaluated; a set of scores, ratings, etc., that a test is designed to correlate with or to predict.

CRITERION-REFERENCED TEST   A test whose items are tied to specific objectives. Usually used when mastery learning is involved. Variability of scores is of little consequence. Emphasis is on an individual's performance relative to an absolute rather than a normative standard, i.e., an individual's performance is compared with an *a priori* criterion instead of with the performance of other people. (See Mastery Test.)

CRITERION-RELATED VALIDITY   Label for a test-use category which refers to how well test scores match (correlate) with measures of criterion performance. Measures of criteria may be gathered concurrently (Concurrent Validity). Examples: comparing distribution of scores for men in an occupation with those for men-in-general, correlation of personality test scores with estimates of adjustments made in the counseling interviews, correlation of end-of-course achievement or ability test scores with school marks. Measures of criteria may be gathered at a later distant time (Predictive Validity). Examples: correlation of intelligence test scores with course grades, correlation of test scores obtained at beginning of the year with marks earned at the end of the year. (See Concurrent Validity, Predictive Validity, and Validity.)

CROSS-VALIDATION   The process of checking whether a decision derived from one set of data is truly effective when this decision process (or strategy) is applied to another independent, but relevant set of data.

CURRICULUM EVALUATION   The process of collecting and processing data aimed at decision making pertaining to an educational program. Data may include (1) objective description of goals, environments, personnel, methods and content, and results, and (2) recorded personal judgments of quality and appropriateness of goals, inputs and outcomes. (See Evaluation Program.)

DECILE   Any one of the nine percentile points (scores) in a distribution that divide the distribution into ten equal parts; every tenth percentile. The first decile is the 10th percentile, the ninth decile the 90th percentile, etc.

DERIVED SCORE   A score that has been converted from a qualitative or quantitative mark on one scale into the units of another scale (e.g., standard score, percentile rank, intelligence quotient, IQ etc.)

DEVIATION   The amount by which a score differs from some reference value, such as the mean, the norm, or the score on some other test.

DEVIATION IQ   A measure of intelligence based on the extent to which an individual's score deviates from a score that is typical for the individual's age. (See Intelligence Quotient.)

DIAGNOSTIC TEST   A test used to locate specific areas of weakness or strength and to determine the nature of weaknesses or deficiencies; it yields measures of the components or sub-parts of some larger body of information or skill. Diagnostic achievement tests are most commonly prepared for the skill subjects—reading, arithmetic, spelling.

DIFFICULTY INDEX   The percent of some specified group, such as students of a given age or grade, who answer an item correctly or score in a particular direction.

DISCRIMINATION INDEX   The ability of a test item to differentiate between individuals possessing much of some characteristic (skill, knowledge, attitude) from those possessing little of the characteristic.

DISTRACTOR   Any of the plausible but incorrect choices in a multiple-choice or matching item. Sometimes called foil, alternative or option. The choices are "distracting" and appear equally attractive to the less knowledgeable or skillful examinee, thereby reducing the effect of guessing. (See Foil, and Option.)

DISTRIBUTION   See Frequency Distribution. An ordered tabulation of scores showing the number of individuals that obtain each score or fall in each score interval.

DUAL STANDARDIZATION   The procedure of norming or standardizing two tests simultaneously on one sample, thereby integrating the two instruments, e.g., norming a group intelligence test and an achievement battery on the same population sample.

ERROR OF ESTIMATE   See Standard Error of Estimate.

EQUIVALENT FORMS   Any of two or more forms of a test that are closely parallel with respect to the nature of the content and the difficulty of the items included, and that will yield very similar average scores and measures of variability for a given group.

EVALUATION   The process by which quantitative and qualitative data are processed to arrive at a judgment of value, worth, or effectiveness.

EVALUATION PROGRAM   Testing, measuring, and appraising adjustment status, growth, and/or achievement of the learner by means of tests and non-test instruments and techniques. The program tends to involve the identification and formulation of a comprehensive set of major objectives of a curriculum, their definition in terms of pupil behavior, and the selection and construction of valid, reliable, and practical instruments for appraising specified phases of pupil behavior. Evaluation includes integrating and interpreting the various evidences of behavior stability and behavior changes into multifaceted description of an individual or of an educational situation. An adequate educational evaluation program is one that is (1) comprehensive and well-balanced in terms of both the learner and the curriculum, (2) continuous and well-articulated from the first grade through the secondary grades, (3) functional and practical for those using it, and (4) integrated and uses scientific measuring instruments and techniques. Evaluation and measurement are not synonymous terms. The emphasis in measurement is upon single aspects of subject-matter achievement or specific skills and abilities; emphasis in evaluation is upon broad personality changes and major objectives of the educational program. (See Curriculum Evaluation.)

EXPECTANCY TABLE Generally a two-way grid or bi-variate table expressing the relationship between two (or more) variables by stating the likelihood or probability that individuals who belong to each of a set of subgroups defined on the basis of one (or more) variables will belong to each of a set of subgroups defined on the basis of another variable. A method of expressing the validity of a test, as usually one of the variables will be the predictor and the other the criterion.

EXTRAPOLATION As applied to test norms, the process of extending or estimating a norm line beyond the limits of actually obtained data in order to permit interpretation of extreme scores. This extension may be done mathematically by fitting a curve to the obtained data or by less rigorous graphic methods.

FACE VALIDITY Term used to describe the acceptability of the test and test situation by the examinee and to some extent user in terms of apparent uses to which the test is to be put. A test has face validity when it appears to measure the variable to be tested.

FACTOR In mental measurement, hypothetical trait, ability, or component of ability that underlies and influences performance on two or more tests and hence causes scores on the tests to be correlated. The term "factor" strictly refers to a theoretical variable, derived by a process of factor analysis, from a table of intercorrelations among tests, but it is also commonly used to denote the psychological interpretation given to the variable, i.e., the mental trait assumed to be represented by the variable, as verbal ability, numerical ability, etc.

FACTOR ANALYSIS A set of methods for analyzing the intercorrelations among a set of variables such as test scores. With factor analysis we may attempt to account for the interrelationships in terms of some underlying "factors," preferably fewer in number than the original variables. It reveals how much of the variation in each of the original measures is associated with each of the hypothetical factors.

FOIL See Alternative, Distractor, and Option.

FORCED-CHOICE ITEM Broadly, any multiple-choice item in which the examinee is required to select one or more of the given choices. The term is best used to denote a special type of multiple-choice item, in which the options, or choices, are (1) of equal "preference value," i.e., chosen equally often by a typical group, but (2) of differential discriminating ability, i.e., such that one of the options discriminates between persons high and low on the factor that this option measures, while the other options do not.

FORMATIVE EVALUATION   The use of evaluation data to modify, revise, and generally improve an educational program during its developmental stages. Such uses include improving curriculum and instruction for individuals and for groups. (See Summative Evaluation.)

FREQUENCY DISTRIBUTION   An ordered tabulation of scores showing the number of individuals that obtain each score or fall in each score interval. (See Class Interval.)

GRADE EQUIVALENT   The grade level for which a given score is the real or estimated average. A grade equivalent of 6.4 is theoretically the average score obtained by students in the fourth month of the sixth grade. Grade equivalent score units are subject to much distortion to variations in curriculum, individual aptitude, and learning.

GRAPHIC RATING SCALE   A scale which presents the rater with a continuum of descriptive phrases for a particular trait. The rater makes a judgment about the individual or object with reference to the trait, and places a mark on the line indicating his opinion.

GROUP TEST   A test that may be administered to a number of individuals at the same time by one examiner.

GUESSING   See Correction for Guessing.

INCREMENTAL VALIDITY   The increase in relationship between the predictor(s) and the criterion measure when another predictor is added to the set.

INDIVIDUAL TEST   A test that can be administered to only one person at a time.

INTELLIGENCE QUOTIENT   This now outmoded index was originally the ratio of a person's mental age to his chronological age (MA/CA) or, more precisely, especially for older persons, the ratio of mental age to the mental age typical for chronological age (in both cases multiplied by 100 to eliminate the decimal). More generally, IQ is a measure of "brightness" that takes into account both the score on an intelligence test and age. A deviation IQ is such a measure of "brightness," based on the difference or deviation between a person's obtained score and the score that is typical for the person's age. Usually expressed as a type of standard score. (See Deviation IQ.)

INTERNAL CONSISTENCY   The extent to which items on a test are correlated with each other (implying the measurement of common content skill, behavior, or other factor).

INTERPOLATION   In general, any process of estimating intermediate values between two known points. As applied to test norms, it usually refers to the procedure used in assigning values, e.g. grade or age equivalents, to scores between the successive average scores actually obtained in the standardization process. In reading norm tables, it is necessary to interpolate to obtain a norm value for a score between scores given in a table.

INVENTORY TEST   As applied to achievement tests, a test that attempts to cover rather thoroughly some relatively small unit of specific instruction or training. The purpose of an inventory test, as the name suggests, is more in the nature of a "stocktaking" of an individual's knowledge or skill than an effort to measure in the usual sense. The term sometimes denotes a type of test used to measure achievement status prior to instruction, or general mental health or personality status.

ITEM   A single question or exercise in a test.

ITEM ANALYSIS   Any one of several methods used in test development and refinement to determine how well a given test item discriminates among individuals differing in some characteristic. The effectiveness of a test item depends upon three factors: 1) the validity of the item in regards to an outside criterion, curriculum content, or educational objective; 2) the discriminating power of the item in regards to validity and internal consistency; 3) the difficulty of the item.

ITEM SAMPLING   Technique used in standardization of tests and in curriculum evaluation. Instead of requiring all individuals to respond to all items, subgroups take subsets of items (e.g., instead of requiring 100 individuals to answer 70 items, have ten groups of ten individuals each answer seven items).

KUDER-RICHARDSON FORMULA(S)   Formulas for estimating the reliability, specifically internal consistency, of a test from (1) information about the individual items in the test or (2) the mean score, standard deviation, and the number of items in the test. Because the Kuder-Richardson formulas permit estimation of reliability from a single administration of a test, without dividing the test into halves, their use has become common in test development. The Kuder-Richardson formulas are not appropriate for estimating the reliability of speeded tests.

MASTERY TEST   A test of the extent to which a student has mastered a specified set of objectives or met minimum requirements set by a teacher or examining agency. Usually a criterion-referenced measure. (See Criterion-Referenced Test.)

MATCHING ITEM   A test item calling for the correct association of each entry in one list with an entry in a second list.

MEAN   The sum of a set of scores divided by the number of scores.

MEASUREMENT   The process of quantifying according to a standard. The assignment of numerals to represent objects, individuals, or phenomena.

MEDIAN   The 50th percentile; the point that divides the group into two equal parts. Half of the group of scores fall below the median and half above it.

MENTAL AGE (MA)   The age for which a given score on an intelligence test is average or normal. If a score of 55 on an intelligence test corresponds to a mental age of 6 years, 10 months, then 55 is presumably the average score that would be made by an unselected group of children 6 years, 10 months of age.

MODE   The score or value that occurs more frequently in a distribution.

MULTIPLE-CHOICE ITEM   A test item in which the examinee's task is to choose the correct or best answer from several given answers, options, foils, distractors, or alternatives.

MULTIPLE CORRELATION   The relationship between one variable and the weighted sum of two or more other variables.

MULTIPLE REGRESSION   A method of combining two or more predictors to estimate a single criterion measure (e.g., freshman grade point average may be predicted from a combination of high school rank, intelligence test score, and interest inventory scores).

MULTIPLE-RESPONSE ITEM   A special type of multiple-choice item in which two or more of the given choices may be correct.

N   The symbol commonly used to represent the number of cases in a distribution, study, etc. The sum of the frequencies = N.

NORMAL DISTRIBUTION   A derived curve based on the assumption that variations from the mean are by chance. It is bell-shaped in form and accepted as a representational model because of its repeated recurrence in measurements of human characteristics in psychology and education. It has many useful mathematical properties. In a normal distribution curve, scores are distributed symmetrically about the mean with cases concentrated near the mean and decreasing in frequency the further one departs from it. One cannot tell if a particular distribution is "normal" by simply looking at it, but must determine if the data fit a particular mathematical function.

NORMALIZED STANDARDIZED SCORE   Usually called T-scores, made to conform to standard score values of a normal distribution curve by use of percentile equivalents for the normal curve and most frequently expressed with a mean equated to 50 and a standard deviation equated to 10. (See Stanines.)

NORM REFERENCED MEASURE   A measure which is used to distinguish among members of a group, comparing a person's performance with the performance of others in the group.

NORMS   Statistics that describe the test performance of specified groups, such as pupils of various ages or grades in the standardization group for a test. Norms are often assumed to be representative of some larger population, as of pupils in the country as a whole. Norms are descriptive of average or typical performance; they are not to be regarded as standards, or desirable levels of attainment. Grade, age, percentile, and standard score are the most common types of norms.

OBJECTIVITY   Consistency in scoring. A characteristic of a test in the scoring of which there is little or no possibility of difference of opinion among scorers as to whether responses are to be scored right or wrong. It is contrasted with a "subjective" test, e.g., the usual essay examination to which different scorers may assign different scores, ratings, or grades. Objectivity is a characteristic of the scoring of the test, not the form, e.g., multiple-choice. Another definition of an objective test is one in which the method of gathering the data does not distort what it is that is being measured.

OMNIBUS   A test (1) in which items measuring a variety of mental operations are all combined into a single sequence rather than grouped together by type of operation, and (2) from which only a single score is derived, rather than separate scores for each operation or function. Omnibus tests make for simplicity of administration: One set of directions and one over-all time limit usually suffice.

OPTION   See Distractor.

PERCENTILE   One of the 99 point scores that divide a ranked distribution into groups, where each group is composed of 1/100 of the scores. A point below which a certain percentage of the scores fall. For example, the median (the 50th percentile) is the point in a distribution below which 50% of the scores fall. (See Centile.)

PERCENTILE RANK.   The percent of scores in a distribution equal to or lower than the score being described. If a person obtains a percentile rank of 70, his standing is regarded as equaling or surpassing 70 percent of the normative group on which the test was standardized.

PERFORMANCE CONTRACT   Agreement to bring about specified changes in individuals or groups. Criteria are detailed and level of payment is tied to performance.

PERFORMANCE TEST   Usually a test requiring motor or manual response on the examinee's part, generally but not always involving manipulation of concrete equipment or materials. As contrasted with paper-and-pencil test. "Performance test" is also used in another sense, to denote a test that is actually a work-sample, and in this sense it may include the paper-and-pencil test, as, for example, a test in accountancy, or in taking shorthand, or in proofreading, where no materials other than paper and pencil may be required, but where the test response is identical with the behavior about which information is desired.

PERSONALITY TEST   A test intended to measure one or more non-intellective variables. Personality tests include the so-called *personality inventories* or *adjustment inventories* which seek to measure a person's status (on such traits as dominance, sociability, introversion, etc.,) by means of self-descriptive responses to a series of questions; *rating scales* which call for rating, by one's self or another, of the extent to which a subject possesses certain characteristics; situation tests in which the individual's behavior in simulated lifelike situations is observed and evaluated (by one or more judges) with reference to various personality traits; and opinion or attitude inventories. Some writers also classify interest inventories as personality tests.

PLACEMENT   Classifying a person into one of two or more treatments, programs, etc. (See Selection.)

POWER TEST   A test intended to measure level of performance and sample the range of an examinee's capacity rather than speed of response, hence one in which there is either no time limit or a very generous one. (See Work-Limit Test.)

PRACTICE EFFECT   The influence of previous experience with a test on a later administration of the same test or a similar test, usually resulting in an increase in the score on the second testing that is attributed to increased familiarity with the directions, kinds of questions, etc. Practice effect is greatest when the time interval between testings is small, when the materials in the two tests are very similar and when the initial test-taking represents a relatively novel experience for the subjects.

PREDICTIVE VALIDITY   See Concurrent Validity, and Criterion-Related Validity.

PRODUCT-MOMENT COEFFICIENT   See Correlation Coefficient.

PROFILE   A graphic representation of the results on several tests, for either an individual or group, when the results have been expressed in some uniform or comparable terms. This method of presentation permits easy identification of areas of strength or weakness.

PROJECTIVE TECHNIQUE (PROJECTIVE METHOD)   A method of personality study in which the subject responds as he chooses to a series of ambiguous stimuli such as inkblots, pictures, unfinished sentences, etc. So called because of the assumption that under this free-response condition the subject "projects" into his responses manifestations of personality characteristics and organization that can, by suitable methods, be scored and interpreted to yield a description of his basic personality structure. The *Rorschach* (inkblot) *Technique* and the *Murray Thematic Appreception Test* are the most commonly used.

Q-SORT   A technique used to measure personality requiring the subject to sort a large number of statements into piles representing degrees to which the statements apply to him.

QUARTILE   One of three points that divides the cases in a distribution into four equal groups. The first quartile, is the 25th percentile, the second quartile is the 50th percentile, or median, and the third quartile, is the 75th percentile.

RANDOM SAMPLE   A sample of the members of a population drawn in such a way that every member of the population has an equal chance of being included. That is, the sample is drawn in a way that precludes the operation of bias in selection. One reason for such a sample is, of course, to assure that the sample be fairly "representative" of the total population, so that sample findings may be generalized to the population. (However, a random sample may still be atypical and unrepresentative of the population.) A great advantage of random samples is that formulas are available for estimating the expected variation of the sample statistics from their true values in the total population; in other words, we know how precise an estimate of the population value is given by a random sample of any given size.

RANGE   The difference between the highest and the lowest scores obtained on a test by a particular group.

RATING SCALE   A data gathering method involving the use of numerals or phrases describing points along a continuum. An instrument may have several such scales.

RAW SCORE   The first quantitative result obtained in scoring a test. Usually the number of right answers, the time required for performance, number of errors, or similar direct, unconverted, uninterpreted measure.

READINESS TEST   A test that measures the extent to which an individual has achieved a degree of maturity or acquired certain skills or information needed for undertaking successfully some new learning activity. Thus a *reading readiness test* indicates the extent to which a child has reached a developmental stage and possesses the prerequisite skills so that he may profitably begin a formal instructional program in reading.

RECALL ITEM   An item that requires the examinee to supply the correct answer from his own memory or recollection, as contrasted to a *recognition item*, in which he need only select or identify the correct answer.

RECOGNITION ITEM   An item requiring the examinee to recognize or select the correct answer from among two or more given answers.

REGRESSION EFFECT   Tendency for a predicted score to be relatively nearer the mean of its series than the score from which it was predicted is to the mean of its series. For example, if we predict school marks from an intelligence test, we will find that for all pupils who have IQ's two standard deviations above the mean, the mean of their predicted school marks will be less than two standard deviations from the mean of the school marks. There is a regression effect whenever the correlation between two measures is less than perfect.

RELEVANCE   The extent to which specific items are in fact measures of specific objectives. In a real sense relevance refers to item validity.

RELIABILITY   The extent to which a test is accurate or consistent in measuring whatever it does measure; dependability, stability, relative freedom from errors of measurement. Estimating reliability generally involves examination of internal consistency, equivalence of forms, and stability of scores over time.

RELIABILITY OF A DIFFERENCE   The extent to which a difference between scores is consistent. For example, the extent to which differences between pre- and post-test scores using one form of a test would be related to pre and post differences using another form of the test.

REPRESENTATIVE SAMPLE   A sample that corresponds to or matches the population of which it is a sample with respect to characteristics important for the purposes under investigation. For example, in an achievement test norm sample, representation might be according to proportion of pupils from each state, from various regions, etc. etc.

SCALED SCORE   A unit in a system of equated scores established for the raw scores of a test so that the scaled score values may themselves be interpreted usually as representative of the mean performance of certain reference groups. It is also intended that intervals between any pair of scaled scores may be interpreted as differences in terms of the characteristics of the reference group.

SCALED TEST   (1) A test in which the items are arranged in an order of increasing difficulty or on some other basis. (2) This term may also be used to describe a test whose items are assigned weights or values according to the difficulty of the item. Scaled tests are used in evaluating individualized learning programs.

SCHOLASTIC APTITUDE   See Academic Aptitude.

SELECTION   Deciding to accept or reject an individual for a treatment, program, school, etc. (See Placement.)

SEMANTIC DIFFERENTIAL TECHNIQUE   A method requiring individuals to express their feelings about a particular concept by rating the concept on a series of bi-polar adjectives, e.g., good-bad, strong-weak, and fast-slow. Format usually involves a seven interval scale. Three major dimensions are generally involved: evaluation, potency, and activity.

SKEWNESS   The tendency of a distribution to depart from symmetry or balance around the mean. For example, a negatively skewed distribution has more extreme low scores than high scores, with the mean being lower than the median.

SOCIOMETRY   Measurement of the interpersonal relationships prevailing among the members of a group. By means of sociometric devices, e.g., the *sociogram*, an attempt is made to discover the patterns of choice and rejection among the individuals making up the group—which ones are chosen most often as friends or leaders ("star"), which are rejected by others ("isolates"), how the group subdivides into clusters or cliques, etc.

SPEARMAN-BROWN FORMULA   A formula giving the relationship between the reliability of a test and its length. The formula permits estimation of the reliability of a test lengthened or shortened by any amount, from the known reliability of a test of specified length. Its most common application is in the estimation of reliability of an entire test from the correlation between two halves of the test, an estimate of internal consistency.

SPECIFICITY   The extent to which items on a test represent course-specific learnings. Experts should receive near perfect scores, and test-wise but course-naive students near chance scores.

SPEED TEST   A test in which performance is measured by the number of tasks performed correctly in a given time. Items are near same level of difficulty, generally easy.

SPLIT-HALF COEFFICIENT   A set of methods for estimating the internal consistency reliability of a power test by splitting it into comparable halves (usually the odd-numbered items, and the even-numbered items). The most common method involves correlating the scores of the two halves and applying the Spearman-Brown prophecy formula to estimate the correlation.

STABILITY   As applied to the examination of reliability the method involves two administrations of the same test to the same group on two different occasions, and correlating the scores. (See Test-Retest Coefficient.)

STANDARD DEVIATION   A measure of the variability of dispersion of a set of scores. The more the scores cluster around the mean, the smaller the standard deviation.

STANDARD ERROR OF ESTIMATE   An expression of the degree to which predictions or estimates of criterion scores are likely to correspond to actual values. (Standard deviation of the criterion times the square root of the quantity, one minus the correlation coefficient squared). A method of expressing the validity of the test. All other things being equal the smaller the Standard Error the better the validity. (See Standard Error of Measurement.)

STANDARD ERROR OF MEASUREMENT   A measure of the estimated difference between the observed test score and the hypothetical "true score," i.e., errorless score. A method of expressing the reliability of the test. The smaller the error of measurement, in general, the higher the reliability (all other things being equal). (Standard deviation of the test times the quantity the square root of one minus the reliability coefficient). Used in estimating the true score. (See Standard Error of Estimate.)

STANDARD SCORE   A general term referring to any of a variety of "transformed" scores, in terms of which raw scores may be expressed for reasons of convenience, comparability, ease of interpretation, etc. The simplest type of standard score is that which expresses the deviation of an individual's raw score from the average score of his group in relation to the standard deviation of the scores of the group. Thus:

$$\text{Standard score } (z) = \frac{\text{raw score } (X) - \text{mean } (M)}{\text{standard deviation } (S.D.)}$$

Standard scores do not affect the relative standing of the individuals in the group nor change the shape of the original distribution. More complicated types of standard scores may yield distributions differing in shape from the original distribution; in fact, they are sometimes used for precisely this purpose.

STANDARDIZATION SAMPLE   Term used to describe the reference sample of individuals (or schools, or other units) selected for use in norming a test. This sample should be representative of the target population and therefore should be concerned with essential characteristics such as geographical representation, age, and grade.

STANDARDIZED TEST   A systematic sample of performance obtained under prescribed conditions, scored according to definite rules, and capable of evaluation by reference to normative information. Some writers restrict the term to tests having the above properties, whose items have been experimentally evaluated, and/or for which evidences of validity and reliability are provided.

STANINES   A unit that divides the norm population into nine groups. Except for Stanines 1 and 9, the groups are spaced in half-sigma units, with the mean at Stanine 5, and those scoring the highest at Stanine 9 are usually normalized standard scores. (See Normalized Standardized Score.)

Stanine	1	2	3	4	5	6	7	8	9
% in Stanine	4	7	12	17	20	17	12	7	4

STENCIL KEY   A scoring key which, when positioned over an examinee's responses either in a test booklet or, more commonly, on an answer sheet, permits rapid identification and counting of all right answers. Stencil keys may be perforated in positions corresponding to positions of right answers, so that only right answers show through when the keys are in place, or they may be transparent, with positions of right answers identified by circles, boxes, etc., printed on the key.

STRIP KEY   A scoring key arranged so that the answers for items on any page or in any column of the test appear in a strip or column that may be placed alongside the examinee's responses for easy scoring.

SUB TEST   A collection of items in a battery or test which have distinct, similar characteristics or functions. A separate score is usually provided.

SUMMATIVE EVALUATION   The use of evaluation data to make an end-of-unit, -course, or -program judgment about effectiveness. Total effectiveness or worth is the focus. (See Formative Evaluation.)

SURVEY TEST   A test that measures general achievement in a given subject or area, usually with the connotation that the test is intended to measure group status, rather than precise measures of individuals.

T-SCORE   A derived (normalized standard) score based upon the equivalence of percentile values to standard scores, thus, avoiding the effects of skewed distributions, and usually having a mean equated to 50 and a standard deviation equated to 10.

TABLE OF SPECIFICATIONS   Usually a two way grid summarizing behavioral outcomes and content of a course or unit of instruction. Percentages in cells of table indicate importance of sub-topics dictated by value judgments, instructional time spent on topic, etc. Used to guide achievement test development and selection. Specifications may also call for particular type of item, specific behaviors, etc. Tables of Specifications are also used in development of tests other than proficiency.

TEST   A systematic procedure for gathering data to make intra- or inter-individual comparisons.

TEST-RETEST COEFFICIENT   A type of reliability coefficient obtained by administering the same test to the same sample a second time after an interval and correlating the two sets of scores. (See Stability.)

TRUE SCORE   The average score of an infinite series of measurements with the same or exactly equivalent tests, assuming no practice effect or change in the examinee during the testings. A score for which errors of measurement have been averaged.

VALIDITY   The extent to which a test does the job for which it is used. Validity, thus defined, has different connotations for various kinds of tests and, accordingly different kinds of validity evidence are appropriate for them. For example: 1) The validity for an achievement test is the extent to which the content of the test represents a balanced and adequate sampling of the outcomes (knowledge, skills, etc.,) of the course or instructional program it is intended to cover (content, face, or curricular validity). It is best evidenced by a comparison of the test content with courses of study, instructional materials, and statements of instructional goals, and by critical analysis of the processes required in responding to the items. 2) The validity of an aptitude, prognostic, or readiness test is the extent to which it accurately indicates future learning success in the area for which it is used as a predictor. It is evidenced by correlations between test scores and measures of later success. 3) The validity of a personality test is the extent to which the test yields an accurate description of an individual's personality traits or personality organization. It may be evidenced by agreement between test results and other types of evaluation, such as ratings or clinical classification, but only to the extent that such criteria are themselves valid. The traditional definition of validity as "the extent to which a test measures what it is supposed to measure," seems less satisfactory than the above, since it fails to emphasize that the validity of a test is always specific to the purposes for which the test is used, that different kinds of evidence are appropriate for appraising the validity of various types of tests, and that final responsibility for validation is with the test interpreter and user. (See Content, Construct, and Criterion-related Validity.)

WORK-LIMIT TEST   A test on which sufficient time is allowed for all or nearly all pupils to complete their work. (See Power Test.)

WORK SAMPLE TEST   A high relevance performance test which provides for an actual try-out of examinees' behavior in a realistic setting.

SUBJECT INDEX

389

NAME INDEX